W9-AXU-940

Inside

Inside

The Biography of John Gunther

Ken Cuthbertson

Bonus Books, Inc., Chicago

96 95 94 93 92 5 4 3 2 1

Library of Congress Catalog Card Number: 91-77020

International Standard Book Number: 0-929387-70-8

Bonus Books, Inc.
160 East Illinois Street
Chicago, Illinois 60611

Printed in the United States of America

To
Marianne, who understood

FOREWORD

Now that I stop to think about it, John Gunther tried all his life to get on the inside of things. It was a disease with him and a passion. By the time I caught up with him in 1930 in Vienna, where we both represented Chicago newspapers, the disease and the passion had consumed him.

I suppose that was why he was never much interested in covering merely "spot" news, the happening of the moment that gets the big front-page headline. Most of us correspondents used to boast of having obtained a "world scoop" now and then. Gunther always maintained that he was probably the only reporter who had never had a scoop on spot news—or at least the only one who ever admitted it. What interested him far more was to delve behind the news and get inside the situations, which in Austria, or Syria, or India or a hundred other places on this sorry earth confused mankind and especially the readers back home. Getting the news was not enough. Understanding it and trying to make others understand it was more important. For that you had to dig and dig for a thousand facts and then relate them.

So far as I can gather, this trait, which made him one of the outstanding reporters in a generation of pretty good American foreign correspondents, developed at a ridiculously early age. He had turned all of eleven and had reached the fifth grade in a public school in Chicago, the city of his birth, when he decided it was time to write an encyclopedia—no less. He proceeded to do so and, as I recall, got through the first four sections, a matter of a hundred pages, with such fancy titles as "All the Necessary Statistics of the World," "The World's Battleships," "Greek and Roman Mythology with Genealogical Tables of the Gods" and "List of Species of the World's Animals" before he decided that such extracurricular activity, though fascinating and exciting, would have to be dispensed with if he were ever to pass his examinations in more prosaic subjects for the sixth grade.

But the encyclopedic turn of mind stuck and helped to make him the kind of journalist and authority that he became.

Like a good many other American foreign correspondents (including the writer), Gunther made his first trip to Europe on a cattle boat. I don't know what there was about working your way across the Atlantic on a boat full of cows that paved the way to a newspaper career abroad, but there must have been something. In Gunther's case, the effect was slightly delayed. He quit his cattle boat in Liverpool, bicycled to London and promptly applied for a job with the local office of the now defunct *Chicago Daily News*. The resident correspondent thought he was too young (he was twenty, and had just graduated from the University of Chicago) and told him to come back in a year or two.

This he did—in 1924—after a couple of years as a local reporter on the *News* in Chicago. The London office of the *News* rejected him again, this time for lack of experience. So he went to work for the United Press until the *News* finally gave in and took him in as assistant Paris correspondent under the venerable Paul Scott Mowrer.

In those good old days, the *News* was a great newspaper for a beginner in Europe to work on. All the *News* men were brought home regularly for three-month leaves-of-absence so that there was usually an important bureau to be taken over temporarily by the second-stringer from Paris. Thus Gunther found himself covering the next few years London, Berlin, Rome, Geneva, Moscow, Scandinavia, the Baltic and the Balkans, and thus early acquired a first-hand knowledge of all of Europe that was to serve him in good stead in writing his first "inside" book in 1936.

What would he call it? He didn't know. He felt a title was important. But he couldn't think of one. His publisher and friends suggested a dozen. He didn't much like them. Finally it was decided to call it *Thunder Over Europe*—or something over Europe, at any rate.

One dismal afternoon sitting in a decrepit diner on a train taking him back to London from Wales, where he had been investigating conditions in the Welsh coal mines, an idea struck him out of the blue. He sat facing some cold mutton, a glass of lukewarm British beer and the *London Times*. The dispatches in that journal, he reflected, somehow got *inside* a situation. That was what he had tried to do in the book—get *inside* Europe.

On the margin of the *Times* he scribbled a couple of words: "Inside Europe." That night in London he cabled them to his American publisher.

For the next thirty-four years the inspiration of that winter afternoon kept him busy. There were to be eight more *Inside* books. I had an idea at the time that Gunther had his work cut out for him, whether he knew it or not.

---William L. Shirer

Mr. Shirer, who was born February 23, 1904, in Chicago, is the author of The Rise and Fall of the Third Reich *(1960) and fourteen other books. He was one of America's most distinguished foreign correspondents. Now eighty-eight years of age and retired, he lives in Lenox, Massachusetts. This foreword is a revised version of an article originally written for the* Book of the Month Club News.

ACKNOWLEDGMENTS

I wish to thank my wife, Marianne Hunter, for her love and understanding during the more than five years that it took to research and write this book.

I also wish to thank the following individuals, businesses and institutions for their kind assistance: Ms. Nancy Barnett, Great Barrington, Mass; the Book of the Month Club, New York, N.Y.; Mrs. Jean Bennedsen (nee Brand), Orinda, Ca.; Mr. Carl Brandt, Jr., New York, N.Y.; Mrs. Bertha Brenner, Washington, D.C.; Mr. Cass Canfield, Jr., New York, N.Y.; Chicago Board of Education, Chicago, Ill.; Cook County Vital Statistics Office, Chicago, Ill.; Mrs. Gretchen Corazzo, Chesterton Ind.; the late Mr. Malcolm Cowley, Sherman, Conn.; Ms. Marcia Davenport, Pebble Beach, Ca.; Ms Anne Louise Davis, Plainfield, N.J.; Dr. Henry Eisner, Philadelphia, Pa.; Mr. Clifton Fadiman, Santa Barbara, Ca.; Mr. Denis Fodor, Munich, Germany; Mr. William Forbis, Big Arm, Mont.; Sen. William Fullbright, Washington, D.C.; Mr. John Gershgorn, Beverly Hills, Ca.; Mrs. Judith de Mille Donelan, Easton Md.; Ms. Alice M. Gibb, London, Ont., Canada; Mrs. Victoia Glendinning, London, England; Dr. S. Gopal, New Delhi, India; Graceland Cemetary & Crematorium, Chicago, Ill.; Mrs. Emily Hahn (Boxer), New York; the late Helen Hahn (Smith), New York; Mr. Kenneth Hartung, and the staff of the Classification/Declassification Center, U.S. Department of State, Washington, D.C.; Mrs. Donna Haskell, and the staff of the Newberry Library, Chicago, Ill.; the Jerusalem Post, Jerusalem, Israel; Mr. Kenneth Knickerbocker, Knoxville, Tenn.; Mr. Herman Kogan, New Buffalo, Mi.; Ms. Sharon Kotok, Chief, Information Access Branch, U.S. Department of State, Washington, D.C.; Mr. Buddy Lewis, Chicago, Ill.; Mr. Arvide Lunde, Park Ridge, Ill.; Mr.

Jim Marksbury, Alumni Secretary, Deerfield Academy, Deerfield, Mass.; Mr. Daniel Meyer, Associate Curator, and the staff of the Special Collections Unit, Regenstein Library, University of Chicago, Chicago, Ill.; Mr. Emil Moschella, Chief, FOI-Privacy Acts Section, Records Management, FBI, Washington, D.C.; Mr. Richard Mowrer, Chocorua, N.H.; Random House, New York, N.Y.; Mr. K. Natwar-Singh, Secretary, Jawaharlal Nehru Memorial Fund, New Delhi, India; Ms. Luise Rainer, Viso Morcote, Switzerland; Mr. Joseph Schoeninger, Dealfield, Wisc.; Mr. Bob Sharp, Communications Coordinator, Galveston Independent School District, Galveston, Tex.; Ms. Virginia Shaw, Registrar of Barnard College, New York; Mr. Dudley Siprelle, U.S. Consul General, Embassy of the United States of America, Rome, Italy; Mr. B.C. Smith, Kingston, Ont., Canada; the late William Stoneman, St.-Germain-En-Laye, France; Mr. C.L. Sulzberger, Paris, France; Mr. Craig Tenney, Harold Ober Associates, New York, N.Y.; Mr. Evan Thomas, New York, N.Y.; the staff of the alumni office at the University of Chicago, Chicago, Ill.; and, Mrs. Marco Zur, Stratford, Conn.

Thanks to my colleagues and friends at Queen's University in Kingston, Ont., Canada, particularly to Ms. Alison Holt, Assistant Editor of the Queen's Alumni Review, for reading (and sometimes rereading) portions of the manuscript, and for her invaluable comments and criticism; Ms. Cathy Perkins, former Editor of the Alumni Review; and Dr. Geoffrey Smith, Department of History.

Special thanks to the following individuals: novelist Mrs. Leonora Hornblow, New York, N.Y., John Gunther's longtime friend, for her insights into John Gunther's life and work, and for her generosity in commenting on portions of the manuscript; Mrs. Dorothy Olding, Harold Ober Agency, New York, for all her encouragement, but mostly for believing in me, and in the merits of this project. She's the epitome of all that a literary agent should be; Dr. Alexander Rafaeli, Jerusalem, Israel, Frances Gunther's executor, for providing me with invaluable information from the papers of Frances Gunther, and for all of his generosity and support from across the seas; Mrs. Mary von Euler, Washington, D.C., for her hospitality, for providing me with access to some of the papers of Frances Gunther, and for opening my eyes to aspects of Frances' life and personality that I otherwise might well have overlooked.

And finally, special thanks to two of the most remarkable gentlemen whom I've ever had the good fortune to meet: Mr. George Seldes, Hartland-4-Corners, Vt., and Mr. William Shirer, Lenox, Mass. They have awed me with their wisdom, inspired me with their professionalism, and astounded me with their boundless zest for life.

At more than 100 years of age, George Seldes is the undisputed dean of American foreign correspondents. Mr. Seldes selflessly gave of his time to read and critique portions of my manuscript, engage in several early morning telephone conversations when I was in need of help, and proved to me that old age is nothing more than a state of mind.

Mr. William L. Shirer, John Gunther's friend and colleague, shared with me his memories of John and Frances Gunther, and of those "bubbling, blazing days of American foreign correspondence." I'm deeply honored that he has allowed me to reprint his tribute to John Gunther as the foreword to this book.

INTRODUCTION

Manhattan was bathed in sunshine on the morning of June 2, 1970. It was the kind of day that songwriters Burton Lane and Ralph Freed might have had in mind when they wrote the popular tune *How About You?* ("I like New York in June, how about you?"). The streets were bustling with cars and people. At newsstands, the morning's *New York Times* told of an earthquake in Peru; from Cambodia, correspondent Sydney Schanberg reported that eight more western newsmen were missing, presumably captured by the North Vietnamese and Vietcong. In Central Park, nature had splashed the flower beds with a rainbow palette of colors, and the trees were bursting with lush greenery.

A block away, at Madison Avenue and East Seventy-first Street, the mood outside St. James Episcopal Church was somber. It was a few minutes before eleven o'clock, and a funeral was about to begin. Passers-by could spot some well-known faces among the crowd filing into the church. Publisher Cass Canfield was there. So, too, were journalists Theodore (Teddy) White, Whit Burnett, Hamilton Fish Armstrong, and Hobart Lewis, as well as the CBS news broadcaster Eric Sevareid, financier John D. Rockefeller, III, orchestra leader Andre Kostelanetz, and Lord Caradon, the British ambassador to the United Nations.

Four hundred mourners had gathered to bid a loving farewell to John Joseph Gunther, a man whom Sevareid would describe in his CBS radio newscast that evening as being "in his day probably the most famous American newsman of them all."[1] Gunther's life had come to an abrupt end four days earlier, on May 29, 1970. Liver cancer had claimed him at age sixty-nine.

New York Post columnist Pete Hamill wrote of Gunther's funeral: "At one point during the reading of the 27th Psalm, I realized that for the first time in several years I was among the youngest persons at a gathering. When Gunther made friends, they apparently lasted."[2]

Born in Chicago in 1901, John Gunther's mother was a school teacher, while his father was a ne'er-do-well "who dabbled in real estate and excelled at drinking." Gunther won his spurs in journalism during the crazy, colorful 1920s as a reporter at the old *Chicago Daily News*, where he worked alongside Ben Hecht and Carl Sandburg. But like so many other members of Gertrude Stein's celebrated "Lost Generation," he ran off to Europe in pursuit of fame and fortune as an expatriate novelist. His first book, *The Red Pavilion* (1926), earned him a spot on one critic's list as one of the "Five Most Promising Young Novelists of the '20s." One of the other names on the list was another young Chicago native, Ernest Hemingway.

However, John Gunther's youthful dreams faded as it gradually became clear that his talents were not as a writer of fiction, but rather as a reporter. Despite his early promise, none of Gunther's subsequent attempts to write the Great American Novel measured up to his journalism, creatively or commercially. By 1936 he was making so much money from his non-fiction writing and radio broadcasting that he could not afford to devote proper time or energy to the writing of good fiction; Gunther's novels became casualties of his journalism success.

In the course of an astounding career that spanned almost half a century, "the most famous American newsman of them all"—as Eric Sevareid described him—traveled more miles than any journalist ever before. He met, interviewed, and from 1924 to the time of his death was on a first-name basis with many kings and queens, presidents and prime ministers, artists and entertainers, scholars and scoundrels.

Gunther made hundreds of broadcasts during his career, many during the pioneering days of radio (and, to a lesser extent, television). Yet broadcasting was never more than a diversion to him. "Nothing is real to me unless it is a book," he once said.[3] So he wrote, and oh, how John Gunther wrote.

In addition to countless newspaper and magazine articles, he created more than two dozen popular books, including his trademark *Inside* series, biographies, novels, and *Death Be Not Proud*, a moving account of his son's tragic death (still in print today, five decades after it was written.) All told, Gunther's books were translated into ninety languages, and sold more than 4.5 million copies at a time when a sale of 100,000 copies was still considered extraordinary. His name appeared on the international best-seller list seven of the eleven years between 1936 and 1947. At the height of his popularity, John Gunther was one of the world's best known and highest paid writers. As Richard Rovere of *The New Yorker* observed in 1947, Gunther occupied an exalted position alongside Franklin D. Roosevelt and Charles Lindbergh as "one of a half-dozen or so authentic international celebrities" of the era.[4]

Egypt's fiery President Gamel Abdel Nasser once told an American interviewer, "You have to take Gunther seriously because he tells both sides"[5]

The future first prime minister of an independent India, Jawaharlal Nehru, made his radio debut in 1938 to introduce Gunther to an India-wide audience.[6]

King George II of Greece, an unabashed Gunther fan, awarded him the decoration Virgin Eagle (Second Class), one of that country's highest peacetime honors.[7]

A revised edition of Gunther's 1939 book *Inside Asia* was on President Harry Truman's desk as he broadcast his V-J Day speech in 1945.[8] And when then Vice-President Richard Nixon traveled to Moscow in 1958 to confer with Soviet leaders, he carried with him as resource material a copy of Gunther's *Inside Russia Today.*

A bar was even named for him in the Iraqi capital, Baghdad.[9]

But all that is now virtually forgotten.

In the frenzied rush to prosperity that followed World War II, life's pace and tenor have become so quickened, so glib, that it sometimes seems that virtually nothing of interest or importance happened in the "distant" past. Nowadays, when everything happened recently, if not this morning, fame has the shelf life of a supermarket tabloid; the icons of today's pop culture are tomorrow's trinkets of trivia.

Ten years, twenty years, even a half century are but a few beats in what poet W.B. Yeats called, "the endless song" of time. But the momentous events of our grandparents' (and even our parents') day have long since been washed with the sepia hues of time. Thus, by the time he died in 1970, John Gunther, like most of his peers—people such as Walter Winchell, Dorothy Thompson, and H.R. Knickerbocker—had largely been forgotten. Even so, word of Gunther's death was front page news in the *New York Times* and many other newspapers around the world.[10] Those who remembered, who knew about such things, were aware that the residual effect of Gunther's phenomenal popularity was still as significant as it had once been pervasive.

John Gunther was a product of the school of individualistic journalism that blossomed in the 1920s and 1930s. Eric Sevareid said it best, when in his obituary of Gunther he noted that "[He] was the leader in that original extraordinary band of American journalists, some with Midwest hayseed still in their hair. . . scholars and linguists who rampaged through Europe in the twenties and thirties, and somehow ended up on a first-name basis with kings and bartenders. . . More than diplomats or politicians, it was they who told America what was happening and what was going to happen to the civilization of the west."[11]

The years between the two great wars were a golden age of journalism. Gunther, himself, termed them "the bubbling, blazing days of American foreign correspondence."[12] In retrospect, life in those halcyon times seems simpler—even though it did not seem that way at the time.

Many intellectuals were preoccupied with concerns that life had grown too complex, that the scientific knowledge and artistic impulses of Western civilization had become "perilously esoteric," as the British historian Arnold Toynbee put it. The mass media responded with a vigorous campaign to popularize and make accessible all aspects of knowledge, to show that *everything* and *everyone* were the threads of a vast, disparate cultural tapestry. The result was the appearance of distinctly American, mass-oriented, middle-brow magazines such as as *Reader's Digest* and *Life*. And, of course, John Gunther's *Inside* books (the first of which, coincidentally, appeared in 1936—the same year that Henry R. Luce launched *Life* magazine.)

Time and tastes changed. Despite their early enthusiasm, many critics would eventually dismiss Gunther, the master popularizer, as the "Marco Polo of the Book Club." His strength became his literary liability; he was *too* accessible and *too* entertaining. He made good writing look deceptively simple. Author-critic Clifton Fadiman acknowledged as much when he pointed out: "Gunther is a born teacher. He doesn't miss a fact trick. His books are almost too easy to read, and because of that, they seem superficial. But he's taught us a hell of a lot about our world, in primer terms. He's drawn the maps for us."[13]

It is easy to forget just how much history has happened in two short generations. It is easy to forget that within living memory the miracle of the jet engine has made mass air travel a reality. And television has put us on the front lines of history. Whether it's war in the Persian Gulf or a hurricane in Florida, we turn on the TV expecting to see on-the-spot reports, live. Our grandparents would have been astounded to find that the big, mysterious world that they inhabited has grown crowded.

In the 1920s and 1930s it was the roving correspondent who gave Americans whatever world consciousness had after long years of isolationism. Foreign reporting was the province of scrupulous writers who became famous as they informed and entertained readers with their subtly styled points of view. Ernest Hemingway first came to the world's attention while working as a foreign correspondent. So, too, did William Shirer, Edward R. Murrow, Ernie Pyle, Jimmy Sheean, and, of course, John Gunther (to name just a few); the list reads like a roll call of some imaginary Hall of Fame for American journalists.

It is a measure of how much our society, and the profession of journalism have evolved that today the substance of the news has become secondary to the technology of the God known as TV; great world events today are presented to us by globetrotting television performers *cum* news people. Network news anchors—people such as Peter Jennings, Dan Rather, and Tom Brokaw—are household names across America. (Military coup in Moscow? No problem. Diane Sawyer is there with reports from Boris Yeltsin's elbow. American planes bombing Baghdad? "A CNN reporting team will bring it to you live, but first a word from our sponsor. . . .")

In the years between the wars, foreign reporting was more substance than style. Not that the quality of journalism was necessarily better (although on the whole it was unquestionably more literate and possibly more comprehensive), but it was different. Foreign correspondents, the glamour figures of their era, were a special breed of men. (As Julia Edwards points out in her book *The Women of the World: The Great Foreign Correspondents* (1988), the field was then—and remains—dominated by males. Even in 1987, 50 per cent of the broadcast and print reporters and editors in the United States were women, yet 80 per cent of the foreign correspondents were men!)[14]

Having escaped the responsibilities of home, family, and country, America's foreign correspondents were an informal fraternity to whom personal excess was the rule, not the exception. It was the rare man who resisted the temptations of the itinerant lifestyle: drinking, smoking, and philandering. Many kept at least one mistress who filled a variety of roles: lover, companion, translator, and knowledgeable source of political gossip.

"A good many newspapermen of the time and place could have been said to be without private lives," John Gunther's friend and colleague Jimmy Sheean explained in his memoir, *Personal History* (1935), "or to treat their private lives with indifference—to marry and beget absent-mindedly, see their wives sometimes once a week, and live, in all the keener hours of their existence, in the 'office,' a place taken to comprise most of the other offices, bars, cafes, and meeting places of the press and politicians."[15]

In the 1920s and 1930s, all of the news from Europe, the Soviet Union, and the Middle East was funneled into North America through just three news agencies and seven large newspapers that maintained complete overseas news services. It was the 300 or so journalists staffing these news operations who controlled the flow of information to the whole continent. John Gunther's syndicated reports, which were carried by more than 100 newspapers across North America, exerted a profound influence on public opinion. For better or worse, America's view of the world was the WASP, male, middle-class view of the world which Gunther and most of his colleagues shared.

The hallmark of this view was an unwavering mid-Western faith in the virtues of the American way of life. This messianic urge was an outward looking, updated version of the nineteenth century doctrine known as Manifest Destiny. At its best, it gave rise to such altruistic foreign policy initiatives as the Marshall Plan—the Truman administration's aid package that rebuilt Europe in the wake of the Second World War. John Gunther and other liberal-minded commentators, would come to argue that at its misguided worst, the same impulses fostered the so-called "Ugly American syndrome," and planted the seeds for involvements in

Vietnam and Central America.

But all of that was still years in the future when in 1936 John Gunther profiled Hitler, Mussolini, and Stalin in a book called *Inside Europe.* America suddenly began to take serious notice of the crazy men who had seized sanity hostage and were prodding the world towards the bloodiest war in history. *Inside Europe* became a runaway international best seller, and that six-letter preposition—"i-n-s-i-d-e"—forever changed Gunther's life. It also redefined the essence of modern journalism. The word took on a new meaning overnight, one that reflected itself in the way we view our society, and the world around us; the public's appetite for "inside" information became insatiable.

The Gunther formula was often imitated, although never duplicated in the years immediately following publication of *Inside Europe.* No fewer than thirty "inside" books were published about everything from countries to institutions, and even modern medicine. (*Inside Medicine* was a laymen's guide to intestines!) The magazine and newspaper adaptations of Gunther's approach numbered in the thousands.

What had formerly been the kind of chatty background information—indeed, superfluous information—that no one had ever bothered or *dared* to report suddenly was deemed essential to any well-written news story. Small wonder that *Inside Europe* created a sensation, shattering sales records on both sides of the Atlantic, and garnering its author kudos and condemnation. Winston Churchill praised the book as a journalistic *tour de force,* while Adolf Hitler (in a gesture reminiscent of the Ayatollah Khomeini's death decree against British author Salman Rushdie) ordered the Gestapo to liquidate Gunther whenever and wherever he was caught.[16]

If the "inside" story of John Gunther be known, there was never a stranger candidate for any dictator's death list.

Gunther was an amiable, fair-haired bear of a man. His abiding passions in life were not political, but rather good company, gourmet food and drink, fine clothing, and beautiful women. As someone once noted, he had no friends, only *best* friends.

John Gunther was a larger-than-life figure who embraced life with passion. During the post-war years (he escaped the Gestapo's long arm) his elegant New York apartment was renowned as a cultural and political salon where prominent authors, artists, journalists, politicians, and Hollywood film stars gathered. When the sultry actress Tallulah Bankhead met Gunther for the first time, she purred, "I'm in a helluva fix, because I think you're a writer, yet you look like a football player." Asked why that mattered, she sighed, "Because I don't know whether to be witty or sexy."[17]

At one of Gunther's gala parties, co-hosted by Claude Phillipe of the Waldorf-Astoria Hotel, liveried footmen carried scrolls bearing an invitation to each of the eighty guests.[18] Visitors to the Gunther apartment during those golden years in the late 1940s and the 1950s included the Duke and Duchess of Windsor, Eleanor Roosevelt, Wendell Willkie, Adlai Stevenson, Greta Garbo (to whom Gunther dedicated his 1958 book *Inside Russia Today*), Marlene Dietrich, William L. Shirer, Edward R. Murrow, Bennett Cerf, and Arthur Rubenstein.

To his fans and colleagues, John Gunther appeared to be someone who had it all—fame, wealth, adventure, and romance. But that was only half of it. Those who knew the "inside" story knew that his life wasn't all champagne and filet mignon. Family and close friends knew that Gunther's success was proof of Thomas Edison's maxim: "Genius is one per cent inspiration and 99 per cent perspiration." John Gunther paid the price for for fame and fortune.

His fast-paced, happy-go-lucky lifestyle ensured that he was perpetually strapped for cash. He once told an interviewer, "I've eaten every book before it's published," yet Gunther's biggest problem was not money. He was a man who was bedeviled at various times during his life by self-doubt, the memories of having grown up aching for the love of a father he never really knew, by artistic frustrations, a doomed first marriage, the tragic deaths of his only two natural children, his own precarious health, and an ill-fated love affair with the wife of a close friend.

Despite the devoted love of his second wife, and an adopted son, he was a man not entirely at peace with himself or the world when death took him. His autobiography, in the planning stages, was never written.

Edward R. Murrow, Gunther's long-time friend and colleague, once asked him to write a short statement of his beliefs for inclusion on a long-playing record and in a book. Gunther responded by stating that he believed in truth, hard work, a God of man's making, and in himself. "Logically, before believing in anything else at all, I am compelled to believe in my own self—whatever its manifest imperfections and shortcomings—or my life would hardly be worth living," he said.[20]

The ultimate irony of Gunther's life was that he forgot those words. How else does one explain his admission to a *Time* reporter a few years later? "I'm terribly limited. I completely lack intensity of soul. I'm not original. "I'm really only a competent observer who works terribly hard at doing a job well."[21]

Not everyone agreed with that humble self-assessment—certainly not the mourners who gathered at St. James Episcopal Church that glorious June day to pay their last respects to John Gunther, and certainly not that generation of Americans who learned about the world from him. He was a person fascinated by the past, someone voraciously interested in people and ideas.

"What I sought was to grasp the flavor of a man, his texture, his impact, what he stood for, what he believed in, what made him what he was, and what color he gave to the fabric of his time," Gunther once explained.[22] In so doing Gunther, too, became enmeshed in that marvelous, terrible tapestry that is the history of our times.

In many ways, the story of his remarkable life is a metaphor for America's own coming of age. John Gunther's career spanned a period of astounding change in the world. That idea provided both the impetus and a theme for an exhibition of Gunther papers, photos, and memorabilia which was presented by the Special Collections Unit of the University of Chicago Library in the fall of 1990. Acting Curator Daniel Meyer pointed out in the preface to a catalogue prepared for "John Gunther: Inside Journalism," that during the forty-six years of Gunther's journalism career, numerous developments had forever altered the tone and character of modern life: the growth of totalitarianism, the transformation of political ideologies, the collapse of the great colonial empires, the proliferation of wars and revolutions, and the emergence of the United States as a global superpower. Coming to grips with these stark new geopolitical realities was a matter of pressing concern to an America newly shed of its inhibitions and uncertainties. John Gunther's popular books helped Americans (and millions of other people around the world, too) to do exactly that.[23]

However, as author Jay Pridmore noted in that same exhibition catalog, "Behind a reporter known for evenhandedness and objectivity was a searing romanticism of the most emotional kind. How these qualities were all contained in a single life, a single career, is one of the great stories of American journalism in this century."[24]

This book examines that story.

CHAPTER ONE

Just after three o'clock on the afternoon of April 25, 1947, the jangle of the telephone interrupted the tapping of the typewriter in the Park Avenue apartment of journalist John Gunther. He rose from the desk in his study.

Ordinarily, an afternoon phone call would have been an irritation. Not today. John had just completed the first four chapters of his latest book, *Inside U.S.A.* It was to be a sprawling, complex literary snapshot of America, "the greatest, craziest, most dangerous, least stable, most spectacular, least grown-up and most powerful nation ever known."[1] It was to be a book the likes of which no one had attempted in the 100 years since Count Alexis de Tocqueville wrote *Democracy in America, 1835-39.*

Who better to tackle this formidable task than John Gunther?

After all, his popular *Inside* books and radio show had earned him fame and fortune as one of America's highest paid journalists. The Gunther apartment, the epitome of 1940s chic, was decorated with paintings by Picasso, Matisse, and Cezanne, and other modern masters, which John Gunther had the foresight to collect during a dozen years in Europe as a *Chicago Daily News* foreign correspondent.

Physically, Gunther had never felt better. There was no question that his fondness for the good life and a few too many nights on the town had added some extra pounds to his six-foot-two frame. But apart from occasional bouts with asthma, which were not helped by the cigarette that was perpetually between his lips, he was hale and hardy. At forty-six, John had the energy and stamina of a man half his age. Richard Rovere of the *New Yorker* described him about this time as being "tall and blond, with a bulldozer frame, blue eyes, a ruddy complexion, and incongruously delicate features."[2]

John took a drag on his smoke and lifted the telephone receiver.

In the instant that followed, the voice on the other end of the line dispelled the euphoria that John had been feeling. It was the doctor at Deerfield Academy, his sixteen-year-old son's boarding school. The man informed John that a neurologist from nearby Springfield, Massachussets, had just examined Johnny, Jr. The neurologist then came on the line to report his diagnosis.

"I think your child has a brain tumor," he said. The words were a spike of fear thrust into John's heart.

"But that's very serious, isn't it?" he blurted.

It was all he could think of to say. John was too stunned to make sense. That instant was his worst nightmare come true.

Johnny had seemed fine at Christmas. Three months later, during March break, he had complained of tiredness and a stiff neck. Neither John nor his ex-wife Frances had been much concerned. Any real fear they had centered on a recent case of polio at Deerfield. As a precaution, Johnny had been examined by the family doctor, who pronounced him a fit, healthy teen-ager.

John immediately telephoned Frances with the grim news. He then rang Dr. Tracy Putnam, a prominent Columbia University neurologist who had been recommended to him by the doctor from Springfield. Less than two hours after receiving that terrible phone call, John and Putnam were in a car racing north out of New York. They picked up Frances in Connecticut on the 150-mile drive to Deerfield. It was a grim, foggy night, with an icy sleet falling.

The world into which John Gunther had been born in 1901 was the America of that bygone era. Now beyond the realm of living memory, it was largely a sprawling, undeveloped agrarian frontier. From the Alleghenies in the east to the Pacific in the west, most of the 76 million citizens were still "down on the farm" or in thousands of small towns, where life revolved around the seasons, and the values that counted were self-reliance, thrift, hard work, and religion. Isolation was the norm. So, too, were a deeply rooted self-righteousness, and a suspicion of all things "big city."

Most Americans still rarely ventured more than a few miles from home. Only the well-to-do traveled regularly. And when they did it was in private railroad cars known as "varnishes." Or else they crossed the Atlantic in luxury aboard the scores of ocean liners that plied the shipping lanes between New York and "the Continent."

Two years before the Wright brothers made that first tentative flight in their flimsy wooden plane they called the *Kitty Hawk*, horses were America's favored means of locomotion. Not one person in two had even *seen* an automobile, much less owned or driven in one. It would be another decade before Henry Ford opened his assembly line at Highland Park, Michigan, and changed America forever. In 1901, many people still considered the newfangled "horseless carriage" a curiosity at best, or an outright menace. Woodrow Wilson, president of Princeton University, dismissed the motorcar as the plaything of the rich; in 1906, six years before his election to the White House, Wilson gave voice to a widely held sentiment when he stated, "Nothing has spread socialistic feelings in this country more than the automobile. It offers us a picture of the arrogance of wealth."

In the world of John Gunther's youth the marvels of electricity, telephones, paved roads, and moving pictures were still just rumors for most people. Women's suffrage, air conditioning, radio and television, computers, and space travel were the visions of utopian fantasy. The grim realities of our age—world wars, environmental destruction, drugs, AIDS, and international terrorism—were nightmares which not even the most alarmist of visionaries prophesied.

Republican William McKinley had begun his second term as president. Prosperity was only now returning after a great depression that had ravaged the economy in the mid-1890s, when "Businessmen died like flies under the strain," as economist Henry C. Adams put it. Banks failed. Labor unrest swept the nation. Railroads went broke, and the federal government staved off bankruptcy only because banker J.P. Morgan lent the treasury $65 million in gold. The price of grain and other Midwestern crops had plummeted, driving many farmers off the land; in Kansas alone 11,000 farms were lost to foreclosure. The poor and the homeless had little choice but to flock to the cities in search of work to feed their families. For many of them, Chicago was a logical destination.

By the turn of the century, the Great Fire of 1871 was the stuff of legends; the city that poet Carl Sandburg would dub the "City of Big Shoulders" was a magnetic, sprawling frontier capital. With a population of 1.7 million, Chicago was the economic hub of the rich hinterlands. Most of the great railroads that fanned out across the continent, to both east and west, used the city as a terminus. All roads seemed to converge here, at the southern tip of Lake Michigan. Chicago's railyards, wharves, factories, and grain elevators hummed with activity. The stockyards on the South Side were the world's largest.

With all this prosperity and rude sophistication, Chicago was still a rip-roaring, rough, tough kind of place a century after its founding as Fort Dearborn, a frontier military outpost. William T. Steed, a British journalist who visited in the 1890s, observed that hell would surely be just "a pocket version" of Chicago's brothels, gambling joints, saloons, and squalid slums. "Loving Chicago," novelist Nelson Algren would state, "is like loving a woman with a broken nose."

This was a city where the nineteenth century collided head-on with the twentieth, a vibrant, teeming metropolis of cobblestoned streets, trafficked by horse-drawn carriages and wagons cheek-by-jowl with electric trolleys and a wondrous elevated steam railroad (dubbed the "El" by locals) that "looped" Chicago's business core. These same streets were crowded with people from every part of

America and the globe; three out of four residents were either foreign-born or first-generation American. This was the American melting pot in all its reality; Germans, Swedes, Poles, Irish, English, Italians, Russians, and blacks. All had been drawn to Chicago by the dream of a better life. There was money to be made by anyone with the enterprise and guts to go out and either make—or take—it. It was inevitable that John Gunther's father would be drawn here. He was a man forever in search of easy money.

Eugene McClellan Guenther had been born in Philadelphia on February 5, 1866, to Louise (nee Kraeger) and John Guenther,[3] a blacksmith turned boilermaker. Eugene's father was a big, stocky man with chiseled, noble features and a thatch of dark, black hair. Not much more is known about John Guenther's background, other than the fact that he probably emigrated to America from the Alsace region of Germany sometime around 1850. Like his son after him, John Guenther was more concerned with meeting the future than recalling the past.

Family legend had it that he died while fighting for the Union side in the Civil War. While that would have been a suitably romantic end to a man who gave his son a middle name after erstwhile Union commander Major General George B. ("Little Mac") McClellan, one of Philadelphia's favorite sons, no factual basis exists for that notion. The records show that Eugene was born about ten months after General Robert E. Lee's surrender at Appomattox on April 9, 1865. John Guenther fought in the Union Army all right, but if he died in battle, it could only have happened in the war's closing hours. More likely, later generations confused his fate with that of his brother-in-law, William Kraeger, who fell wearing Union blue.

Although Guenther might have chosen to give his son Eugene the middle name of a more successful military leader, his choice turned out to be apt in one important regard: temperamentally, Eugene Guenther and the general were alike. While McClellan was a man of indisputable charm and talent, he was also a man possessed by a seething, unbridled ambition that ultimately proved to be his downfall.

From the time he was a lad, Eugene was intoxicated by dreams of wealth. He quit school in Philadelphia at an early age, and then worked for a few years before drifting west. He arrived in the Windy City about 1886. Here he lived in rooming houses on Chicago's North Side, and found work as a "commercial traveler." Eugene soon saved enough money to open a small cigar making business in the downtown loop, not far from the Chicago Opera House. Unfortunately, when the venture failed in 1888, Eugene was obliged to return to sales. It was an occupation that he pursued from time to time for most of his life.[4] Sometimes he sold cigars or liquor, sometimes real estate. Other times it was anything that he could on sales trips that took him throughout the Midwest.

Family members recall that like his father before him, Eugene McClellan Guenther was a portly, big-boned man with the family's jet black hair. Eugene loved natty clothes and proudly wore an elk's tooth—the symbol of his fraternal lodge—on a gold vest chain.[5]

Another Guenther trait was a love of good food and drink. Eugene ballooned to about 300 pounds as he hit middle age. The combination of excess weight and an arthritic knee caused him to limp noticeably, and he walked with the help of a cane.[6] It did not help his health that he chain-smoked cigars when he could afford to do so. He also suffered from high blood pressure. "Eugene Guenther wasn't a well man," one of his nieces recalls; another vividly remembers his "red, florid face."[7]

To his acquaintances and customers, he was a Falstaffian character, possessed of an ingratiating gregariousness and charm. Family members were familiar with another, darker side to his character. Like his famous military namesake, Eugene's ambition exceeded his grasp. Frustration was the inevitable result. Years later, his son John described him as "a robust ne'er-do-well, vain [and] sanguine."[8]

In 1900, Eugene Guenther was thirty-five and frustrated that he was no closer to making his fortune. He decided the time had come to marry. Although he fancied himself a ladies man who did his best to look and dress the part, Eugene's circle of eligible female acquaintances was not large. His nomadic life left little time for proper socializing. He began spending a lot of time at the home of his mother's younger sister, his Aunt Lisetta. Here Eugene ate home-cooked meals, and began courting his spinster cousin Lizette.

At age thirty, Lizette was the second of the four Schoeninger children and eldest of the two daughters. The family despaired of ever finding "Ett" a husband, and while Eugene Guenther was not a rich man, he seemed at least to be one with prospects: he dressed well, got along with people, and came from an "acceptable" family background.

Lizette Gunther was about five-feet-six-inches in height, which was considered tall for the time, with beautifully smooth, clear skin, blonde, naturally curly hair, and distinctively angular Germanic features, all of which were typical of the Schoeningers. The family traced its roots back to the Stuttgart area of southwest Germany (where their surname was originally von Schoeninger). John Gunther years later remembered his mother's family as closely knit, comfortably "bourgeois," and "much more stolid, less nomadic than my father's."[9]

Life in the Schoeninger home revolved around Lizette's father. Joseph Schoeninger was a broad shouldered, patriarchal figure with a mane of wavy blond hair, a bushy Vandyke beard, and an amiable, easy disposition. Born in Germany in 1839, he had emigrated to America in 1856, at age seventeen. After working for a time as a farmhand, he enlisted in the Union Army during the Civil War and saw action at Shiloh in April 1862. Following the war, he lived briefly in Philadelphia, where he married the teenaged Lizetta Kraeger.

Not much is known about her family other than the fact that she was one of four children. A lone brother named William—the one family members later seem to have confused with John Guenther—died fighting in the Civil War; sister Philomena (1833-1913) married a man named Charles H. Bohnstedt; and her other sister, Louise (1839-1915), married Joseph Guenther and bore the baby Eugene.

Joseph and Lizetta Schoeninger had four children in quick succession: Joseph, Jr. (1869), Lizette (1872), Julius (1873), and Mae (1875). The young family joined the great post-Civil War migration westward, settling in the burgeoning German community in the north Chicago suburb of Lakeview. Joe Schoeninger found work in the Chicago Mint. After the children reached school age, Lizetta took her teaching diploma and taught primary school for a time. Lizette and her siblings grew up in a loving, closely knit household, where books, music, bridge, and conversation were the nightly pastimes, and a man with an education was respected. After all, this was an era when knowledge seemed to make all things possible. These were the values that Lizette took with her as she began life with cousin Eugene following their marriage in 1899.[10]

In those days, for $6,500 one could buy an eight-room home with steam heat and large shady lot on comfortably middle class North Magnolia Avenue in Chicago's booming northern Lakeview suburb. It was one of these homes that Eugene Guenther coveted, but a few blocks distant, the neat, less costly and decidedly less fashionable houses of the immigrant working class were springing up almost as fast as the crops in their front yard celery gardens. Row upon row, the simple frame homes crowded the streetscapes of the avenues off Chicago's North Clark Street. It was here that Eugene and Lizette began their life together.

And it was here, in a second-floor bedroom of one of those houses, at 1422 Wellington Street, on a sweltering hot Thursday, August 30, 1901, that Lizette Guenther gave birth to her first child. Downstairs, in the crowded kitchen, friends, neighbors, Lisette's parents, and the rest of the Schoeninger family fanned themselves as they waited anxiously for the doctor to emerge from the upstairs bedroom. When Dr. Julius H. Oswald finally did so, he smiled, nodded his head, and announced, "Congratulations, it's a boy." The tiny kitchen erupted with shouts of joy, laughter, and the clapping of hands. "A son!" shouted Eugene.

CHAPTER TWO

Almost from the beginning, the marriage of Eugene and Lizette Guenther was unhappy. Although there seems to have been enough money for them to live a comfortable middle class life style, they had little in common and argued frequently. Whether by design or necessity, Eugene's sales trips took him away for weeks at a time. Lizette must surely have wondered how he passed the long nights in countless dusty prairie towns. But the memories of his experiences were not something he shared with his wife and family. "Often now I wonder about the infinity of experience he must have had wandering through the Middle-West," his son John wrote years later. "I am curious about much of his life that is unknown to me."[1]

Despite the distance that often separated them, young John's earliest letters to Eugene reflected a young boy's love for his father.

They also displayed his facility with the written word. At age five, John described an intricate trick that he had seen a circus elephant perform. At age ten, he mused about Teddy Roosevelt's delegate support at the 1912 Republican convention, and commented on the fortunes of Chicago's two professional baseball teams.[2]

During her husband's long absences Lizette spent a lot of time at her parents' home. She had hoped that with the birth of the baby John on that hot August day in 1901 her marriage would improve. It did not. Accentuating the couple's marital problems was the fact that because Eugene was away from home so much, he seldom took part in Schoeninger family gatherings. On the rare occasions when he did, his presence caused tension. One of Lizette's nieces recalls, "Of course, nothing was ever said to us children, but I can remember my parents speaking disdainfully about Uncle Gene, how he gambled, and how he embarrassed Aunt Ett in front of the family by chastising her for her spending habits and asking her to account for money he'd given her."[3]

Despite these difficulties, the couple's second child was born on November 4, 1905.[4] They named the baby girl Jean. Afterwards, life reverted to the familiar pattern. With Eugene away much of the time, young John and his baby sister were raised by Lizette. Neither of the children really knew their father, other than as the near-stranger who periodically came to the house to spend a few days, leave some money, and collect a suitcase full of clean clothes. As a result, Jean became totally devoted to Lizette, and following her mother's death many years later, she refused even to utter her name for a long time. In her old age, if asked what it was that her father did for a living, Jean would smile and shrug. "He was a traveling salesman, so he was away a lot. I truly don't know what he sold or even where."[5]

If anyone was capable of raising two young children alone, however, it was Lizette Guenther. She did all that she could to provide a loving home environment for her son and daughter. "She was an exceptionally modest and cultivated woman," John would recall, "very receptive and intelligent, infinitely loving of books and pictures, infinitely eager to know more to improve herself. My sister was much more on her side too. My mother took care of both of us."[6]

Being suspicious of the quality of Chicago's burgeoning public school system, Lizette for a time taught both children at home. In fact, this proved to be for the best, since neither of them was in good health. John suffered from asthma, while Jean's problems were the result of an accident.

One day in the summer of 1910 she was hit by a car as she roller-skated on the street in front of the family home. When the broken bones in her leg failed to heal properly, she was left with one leg shorter than the other. Jean, who was by nature shy and introspective, walked with a limp for the rest of her life. Emotionally, her scars ran even deeper.

Lizette Guenther compensated for her children's frailties—overly so—by sheltering and immersing them in a world of her extended family, music, books, and pictures. John developed a lifelong aversion to exercise and group activities. "We were lonely children. We both disliked games," he once recalled.[7]

Lizette read to her children for hours on end. The Greek poets and mythology, Dickens novels, and Kipling's Jungle Books were favorites. Everyone in the family had a nickname drawn from the Kipling stories. John's nickname has been forgotten. Jean remembered that her mother became "Shere Khan," the tiger, while she was "Billi"—a moniker that stayed with her permanently.

John became a self-admitted "book-worm." By six or seven, he delighted his elders with his ability to recite much of the translated version of the Greek poet Homer's epic poem *The Iliad*. An early fascination with ancient life evolved into a lifelong love affair with history in general, and with the natural sciences. Young John Gunther spent many hours in his book-lined bedroom reading the volumes of the popular *Standard American Encyclopedia* (1897) by John Clark Ridpath, laboriously plotting and writing out lists of kings and queens, dynasties, revolutions, great battles, and events of the past. When he was eleven, he set out to write his own encyclopedia, which consisted of 200 pages divided into five sections: Greek and Roman Historical Characters, Animals, World Statistics, Events in American History, and Battleships.

This period of sheltered childhood ended about 1910 for both John and Jean. Eugene Gunther's sales income plummeted during a period of failing business, and the family suddenly found itself short of money. Although she was already forty, and well beyond the usual age for doing so, Lizette (like her mother before her) went to normal school, got her teacher's certificate, and then helped support her family by teaching. John, now ten, was enrolled at nearby Morris School in the fall of 1911.[8] The younger, more fragile Jean was placed in Francis Parker School, a small, private institution on North Clark Street. Eugene drove her to and from classes in a secondhand Buick he owned.[9]

Lizette had taught her children well. They excelled academically, and in 1914 John progressed to nearby Lake View High School, an imposing, fortress-like structure built in 1874 at the bustling intersection of Irving Park Road and Ashland Avenue. One of the first township high schools built in Illinois, it was also one of the largest. The four years that John spent here were not happy. "I was afraid of the older boys," he once explained. "I didn't know how to scrap back. I had been far too deeply cloistered at home. I couldn't bat a ball or catch a pass. My father despaired of me."[10]

The upturn in the economy in the years prior to America's entry into the First World War and the presence of two breadwinners in the home improved the Guenther family's finances. Eugene saved and borrowed enough money so that in 1916 he could quit his sales job and go into business for himself once again. He and a partner named Harry Bernstein opened Guenther's & Bernstein's saloon at 1556 North Clark Street. Business was good, and the next year he bought a comfortably spacious, two-story frame home at 4223 Kenmore Avenue, just north of the baseball park that would later become Wrigley Field, and adjacent to Graceland Cemetery and the "El" tracks. Eugene felt the larger home was more in keeping with his elevated status in the community. So, too, was his decision, following the nation's entry into the Great War, to patriotically "Americanize" his German-sounding family surname by dropping the first "e." Thereafter, Guenther became "Gunther."

Eugene spent most of his time at his saloon. When he came home early, it was to sleep or flop in his favorite chair, and talk with a young male boarder the family had taken in to help pay the bills. The children adopted the man as "Uncle Tony" and held him in great affection because of his trick of standing on his head while coins for them rolled out of his pockets.

Relations between Eugene and Lizette remained distant. The couple continued to sleep in separate bedrooms at opposite ends of the upstairs hallway. If Lizette was more content, it was only because she now had the money to enjoy life. She bought a player piano for the parlor, employed young German immigrant girls as maids, traveled to Germany to visit family, and even joined in the Schoeninger family's annual expeditions to rented summer cottages. "My mother, John, and I spent a series of summers with the Schoeningers at Mackinac Island, at the head of Lake Michigan," Jean Gunther recalled. "Sometimes we drove up in cars. Sometimes we went by lake boat. It was really a lot of fun because in those days there were no cars on Mackinac Island, just horses and buggies."[11]

It was also about this time that another important development occurred in young John's life: he discovered his talent for writing. In a foreshadowing of things to come, his current events essay on the recent Russian Revolution won praise from his teachers, and it was printed in a 1917 edition of the Lake View High School magazine, *The Red & White*. John's first byline spurred him to begin writing short stories, poems, and articles. "My writing had . . . a political bent at the very beginning," he remembered many years later.[12]

John's literary interests (like those of classmate Margaret Saunders, who became known for her novels under the pen name Rakham Holt) were encouraged at school by an English teacher named Margaret S. Harding, who would become a distinguished author and editor in her own right, and who in the 1940s headed the University of Minnesota Press.

At home, John was nurtured both by his mother and by his uncle, Julius Schoeninger. During John's high school years, Uncle Julius bought small, hard-cover blank diaries and encouraged the boy by challenging him to reading "contests." Any time either of them finished a book, its title, author, and the date were duly noted in the alphabetical listings. Often John made jottings about what he had read. These comments reveal his precocity. Of *Treasure Island*, the Robert Louis Stevenson book, young John wrote, "This book, as everyone knows, is a classic of juvenile literature, and after I had read it, I fully agreed because it certainly is fine."[13]

Between November 15, 1917, and the early months of 1919, John filled five of these blank books. Although no record of Uncle Julius' performance survives, the impact of the reading contests he instigated was clear: John became convinced that "to make something" of his life he would continue his reading and his education.

CHAPTER THREE

With a dream of becoming a chemist, John Gunther enrolled for his freshman year at the University of Chicago (U of C) in October 1918. Eugene Gunther did not approve. He preferred that his son find a job. But John continued to live at home and each day rode the "El" on the long, noisy trip to and from the U of C campus.

"College was to be a purely vocational interlude. Why I chose chemistry I have no idea," John wrote years later. "I had no talent for it since chemistry, in its non-stink phase, is largely physics and mathematics, and I was never able to learn to add or subtract. I did chemistry for two years at the university, then gave it up, and turned to the things I liked, English and History."[1]

When John did well in his studies in his first year, he was awarded a scholarship. He also found part-time work in the university library during the school year. His summer jobs were typical student labor: selling shoes, sorting mail, and working in a chemical factory.

Lizette Gunther had by now emerged as the family's chief breadwinner. Eugene's health was failing. So, too, were his fortunes. With the coming into force in February 1918 of the Eighteenth Amendment, "the noble experiment" (as Herbert Hoover called it) that made Prohibition law, the bottom dropped out of the saloon business. In one of his widely read columns, Chicago newspaperman Finley Peter Dunne reflected the gloom felt by Eugene Gunther and a great many other Americans when he had his popular fictional bartender, Mr. Dooley, suggest to his friend, Mr. Hennessey, that grim times lay ahead. "King Alcohol no longer rules th' sea or th' land. Th' ladies have got that benevolent o' dishpot (President Woodrow Wilson) on his knees beggin' f'r mercy . . . Take a dhrink, me boy, whether ye need it or not. Take it now. It may be y'er last."[2]

John was not much happier than the fictional Mr. Dooley, for his freshman days at university proved to be as lonely and miserable as those of his initial experiences at Lake View High. He was still painfully shy. John knew almost no one, even though most U of C students in those days came from the city and surrounding area. It was on the advice of their "elders" that freshmen got involved in campus life. Not surprisingly, John took part in no extracurricular activities in his first year. He joined no fraternity, at a time when campus social life for many of the 5,000 students centered around these tightly-knit, socially stratified groups. Fortunately, John was not alone in his non-status.

Although Jews were a sizable minority at the U of C, antisemitism was rampant. All Jews, "Christers" (religious Fundamentalists), and "queers"—people like John, who seemed different or at all individualistic—were referred to as "barbs," which was short for barbarians. All were social pariahs, deemed ineligible to join most social campus groups. It was mostly other barbs with whom John became friends.

"The U of C, one of the largest and richest institutions of learning in the world, was partly inhabited by a couple of thousand young nincompoops whose ambition in life was to get into the right fraternity or club, go to the right parties and get elected to something or other," John's friend and later colleague Vincent

"Jimmy" Sheean wrote in *Personal History*, his 1935 memoir of his student days. "The frivolous 2,000—the undergraduate body, the 'campus'—may have been a minority, for the University contained a great many solitary workers in both the undergraduate and graduate fields; but the minority thought of itself as a majority, thought of itself, in fact, as the whole of the University."[3]

The U of C had been founded just twenty-six years earlier, in 1892, as a Baptist institution, mainly on the strength of a $600,000 endowment from industrialist John D. Rockefeller. By 1918, when John Gunther enrolled as a seventeen-year-old freshman, the overt Baptist influence had faded, and the school was renowned as one of America's leading academic institutions. A degree from the Chicago school was among the most respected in the land. Even the campus itself *looked* like the archetypal college campus, with its Oxford-style quadrangles, its towering spires, red slate roofs, and ornate, ivy-covered halls. Jimmy Sheean aptly described it as "that mountain ring of 20th Century Gothic near the shores of Lake Michigan."[4]

Many years later, in a 1965 magazine article, John Gunther looked back ruefully on his student days at U of C. They were, he recalled, a period of "electivism gone wild"[5] on America's campuses. John was obliged to take only two compulsory courses in his four years of studying for a bachelor's degree: English composition and Shakespeare. He was free to choose any courses he liked, as long as he fulfilled his requirement in English, his major. Like most of his classmates, John studied either what appealed to him or seemed easiest. In later life, he would lament the fact he had received no education at all in Languages, the Arts and Humanities, and only the barest of training in such disciplines as Economics, Political Science, Philosophy, and Sociology.

By his sophomore year John Gunther had began to shed his shyness. He became friendly with a group of like-minded young men, barbs who shared his interest in literature. Among them were William N. Fuqua, who went on to enjoy a successful career in the Chicago advertising industry; Leonard Weil, who also worked in advertising and occasionally wrote for the *New York Times*; and James (Herc) Mulroy, a campus correspondent for the *Chicago Daily News*. It was Mulroy who opened the door for John to begin writing for the newpaper, and then to join the reporting staff after his graduation.

Mulroy achieved fame early in his journalism career, teaming up with a co-worker to win the 1924 Pulitzer Prize for investigative reporting when they helped to solve the infamous Leopold-Loeb murder case. For two years before his premature death in 1951 at age fifty-two, Mulroy was Illinois Governor Adlai Stevenson's executive assistant. When Mulroy introduced him to the governor, John became one of Stevenson's staunchest supporters.

John, Herc Mulroy and their friends formed their own fraternal society called the "Green Chalybeate." The Greek name, which had no significance other than its mysterious sound, means "impregnated with iron." The Green Chalybeate met regularly for nights out on the town, youthful girl chasing, general merriment, and "bull" sessions. John sometimes got carried away. In some of these guys-only outings, he boasted about his relationships with various campus co-eds. Tongues wagged, and one anonymous young lady responded by penning a caustic poem entitled, "Why Don't You Speak for Yourself, John?" which appeared in the campus newspaper, *The Daily Maroon.*

Far more significant than these student shenanigans was the group's keen shared interest in books and writing. John and his friends together became attuned to the ferment that was bubbling through American literature. "What bedazzled us, enchanted us, and bewildered us were the metrical innovations of Edna St. Vincent Millay, the short story techniques of Cardoc Evans or A.E. Coppard," John remembered in a 1965 magazine article. "The giddy glory of those days! The explorations, the discoveries, the excitements!" What was inspiring was the fact that so much of what was new and exciting was taking place right in Chicago; for a time, the city displaced New York as America's literary mecca. Novelist Theodore Dreiser spoke for the generation of writers who came of age in these post-war years when he wrote, "Chicago was so young, so blithe, so new that just to be a part of it made me crazy with life."[6]

Among the prominent Chicago writers of the day were Edna Ferber, Upton Sinclair, Sherwood Anderson, and James T. Farrell. Poets Carl Sandburg and Edgar Lee Masters received international acclaim for their distinctively Midwestern voices. *Poetry: A Magazine of Verse*, founded in Chicago in 1912 by Harriet Monroe, had a liberating impact on American writing, as did Margaret Anderson's innovative literary magazine *The Little Review*, which began publishing in 1914. Among the then-unknown writers who contributed were T.S. Eliot, Ford Madox Ford, Ernest Hemingway, Hart Crane, Gertrude Stein, William Carlos Williams, Marianne Moore, Ezra Pound, James Joyce, and William Butler Yeats.

One writer more than any other influenced idealistic young people of the day: Sinclair Lewis. John Gunther and just about every other college student had read Lewis' brilliant satiric novel *Main Street*, which scoffed at and questioned the morality of small town, middle-America. Published in 1920, the controversial book sold 400,000 copies in its first year alone.

Sinclair Lewis evoked emotions no less intense in those whom he met. Born in 1885 in rural Minnesota, he graduated Yale and spent several years in journalism before writing *Main Street*. As his biographer, Mark Schorer, has noted, most people were repelled by Lewis' appearance: he was gaunt, with a tuft of carrot-red hair, and his ruddy face was pitted by pre-cancerous lesions. But those who knew him were fascinated by the quickness of his mind, his compassion, and his amusing gift for mimicry.[7]

Like many old newspapermen, Lewis had an alcohol problem; it brought out his Jekyll-and-Hyde nature. A delightful companion when sober, he was a brooding boor when drinking. It was also while he was drinking that Lewis unleashed his acerbic wit, which otherwise was deftly channeled in his writings. Though widely traveled, Lewis' best work caricatured his small town roots, and many of his contemporaries regarded him as being at heart as provincial as the characters he created. Writer Anita Loos once wrote, "[H.L.] Mencken and I used to laugh about him. He was so *square*."[8]

The cynicism of Lewis' *Main Street* proved as fashionable among young intellectuals as it was contagious. John Gunther and his friends at the U of C read and digested the book. Despite the fervor of the artistic flowering taking place around them, they came to regard Chicago as "stiflingly provincial"; they began to affect a studied pose of youthful intellectual scorn. Jean Gunther remembers her brother, Herc Mulroy, and their friends gathering, sometimes at the Gunthers' Kenmore Avenue home, sometimes at the rented summer cottage, to argue long and loud about literature or to work on a play they claimed to be writing. It was evident to Jean that even then her brother had grown serious about becoming a writer. That was further illustrated by an incident that occurred in the spring of 1920.

John was encouraged in his sophomore year by James Weber Linn, his favorite English professor and mentor, to enter one of his critical essays in the annual McLaughlin undergraduate literary competition. First prize was fifty dollars, a significant sum in those days. John chose as his subject the work of a now largely forgotten American novelist named James Branch Cabell (1879-1958). Cabell's complex, mannered, and ironic fantasies, which were considered daring in 1920, were praised by people like Mark Twain, Sinclair Lewis, and H.L. Mencken. When Cabell's 1919 novel *Jurgen* was surpressed two years after its publication on grounds of obscenity, the author became an anti-establishment hero to many students.

John's essay, which pre-dated Cabell's notoriety, did not win the campus essay competition. Undaunted, however, he sent it to *Bookman*, a prominent, scholarly New York literary magazine. To his delight, the editors accepted the essay for publication. What is more, based on the number of words multiplied by the going-rate per word, they sent him a check for exactly fifty-one dollars—a dollar more than the McLaughlin prize! When the essay appeared in the magazine's November 1920 issue,[9] John became a campus celebrity to all the barbs. This unexpected success also convinced him that he could make his living as a writer.

In his third year, John joined both the Drama Club and the campus literary magazine, *The Chanticleer.* Then, in the fall of his senior year, he and Leonard Weil "went out for" the staff of *The Daily Maroon*. The paper's senior editorial jobs were highly coveted on campus, and the incumbents jealously guarded their positions against "barbs." For that reason, all would-be staffers were carefully screened. To the surprise of many people, John and Leonard Weil were not only accepted, managing editor Herbert Rubel appointed them to prominent jobs. Weil became an associate editor, John became the paper's first literary editor, a title he was quick to put to good use.

The Daily Maroon, usually a four-page broadsheet, was published Tuesday through Friday during the school year from a couple of offices in Ellis Hall on the U of C campus. Officially, the newsroom staff consisted of fourteen student editors and about two dozen student reporters, but, in actual fact, only about a dozen students regularly worked on the paper. Those who did got to know one another by working at close quarters formed friendships that were as intense as the animosities.

Arvid Lunde, athletics editor that year, does not remember the first time he met John Gunther in the *Maroon*'s offices, only that he liked him instantly, as did everyone else on the staff. "John was rather big physically and not the most handsome guy, although I'm not one to talk," Lunde recalls with a laugh. "He was always neatly dressed, very likable, and you could tell he was intelligent; I'm not just saying this, but I actually felt kind of stupid next to him. His talents showed and I remember thinking that he'd amount to something. Others did, too, I think."[10]

Jean Brand (now Bennedsen), whose *Daily Maroon* newsroom desk was right behind John's, agreed. "He was a biggish man, with nice, regular features and he always dressed neatly," she said. "He was rather quiet, but people seemed to like him."[11]

From the outset of his journalistic career, John had a knack for sensing where things were about to happen and for knowing what would appeal to his editors and readers. No sooner had he been appointed literary editor than he set about writing every major book publisher in the country asking for new books to review. He was delighted when many began shipping him their latest titles. John carried his idea one step farther when he contacted the publishers of daily newspapers throughout the Midwest, offering to sell them his *Daily Maroon* column. Six said yes, among them a local paper in Evanston, Illinois. The *Chicago Daily News* sometimes picked it up, too. "So—this was in 1921 and I was still an undergraduate—I became a syndicated book reviewer," John said proudly years later.[12]

The new weekly column, "Literary Leaders: The Latest Books Reviewed by John Gunther," made its debut in the *Maroon* on Friday, October 7, 1921. An editorial by the paper's senior editors promised that the column was the first move in revising the *Maroon*'s reputation as a "glorified bulletin board"[13] and promised that the "Literary Leaders" would "startle and shock" its readers "with snappy reviews of the best in contemporary literature." John Gunther, the editorial enthused, was "a man well able to cope with the influx of literature from the more than 25 publishers who are mailing us their best."

"Literary Leaders" attracted a wide readership, as John reviewed any books that were sent to him. His inaugural column proved typical. He offered thumbnail reviews of seven books: two novels, two collections of obscure essays, and three books of poetry.

While John's writing in the column was not always as polished as in the *Bookman* essay, it was seldom dull. John proved that he had both the journalistic skill and critical saavy to handle a column. That first week, he brazenly dismissed Ben Hecht's new novel, *Erik Dorn*, as lacking sufficient "solidity to carry its brilliance," and commented that the subject of one of the essay collections in the hands of a lesser-known writer "might be characterized as fit . . . for literary monkey glands." He also rhapsodized that poet Edna St. Vincent Millay combined "in her lyrics a lusty exaltation, a fine impudence, even, with beautiful phrase patterns and clean passion."[14]

"Literary Leaders" quickly became the *Maroon*'s most widely read column, and its author a campus celebrity. James Weber Linn, John's favorite English professor, praised the column as "the best of its kind in Chicago."

John's self-confidence received a further boost when, after a little prompting on his part, readers well beyond the confines of the university campus began taking note of "Literary Leaders." In 1921 John solicited comments from no less an authority than H.L. Mencken, who at the time was editing a magazine called *Smart Set*. Mencken, known for his crusty temperament, praised the "Literary Leaders" column. Furthermore, when John proposed an article on the U of C, Mencken agreed to publish it. "Higher Learning in America: The University of Chicago" appeared in the April 1922 edition of *Smart Set*.[15]

Mencken evidently liked what he read, for he assigned John another article in August of that year. This one dealt with the decline of the Chicago literary scene. "[Ben] Hecht is now writing detective stories, [Carl] Sandburg is getting degrees from silo colleges . . . ," Mencken scoffed in a letter to his young admirer.[16] Adopting that same haughty tone in his article, John chided Edgar Lee Masters for "self-imitation," and took pot shots at Sherwood Anderson, Hecht, and Sandburg, among others. In the end, he devoted so much time to critical sniping that he never got around to explaining why Chicago's literary scene had supposidly declined.

The article would doubtless have created a stir and made John some powerful enemies. But it was never published. When editors at the *Daily News* got wind of what John had written, word spread quickly. When the gist of the piece was leaked by a writer in the *Brooklyn Eagle* in distant New York, Mencken was irate. He wrote to John complaining that his "blabbing" had dulled the article's impact. Though the rebuke wounded John's pride, he and Mencken continued to correspond.[17]

As it turned out, far more significant than John's friendship with H.L. Mencken was the fact that John's column caught the eye of Harry Hansen, the literary editor of the *Chicago Daily News*. Hansen, who had graduated from the U of C himself in 1909 and briefly worked overseas as a war correspondent, invited John to write reviews for the Wednesday book page. Hansen also suggested to his boss, news editor Henry Justin Smith, that John Gunther be hired as a campus correspondent. Smith, a part-time novelist, passionately believed in the vitality of Chicago's literary flowering. He championed homegrown talents whenever possible. Thus John's byline began appearing in the *CDN* with regularity.

This sudden celebrity got him elected to the campus chapter of Phi Beta Kappa fraternity. However, despite his "years in semi-Coventry," as he later recalled them, and his "yearning to be liked," John was reluctant to join campus organizations, clubs, or political groups. He was no longer the shy, uncertain youth of his freshman year. His graduation photo in *Cap & Gown*, the U of C yearbook, depicts an intense twenty-one-year-old man peering out from behind round, wire-framed glasses, with his fair hair combed straight back off a high forehead in the style of the day.

A *Cap & Gown* lampoon of the "Literary Laggards—The Earliest Books Reviewed by John Grunter," suggests that John at this point had begun taking himself a tad too seriously. An anonymous classmate parodied John's writing style and poked light-hearted fun at his success. Among the fictional volumes reviewed by "Grunter" were *Gusto* by Knot Handsome (Knuff), and *Hellish* by F. Suit Fitztightly. "Personally," Grunter intoned, "I consider his taste in cigarettes abominable."[18]

The young literary critic graduated in the spring of 1922 with a Bachelor of Philosophy (Ph.B.) degree, with honors in English. On Harry Hansen's recommendation, he was hired as a reporter by the *CDN*. John opted to take a summer vacation rather than start work immediately, and he arranged to have his degree and Phi Beta Kappa key mailed to him.

Using money he had saved and some that he borrowed from family, John and three Green Chalybeate friends, Vorries Fisher, Francis Bitter, and Franklin Barber, joined the crush of idealistic young Americans who were rushing off to Europe. The four held their travel expenses down by working their way from Boston to Liverpool on the SS *Winifredian*, a cattle boat. John recorded in his diary how the four friends cycled first to London, then through France, Italy, and Switzerland before stopping in Paris, the beautiful City of Light. Here they soaked up the atmosphere, saw all of the sights, and sipped wine in the same sidewalk cafes where Hemingway, Fitzgerald, Picasso and other artists gathered nightly. John even encountered his friend Jimmy Sheean, who was also traveling in Europe. "Met, of all people, J.V. Sheean!" John wrote in his diary. "Good boy, though an ass."[19]

These were magical days for John, who had been inspired by his mother from his childhood to dream of travel to exotic places. Paris certainly qualified.

As the last days of that idyllic summer of 1922 slipped away, John resolved to return to Europe one day soon as a foreign correspondent. After that, he would write the Great American Novel that he and his friends had so often talked about. But first he faced the more immediate challenge of winning his spurs in the rough-and-tumble world of the *Chicago Daily News*.

CHAPTER FOUR

The *Chicago Daily News* (*CDN*) was the cities, largest daily newspaper (circulation 375,000), and the owner of WMAQ, one of America's first commercial radio stations. The newspaper, which billed itself as a "family" publication, was also an outspoken critic of gangsters and their corrupt friends among the police, judiciary, and civic officials who ran the town. "Minor items from the police blotter, any of which might have suggested a novel to Dostoyevsky, we held down to a few lines each," veteran *CDN* reporter and editor Paul Scott Mowrer wrote in his memoirs, "for ours was a 'home' newspaper, decent and respectable."[1] It was also one of the country's most reputable journalistic voices. John Gunther recalled it years later as a "grand shop" where he got "more education in a year . . . than in four at the university."[2]

The *CDN* offices were located in an undistinguished four-story, red brick office building at 15 North Wells Street. It was in the shadow of City Hall and right next door to Schlogl's, a greasy spoon restaurant that served as the ersatz home for John as well as many other reporters and their editors.

The city newsroom was on the top floor of the *CDN* building, up four creaky flights of wooden stairs. The scene here would have been familiar to Hildy Johnson and Walter Burns, the lead characters in Charles MacArthur's and Ben Hecht's classic 1930 play *The Front Page*. Hecht was a member of a colorful and distinguished *CDN* reporting staff that in the fall of 1922 included Junius Wood, Robert J. Casey, Charles Vincent Starrett, and the poet Carl Sandburg.

The west wall of the long, crowded and starkly lit newsroom was taken up by three large, dust-caked windows. From them one gained a bird's-eye view of the elevated trains that roared past, along North Wells Street. On a newsroom bench sat the copy boys, who served as runners between the newsroom and the typesetting shop. The editors' frantic summons: "Copy Boy!" periodically roused them from inertia.

During the day, the air was filled with a cacophony of ringing telephones, clattering typewriters, and teletypes. A slightly elevated platform in the middle of the squeaky, unswept wooden floor housed the "local" desk, the newsroom's nerve center. It was here that green-visored copy editors and paste-up men rolled up their sleeves to labor over the editing and layout of pages for the eight daily editions.[3]

Managing editor Charles Dennis, the man who presided over this organized chaos, was a meticulous taskmaster who demanded excellence from his staff. Legend had it that Dennis had once edited a 300-word editorial and left untouched only three words. Surprisingly, the author conceded that Dennis had done a good job in wielding his red pencil!

John quickly discovered that while reporters respected and feared Dennis, they revered his subordinate, Henry Justin Smith. It was Smith who ran the newsroom. He succeeded Dennis as managing editor in 1926, and spent the last ten years of an abbreviated life in the job. Smith was a genuine legend in a city crowded with newspaper legends. In his 1954 memoir, *Child of the Century*, Hecht remembered the bespectacled Smith as "tall, thin and fastidious, with flushed lean cheeks and a royalist droop to his mouth and thin-lined mustache . . . scanty-worded, hiding a childlike sensitivity in a chronically fretful air so that he might seem like an executive rather than a moon-struck wonderer; bending over to pick up pins from the floor as he walked; incapable of oath or obscenity, scorning liquor and personal scandal and passionately in love with a newspaper."[4]

When John Gunther joined the *CDN* reporting staff in the fall of 1922, Smith held the title of news editor. Slotted into the editorial hierarchy between city editor Brooks Beitler (whose job it was each day to assign reporters and editors to stories) and managing editor Charles Dennis (who oversaw all editorial operations), Smith had responsibility for all routine editorial and personnel matters, including staffing of the *CDN*'s five overseas bureaus and its extensive network of foreign correspondents.

The soft-spoken Smith was the son of a prominent Baptist minister who had helped found the University of Chicago, but he was no wide-eyed innocent. Despite an academic demeanor, he was a shrewd, tough administrator with a knack for spotting and nurturing raw journalistic talent. More than anyone else at the *CDN*, it was he who honed John Gunther's nascent skills and guided him in formulating his own distinctive writing style.

Smith regarded news as "unrhetorical essays on life."[5] He felt that to be a first-rate writer, one also had to be a first-rate person, with an abiding interest in people and the human element of every story. Good writers were self-made through sheer hard work, and a passion for the reading and writing of literature. Although Smith's philosophy of journalism was to "keep it short and simple," he valued imagination and enterprise above all else. On one occasion, Smith was so taken with a story in the Minneapolis newspaper that he immediately cabled a job offer to Robert Hardy Andrews, the young reporter responsible. Andrews sheepishly admitted in his reply that he had fabricated the story Smith had so admired. Unfazed, Smith promptly responded with a second cable reading: "Accuracy can be taught. Imagination cannot. We can use both. Offering you a job immediately. Confirm."

Five years before John Gunther joined the *CDN*, Smith had hired and retained on staff both Ben Hecht and Carl Sandburg. Smith hired Hecht away from the rival *Chicago Journal* in early 1917, as a $45-per-week police reporter. In August of that year, on

Hecht's recommendation, Smith gave Sandburg a job, despite objections by some copy editors. Sandburg, then thirty-nine years old, was already an eccentric, even among his free-wheeling newsroom colleagues. Temperamentally and physically, he was markedly different from his co-workers, one of whom dubbed him "John Guts" presumably because of his talent for penning earthy poetry. Beetle-browed, with unruly shocks of hair falling over his ears, Sandburg was fond of wearing a battered baseball cap and half-laced, stub-toed shoes that had been out of vogue for a half century.

During Sandburg's first day on the job, the poet was sitting at his city room desk, emptying the contents of the drawers and refilling them with the pamphlets of radical political groups with whom he sympathized. One of the editors commented to Hecht, "Sandburg? Never heard of him. But he looks peculiar enough to work on this paper. Where's he from—the Ozarks?" Hecht responded that Sandburg was a radical, and a poet. He had also once played semi-professional baseball. "You don't say," sniffed the editor. "A good spotted terrier would round out the staff."

Henry Smith admired Sandburg's literary talents, and was fond of pointing out to cynical editors that the poet was a genius who "traveled in his own orbit." John Gunther, who certainly knew of Sandburg's literary reputation, was in awe of him, particularly after Smith issued instructions to the city desk copy editors that Sandburg's news stories were to be published "just as he wrote them." Smith even shielded his star reporter from the wrath of crusty city editor Brooks Beitler. Once, when Sandburg covered an American Federation of Labor (AFL) convention in Minneapolis, nothing was heard of him for four days. The poet later explained that he'd gotten caught up in the excitement of the event and forgotten to write a story.

Sandburg was not a news reporter in any conventional sense, yet Smith gave him the time to find his niche, which turned out to be writing film reviews and columns. Harry Hansen mused years later that the only reason eccentrics like him and Sandburg kept their jobs at the *CDN* was because of "the unusual protection assured us by Smith."

John Gunther also had reason to thank the paper's kindhearted news editor. It was Smith who, at Harry Hansen's urging, launched John's career with a $15-per-week job as cub reporter. Smith may have seen something of himself as a young man in John, who in the fall of 1922 was still very much a quiet, studious college graduate with a passion for literature. John and Smith shared an appreciation for good writing and, while theirs was at first a mentor-student relationship, they became fast friends. It was Smith who pegged John as a clever young man with a real future in newspapers.

Smith encouraged John, and all of his reporters, to write in their spare time. John, an avid accumulator of both books and literary acquaintances, was welcomed at the "round table" that met daily over coffee at Schlogl's restaurant; *Daily News* literary editor Harry Hansen designated him as "the critical spokesman for the younger generation."[6]

John also began accompanying Henry Smith on visits to a small, cluttered used book shop and literary publishing house on Washington Street, not far from the CDN building. He became a regular amidst the gloomy cul-de-sacs of Covici-McGee Booksellers. Ben Hecht recalled that the customers there "did not come and go like customers in other stores but took up positions and held them through the day." The shop was a local "mecca of the arts," as much as a place of business. A varied and illustrious clientele dropped by to talk literature and banter with the owners, Pascal Covici and Billy McGee. In addition to *Daily News* regulars as Hecht, Sandburg, and Hansen, the Covici-McGee circle included poets Sherwood Anderson, Edgar Lee Masters, and Lew Sarett, the celebrated trial lawyer Clarence Darrow, and a troupe of assorted young literary talents, some of whom were destined for great things.[7]

Inspired by such heady company, John moved beyond the academic exercises of his student days and experimented with short fiction. Like most young newspapermen of the day, he dreamed of becoming a great novelist. "Being a journalist is like being a chorus girl," he would write in his diary a few years later. "There are few pure 'pure' journalists, just as there are few chorus girls who expect to *stay* chorus girls. Each profession is essentially a step to something beyond . . . men get jobs on newspapers because they want to be writers."[8]

Most of John's co-workers were bent on following in the literary footsteps of fellow Chicagoan, Ernest Hemingway. Not John. He dreamed of emulating the success of the stylish English novelist

Aldous Huxley, whom he idolized.

That John Gunther had some distance to go before he could ever hope to do so was made clear to him by the young woman who now entered his life.

CHAPTER FIVE

One hot afternoon in July 1923, John Gunther visited the Soberman-Sayers book shop not far from the *CDN* building, to buy a crossword puzzle book. Puzzles were all the rage at the time, and Harry Hansen had told John about a pretty twenty-two-year-old art student who was clerking at the book shop for the summer and loved to do puzzles. Helen Hahn, an older sister of Emily (Mickey) Hahn—who would make her name as a member of the *New Yorker* magazine's stable of writers—sold John a puzzle book, and captured his heart at the same time.

Helen was a young woman who turned men's heads. Sister Emily surmised that it was because of Helen's apparent vulnerability; she showed her feelings, and men were flattered. John was no exception. He fell for her the moment they met. Helen Hahn recalled that John "had a big bag of cherries, which we ate while standing at the door, seeing who could spit the pits the farthest out into the street. It was a very good beginning to our relationship."[1]

John waited around to walk Helen home after work, and they began dating. Helen had occasionally gone out with Harry Hansen, and over lunch one day he and John cooked up a scheme to convince their bosses to hire her as the newspaper's first-ever puzzles editor. The two agreed to approach Charles Dennis and to arrange a job interview for her the next day. Helen appeared at the *CDN* newsroom at the appointed time, to discover that John was nowhere to be seen, and Hansen was hiding his face in embarrassment. Both men had forgotten to broach the idea with the managing editor. Helen was not discouraged.

Dennis, who was won over by Helen's enthusiasm, agreed to let her test some of her ideas. The newspaper ran a contest, in which readers were invited to submit crossword puzzles. To everyone's surprise, so many did that Helen had only to edit one for each Sunday's paper to hold a job.

Helen Hahn was as ambitious as she was talented. Before long, John was asking Helen to critique his efforts at fiction. When he sold one of his first short stories, he gave her part of the money. "He seemed to need some sort of guidance with his writing," Helen recalled. "John was quite talented, but I told him I thought he had a tendency to point out the 'cows.' It was as if when passing a field filled with cows he'd stop and say, 'There's a cow.' I used to read his stuff and point out the 'cows' to him. He remembered that line and used it in his first novel, *The Red Pavilion* (1926)."[2]

These were years when, as Scott Fitzgerald noted in a famous essay he wrote about the 1920s, "Writers were geniuses on the strength of one respectable book or play."[3] John Gunther, who was keen to test the truth of that theory, made clear to Helen and other friends that he regarded newspaper work as a stepping stone to fame as a novelist. In his own estimation, he was a mediocre news reporter. "I had little sense of news as news, and small talent for digging out facts. I don't think I ever had a scoop," he once confided.[4] He was undoubtedly casting his mind back to his first day at the *CDN*.

Upon entering the newsroom John had been summoned by Beitler, the city editor, a gruff, newsroom drill sergeant who wore his hair in a "pineapple" cut—close-shaved on the sides and in a thick tuft on top. Beitler, who added emphasis to his words by stabbing the air with his cigarette holder, gave John his first assignment and then listened in bemused silence to his request for change for a quarter to use one of the telephones in the city room. John had never had free access to a telephone before. For months afterwards, Beitler and his assistant city editor kept a slug on a piece of string, and any time their cub reporter approached the local desk they guffawed as they waved it at him.[5]

Thrown headlong into a dizzying world of Rotary Club speeches, conventions, brothels, speakeasies, tough cops, and four-alarm fires, John learned his craft on the run. This journalistic rite of passage opened his eyes to the sordid realities of life in a city of 2.7 million people. It also taught him the skills needed to make a living as a newspaper reporter. That John Gunther was a quick learner is shown by a breathless, front-page account he wrote on December 27, 1923, of a fire at a Chicago insane asylum.

Most young reporters would have focused on the grim details of the deaths that occurred. Instead John wrote about a patient, an ex-fireman, who rose above his illness long enough to be a hero battling the blaze. John's story, "The Return of Joe Vesley," was reprinted in a hardcover book entitled *The Best News Stories of 1923*. Typically, the writing was crisp, colorful, and flavored with a good dash of sensationalism. "Insanity stalked through the red gloom hovering over Dunning last night," John wrote, "playing queer tricks with human minds and human bodies through the chaos of horror and heroism and despair."[6]

Despite a gift for this kind of vivid writing, at age twenty-three John was keen to show off talent, and his education. Where this tendency in others was often grating, it was tolerated in his case. Co-workers respected, even admired, his determination and boundless energy. His self-discipline was astounding, his energy boundless. John spent long hours reading in *CDN*'s clippings morgue, and polishing his writing skills by doing endless rewrites on the night shift. The work, tedious and often boring, "shook some of the pedantry away," John wrote years later.[7]

Most mornings he crawled home to bed after work just as the sun was rising. John's cousin, Gretchen Corazzo, recalls visiting the Gunther household one sunny fall afternoon about this time. John's sister, Jean, was hosting a teddy bear party for a half dozen of her younger cousins. The noisy children were hushed by Aunt Lizette. "Cousin John has a job," she told them. To emphasize why they should be quiet, she trooped them all upstairs, where they were allowed to peek inside John's darkened bedroom. They could barely make out the form of the cub reporter as he lay sleeping after another long night's work.[8]

For a time, John saved money by living with his family. The fact that the Gunthers were still in their home and by now were relatively stable financially was due at least in part to Lizette Gunther's job as a substitute teacher. After the failure of his saloon, Eugene Gunther had worked at a variety of jobs while dreaming up schemes to get rich quickly. Faced with the reality that his health was failing as steadily as his marriage, he derived quiet satisfaction from his son's success. After all, John was a young man with an education and a promising career—two things Eugene admitted that he had never achieved.

Both John Gunther and his employer realized that his journalistic talent lay not in the hard news that came from chasing firetrucks or reporting city hall, but rather in personality interviews and feature articles which provided background color on the news or newsmakers. John displayed a keen eye for the human interest stories. He had a knack for seeing aspects of a situation that others overlooked.

When the infamous Teapot Dome scandal broke late in 1923, John hit upon the idea of going to the Wyoming wastelands, near Casper, to describe firsthand the rock formation known as Teapot Dome. In retrospect, it seems like an obvious story, yet no one else thought of it. Many years later, John described its genesis to a *New York Times* reporter.[8] One day in mid-March 1924, he had gone to Charles Dennis with the suggestion. "Look," he pointed out, "we're running thousands of words about Teapot Dome, but has anyone ever seen it?"

"What of it?" Dennis barked.

"Well, I could go and look at it," John volunteered.

Dennis, who was enthusiastic about the possibilities, set his young reporter to work on the story. The reward for John's imagination was his first trip to the American West, which resulted in a breezy feature entitled, "A Visit to the Teapot Dome" (March 24,

1924). More a triumph of substance than style, the story reported that the "Teapot Dome has no resemblance whatever to a teapot or a dome." Nevertheless, the story found wide readership, and it showcased John Gunther's greatest journalistic talent—a gift for making the mundane, the complex, or the obscure interesting and understandable to average readers.

John's Teapot Dome story was chosen as one of the year's best news features, and was reprinted in *The Best News Stories of 1924*. It was the second consecutive year that one of John Gunther's stories was included in that annual collection.

Not surprisingly, John graduated from spot news to the writing of bylined feature articles which, as he put it, "gave me glimpses of many sorts of people." He also continued doing book reviews for Harry Hansen's Wednesday book page. John had lost neither his interest in reviewing nor his critical bite. The writing skills drilled into him by the newspaper's copy editors made him a better critic than he had been in his student days.

In one review, he considered the merits of *The Green Hat*, a lurid bestseller that exposed the supposed promiscuity of glamorous English ladies. John gave his readers, in point form, "the Cold Dope" on the book's author Michael Arlen, an Armenian expatriate whose real name was Dikran Kuyumjian. This was the sort of writing, making liberal use of street jargon, that John had never dared to try as a student critic. The gesture hints at a growing self-confidence. Feeling free for the first time both from the restraints of academia and adolescence, John was eager to make his own way in the world, and to achieve the kind of success that had always eluded his father.

Despite John's uneasiness—or was it shame?—at the realities of Eugene's life, the parallels between father and son were as striking as were the differences. The subject was one John never cared to discuss. Helen Hahn recalled that he did not talk about his father.

John's friends from these days recalled that away from the newsroom he was an easygoing, gregarious companion with an infectious love of life. Like Eugene, he made friends easily and related well to women, who found him attractive. John was most at ease in the presence of females, having been raised by his mother, and having spent a lot of time in the company of his sister and aunts.

Leonora Hornblow, the wife of prominent Hollywood film producer Arthur Hornblow, came to know John well when he lived in New York in later years. She remembers his easy appeal and speculates, "One of the reasons he was attractive to women, I guess, was the fact he was crazy about them. He simply *liked* female company. But there was something about John that brought out the cruel side in some women, and they'd sometimes say cutting things to him. I don't know why."[10]

Helen Hahn had the same feeling. Some girls she knew swooned over John's boyish features. "He was considered a good-looking man," she said.[11] Blond-haired, blue-eyed and bespectacled, he was physically imposing even then. However, at six-foot-two and 190 pounds, he was not yet the commanding presence he would became in middle age. His passion for good food and drink, and his pronounced aversion to exercise, resulted in a distressing tendency to gain weight. An interviewer once asked his favorite color; "smoked salmon," he replied without pause. "Prunier's, of course, not Reuben's."[12]

Typical of John's gift for charming members of the opposite sex, even when in an embarrassing situation, was an incident that occurred in the autumn of 1924. Helen Hahn's sisters, Emily and Dauphine, were by this time attending the University of Wisconsin, at Madison. When John was assigned the task of securing an exclusive interview with the touring Prince of Wales (the future Edward VIII), he headed for Duluth to intercept the prince's special train, en route to Chicago from western Canada. John, who had always been fond of Emily, telephoned the Hahn sisters to suggest that because Madison was on the way to Duluth, they should meet him when his train stopped there about nine o'clock that evening.

When Emily and Dauphine did so, they had such a good time that John suggested they ride with him to the next stop, a small town just a few miles down the line. He assured them that they could catch a return train and then be back home in time for bed. Unfortunately, there were a few problems. John did not have enough money for tickets for the two young women. Nor had he checked the train schedule; the overnight train did not stop at the next town! Emily Hahn recalls what happened: "Dauphine started to cry and complain about stomach pains. I told her to stop sniveling, things would work out. There was quite an uproar, until an old man sitting across from us in the Pullman car volunteered to pay our fares."

It was the wee hours of the morning by the time the Hahn sisters got back to Madison. Dauphine's pains were worse, and a doctor diagnosed her trouble as appendicitis.[13]

John, unaware of the drama that had unfolded behind him, continued on to Duluth alone. Once there, he donned a derby and "gates ajar" collar and stowed away on board the prince's train. It was not until one of the aides in the Royal party noticed his socially incorrect tan shoes and tweed trousers that his ruse was discovered. The Prince of Wales, himself a young man, was so amused by John's stunt that he allowed him to remain on board the train all the way to Chicago.[14] John got his story, and although the Hahn sisters were miffed with him for a time, their anger eventually faded as the humor of the situation grew with each telling of the tale.

An ingratiating charm was not the only paternal characteristic that John Gunther inherited. He also took his father's happy-go-lucky attitude towards money, and a taste for expensive, tailored clothing. In the words of the dapper Scott Fitzgerald, a gentleman's clothes were "a symbol of the power that man must hold and that passes from race to race."

Even in his days as a fledgling newspaperman, John found the money to dress smartly. In later years, after he became successful, John patronized only the best tailors in New York and on London's Savile Row. Nevertheless, friends recall his "built-in" rumples; no matter how expensive or well-made his suit was, it usully seemed as though he had slept in it. Journalist William Shirer vividly remembers John's dress habits. "He may have been wearing a good shirt and a tie and expensive jacket, but it was *always* rumpled," Shirer says. I don't know if he ever sent things to be pressed."[15]

John, himself, said it best when he wryly described a character in one of his novels, who is himself thinly disguised, as "two hours after getting into a new suit [looking] as if he were dressed in a baked potato skin."

Dressed like a young swell, John took to living like one. Working almost regular office hours as a features writer left him with most nights and weekends free to write fiction, date Helen Hahn, or socialize with a diverse circle of friends. Apart from his relationship with the Covici-McGee group and his newsroom colleagues, John maintained his friendship with the former university classmates who had founded the Green Chalybeate. Like John, most of them had graduated and now held steady jobs.

Helen Hahn recalled how these young "parlor snakes"—as her parents sometimes referred to them—pooled their resources to rent a "clubhouse." It was nothing more than a sparsely furnished room above a corner drugstore on the south side of town, near the campus. Among the furnishings was a battered old sofa with a nondescript, framed picture hanging on the wall above it. "The Green Chalybeates took their girlfriends here singly," Hahn said. "They kept track of their sofa 'successes' by marking a line on the wall behind the picture. John and I were very good friends; I guess that's why he took me there to show me the marks on the wall. We laughed about it."[16]

John and his Green Chalybeate friends were also regular guests for a time at the suburban home of Roy Gobel, a wealthy businessman, who threw lavish drunken parties to which he invited crowds of university students and other young people. Helen Hahn remembered visiting Gobel's home a few times. "The parties were very good, but I never cared for them. I didn't drink much and didn't care for crowds of people around me," she explained.[17] Gobel, who was gay, used the parties as a venue for meeting young men. While John attended several of these gatherings, and on at least one occasion accompanied Gobel and a group of revelers to a local movie theatre to watch the German silent film classic, *The Cabinet of Dr. Caligari*, that was the extent of his relationship with Gobel. Helen noted that his sexuality was never in doubt.

Although he was still making a pretense of dating various women, John was deeply and hopelessly in love with Helen Hahn. He was also jealous of her many other suitors. John was determined to marry Helen, and during a year of dogged pursuit he became a familiar figure around the Hahn's North Side home. With five pretty sisters and a teen-aged brother in the house, the social activity there was constant. It reminded John of the happy times he had spent with his mother's family as a boy. When Helen was working or otherwise engaged, John dated her two older sisters, Rose and Dauphine, and occasionally the younger Emily. The fifth sister was still considered too young to go out with boys.

Helen eventually made it clear to John that she regarded their relationship as mostly platonic. He was insistent that it be something more. Helen, pretty and more cosmopolitan than many other young Chicago women of her age, never lacked for male company. She had spent two years at Smith College in Massachusetts, leaving school after her sophomore year to return home and study art. Emily Hahn joked that after her sister came home it suddenly became difficult for the other Hahn girls to retain suitors. Helen had a knack for stealing male hearts.[18] But she never really intended to steal John's, nor to marry him—or anyone else at that time. She enjoyed his company and spent much time with him, but she did not find him physically attractive; the chemistry just was not there.

John was aware of Helen's feelings, but he refused to accept them. Recalling their relationship two years later in *The Red Pavilion*, he wrote: "That was the strange thing about the year . . . Nothing was important. Nothing was significant. It was like a haze of days, interminably floating past, like a vague tapestry of pain, with rare, sudden illuminations of happiness when [Helen] smiled; many moments of pain when she was remote and elusive with her eyes vague."[19]

The love affair, and John's life, took a decisive turn one afternoon in the fall of 1924. He and Helen were at a concert by the touring Polish composer-pianist Ignace Paderewski. Helen, feeling increasingly chafed and uneasy by the intensity of John's attentions, sat brooding. Finally, at the interval, John demanded to know what was troubling her. She told him: she *liked* him a lot, but she did not *love* him.

"I'm not hurt. I'm not hurt," he stubbornly repeated over and over.

"You're not hurt, John, but your vanity is—and somehow I don't think that it's anything but your vanity. No, John, *you're* not hurt," Helen snapped.[20]

That confrontation was the death knell of the relationship. But John refused to concede that the romance was over. He decided to avoid Helen for a while, immersing himself in his work at the *CDN* and spending his spare time with his Green Chalybeate friends in fitful bouts of drinking and melancholia. Recalling this period of his life in later years, he was vague. Without mentioning Helen, he wrote of his "blinding unhappiness, a choking frustration, a bitter and lonely yearning for something I could not define, that soon made Chicago unbearable."[21]

Many young artists and writers of the day, Gertrude Stein's celebrated "Lost Generation," felt spiritually suffocated by what they regarded as American society's gaudy materialism and intellectual bankruptcy. As the literary critic Malcolm Cowley explained in his memoir, *Exile's Return* (1934), "Society was something alien. It was a sort of parlor car in which we rode, over smooth tracks, toward a destination we should never have chosen for ourselves."[22] While John's miseries owed as much to the pain of unrequited love as to such lofty philosophical musings, the Old World's quixotic call was every bit as enticing for him as it was for Hemingway, Fitzgerald, Cowley and thousands of other idealists.

John decided the time had come to join the exodus. He would go to Europe, he decided, and become a foreign correspondent. Then he would write the Great American Novel. *That* would prove to Helen just how foolish she had been to reject him. The depth of his disillusionment was reflected in an October 1, 1924, review of poet Edgar Lee Master's book *New Spoon River,* the sequel to the classic *Spoon River Anthology.* Echoing the unpublished criticism that he had written in the article for H.L. Mencken, John quipped, "Mr. Masters has been close to the front (of Chicago's literary scene) for a decade. He was in at the beginning. And he is in at the death."

John had decided to make a dramatic break both with his own painful past and with a city whose literary tide had ebbed. His main difficulty was in finding a way to take his leave.

Even with a $55-per-week salary, John's liberal spending habits made it difficult to save money. Thus it seemed like a perfect solution to his problems, when he hit upon the idea of finding work with the *CDN*'s overseas news service. The staffing of this network of more than 100 part-time correspondents and five bureaus (in London, Paris, Rome, Berlin, and Peking) was the responsibility of John's mentor and friend, *CDN* news editor Henry J. Smith.

Begun by *CDN* founder Victor Lawson in 1898, during the Spanish-American War, the service reflected America's changing role in the world's economic and political structure. A new martial spirit fueled by a revival of the old doctrine of Manifest Destiny had gripped the nation and found expression in a succession of chauvinistic outbursts; "jingoism" it was called. That Victor Lawson subscribed to such messianic sentiments is clear. "The U.S. has entered on a new era," he proclaimed. "Whether we Americans like it or not, the nation henceforth must shoulder the responsibilities and discharge the duties of a world power."[23] To do so, Lawson and his rivals William Randolph Hearst and Joseph Pulitzer felt it was imperative that the nation have its own sources of international news, rather than foreign agencies that were often subsidized by foreign governments.

While the *CDN* overseas cable service was by no means the first to be inaugurated by an American newspaper—that distinction belonged to the now-defunct *New York Herald*—it was the first to adopt as its goal comprehensive in-depth reporting of events that occurred beyond the traditional capitals. By 1924 the *CDN* service, with its well deserved reputation for excellence, was syndicated to thirty-nine North American newspapers, and the *London Daily Telegraph*.

Smith was not receptive to John's request for an overseas posting; only a few years earlier he might have been. Such jobs had been considered a dead end. In fact, Smith had warned Paul Scott Mowrer in 1910 that if he took the Paris bureau job he would be putting himself in a kind of journalistic "limbo." But by 1924 it had become fashionable to work in Europe, and the *Chicago Daily News*, like all American newspapers, had a lineup of experienced staff eager to work abroad.

For that reason, in rejecting John's application, Smith reminded him that he was still a young man with a mere two years reporting experience. Undeterred, John pressed ahead with his plans. By early October, when he had saved $150, he gave his notice. On October 22, Harry Hansen bid him fond farewell in his weekly literary column. Wrote Hansen: "John Gunther, who reviewed for the book pages, has departed for London, England, to collaborate with Thomas Hardy on a crossword puzzle book."

Buoyed by the send-off, John was bubbling with youthful optimism and keen for adventure. However, even he could not have suspected how dramatic would be the turns his life would take. As the noon train to New York City, *The Century*, pulled out of the Chicago railroad yards, John pressed his nose to the window. He whispered good-by to the city of his birth, never suspecting that he would never return there to live. He would spend the next dozen years in Europe.

CHAPTER SIX

A few minutes after one o'clock on the morning of Sunday, October 26, 1924, Captain Frank B. Haworth gave two long blasts of the RMS *Olympic*'s steam whistle. The bass bellow echoed through the streets around Manhattan's West Seventeenth Street pier as tugs, laboring like ants, pulled the great ship free of her Hudson River berth. The majestic *Olympic*, launched in 1908 as one of the ill-fated *Titanic*'s two sister ships, was the pride of the White Star line. Almost three football fields long, every inch of her 882-foot long hull was freshly painted a gleaming white, and her brass fittings and sweeping mahogany and walnut decks shone like glass.

"It is enormous! It is magnificent!" John wrote to Helen Hahn. "It is also grotesque; the thing is not a boat, it is a strange, movable palace using waves for wheels. Imagine a floating Biltmore—palm gardens, elevators, swimming pools, tennis courts. If one peers out very cautiously from one of the upper decks, one may look down far and long enough to witness the sea. Not otherwise."[1]

A festive mood enveloped the *Olympic*. Despite the hour, many of the 2,000 passengers stood on deck waving and shouting goodbyes to relatives and friends. The night air was cool and tangy with the smell of salt water. As the *Olympic* glided past the Statue of Liberty and out through the Narrows into the Atlantic Ocean bound for Southampton, the bright lights of the Manhattan skyline receded into the wake. It was not long before they were just a dim glow on the western horizon. The chill of a northerly breeze prompted those who had come on deck from the ship's ballroom to return to their reveries. Other passengers retired to their cabins for the night, among them a bone-weary Prince of Wales on his way home to England after a two-month North American tour. The prince had tried to slip quietly on board in late afternoon, only to discover a crowd of reporters awaiting him; John was among them. The prince nodded, having recognized him after their meeting in the Midwest. Then, after reading a press statement and posing for a few photographs with some official well-wishers, the future king disappeared to his suite to nurse a cold.

Long after most of the other passengers had gone inside for the night, John remained on deck in the darkness. He stood at the railing with a cigarette and his thoughts. Cocky, confident, and just twenty-three years old, he savored the excitement of the adventure. But as he stared at the rolling black expanse of waves, even someone as cocksure as John had doubts about the bold course that he had chosen. His family and friends, a good job at the *Chicago Daily News*, and the safe, insular world of the Midwest suddenly seemed far away.

Despite his best efforts, most of the $150 that had been in his pocket when he left home a few days before was already gone. Arriving in New York, John had just eighteen cents spending money left. He booked steerage-class passage on the *Olympic*, which was the cheapest fare possible. Discovering that the Prince of Wales was also going to be on board was a stroke of luck. John had rushed over to the United Press (UP) wire service office where, armed with a letter of introduction from Harry Hansen, he talked manager Karl Bickel into paying to raise his passage from steerage- to second-class as payment for news coverage "in case HRH should fall down a hatchway or something." John promptly dug into his small reserve fund of traveler's checks for the $50 for a first-class ticket. "Circumstances warranted it," he observed.[2] John had also worked out a loose arrangement with Henry J. Smith. His dispatches during the five-day voyage appeared in the *Chicago Daily News* under the placeline "Special Dispatch from a Staff Correspondent."

Given his financial situation, John glumly contemplated the prospect of arriving in England broke. Such thoughts provided him with incentive not to forget his responsibilities as a free-lance correspondent. After filing a 550-word cable to Chicago early that first day at sea ("Wales Says Goodby and Goes to Sleep"), he scanned the 300 names on the ship's first-class passenger list for possible interview subjects.[3] With many Britons on board, and the prince among them, John found endless amusement in observing the social dynamics at work. Especially intriguing were the quaint dress habits of the British upper class. "Mauve spats, taupe knickers wide enough to drive a Ford through, dinky caps, rugs for capes, monocles, and Piccadilly accents. One old Duke wears pink bedroom slippers while strolling," John reported in a letter to Helen Hahn.[4]

He went on to describe some of his fellow passengers. One with whom he spent time was a young London literary agent named Peters. The man had sought out John at the urging of Carl Brandt, a New York literary agent who was a friend of Harry Hansen; Brandt had agreed to represent John should he write anything worthwhile. Another passenger with whom John became friendly was an effeminate Englishman named Selden, who was fond of drinking champagne for breakfast. "He clasps your hand tightly when you meet him and invites you down to his cabin to see his 'traveling outfit,'" John told Helen. "It consists mostly of mauve and burnt orange pajamas. Also, he has dozens of roses sent to him. I got out of the cabin as soon as possible and have been heartfully avoiding him."[5]

The Prince of Wales, "buttressed off like a Hindu virgin or a case of leprosy," spent most of the five-day voyage swimming in the ship's pool, or playing shuffleboard and squash. In the evenings, he was seen dancing with young women in the ballroom. The prince's aides for the most part kept other passengers away from him, except while he was on the dance floor or strolling on deck, where he mingled freely. In doing so, the bemused royal noticed "that young chap from Chicago" lurking nearby, note pad in hand.

Nervous, headstrong, and stubborn, yet possessed of extraordinary personal charm, the twenty-nine-year-old future King Edward VIII was already displaying the defiance of stuffy convention that would be his ruin. For one thing, the prince had begun to drink in public, although seldom to excess and certainly not enough to concern his associates. Nevertheless his father, King George V, was not amused by this impropriety. Nor was he amused by his son's impatience with public engagements. On occasion, the prince was boredom personified—he hung his head while talking with people, mumbled around the cigarette that dangled ever-present from his lip, or toyed with his necktie or fly. Some appointments he was simply late for; others he broke without warning or explanation.

The king received confidential reports about his son's behavior on the tour. He was not amused. "You have had a much freer life than I ever knew, but don't think this means that you can act like other people! Never forget your position and who you are!" the king had admonished his son.[6]

This awareness that he was under parental scrutiny may have contributed to the prince's edginess where journalists were concerned. Or he may have been bothered by the tone of American press reports about him, for he instructed his secretary, Captain Alan Lascelles, to vet all future stories. If John or the handful of other reporters on board the *Olympic* wrote any more stories about the prince's voyage, their efforts were for naught; Lascelles approved nothing. Even Lord Mountbatten, the prince's cousin, described Lascelles as a "difficult, disapproving prissy."[7] In one dispatch, John innocently mentioned that HRH sometimes strolled on deck alone at night. "We'd better cut that out," Lascelles snarled. "It panders to the more *romantic* of your readers." No more of this "inside" information about the prince appeared in the newspapers on either side of the Atlantic until October 31, the day the *Olympic* docked at Southampton.

John's train arrived in London at five o'clock that afternoon. It was already dark, and a cold rain was falling. After taking the "tube" to the area of the British Museum, he hurried along Great Russell Street, stopping at the first hotel he came to. It was a cheap, dingy place called the Kenilworth Hotel. To revive his flagging spirits, John went to the kitchen for a shot of brandy. To his dismay, he discovered the Kenilworth was a temperance hotel! Thus his first night in London was long, lonely, and dry—in at least one sense of the word.[8]

Early on the morning of November 1, 1924, John took his new umbrella and set off on the twenty-minute walk to the *CDN* office on Trafalgar Square. It was a Saturday, and bureau chief Hal O'Flaherty was not in yet. John left a note for O'Flaherty explaining his silence of the last five days by citing the "extraordinary censorship on the *Olympic*."

John also left O'Flaherty a 450-word story ("Wales Denies Story that He'll Renounce")[9] reporting that the prince had denied a shipboard rumor he would renounce his claim to the English throne. John's story mentioned the presence on the voyage of a magnificently dressed "mystery woman"—actually Ann Dunlop, a married American newspaper reporter who was traveling alone. She was seen dancing and dining with the prince on several occasions. (The irony of this could not have escaped John a dozen years later, in 1936, when Edward shocked the world by abdicating his throne to marry Mrs. Wallis Simpson, an American divorcee.)

His free-lance obligations fulfilled, John made his way to the office of Associated Press, where he was told there were no jobs. At United Press, bureau chief Edward Keen was more optimistic, offering the possibility of work "in a few weeks." With his spirits revived, John ate a pub lunch, then browsed in the National Gallery. Then, on the spur of the moment, he went into Thresher & Glenny "Gentlemen's Clothier" on Savile Row, where he ordered two suits, an overcoat, and accessories, all on credit. It was a gesture typical of his sunny outlook on life. With only dreams in his pockets, John was confident that he would not "starve on Fleet Street." He was right.

A note from Hal O'Flaherty awaited him at the Kenilworth. "Please see me," it read. It was still raining, and John almost did not bother to trudge back to Trafalgar Square. Fortunately he did. O'Flaherty spent the next two hours talking with him before a warm grate fire. O'Flaherty's English assistant had just quit, and he needed help. He offered John a job starting on Monday morning.[10] Many years later, in an interview with the *New York Times*, John recalled O'Flaherty's offer as "the most wonderful gesture any one has ever made to me."[11]

Hal O'Flaherty, thirty-four years old and compactly built, was Irish as a shamrock. John informed Helen Hahn in one of his now daily letters that his new boss cussed "better than any man I've heard since Herc (Mulroy)."[12] A native of a small Iowa town with the wonderfully evocative name of What Cheer, O'Flaherty was also a graduate of the University of Chicago. After being in Europe for eight years, he was growing impatient to return to the States.

O'Flaherty empathized with the young man from Chicago who had appeared at his office door hungry for adventure. He had been the same way in 1916. O'Flaherty had arrived in London as a $30-per-week reporter with the UP wire service. After working as a war correspondent, he had joined the *CDN* foreign staff in 1919. Three years later, he took over the London bureau from Paul Scott Mowrer, who was promoted to head the newspaper's European operations.[13]

Mowrer had not disguised his joy at being freed from the daily grind of the London job. Writing in his memoir, *The House of Europe* (1945), he recalled that the day he had turned over the office to O'Flaherty he "all but sang in the streets. No more cares! No more fussing with other people's copy and cable quotas and accounts."[14] By late 1924, Hal O'Flaherty was feeling burned out, and he welcomed the chance to delegate work to someone from the home office who came as well recommended as John did.

Leaving the *CDN* office, John was giddy. He went straight to Simpson's, one of London's finest restaurants, to order a roast beef dinner with all the trimmings. That done, his next priority was finding a proper place to live. This, too, proved to be surprisingly easy. Armed with his letters of introduction, he sought out the friend of a friend. The man kindly arranged lodging for him at the Connaught, one of the hundreds of private gentlemen's clubs in London. The room was large and bright, while the club had a good, inexpensive restaurant, lounge rooms, a reading room, and even a valet service. The rate for all this was just $9 U.S. per week. Given that he was now being paid $70 per week, John was again optimistic that he had done the right thing in leaving Chicago. He would prove to Helen Hahn, and to the rest of the world, that he was a young man with a bright future.[15]

CHAPTER SEVEN

John began a crash course with Hal O'Flaherty on the workaday routine of running an overseas news bureau. O'Flaherty set him to work on a variety of reporting assignments: a brief article about the reaction of visiting Chicagoans to news of Calvin Coolidge's election as president, stories about British foreign relations, and a series of feature articles entitled, "Is London Finished?" The latter was in response to some controversial remarks made by Frank B. Kellogg, the American ambassador to England.

In off-hours, John wrote to prominent British literary figures. He requested interviews for a series of profiles he planned to write. In this way, during his very first week in London, he was invited to tea by novelists Hugh Walpole, the visiting Sinclair Lewis (whom John had already interviewed once in Chicago), and critic-novelist

Frank Swinnerton, "a shy man with a beard and a chuckle." Swinnerton good-naturedly advised John that London society was still very formal, and so it would be "prudent" to use his social contacts when seeking interviews. John heeded the advice to wrangle exclusive interviews with politicians, soldiers, writers, artists, and entertainers who normally shunned the press.[1]

He also began seeking out business contacts. On November 11, a letter from Harry Hansen got him an invitation to lunch with Cass Canfield, the London representative of Harper & Brothers, the New York publishing house. Of all the friendships that John struck up in London during this period, this one proved to be the most significant. The two men hit it off, and years later it was Canfield, more than anyone else, who was responsible for the turn of events that earned John the fame and fortune he craved.

John also became friends with former *CDN* Berlin correspondent Raymond Gram Swing. During the 1940s, Swing would became one of America's most popular radio commentators. In 1924, however, he was working at the London bureau of the *Philadelphia Public Ledger* and the *New York Evening Post*. Despite a fourteen-year age difference, John and Swing became instant friends, primarily because of their shared love of literature and classical music. Swing wrote in his 1964 memoir, *Good Evening!*, that John "came to see me as a *Daily News* alumnus, and in that first week of our acquaintance, we walked the streets every night, talking with a candor and excitement that adults seldom achieve with each other."[2]

It was Swing who introduced John to Dorothy Thompson, another figure of towering importance in the early years of his career. This imposing, handsome, "blue-eyed tornado"[3] had been born on July 9, 1893, in Lancaster, New York. She was the eldest of the three children of Peter Thompson, a poor British-born Methodist clergyman, and Marion (nee Grierson) Thompson. According to Thompson's biographer, Marion K. Sanders, when Dorothy was eight her mother died from blood poisoning after a bungled abortion performed by Dorothy's maternal grandmother.[4] Dorothy rebelled in the wake of her mother's death, and her father in frustration sent her off to Chicago to live with an aunt. She returned to upstate New York in 1910, enrolling at Syracuse University on a scholarship funded by the Methodist Church.

After graduating in 1914, she had worked for a time as a teacher. Then, in 1920, Thompson and a girlfriend sailed to Europe on an extended holiday. On the boat over, she met a group of American Jews on the way to a Zionist conference. Her journalism career began when she convinced the International News Service (INS) to let her cover the event. Early the next year, at age twenty-five, she landed an unsalaried position as Vienna correspondent of the *Public Ledger*—making her one of the few female foreign correspondents in all of Europe. She made the most of her opportunity. By 1925, she had been married and divorced, and had become the newspaper's Berlin bureau chief

Thompson became an international celebrity in 1928, when she wed novelist Sinclair Lewis (who two years later would become the first American ever to win the Nobel Prize for Literature). During the Second World War, Thompson's syndicated newspaper column, *On the Record*, earned her a reputation as one of America's most influential women—the nation's "first lady of journalism," as one observer hailed her. It was a status in which she reveled. But many people found her *grande dame* persona overpowering.

Despite the fact Dorothy Thompson had been given the prized Berlin posting ahead of Swing and several other more veteran male colleagues, she remained on good terms with all of them.

Thompson, who was taken with John Gunther, befriended him both as a young man and a pupil. Theirs was an intimate, albeit platonic (as far as is known), relationship which endured through good times and bad, until Thompson's 1961 death by a heart attack.

While there may have been an element of mystery to John's relationship with Dorothy Thompson, there was none about his relationship with the literary critic and novelist Cicily Fairfield, better known by her pen name: Rebecca West. She had first met John on a 1923 visit to Chicago, when he interviewed her on behalf of the *CDN*. That John made a strong impression both upon West and her friend the novelist Marcia Davenport is clear, for West referred to John in a letter to her friend as that "young and massive Adonis with curly blond hair."[5]

A short time after he began to work at the *CDN*'s London bureau, John reported on a dinner West gave for the American feminist and anarchist Emma Goldman. Spotting John there, West sent him a note. They began an affair. John confided in his letters to Helen Hahn that while he liked Rebecca West he was "a little afraid of her."[6] Nine years his senior, she had an aura of glamor and mystery, being the long-time mistress of British writer H.G. Wells, one of the world's most famous novelists. John was shocked to hear West sarcastically refer to Anthony, her illegitimate son by Wells, as "H.G.'s brat."

According to Victoria Glendinning, one of West's biographers, "Rebecca entertained John Gunther, smothered him in maternal affection, and introduced him to writers and loved him dearly in a carefree way."[7] When John took her to lunch at the Ritz, a gesture that strained his meager finances, she reciprocated by "opening doors" for him with a glittering literary luncheon in his honor at Claridges. Given his fondness for such establishments, John devoted most of his spare time to writing free-lance articles. This earned him vital extra income, while enhancing his growing reputation.

Among the famous people John interviewed was novelist Michael Arlen, the author of the *Green Hat*, a book John had admired during his college days. Arlen was polite, but John was disappointed to find that his onetime hero was "vain, a bit pompous, excessively sophisticated, and somehow, I thought, rather untrustworthy."[8]

Another interview subject was Sir Arthur Conan Doyle, the creator of the Sherlock Holmes mysteries. Doyle, silver-haired and enigmatic, was a true literary aristocrat—both in reputation and temperament. John meekly agreed when Doyle, like the Prince of Wales, demanded to read any article before publication. Doyle did not like what he saw, of course. He savaged the story with his editing pencil, then wrote Hal O'Flaherty to complain that he had been misquoted. "Doyle is a b-st-rd," John told Helen in one of his letters.[9]

The famed literay connoisseur Gilbert Keith (G.K.) Chesterton was decidedly more cordial, making what was literally a "big" impression on John. "It is a lie that Chesterton is fat," John quipped. "He is enormous . . . The strange thing is to hear him talk. He is such an enormous man. And his voice is slight and squeaky, drifting to you from great heights. Also he laughs a great deal: charming, bubbling laughter. His talk is brilliant, just like his writing, the epitome of paradox, everything upside down. Such stuff flows from him naturally."[10]

John encountered playwright George Bernard Shaw one day while dining in a London restaurant. John's companion introduced him to the grand old white-haired gentleman. "My chief impression shocked me," John told Helen in a letter. "I had no idea GBS [Shaw] was such an old man. He looks 80, and as wise as the sea."[11]

Meeting such well-known writers provided ample material for the series of biographical sketches that John was writing. It also gave him insight into the ways of the British literary establishment, which he concluded was every bit as parochial and stodgy as the society portrayed in Sinclair Lewis's novel *Main Street*.

John's articles attracted mostly favorable attention. One notable exception was an article that he wrote for the New York-based *Saturday Review of Literature*. Reacting to the snubs to which he had been subjected, and in a piece reminiscent of the article about Chicago's literary scene that he had written for *Smart Set*, John suggested that English reviewers conspired to decry American books. He went on to say that American writers had little chance of being published in London. The city's critics were outraged. Fortunately for John, by the time the article appeared in the April 18, 1925, issue of the magazine, he had left London.

Hal O'Flaherty went away for a week in mid-November 1924, leaving his young assistant in charge of the bureau. It was grand fun. "I write in pompous, lordly fashion of the politics of Europe, and I don't know a damned thing about them" John confided in a letter to Helen.[12]

John's byline began appearing in the *Chicago Daily News* as often as it had when he had worked in the city room. This created a dilemma for the editors: John was doing a first-rate job, but they feared if he was allowed to remain on staff in London it would be an obvious invitation to others to follow in his footsteps. To save face, the decision was made to let John work elsewhere for a time, and then to rehire him. Paul Scott Mowrer recalled in his memoirs what happened next: "As we couldn't let people go on appointing themselves this way, we held John off for a while, but to tide him over found him a place with the United Press."

This new job paid $65 per week, almost what John had earned with the *CDN*, and he got on well with his new boss, Ed Keen. Still he was not content. Stuck in the office editing cables all day long, he could no longer have lunch with authors he had arranged to interview. Only Hal O'Flaherty's fatherly admonitions dissuaded him from quitting to try his luck at free-lancing full time. John decided to remain with UP for three months, then he would resign and go to Paris to spend the summer writing a novel. In the autumn, he planned to return to London briefly before sailing for the States. With this in mind, he began banking about $15 per week.[14]

John's plans changed when luck again smiled on him in early February 1925. Hal O'Flaherty called to say that the *CDN* management would rehire him the first week in July. O'Flaherty was going on vacation again, and Paul Scott Mowrer was to relieve him, with John acting as his assistant. This meshed perfectly with John's plans.

He had become fast friends with Eric Maschwitz, a young would-be novelist he had met through Rebecca West. "Tall, 25, black hair falling down over his forehead, tortoise shell glasses," as John described him, Maschwitz lived with his wife, Toni, in an attic. Like John, they were perpetually short of money, but aspired to a life of leisure.[15]

John and Eric planned a fall walking tour of the Alps, and Eric suggested that instead of spending the summer in Paris, John should make for the Mediterranean island of Porquolles, just off the French coast at Hyeres. John was keen on the idea, especially after Frank Swinnerton one day introduced him to novelist Arnold Bennett. John and Bennett fell to chatting about Porquolles, and the writer announced that he had glimpsed the island while out cruising on his yacht. Informed by John that it was a volcanic isle just three miles long and three miles wide, Bennett smiled. "I don't think that it will be big enough for you," he said.[16]

Apart from Porquolles' exotic image, the island appealed to John for other reasons. For one, Joseph Conrad had retreated there the previous year to write his novel *The Rover.* For another, Porquolles was inexpensive. Eric Maschwitz assured John that he could spend a couple of weeks in Paris and then go to the island for three or four months on the $300 he had saved.

With that in mind, John gave his notice on February 16 and began preparing for the trip. The next few weeks were a whirl of lunch and dinner engagements and parties. At one such function, John met a young English critic-novelist named J.B. Priestley. "Please put him down in some book and underline him with red ink," John advised Helen Hahn in one of his letters. "Then, 20 years from now, thank me for first discovering a great critic. I mean this very seriously—Priestley is a comer."[17]

John bid farewell to Rebecca West, who saw him off on March 24 by treating him to a wild, wonderfully carefree shopping spree in the smart shops along Bond Street and through Mayfair. "We went into dress shops and saw mannequin parades, we tried on hats," he recalled. "I fingered a huge elephant gun in an army store, we tried perfume shops, tobacconist shops, china shops . . . everything in the world, bubbling with laughter most of the while. It was fun!" They bought armloads of "great glowing" daffodils from the street corner vendors, loaded a cab until "it looked like a funeral cortege," and then raced back to West's Kensington flat to receive a guest for tea. After the guest departed, John and Rebecca decorated her white-paneled rooms with bunches of flowers and talked about their relationship and about life "very seriously for an hour or more."[18]

That night in his room at the Connaught, John contemplated the future. Seated before a blazing fire, he re-read 100 pages of a semi-autobiographical novel that he had diligently worked at every evening since his arrival in London. The prose that had seemed so vibrant and clever now seemed verbose, sophomoric, and overwritten. It was "bad, thoroughly bad . . . a juvenile exercise. Also, it was entirely, totally, you-and-I," John wrote Helen. "Reading it made me feel undressed." John had matured in the six months since leaving home—both as a writer and a man. It was now clear to him that no matter how many unanswered letters he wrote to her, no matter how sophisticated he might become, Helen would never love him. In his head, he knew that it was over between them; in his heart he hoped against hope. After sitting a long while, wallowing in his melancholia, John came at last to a monumental personal decision. "I tossed [the manuscript] in the fire which burns with such a smacking lusty red glow in my little grate," he recalled. "And I watched it burn—the flames licking along the outside papers, and then boring into the dead white of the middle, devouring the whole thing—and I was very glad."[19]

John had made plans to rendezvous in Paris with Leonard Weil, one of his Green Chalybeate chums, who was traveling in Europe. Then, Eric and Toni Maschwitz decided to go along, too. The only problem was that they had no money. That problem was solved unexpectedly and dramatically on John's last afternoon in London. He and Hal O'Flaherty were in John's room having a farewell drink when Eric came along. Following introductions, the three men talked. It came out that Eric's plans to accompany John to Paris had fallen through for lack of money. O'Flaherty, sitting on the bed with his drink in hand, asked Eric how much it would cost him to go to Paris. "About 20 pounds" ($100 U.S.) came the reply.

"Tell me," O'Flaherty said, "are you one of John's friends?" Maschwitz smiled and nodded.

"Hell, why didn't you tell me before?" O'Flaherty snorted. "Here, I'll lend you the money."[20]

With preparations for the trip thus completed, John was exuberant on his last evening with Rebecca. They had dinner, walked in Hyde Park, and sat in front of a fire sipping wine. Two days later, on the morning March 30, a cool, gray spring mist was falling as John, Eric, and Toni boarded the morning train bound for whatever wild and wonderful adventures awaited them in Paris.

CHAPTER EIGHT

Early on the evening of March 29, John and Eric and Toni Maschwitz arrived at the Gare du Nord in Paris. Leonard Weil was waiting for them on the platform. Carrying a mountain of luggage, they piled into a cab to begin the search for a hotel. They found what they needed at the Grand Hotel de Turin: a couple of rooms, each costing sixty cents a day. The accommodations were clean and bright, and the fact that the hotel was a brothel served to heighten the sense of adventure.

Spring was in the air, and the perfume of the blossoming chestnut trees along the Champs Élysées pervaded the city. The four young people walked endlessly. They sipped wine and talked in the sidewalk cafes, and sat watching the whores soliciting business. They went to the Folies-Bergere and passed many evenings in the cabarets. "For a second," as he recorded in his diary, John fell madly in love with an Algerian dancer. Fortunately, he was rescued by his friends.[1]

John took time out from his revelries to drop in at the *Chicago Daily News* office, "smack in the middle of the city, with the world buzzing beneath the wide windows," as John described it.[2] The resident correspondent, Iowa-born Constantine Brown, spoke English with an accent that made him sound like Maurice Chevalier. Both Brown and Paul Scott Mowrer treated him to a good meal; both assured him that a job awaited him on his July return from Porquolles.

John's time in Paris ended abruptly after just a week. Eric and Toni Maschwitz ran out of money. John and Leonard dipped into their own meager resources to pay the Maschwitz's hotel bill when the couple returned to London. Now short of money themselves, John and Lonard stayed in Paris just three more days. On April 7, they took the train to Avignon, where they spent a carefree week as the guests of Weil's parents, who were touring the continent. From there, John and Leonard traveled to Porquolles. The island was everything John had dreamed. The tiny, straggling village, at the foot of the seaside cliffs, consisted of a hotel—"beyond doubt the filthiest place I had ever seen," John noted—a couple of stores, a post office, and a few other buildings. No automobiles were on the island, nor even horse carriages.

John and Leonard rented two rooms in a clean but spartan seaside cottage. The building had once been the police station. "Our rooms are like a Eugene O'Neill set," wrote John to Helen Hahn, to whom he was still writing out of habit. "Red whitewashed walls, red stone floors, two huge (in height) French beds, shuttered windows, and tall wooden doors. It is the most bare and primitive place I have ever seen, but we are perfectly comfortable."[3]

A neighbor named Mrs. Batson was the island's only English resident. Taking pity on the young men, she loaned them sheets and blankets until they could go to the mainland for their own. After "vacationing strenuously" for two days, John settled into a comfortable routine, swimming, basking in the Mediterranean sun, and writing short stories. For amusement, he and Leonard decided to see who could write a novel fastest. "Metaphorically speaking, we set up a big blackboard, and on the blackboard, every idea, phrase, suggestion, name, or other item mentioned in conversation was set down. This was common property," John told an interviewer many years later. "I fear I grabbed more than my share. Anyway, I won. That is, I finished . . . before [Leonard] finished (his) manuscript."[4]

The fruit of John's labors was a stilted, semi-autobiographical novel that he called *High Sat White Helen*. The plot, reminiscent of Aldous Huxley's bohemian novel *Antic Hay* (1925), was based on John's experiences as a college student and on the pain of his unrequited love for Helen Hahn. In his mind, that relationship had by now taken on the melodramatic overtones of great fiction. The title, intended as sarcasm, was drawn from a poem about Helen of Troy by the English poet Rupert Brooke (1887-1915) that read in part: "High sat white Helen, lonely and serene, he had not remembered that she was so fair."[5]

This period of youthful reverie ended unexpectedly in the second week in May. John received a cable from Paris telling him to report to the *CDN*'s office there on May 22, six weeks early. Bureau chief Paul Scott Mowrer was covering a rebellion in Morocco, and Constantine Brown was on leave. John reluctantly tucked the 65,000-word, *High Sat White Helen* manuscript into his suitcase, and he and Leonard returned to Paris.

They found lodgings, and while John reported for work, Leonard set out to explore more of Paris on his own. The day after arriving back in the city he met a pretty, blonde-haired expatriate from New York City named Frances Powell Fineman. Leonard struck up a relationship with her. But when he departed for home, John began dating her. The pair met in a cafe one evening, and John interviewed her about a recent trip she had taken to Moscow. The relationship that resulted quickly grew serious. It was no coincidence that not long before Helen had written to say that she was engaged. "I think I've finally awakened to find your news, apparently, is true," John lamented in a letter to her. "I don't know what my reaction is. Some day perhaps I'll be able to tell you. I can't now."[6]

With Brown away again, John was left in charge of the bureau. "Here I am in terror," he told Helen. "You have no idea what an awful business for me is the matutinal reading of some thirty-odd French newspapers. Miss Murphy, the secretary, is a wonder, and she helps me, but I hate to admit how little French I know."[7]

Feeling lonely and depressed, John began spending all his spare time with Frances Fineman. After dining one night at a romantic sidewalk cafe, she invited him to a party at the home of Ford Madox Ford, the British novelist-critic. Ford had founded *Transatlantic Review*, the influential literary magazine that published early works by James Joyce, Ezra Pound, and Gertrude Stein. Although John did not much like his host, whom he derisively referred to as "England's most promising young man for about 40 years," he had to admit that Ford threw interesting parties. Among the guests that night was Ernest Hemingway. "Put that name down. Ernest Hemingway," John advised Helen in one of his last letters to her. "He can think straight and he can write English. Heaven knows two such joined accomplishments are rare nowadays."[8]

For a time, John and Frances became regulars at Ford's weekly parties. They dined together most evenings, and afterwards strolled hand-in-hand through the streets of Paris. John broke off with a young English girl he had also been seeing, and he and Frances became lovers. Still, John could not bring himself to cut the last tie to Helen. He confided as much in a baleful letter to her in which he explained that his latest romance was "possibly only reaction [to] your news [of engagement]."[9]

Between working the bizarre hours required by his job, and courting Frances, John made time to work on the *High Sat White Helen* manuscript. Both Raymond Swing and Rebecca West told him that it was unpublishable, and so he began rewriting it in earnest. "I always looked on the news as the day's work. My real work, I thought, was what occupied me after I left the office, the novels and stories," he told an interviewer many years later.[10]

Frances had by now assumed Helen's place as John's personal editor and critic. It was she who encouraged him to submit to publishers the rewritten novel, now called *The Red Pavilion*. This exotic new title came from a poem by the English poet Francis Thompson (1859-1907), which read in part: "And thou—what needst with thy tribes' black tents,/ Who hast the red pavilion of my heart?"

After being rejected by several publishers on both sides of the Atlantic, John sent his manuscript to Secker Publishing in London. The firm had been founded in 1910 by a quirky young Englishman named Martin Secker, whom John had met in 1924 in London. Secker had published the early writings of Franz Kafka, Thomas Mann, and D.H. Lawrence. Being more of a dilettante than a businessman, Martin Secker eventually went broke publishing what interested him rather than what made money. But for a time Martin Secker was London's most fashionable publisher of new writers.[11] John was ecstatic when Secker agreed to publish *The Red Pavilion*, thus catapulting him into the front ranks of rising literary talents. It also assured that his book would be reviewed by England's most influential newspapers and magazines. If John anticipated a critical hammering, he was pleasantly surprised.

Simon Pure, the London correspondent for *Bookman*, praised John's talents. Even so, he could not resist chiding him for his controversial *Saturday Review* article. "I have already marked down Mr. Gunther as a star of the future," he wrote, "and I hope that just as the publication of his first novel in England will have cleared his mind of one sort of prejudice, so its reception . . . will clear his mind of the absurd notion that English reviewers are bent upon the deprecation of American work."[12]

Buoyed by the prospects of literary success in England, John pressed ahead in efforts to find an American publisher. When his old *CDN* friend Harry Hansen (who would soon become literary editor of the *New York World*) visited London in the summer of 1925, John enlisted his help.[13]

By coincidence, young Bennett Cerf, who with partner Donald Klopfer had only just recently founded Random House publishing in New York, was in town shopping for manuscripts. John wrangled an introduction to Cerf, and when the publisher sailed home on August 25 aboard the SS *Mauretania*, it was with a copy of *The Red Pavilion* manuscript, which he had agreed to read. Hansen, also a passenger on the ship, at John's urging introduced himself to Cerf. When they fell to talking about mutual friends and acquaintances, Cerf commented that he had been reading a manuscript by a young *Chicago Daily News* reporter named John Gunther. "Can you tell me if he knows a girl in Chicago named Helen Hahn?" Cerf asked. He explained that he knew the Hahn family, and the main female character in John's novel bore an uncanny resemblance to one of the daughters, named Helen. Hansen could only laugh as he explained the situation. Cerf discreetly declined to publish the book.[14]

John would not learn of Cerf's decision for several months. In the meantime, he continued his hectic pace. In early December of 1925, he received an urgent cable from home bearing the news that his mother had fallen seriously ill. John took a leave of absence from his job to go home. Before he left, in a letter dated January 4, 1926, Charles Dennis invited him to call on his return to Chicago to discuss his future with the *Chicago Daily News*. John, accompanied to the dock by Frances, set sail for New York. Despite mutual pledges to meet again soon, their parting was tearful, and for the next few months, they carried on a long-distance romance via the mail.

CHAPTER NINE

John Gunther met with Charles Dennis and Henry J. Smith in Chicago in mid-January, 1926. His bosses informed him that as the junior on the overseas staff, he was being assigned to Paris and permanently designated as a "swing man" in the *CDN*'s European operations. All regular overseas staff were entitled to an annual leave of absence, and so it became John's job to move among the bureaus, filling in for whomever was on vacation or ill.

Being ambitious and brimming with enthusiasm to see the world, John delighted that his letters home seldom had the same postmark. Where others might have carped about the constant travel or about having to live out of a suitcase, John embraced each assignment as an adventure and a learning experience. Like his father before him, John Gunther willingly became a "professional traveler" of sorts. The irony was that while the end results of his wayfaring brought him immeasurably more success and fame than Eugene Gunther's ever had, it ultimately would have the same corrosive effect on his personal life.

He became such an inveterate traveler that soon he was writing free-lance magazine articles with titles such as "Exploring the New Europe" (*Shrine Magazine*, June 1926) and "Travel New Style" (*The Rotarian*, February 1926). John pointed out in the latter article that with the advent of the automobile and airplane "real travel has developed a new style." Previously inaccessible areas were now readily accessible.

Traveling off the "beaten track," John wrote articles with widely scattered placelines. Paul Scott Mowrer had realized that John's strength was the writing of feature stories—known in the business as "mailers." These were usually a series of stories that were mailed to the home office to avoid costly telegraphing charges. "So, when I was not substituting for our senior men in a big capital or covering an emergency," John would remember, "Paul would send me to some country or other to prowl around for a week or two and write my impressions."[1]

John's mandate was to explain the "hows and whys" of the news. Ever mindful of Henry Smith's dictum that journalism is an "unrhetorical essay on life," he focused on the people involved in events, flavoring his stories with as much human interest as possible. This was precisely the sort of colorful analysis that set the *CDN* overseas operation apart from its competition. It was also the sort of crisp, readable writing that appealed to America's growing middle class, hungry for a glimpse of the wider world, and for a sense of the place that they and their country occupied in it.

During the first week of May 1926, John toured Egypt, establishing contacts, reporting on nationalist election victories, and attempting to explain the Middle Eastern political situation, which was hopelessly tangled even then. When a simmering rebellion flared into open war between members of the Druse Muslim sect and French colonial troops in neighboring Syria, Mowrer dispatched John to report on the fighting, preferably from the rebel side of the lines. On May 26, he arrived in Beirut, which was part of Syria at the time. It was instantly apparent to John that talking of going out among the Muslim rebels was easier than doing so. In a letter to Charles Dennis written from Jerusalem on June 11,

1926, John lamented that his efforts to visit the Druse camps had been frustrated. As for the French, he said, "They are courteous and willing, but hopelessly incompetent and muddled. The Latins can't colonize."[2]

John's opinions were colored by his experience dealing with French military officials. In anticipation of being allowed to spend a few days in the field with French troops, John traveled south from Damascus down the Holy Hejaz Railway to Der'a, to the French military headquarters. To John's dismay, the staff officers there shrugged their shoulders when he asked where he could stay while awaiting the word to depart. There was no hotel or lodging in the closest town, except for "an Arab flophouse" near the train station. John made the best of a bad situation, renting a bed there. "I survived," he later recalled. "I expelled two Arab boys, an old man washing his feet, several cockroaches, and a couple of deserted sardines from my bed and went to sleep."[3]

Thus rested, John was among the eight battalions of French troops, mostly Spahis and Senegalese, who set off into the desert on June 5 intent on capturing Druse strongholds at the town of Salkhad, about eighty miles south of Damascus. In a front-page story in the *CDN* on June 8, John described the desolate, sunbaked landscape through which the French force marched eighteen miles that first day. "On either side of the road," he wrote, "were so-called fields sprouting not wheat but black rock—interminable sagging miles of volcanic country strewn with nothing but jutting bowlders [sic], outcroppings and great blocks of basalt the color of lead. There were no trees and no crops, and the only vegetation were a few weeds managing to pierce the rocky terrain. Over our heads beat the merciless sun of the Syrian desert in June."

The French encountered resistance while moving through the villages along their route the second day out. But with artillery and airplanes pounding the retreating Druse, the French advanced quickly. On June 7, they stormed and captured the ancient, walled town of Salkhad in what was a battle between a modern, twentieth century army and a ragtag force of Druse, armed only with scimitars and a few rifles. Defending their homes, the Druse fought with a passion born of desperation. Men and women alike attacked the French armored cars and cannons with their bare hands when the bloody fighting became hand-to-hand. Neither side took prisoners in the day-long battle, which ended inevitably with the tricolor flag flying once more atop the town's citadel.

Exhausted and emotionally drained by the campaign ordeal, John retreated to Beirut. Here he recuperated for a few days and arranged an interview with the mysterious and beautiful Nazira-el-Jumblat, the legendary "Queen of the Druse." Lady Nazira, the leader of the powerful Jumblat clan, had become titular head of the Lebanese Druse following the murder of her husband the previous year. John's audience with her took place in a vaulted room of her mountainside, feudal castle, replete with "blazing rugs and bubbling water in a fountain in the middle of the floor."[4]

John sat on a European-style chair, while Lady Nazira lounged on a divan. He was entranced by her. "She is a legend throughout Syria, and is known not only for her power but her beauty," he reported in a story dated June 14. "And although she was heavily veiled in a long scarf of purple silk shot through with gold, we were able to see from the enormous liquid brown eyes, vivid arched black brows and high piled black hair, black as midnight, that the legend was not by any means untrue."

John's bosses were delighted with the wonderfully colorful—albeit superficial—story, and with his coverage of the Druse rebellion. The praise had not been easily earned; conditions in Syria in 1926 were primitive, especially by American or European standards. While John's family and friends, reading his dispatches in far-off Chicago, were enchanted by the romance and adventure of an exotic Middle East war, the reality was in sharp contrast. He was plagued by fleas, dysentery, and heat prostration brought on by the scorching sun. "I haven't known the thermometer to fall below 95 degrees, except in the evenings" he had complained in a letter to Dennis.[5] Adding to his discomfort was the fact that rival correspondents were in the country. John disliked nothing more than scrambling to outwit other reporters, but he was obliged to do. When French censorship and the inefficiencies of the Beirut cable office frustrated him, he risked his status in the country by sending stories by courier to nearby Haifa or Cairo, where they were quickly wired to Chicago verbatim.

John left Syria in mid-June, stopping in Egypt long enough to visit some American archaeologists at a dig near Cairo, and to report on a Moslem religious conference in Alexandria. He then went to Rome, to fill in for two months for Hiram (Hi) Moderwell, the resident *CDN* correspondent. Awaiting him here, in addition to a stack of letters from home and from Frances, was a copy of his novel, *The Red Pavilion.* It had been published by Secker while he was in Syria, "dodging bullets in the desert back of Damascus, and wiping fleas off my face," as he put it.[6] There was soon good news from New York, too, where Cass Canfield at Harper & Brothers had decided to publish the book. Neither John nor Canfield could have known in 1926 that this decision marked the beginning of a close personal and business relationship which would span forty-four years, and produce more than two dozen successful books.

American sales of *The Red Pavilion* were given an unexpected boost when the book was banned in Boston in 1927, along with such "morally objectionable" novels as Sinclair Lewis' *Elmer Gantry.* While the censors were sure of their opinions of John's first novel, the reviewers were not. The newspaper and magazine reviews were mixed; some praised the story, some did not.

The awkwardly structured plot opens with a dinner party at the posh South Chicago home of Mary Detmers, the widow of a prominent university anatomy professor. John made use of this old literary device as a stage to introduce eight characters: a circle of friends that includes a pert young flapper named Doris Barron, a young Jew named Leon Goodman, who writes bad poetry and seeks to interest himself in life by suffering, and the book's central characters, Shirley Bowdoin and Richard Northway.

Shirley is a thinly disguised Helen Hahn, and protagonist husband Richard is John. Although the nature of their relationship and its ultimate outcome are altered, its essence remains unchanged. Richard and Shirley have became emotionally and physically estranged. He wants children; she is intent on studying art, and runs off to Europe for two years. After abandoning plans to become a chemist, Richard earns a lucrative but unfulfilled living selling bonds. The estranged lovers are reunited at Mary Detmer's dinner party and, of course, get back together after various trials and tribulations.

While the critic for *The Saturday Review* dismissed the story as "exceedingly pretentious and at times irritating,"[7] James Weber Linn of the University of Chicago, John's onetime mentor, opined that, "Gunther has taught himself more than I know. Above his brilliance, however, there seems to hang a slight shimmering mist of miasma."[8]

The British newspaper *The Spectator* hailed *The Red Pavilion* as "one of the best, most cultivated and human of recent American books."[9] The *New York Times* was no less effusive; its critic praised John's apparent worldliness and his mastery of the "technique of the genuinely sophisticated novel."[10] *The Red Pavilion*'s critical success and the promise of John's literary talents inspired a writer for the American magazine *The Bohemian* in a May 1927 profile of "the five rising stars in American fiction," to include John Gunther; another was fellow Chicagoan Ernest Hemingway.[11]

Oddly enough, some of John's potentially most hostile critics enjoyed *The Red Pavilion* immensely. Helen Hahn and her sisters took great delight in rummaging through the book for recognizable anecdotes and characters. There were plenty. "Somewhere in the book is a letter Richard writes to Shirley," Helen said. "I recognized it as one John had written to me. And Mickey [sister Emily] recognized it as one he'd written to her, too! Or at least the phrases were the same. There was one we'd chant occasionally: 'fringed fans of eyelashes.'"[12]

Tempering John's sense of achievement was a controversy that developed over his coverage of events in Syria, which potentially had disastrous consequences for his journalism career. The first hint of trouble came in a letter from Charles Dennis, which reached Rome in early July. Dennis pointed out that William B. Seabrook, the veteran Middle East correspondent for the *New York Sun*, had written to complain that John's Syrian dispatches had plagiarized from his recent articles in *Asia Magazine*. "I have been a bit disturbed by the parallelism between your articles about the Druses and the articles by Seabrook," Dennis chided in a subsequent letter, dated July 22.[13] Even so, he backed John, accepting his explanation that any similarities between his stories and Seabrook's had come about because they had hired the same Druse guide and presumably had access to the same information.

Dennis may have been swayed in John's favor, too, by Seabrook's unsavory reputation—particularly his notorious proclivity for sadomasochistic sex, and a self-professed interest in cannibalism. (Seabrook, deeply troubled and alcoholic, took his own life in 1945.)

Dennis stressed his main reason for pressing the plagiarism issue was to "drive home the lesson of the importance to any correspondent of making his own material as unique as possible, avoiding even the appearance of copying material already published." Whether John Gunther intentionally cribbed Seabrook's articles is impossible to say; there were undeniable similarities between the two sets of articles. What is clear is that John took Dennis's admonition to heart. Never again in his long career was he accused of plagiarism.

John was still smarting when in early August he was sent to London to substitute for Constantine Brown, who had replaced Hal O'Flaherty there in June. O'Flaherty had finally gotten his wish to return to Chicago when there was a management shuffle in the *Daily News* offices. Following the September 1925 death of *CDN* founder and publisher Victor Lawson, a group of investors including Charles Dennis had purchased the newspaper from the trustees to whom Lawson had willed it. In the ensuing reorganization Dennis became publisher, O'Flaherty the foreign editor, and Henry Smith the managing editor. The moves solidified the management situation and, even more importantly, ensured John's future with the newspaper. That his relations with all three men were cordial helps explain why, just a few days after leaving Rome, John received a letter from Dennis telling him that Hi Moderwell had resigned from the staff to return to America. The bureau job was offered to John, who declined. He had grown to love his job as "swing man."

John instead began a three-month assignment in London in late August. Bursting with enthusiasm and ideas for a series of articles on the political conditions in Spain and Greece, as well as one he proposed to call "The Rise of the Dictators." A full ten years before he wrote *Inside Europe*, he was already fascinated by the interlocking themes of political power and personality.

Frances rejoined John during his stay in London, and they resumed their love affair. John seems to have taken little interest in the possible outcome of their intimacies, for when Frances asked him what would happen if she became pregnant, he blithely replied, "That would be an act of God, and we'd have to get married."[14]

He could not have suspected how soon his words would apparently become a self-fulfilling prophecy.

CHAPTER TEN

Frances Powell Fineman, the future Mrs. John Gunther, was born September 14, 1897, in New York City, the second of the two children of Sonia (nee Paul) and Dennis Fineman.[1] Her parents' ancestry is obscure, beyond the fact that they were Russian Jews who had emigrated to America from the Kiev area of the Ukraine in the late nineteenth century. Sonia was a petite, red-haired beauty with the same finely boned, delicate features and strong- willed temperament she bequeathed to her daughter Frances. "Sonia spoke Russian and always emphasized that she was high-born," recalls her granddaughter. "She was quite a free-thinking lady."[2]

That liberality extended to Sonia's relations with members of the opposite sex, for Frances always said that her parents had married about 1896 when Sonia was pregnant with her first child, a son they named Bernard (Bernie). The arrival of Frances the next year was equally unexpected, and the relationship between mother and daughter was never close. Frances grew up a lonely, insecure little girl, obsessed by fears that her mother loved her less than she did her brother.

While that may have been so, it may also have been a case of Frances misinterpreting Sonia's marital unhappiness. In 1911 her mother ran off with a well-to-do Texan named Morris Brown, whom she eventually married. She then took her daughter with her when she went to live at her new husband's home in Galveston. Determined to erase all traces of her former life, Sonia adopted the name Sophia Powell Brown.

Frances had been deeply attached to her natural father. Her feelings of betrayal at the breakup of her parents' marriage turned to hatred for a stepfather who sexually abused her. The depth of Frances' emotional trauma manifested itself in later life in the form of a self-destructive ambivalence towards men. She was filled with a seething mistrust and resentment of males, yet she craved the paternal affection that had been denied her. Frances was haunted by a sense of guilt that she had somehow been responsible for Brown's misdeeds. Incest being a crime not spoken of in 1911, Frances was left to wonder at the meaning of it all. It was a burden that no fourteen-year-old could bear alone, and the scars never fully healed.

When Brown's abuse extended to his spouse, Sonia's second marriage proved as unhappy as her first. Vain and domineering, Brown accused her of infidelities, and the resulting marital strains were painfully obvious to the children. Frances retreated into her own dream world, and threw herself into her school work. She was an excellent student, and in the fall of 1911 began attending Ball High School in Galveston. In her senior year, 1915, she served as an editor of the school yearbook, *The Review,* while graduating fifth overall in her class.[3]

Frances returned to her native New York the following February, enrolling as an English major at Barnard College.[4] Although the sparse jottings in her diaries offer little insight into her experiences during this period (a typical entry in 1919 lists Frances' physical characteristics: "5'1", 110 pounds, size four shoes"), her nomadic existence over the next four years, during which she studied at some of America's best colleges for women, reflects the uncertainties in her life. She transferred to Rice Institute in Houston for the 1917-18 academic year, then studied at Radcliffe in Cambridge, Massachusetts, before returning to Barnard to complete her Bachelor of Arts degree in June 1921. After graduating, she worked briefly for a New York fashion magazine, while musing about a career in journalism. But there were few full-time jobs for women in the business in 1924, and Frances was frustrated in her ambitions.

In the fall of 1924, she and a girlfriend left home for a grand tour of Europe and the Soviet Union, where Frances wrote some free-lance reviews of the Moscow theatre scene for the *New York Times*.[5] By the following summer, when she encountered John Gunther and Leonard Weil in Paris, she was living in a small flat near the Etoile.

Frances, a neat, precise person by nature, was astounded by some of John's slovenly attitudes, especially his cavalier approach to money. She would always recall how one day in Paris they had been window shopping in Paris when John insisted on buying her an expensive evening bag. Frances noticed that he did not bother recording the personal check with which he paid. Asked how he knew the balance on his account, John shrugged and said, "The bank writes me a letter!"

John's answer typified his attitude towards financial affairs. Money itself never much concerned him; he was content, as long as he had enough to pay his bills, which were considerable.

Despite their contrasting personalities, Frances thought John handsome. He was bright, warm, generous, amicable, and seemed bound for a successful career in journalism. What's more, his commanding physical presence promised a physical security she craved. She was irresistibly drawn to him. The irony was that his mannerisms and fair hair reminded her of her hated stepfather.

For his part, John was smitten by Frances' delicate, gamin-like quality, her curly blonde hair, and her intense blue eyes. To someone born and raised amidst staid midwestern propriety, she had an air of the exotic to her. Frances spoke French and German (which she had studied in high school), and some Hebrew. To John it seemed that this young woman led an exciting, cosmopolitan life. She was infinitely better educated than I, with sound attitudes towards politics and a swift and penetrating mind, John later wrote. He told friends that Frances at her best was an absolute sparkler.[6]

While the pair shared a passion for literature and ideas, John felt that he lacked the intellectual discipline for sustained systematic thought. Frances, on the other hand, reveled in such mental gymnastics, to the point of fault. This tendency to analyze things to death, as John put it, resulted in a frustrating inability to finish her writing projects; in later years, it became a major source of tension between John and Frances. But all this was in the future.

That spring in 1925, John was fascinated by Frances. He was drawn by her social charm and feminine vulnerability. He was blissfully unaware that she was not the helpless waif she seemed. He would learn otherwise.

Frances was a determined, shrewd young woman who could be devious when she wanted to get her way. At first meeting she seemed the shiest creature you ever met, almost painfully diffident, John mused many years later, but she always knew exactly what she wanted, and she made a straight line to get to it.

What Frances desired more than anything else was to become Mrs. John Gunther. And, characteristically, she set about achieving that goal with calculated determination.

John's plans for a series of articles on Greece and Spain were shelved when his stay in London in the autumn of 1926 was extended. Word reached Paul Scott Mowrer in Paris of a political crisis in Rumania, and so Constantine Brown, the *CDN*'s resident expert on Eastern Europe, was sent there upon returning from vacation. John was relieved only when Brown got back to London. John and Frances then returned to Paris to spend Christmas together. Such time was precious, given John's peripatetic lifestyle.

Early in the new year, he was rambling around in Greece and neighboring Albania. Frances returned home to New York, heartbroken at the prospect of another indefinite separation. It was at this point that she decided on a bold scheme to induce John to propose marriage.

In mid-February 1927, he was filling in at the *CDN*'s Rome bureau after Hi Moderwell resigned. Recalling John's statement that it would be an act of God if she got pregnant, and that he would have no choice to marry her, Frances sent him a three-word cable. It read: Act of God. True to his promise, John responded with a cable of his own: Marry me?[7] Frances accepted, and they decided to be married in Rome on March 16, 1927. It was a decision that John would regret for the rest of his life. Their marriage was doomed, doomed right from the start, his friend Leonora Hornblow observes. "John felt that a 'good Chicago boy' should marry Frances if she was pregnant, but he never really loved her enough to marry her."[8]

By coincidence, Helen Hahn was now living in New York, and one day in late February 1927, she was invited to an informal cocktail party at the home of a girlfriend named Mary Failor. The party was for a young woman whom Failor suggested Hahn would probably want to meet. Recalls Helen: "When I was introduced to the girl, who was Frances, the four or five other people at the party were watching me closely. I guess they expected me to be startled when Frances announced that she was going to Rome to marry John Gunther. That was supposed to be a bombshell, but it didn't quite have that effect on me.

"Frances went with me later, as I was getting my coat to leave, and she began weeping on my shoulder. She was a pretty little thing with curly blond hair. I was still shockable in those days, and I remember how taken aback I was when she suddenly said, 'I don't know if I'm doing the right thing, but it seems wrong when I wake up and there's a dark head on the pillow beside me.' John, of course, was fair haired. I liked Frances though, and I went with her to help pick out her trousseau. She and I became good friends in the brief interval before she left for Rome."[9]

Frances arrived in Italy the first week of March. She and John obtained a marriage licence March 9. One week later, on the morning of Wednesday, March 16, they were wed in a civil ceremony at Rome's magnificent old city hall.[10] John Clayton, the *Chicago Tribune*'s Rome correspondent at the time, served as best man. The matron of honor was Hi Moderwell's wife, Anna, who afterwards hosted a wedding breakfast at a nearby hotel called the Villa Doria.[11]

Life for Mr. and Mrs. John Gunther quickly settled into a routine, with John perpetually on the move between European capitals. When finances permitted, Frances joined him because, for now, there was no baby. It is unclear whether Frances believed she was pregnant when she sent the Act of God cable to John, or whether she was being devious. When queried by a visiting American girlfriend, Frances supposedly smiled, and then explained that her pregnancy had been taken care of before she left New York.[12]

CHAPTER ELEVEN

Despite the disruptions of a peripatetic lifestyle and any misgivings that John may have had about the circumstances of his marriage, the Gunthers were not entirely unhappy together. After all, they were young, and Paris still was a golden place to be in 1927.

John and Frances rented a tiny studio apartment in the Montparnasse district. Frances devoted herself to helping John with his job. She tended to many of the routine chores that annoyed him: tabulating expense accounts, keeping scrapbooks and clipping files, and retyping his stories in the required quadruplicate for mailing to Paul Scott Mowrer.

With her help, John found he had more time to devote to writing fiction; he was working on two novels. The first to be completed was an "amusement" published simultaneously in the autumn of 1927 by Harper & Brothers in New York under the title *Eden for One* and as *Peter Lancelot* in London.

Intended as an adult "fairy tale," *Eden for One* is the story of Peter Lancelot, a small boy with a penchant for dreaming. When a magician named Mr. Dominy causes Peter's every desire to come true, the boy promptly wishes himself into an idyllic new world for which Mr. Dominy conjures up an island, a garden, a castle, a friend, and a lover. But in a moralistic twist, life in this paradise inevitably goes sour.

Reaction to the book was disappointing, especially after the favorable reviews for *The Red Pavilion*. But the indifference of the critics did nothing to dissuade John from his dream of becoming a full-time novelist, for he had no inclination to brood. John worked at his newspaper job as well as his free-lance writing, which provided vital extra income. Despite the devalued French franc, he and Frances found it impossible to make ends meet on his meager newspaper salary.

Also easing any disappointment John may have felt about reviews for *Eden for One* was the celebrity he now enjoyed in the sizable, yet closely knit, American journalistic community in Europe. The writing of novels, no matter what their critical or commercial reception, afforded the author a certain literary status in the eyes of peers, most of whom were would-be novelists themselves. All had heard of Gertrude Stein's advice to Ernest Hemingway—that in order to write seriously, it was necessary to quit the newspaper business. That was much easier said than done, of course, and few had the dedication or confidence to actually do so.

John liked being a "somebody." After all, he had grown up in a family in which social standing was important. His father had hungered for success all his life. Early in his career, at least, John was similarly preoccupied. It was a concern, so typical of America's burgeoning middle class at the turn-of-the-century, that goes a long way towards explaining why in his youth John cultivated mentor relationships. First they were with older family members and teachers, and later in life with newspaper colleagues. He sought out surrogate father figures.

John's earliest literary stirrings had been encouraged by his uncle, Julius Schoeninger. During his days as a student journalist, he had received encouragement from James Weber Linn, his favorite Engish professor. Later, at the *Chicago Daily News*, Harry

Hansen, Henry J. Smith, and then Hal O'Flaherty had taken him under their wings. Even after he became a well-known foreign correspondent, for a time John sought the advice and reassurance of more experienced colleagues, people such as H.R. Knickerbocker, Dorothy Thompson, Raymond G. Swing, and Marcel Fodor.

As John's celebrity grew and surpassed that of his more senior journalists, these professional relationships evolved into close friendships. His circle of friends became a second family to him. His triumphs, sorrows, and even quarrels were theirs, and vice versa. When Dorothy Thompson's book, *The New Russia*, appeared in the fall of 1928, parts of it bore a strong resemblance to parts of Theodore Dreiser's book, *Dreiser Looks at Russia*. Reviewers pointed out the similarities after Dreiser publicly hinted that Thompson had been intimate with him for a time, and had pilfered material from his notes. These allegations of plagiarism stung John after the 1926 incident with William Seabrook. When word of the Thompson-Dreiser controversy reached John in London, he sent an empathetic letter to Thompson. "My dear, I formally and informally, here and now and forever, reiterate my faith in you," he wrote. "If you want character witnesses (!) cable me and I'll come with a ship-load tomorrow. Rebecca West and the Swings are among ever so many people who agree with you on this—our love to you."[1]

Among the other colleagues who played an important role in John's life were James "Jimmy" Vincent Sheean and William L. Shirer. Both shared John's midwestern background, his passion for the good life, and his devotion to "serious fiction." And like him, both were destined to achieve their greatest fame as journalists, not as novelists. "We were, the three of us, Chicago kids, and we all had a lot of luck," Shirer observes. "Jimmy was the best writer of the three of us and a deeper thinker than John or me, I think."[2]

Jimmy Sheean, a red-haired bon vivant, was in many people's minds the quintessential foreign correspondent: "the classic American innocent" abroad. Born December 5, 1899, in Pana, Illinois, he had attended the University of Chicago, where he first met John Gunther. Sheean had quit school in 1922, his senior year, to work at the *Chicago Daily News*, but was fired for insubordination. He briefly worked for a New York paper before joining the great exodus of Americans to Paris. As the writer of his 1975 obituary in the *New York Times* put it, "He seemed a roan destined to be present at history's turning points—Mussolini's march on Rome . . . the Spanish Civil War . . . (the) assassination of Gandhi."[3]

Sheean was one of the best-known of all American foreign correspondents of his day, and his reflective, highly personalized reporting style influenced a generation of young journalists. It also outraged his enemies. In 1946, while covering the murder trial of a group of blacks in Columbia, Tennessee, Sheean's opinionated dispatches nettled the chief of the state highway patrol, who accosted him and called him "a lying, Communistic son-of-a-bitch." Sheean responded with a smile. "Thank you very much," he said. "I would not want you to say anything else. Any good word from you would be the worst possible condemnation."[4]

Musing on his friendship with Sheean, John wrote in 1937, "[He] is perhaps the most remarkable American of my generation I know. I met him when we were both at the University of Chicago. He was bizarre in those days. He hummed Mozart, wore green pants, spoke better Italian than the Italian professors, read the Talmud, quoted Spinoza, learned German, borrowed money, admired dancing, and wrote a treatise on the Wahabis."[5]

Like Sheean, William Shirer was cerebral, opinionated, and immensely talented. He also seemed to have a knack for being in the right place at the right time. Shirer loved nothing more than getting together with John, Jimmy Sheean, and other friends over a few bottles of wine. The talk about where the next news "hot spot" would be was invariably heated.

Born February 23, 1904, in Chicago, Shirer was educated at Coe College in Iowa prior to working his way over to Europe in 1925, on a cattle boat. After stumbling into a $15-a-week job with the Paris edition of the *Chicago Tribune*, Shirer went on to a distinguished, albeit troubled, career as a print and radio newsman.

Shirer recalls meeting John Gunther in Paris about 1926. He was with the *Tribune* and John was working for the rival *Chicago Daily News*. The two really became friends two years later, when Shirer spent two weeks with John and Frances, at the 1928 Winter Olympics at St. Moritz, France. Their friendship solidified in 1930, when both found themselves based in Vienna. Shirer remembers John's tremendous energy and his ambition to become a successful novelist. Whenever the two crossed paths those days, which was often, they spent countless hours in cafes, hotel rooms, and on board overnight trains talking out their dreams.[6]

In late November 1927, John toured Eastern Europe, and in an expedition reminiscent of his Syrian adventure of the previous year, he spent four eventful days in Bulgaria in mid-December. John tried to interview the Macedonian guerrilla leader Ivan Mihailov, then hiding in the rugged mountains of neighboring Yugoslavia. Mihailov, whom John would later depict as a character in a short story called, "A Macedonian Robin Hood," was a cunning, fanatical nationalist whose intentions were as simple as they were deadly. He hoped to use terrorism and political assassination to touch off another Balkans war, and in the confusion to achieve independence for Macedonia.[7]

John informed Paul Scott Mowrer that while he had met with Macedonian nationalists in Bulgaria, and had been followed everywhere by their spies, bad weather and the perils of crossing the Yugolslavian frontier had prevented him from actually meeting Mihailov. In fact, that report was only partially correct.

Despite letters of introduction from a Macedonian nationalist leader in Paris, the guerrillas did not trust John. They were willing to escort him and to bask in the publicity that he could give their cause in the United States, but they resisted allowing him into their inner circle. Yugoslavian authorities had placed a $100,000 bounty on Mihailov's head.

As John explained in his "fictionalized" account of the trip, most of his time in Bulgaria was spent in a furtive, guided automobile tour of Macedonia's "incredibly barren hills, with the bare rock showing through like dandruff in a giant's scalp." According to an article he wrote for *CDN* entitled "The Hows and Whys of Political Assassination," the Macedonian nationalist in Sofia who arranged his visit was murdered by political rivals a short time later.[8]

John rendezvoused with Frances in Constantinople, where they spent Christmas, and then visited Albania. They were back in Turkey in time for New Year's, and on January 15, John interviewed the Turkish Foreign Minister Tewfik Rouschdy Bey. Officials at the American embassy, keen to know more about the political situation in the region, asked John to brief them. He readily agreed to do so.[9]

At that time, the Central Intelligence Agency (CIA) had not yet been created (its forerunner, the Office of Strategic Services, did not come into being until 1942), and American intelligence gathering operations in Europe were primitive. When Henry Stimson became secretary of state in 1929, one of his first actions was to close down the highly-successful code-breaking unit known as the Black Chamber. In operation since the end of the First World War, the Black Chamber had solved more than 45,000 cryptograms. At one time or another it had broken the codes of Japan, Germany, France, Great Britain, and the Soviet Union. However, in Stimson's view, prying into other country's secrets was improper. "Gentlemen do not read each other's mail," he said.

While there had been American spies during the Revolutionary War, the Civil War, and the First World War, such people were deemed to be unnecessary in peacetime. During the 1920s the United States had retreated into self-imposed isolationism, secure in its own wealth and the vastness of the North American geography. Domestic surveillance of "subversives" was not unusual. But the need for any kind of overseas intelligence apparatus seemed remote and unimportant. Thus, state department officials in foreign postings gathered intelligence in a desultory fashion, or as the need arose. Since not one American embassy had a press or cultural affairs officer, information was obtained through "exchanges" of information, sometimes with foreign correspondents. John was willing to talk, but not all his colleagues were as accommodating. Some were unabashedly hostile to the idea. Among them was George Seldes, the distinguished foreign correspondent and long-time media critic.

Seldes, a diminutive, feisty man who began a distinguished reporting career in Pittsburgh in 1909 and was still practicing his craft long enough and well enough to write a best-selling memoir in 1987, worked as a foreign correspondent from 1916 to 1937. During those twenty-one years, he says he never exchanged information with anyone from the state department. About that, he is adament. "What Gunther did could certainly be considered an exception to the rule," he says.

"Most of the time, they (embassy and consular officials) had no use for American reporters, and we had no regard for them. They didn't know anything anyway. They were more concerned with socializing with Countesses and attending parties. I can tell you this: when we were in trouble, we never, never went to the American Embassy for help. We went to the British; they were more receptive and besides that, they knew more!"[10]

John Gunther was of a different mind. His meeting with embassy officials in Constantinople was not the first time in his career—nor would it be the last—on which he provided American diplomats with information. Writing years later in *A Fragment of an Autobiography*, he recalled, "Naturally, we [American foreign correspondents] cultivated friendships with American officials and diplomats, as well as those of other countries, but not quite in the manner of today. We did not think of ourselves as being instruments of national policy."[11]

John and Frances left Turkey for Paris in late January. They spent several days in St. Moritz, the French ski resort, where John covered the second Winter Olympic games. Their stay in the French Alps, in the company of William Shirer and other American journalists, proved to be as much a holiday as a working assignment. The rest was welcome.

Typically, John was back in Paris no more than a few days when Mowrer sent him on what turned into a five-month assignment. Frances was by now pregnant, and the decision to leave her alone for so long could not have been easy. But at Frances's urging, John left to tour Poland and Sweden, before going on to Moscow to relieve Junius B. Wood, the *Chicago Daily News*'s resident correspondent. John made the most of his first visit to the Soviet Union, traveling along the Volga River and through the Ukraine, and roaming as far afield as Armenia, Azerbaijan, and some of the "shaggy valleys" of the Caucasus.

The Soviet Union was a land that intrigued John. His curiosity was heightened now that Communism had become fashionable with western intellectuals. Lenin's death in 1924 had touched off a power struggle between Stalin and Trotsky that was resolved in

December of 1927 with the triumph of the former and the exile of the latter. When John's visited in the summer of 1928, the Soviets were still eager to show off their accomplishments to the world. The horror of the Stalinist purges and the trauma of forced collectivization were still in the future.

Many American leftists and liberals hailed the Soviet Union as a showplace for fresh thinking. Meanwhile, cynics warned that the achievements of the new state were negated by the paranoia of the Soviet dictatorship, most notably its relentless state propaganda apparatus and a ruthless secret police who made the Tsarist police seem benign by comparison.

John struggled to keep an open mind as he gathered material for a series of five articles about life in Leningrad and Moscow. Away from the carefully staged official tours of model factories, schools, and prisons, John observed the harsh realities of life in a land that had been dragged into the twentieth century. John's articles, which appeared in late August, reflected a midwesterner's profound dismay with the conditions he encountered. The articles reinforced in the minds of ordinary Americans an impression of the Soviet Union as a drab, inhumane land ruled by fanatical Communists. It was an image not without foundation, particularly during the Stalinist era. But over the course of the next half century, the blind acceptance by some American foreign policy makers was to have a profound impact on East-West relations.

The only place in the Soviet Union that John felt at ease was Leningrad (known in pre-revolutionary times—and now, again—as St. Petersburg), the traditional center of Russian culture and the arts. Its sweeping parks, majestic waterways, and leisurely pace reminded him of Copenhagen. "Leningrad is a western city with wide streets rectangularly designed, a city built as a whole and for all time," John wrote.[12] He was sad to note that Leningrad was also a decaying metropolis whose one million inhabitants were outnumbered two-to-one by rats.

The situation in Moscow was even worse. John was dazzled by the architecture he saw there, particularly the towering St. Basil's, a beautiful sixteenth century church on Red Square. John described it as "surely the most fantastic church in the world; Ivan the Terrible blinded the architect so that another church never could be made like it. It has eleven spires and domes in green, red, yellow and gold, scaled pineapple, obliquely burred, convoluted, transversely stripped. To the right, the red wall of the Kremlin stretches between lofty towers."[13]

In sharp contrast to the uplifting effect of Moscow's architectural heritage was the city's oppressive ambience. Chicago was a paradise by comparison.

Life in the Soviet capital had been stripped bare. Here was a dilapidated city of peeling paint, shattered windows, scant consumer goods, and broken spirits. To someone like John, who loved good food and nightlife, Moscow was depressing. "[It] is a dark city at night. Why need lights?" John observed. "There's very little crime and few outsiders are here to lose their way."[14]

In spite of the unrelenting drabness and the uniformity, John amused himself by touring around with Walter Duranty, the free-spirited *New York Times* correspondent. And he found pleasant surprises as he walked the city's rambling, cobbled streets in the blue dusk of the late summer evenings. "Perhaps the first impression is the almost total absence of automobiles," he wrote. "The few that we do see are relics of an almost neolithic past, strange monsters with distorted body lines, paintless fenders, grotesquely fanciful hoods."[15] In place of vehicular traffic, John saw unexpectedly lively street life. He described in vivid detail the colorful scenes at the small, free-enterprise markets and on the street corners, where buskers, hawkers, and a myriad of itinerant sidewalk tradesmen gathered nightly to sell their wares.

As always, it was people who piqued John Gunther's interests. He was fascinated by the clash of personalities in the upper echelons of the Soviet regime. The country was ruled by Joseph Stalin, who had embarked on implementing the first of his Five Year Plans designed to build "Socialism in one country." Oddly enough, the more John saw and learned of this new Russia, the more uncertain he felt in writing about the events unfolding there.

As was so often the case for John, it was the relatively mundane details of everyday life that gave him a sense of history's broader sweep. An incident that occurred one evening in a Moscow restaurant revealed just how much things had changed since the revolution.

John was astounded to see what appeared to be the solid gold crest of the Russian Imperial family on all the restaurant's plates and cutlery. He asked the headwaiter whether or not the articles were genuine.

"Oh yes, it's the real stuff all right, from the palace storerooms," the man explained. "We've got to find some use for all that fancy and useless junk."[16]

Whether the utensils John used to eat his dinner that evening were genuine is not certain. Junius Wood had reported in a 1926 article in *National Geographic* magazine that while the Tsar's linen, silver, and dishes had been on sale in Moscow shops, which catered to foreigners, at least some of the items were facsimiles manufactured using the original designs as a means of earning badly needed foreign exchange.[17]

John breathed a sigh of relief when in early September he left behind the drabness of Moscow to return home to Paris, where Frances was by now almost nine months pregnant. But John barely had time to unpack his suitcases before he was off again, this time on a brief assignment in to London. Here he renewed acquaintances with English friends, including Rebecca West. This was a difficult time for Rebecca, who was in poor health and suffering from a succession of ailments that included flu, colitis, gallstones, and an earache. Compounding her problems was the illness of her son Anthony. The boy had been hospitalized with tuberculosis at a sanatorium in Norfolk.

John did what he could to comfort Rebecca, accompanying her to West Cromer, where she had taken rooms to be near her son. Rebecca responded to John's kindness with a touching letter. "Never, never shall I forget the sweetness of your visit to me," she wrote. "There is something between us that is very real and will never be broken."[18] Rebecca, who had warned John against marrying Frances, had finally warmed to her. Rebecca conceded she had been too harsh in her initial evaluation of Frances, and she expressed hopes for the safe arrival of the baby, which was due any day now.

That child, a girl weighing just over seven pounds, was born on Friday, September 25, at the American Hospital in Paris.[19] The proud parents named her Judith. In the wake of some problems with delivery, it was October 15, almost three weeks later, before the doctors allowed mother and baby to leave the hospital.

A standard joke among American foreign correspondents in Europe at the time concerned a reporter for the Hearst newspaper chain who had gone on a "routine" assignment, leaving his pregnant wife at home; by the time he returned, the child had finished kindergarten. There was more truth in that joke than most news correspondents cared to admit. So John was understandably delighted to have been at home for the birth of his daughter. Raymond Swing added to his joy by presenting him with a silver drinking cup for Judy, and by volunteering to become her godfather.

These were relatively happy days for John and Frances. Sadly, this brief period of happiness would be cut short by tragedy.

CHAPTER TWELVE

Despite John's nagging suspicions that *Chicago Daily News* foreign news head Paul Scott Mowrer disliked him or was jealous of his growing reputation, Mowrer obligingly limited his assignments to nearby turf for the first few months after Judy's birth. Staying close to home gave John time to spend with Frances and the baby, and to concentrate on his fiction writing. He was working on a new novel entitled *The Golden Fleece.* It was the story of a character named Joan Tilford, a young Chicago flapper, vainly seeking meaning in her life through a series of casual affairs. This was a theme that had already been thoroughly explored by F. Scott Fitzgerald, and when *The Golden Fleece* appeared in the spring of 1929, the reviews were generally disappointing.

Being in Paris and London also afforded John the opportunity to expand his journalistic horizons. On December 12, 1928, he made his radio broadcasting debut on Chicago station WMAQ, which was owned by the *CDN*. John stayed up till three o'clock in the morning London time (nine o'clock in the evening midwestern time) to deliver a report on the medical condition of England's ailing King George V. John spoke by telephone to his old friend Hal O'Flaherty, who was working in the home office. Their conversation was broadcast live.

That an "on-the-spot" report from Europe was still very much of a novelty at this time was made clear by newspaper coverage of the event. An item in the next day's paper reported that "The first few words (of the conversation) were fuzzy, while engineers had fumbled with equipment, but then Gunther's voice was heard with remarkable clarity."[1] John had a good, clear radio voice that reminded some people of movie actor Jimmy Stewart. He enjoyed that initial experience, and eventually returned to the airwaves on a regular basis. Like most newspaper journalists, he considered radio easy work, and easy money. He did not regard broadcasting as "serious journalism." The American public felt otherwise, and radio's audience mushroomed as the hours and variety of programming increased. From the beginning, overseas radio news reports were a novelty, and were among the most widely listened to programs.

Among the audience in far off Chicago that snowy Thursday night John reported on the king's failing health was John's mother. His father had died of heart failure on August 23, 1927. John made no mention of the death in his writings or in any of his personal papers. In the years since he had last seen his father, John had simply dismissed him from mind, as had both his mother and his sister, Jean. By 1927, although they still lived under the same roof, John's parents had long since ceased to care for one another. Death found Eugene a sad, lonely figure wasted by a series of debilitating strokes. The day he died, he was in a nursing home. Lizette and Jean were in Paris visiting John and his new bride, Frances.[2]

At just fifty-seven years of age, Lizette, too, was plagued by health problems. Shortly before Christmas 1928, it was apparent to her family that she did not have long to live. John, contacted by relatives, took a leave of absence from work. He caught the first boat home, with Frances and Judy following a few days later. All were en route to Chicago on January 10, 1929, when Lizette Gunther suffered a fatal heart attack. John arrived home ten days later, in time to attend a January 19 funeral service. Lizette Gunther's ashes were laid to rest in the Schoeninger family plot in Graceland Cemetery, a stone's throw across the street from the family's North Side Chicago home on Kenmore Avenue.[3]

John was still grieving over the loss of his mother when, just nine days later, death struck close to him a second time.

He and Frances attended the theatre on the evening of January 27, 1929,[4] leaving the baby Judy at the Kenmore Avenue house in the care of a baby-sitter. They returned home to find the child cold and lifeless in her crib. Judy was dead, the victim of what an autopsy revealed had been an undiagnosed thymus ailment known as status thymicolymphaticus. She was barely four months old.[5]

The Gunthers were crushed. Frances, whose emotional stability seemed at times precarious, groped to come to terms with the death. It was not easy. Tortured by feelings of guilt at having aborted several unwanted pregnancies, she now became obsessed with the notion that Judy's death was a cruel form of divine retribution for her past indiscretions, not the least of which seems to have been the ruse by which she had trapped John into marrying her. John's description of Paula Jarrett, the wife of the protagonist in his 1964 novel *The Lost City*, resembled this side of Frances. "One of [her] puritan characteristics was her persistent fear, even when she was happiest, that all she had might suddenly be snatched away," he wrote. "She adored pleasure, but she could not get over her feeling that she might be punished for achieving pleasure."[6]

At John's urging, Frances tried to relieve her grief by trying to learn more about the probable medical causes of the baby's sudden death. A pediatric specialist at Johns Hopkins Hospital in Baltimore advised her that it was impossible to say for certain what had killed Judy. Another physician told Frances: "There is no question of heredity; it plays no part in the disturbances of the thymus gland. You should have no fear of bringing into this world another Judy. We can honestly say that this death was an unavoidable accident."[7]

Only somewhat reassured, John and Frances left in early February for an extended trip to the West Coast. They took the train west to California, where they visited John's uncle Joseph Schoeninger. Uncle Joe was living at Carmel, then a quiet, unspoiled coastal village south of San Francisco. One of John's cousins recalls the Schoeninger's first impressions of Frances: "she was pretty, intelligent, and seemed to fit in easily."[8]

Away from the grind work pressures, and the disruptions caused by their routine partings, John and Frances were never closer. They began to rediscover the magic that had been there during their first dates in Paris. It was in the Schoeninger's quaint, ivy-covered seaside home in Carmel that the couple conceived their second child.

With a few more weeks before he had to return to work, John and Frances visited her younger brother, Bernie, in Hollywood. A schoolmate and close friend of movie studio whiz kid Irving Thalberg (F. Scott's Fitzgerald's model for *The Last Tycoon*), Bernie Fineman had enjoyed a successful career as a producer of "B" movies in the 1920s, first at Universal Studios and later at Metro-Goldwin-Mayer. Unfortunately for him, like many of his associates, he made the mistake of buying studio stock on margin. The Great Crash of 1929 hit him hard financially. However, at the time of John's and Frances' visit in early 1929 he was on top of the world. Bernie introduced his sister and brother-in-law to well-known film people at parties around the town.[9]

Given Hollywood's voracious appetite for fresh creative talent and the fact that John's third novel, *The Golden Fleece*, had just been published, it was inevitable that he would be offered a job. The attractive screenwriting contract promised him up to $1,500 per month—five times as much as he made at the *CDN*. With another baby on the way, John was sorely tempted to accept the offer. What dissuaded him was the awareness that behind the attractive salaries and the opportunities to work with glamorous film stars, screenwriters were generally regarded as "hacks."

Film, the most American of all art forms, over the years lured West such literary luminaries as F. Scott Fitzgerald, William Faulkner, Aldous Huxley, James Agee, and Nathaniel West. Yet Hollywood had gained a reputation as a dead-end refuge for washed up, would-be or never-were writers. Time spent writing screenplays was regarded by John—and many other "serious" writers—as a form of literary prostitution. The phrase "selling out to Hollywood" was a humorous cliché. So was Jack Warner's quip that writers were nothing more than "schmucks with Underwoods." That is how all but a handful of screenwriters were treated, people such as Robert Riskin, Nunnally Johnson, Dudley Nichols, and Ben Hecht.

CDN Hollywood gossip columnist Jack Casey reported John's

response to the studio contract offer: "Mr. Gunther turned [it] down so abruptly the producer paled. I can imagine Mr. Gunther spending three days or a week awaiting a producer's conference, as do the writers there who never write. The night of the third day, Mr. Gunther would run his fist through the stucco and paper mache that comprises studio walls."[10]

By mid-July, John was back in Chicago, where he did a half-hour live radio broadcast on WMAQ on July 20, 1929, conveying his impressions of life in the Armenian area of Turkey.[11] Then he huddled with his long-time friend James (Herc) Mulroy, who was still working at the *Daily News*. The pair collaborated on an article entitled, "The High Cost of Hoodlums," for the October issue of *Harper's Magazine*.[12] Mulroy provided the information, while John did the writing. The result was an insightful and highly readable behind-the-scenes look at how 600 hoodlums had succeeded in terrorizing Chicago's three million citizens. The easy, personalized writing in the piece foreshadowed the style that John Gunther employed to such good advantage in writing the *Inside* books.

One could have an enemy "bumped off," John pointed out, for as low as $50. The going-rate for a newspaper man, like himself, was $1,000. Despite the fact "The High Cost of Hoodlums" was written nearly sixty years ago, it retains its vitality as a superb historical snapshot of the Chicago of 1929.

John and Frances were back in Paris on November 4, when their second child was born.[13] They named the fair-haired, rosy-cheeked boy John, Jr. They doted on him. Frances was obsessed with ensuring there would be no repeat of Judy's sudden, unexpected crib death. She weighed Johnny, Jr., daily, and for months kept meticulously detailed records of his eating patterns and physical development.

John, feeling the time had come to settle down, now let it be known that he would welcome a bureau job of his own and, in early 1930, he got his wish.

Mowrer offered him the *CDN* Vienna posting. John suspected that his boss was eager to get rid of him by sending him to such a distant posting. But he accepted nonetheless. Vienna had always been one of his favorite European cities, and he was convinced that being there would place him squarely in the middle of the maelstrom that he, William Shirer, Jimmy Sheean, and many other journalists were certain would soon engulf Europe.

CHAPTER THIRTEEN

Vienna had always been a city of consequence. However, by June 1930, when Frances and John Gunther arrived, the Austrian capital's glory days were in the past. The Austrian empire had been shattered, impoverished, and culturally lobotomized by the end of the First World War, which in 1918 brought to an inglorious end 700 years of rule by the House of Hapsburg. In the power vacuum, there was political chaos in which left and right battered one another in bloody street battles.

While conservatives retained control of the national government, socialists took control of the administration of Vienna, where nearly one-third of Austria's six million citizens lived. The union-dominated municipal council, intent on giving working people the good life that had been so long denied them by the monarchy, began a massive urban renewal program. The quicker the pace of change, the more that older Viennese looked to the past for a sense of identity.

In the wake of the Congress of Vienna (1815-16), which ended the Napoleonic Wars, Vienna became the political hub of Europe. "The lilac city" emerged as one of the most civilized, prosperous, and beautiful in all of Europe. The pace of life here was as genteel and unhurried as the Danube River, that undulating ribbon of blue gently wending its way through the wooded foothills of the eastern Alps.

Vienna, a city of sweeping, tree-lined boulevards and spacious parks, seemed like a fairy tale land or a mad architect's dream. Its streetscapes were dominated by imposing neo-classical, Gothic, and baroque buildings capped with their celestial spires, monstrous domes, and facades crowded with likenesses of classical goddesses, chariots, and escutcheons. The soaring Gothic spires of St. Stephen's Cathedral dominated the skyline of the old city, while the immense pillared sprawl of the Hofburg, the grand palace of the Hapsburgs, cast a giant shadow across the city's psyche.

For a time, the Austrian capital displaced Paris as Europe's cultural mecca. Vienna was the city of music—the home of such deities of classical music as Mozart, Beethoven, Haydn, Schubert, and Johann Strauss. Music and baroque were the keys to Viennese life.

By 1848, Vienna's population had swelled to a half million, making it the world's largest and most important German-speaking city. Following the political union of Austria and Hungary in 1867, the Austro-Hungarian empire ruled more than fifty-two million subjects. At its zenith, its empire stretched from the Carpathians in the east, to the Adriatic Sea in the south, Munich in the west, and into what is now Czechoslovakia in the north. The long, inevitable decay of this empire was accelerated by the assassination on June 28, 1914, by Serbian nationalists of Archduke Ferdinand, the heir to the Austro-Hungarian throne. Austria emerged from the ensuing First World War broke and dismembered after being stripped of Bohemia and Moravia. Without its vital industrial heartland, Austria fell on hard times.

The same depression that gripped America was being felt here, too. John and Frances, like most foreign residents, were saddened by the dilapidation of the grand public buildings along Vienna's grand Ringstrasse—the city's equivalent of the Champs Élysées

—and by the sights of many of the magnificent theatres and concert halls in darkness. Most of the smart shops and restaurants were shut tight, and there were long lines in front of the government unemployment offices.

In the midst of such hardship, John and Frances discovered that even with their limited income, they could afford a lifestyle that had been beyond their reach in Paris or London.[1] For 700 shillings (about $100 U.S.), they rented the upstairs of a spacious old villa in the Dobling neighborhood of the city's northern suburbs. The Italianate building, with its peach-colored brick walls and broad pillared windows, was surrounded by an acre of verdant, manicured lawns and gardens. In *The Lost City*, John's 1964 *roman-a-clef* about a foreign correspondent's life in Vienna during this period, he described the Dobling neighborhood as still fashionable, albeit threadbare. "One segment near the greenness of a shiny park was bright with wooded paths and children in starched frock coats accompanied by expensive governesses," he wrote. "Another, flanking on an open market, was a plot of vegetable gardens, where the poorest of poor families lived in tar paper shacks and grew carrots and cabbages."[2]

In better times the Gunthers' landlords had been prosperous bourgeoisie. Faced with economic ruin, they had been reduced to renting the second floor of their home to make ends meet. The whole family—father, mother, grandmother, an uncle, a niece, and two silent, aged women servants, who were retired with the position of family retainers—lived downstairs. At first, it was awkward. But John, Frances, and Johnny became friends with the family, despite the fact that John kept a ping pong table in the apartment. He, William Shirer, and other friends passed many a night playing the game and partying.

John recalled the apartment as six or seven richly paneled, spacious, and sunswept rooms. William Shirer recalls that the first thing a visitor noticed were the presence of two bathrooms and a small electric refrigerator; both were luxuries few Viennese in 1930 could afford.[3] At the urging of Frances, who as the saying goes, "could not boil water," John hired a housekeeper-nanny. For 100 shillings per month (about $14 U.S.), the woman cooked three meals a day, cleaned, ironed, made the beds, and cared for Johnny, leaving Frances free to help her husband with his newspaper work or to pursue her own journalism.

Given the Gunthers' fondness for entertaining, spending weekends in the nearby mountains, and patronizing restaurants, theatres, and pubs, it took every dollar that John and Frances made to maintain this lavish lifestyle. Their financial situation was not helped by John's refusal to accept the modest bribes that the Austrian government paid most foreign journalists in return for favorable news coverage.

Frances began contributing to the family's income when she found work as the Central Europe correspondent for the *London News Chronicle*. The job was easy, given that she had access to all of John's dispatches as well as those by other *CDN* correspondents. For his part, John ignored the admonitions of the home ofice, and used his free time to write free-lance articles for English newspapers and American magazines. The extra income was essential, but there was another motivation. John was easygoing and affable about most things in life. But where his writing was concerned, he was deadly serious. He was a man with definite goals.

John's description of Mason, the protagonist of *The Lost City*, was an exercise in self-portraiture: "One of [his] virtues was that, vague and indeterminate as he often was, restless and diffused, he had the aptitude for progressing from reverie to action once his mind was made up. His ability to detach himself from any background of emotion and apply himself to the typewriter was . . . pronounced."[4]

John felt that his *CDN* editors did not give foreign correspondents respect that was their due. It irked him that after dispatching a long complex story, he sometimes received orders from Chicago for coverage of some news that he regarded as trivial. It was, he complained, akin to having a surgeon clean the operating room after a brilliant operation. That this frustration gave rise to a vague desire to achieve wider recognition as a "serious" journalist was made clear by an incident that occurred one September day in 1931.

John and Frances were hiking at Edlach, a summer resort in the Alps south of Vienna, when they stopped for a drink at a village pub. Here, John happened to pick up a copy of the latest issue of *Vanity Fair* magazine, which featured an article entitled, "America's Leading Foreign Correspondents." While the names of many of his best friends were listed, John's was not. Frances pointed out that everyone mentioned in the article was much older and more experienced than him. It did not matter; there was no consoling John. "I have an unpleasant competitive streak in my nature, and it wounded me that I was not among this chosen dozen," he would explain years later. "I remember driving back to my office in that tired Vienna pseudo-skyscraper, and wondering how I could better myself."[5]

One way was to begin writing serious political articles for such influential, but relatively low paying, journals as *The Nation* and *Foreign Affairs*. Another way was to find fame as a novelist. He confided to colleague Marcel Fodor that it was only a matter of time until he found the elusive "formula" for success, both critically and commercially.

John struck up a friendship with Whit Burnett and Martha Foley, who arrived in Vienna in 1931 as correspondents for the *New York Sun*. Not long afterwards, the couple founded an organization called the Anglo-American Press Association of Vienna, and they began publishing a small literary magazine called *Story*. The Burnetts had keen eyes for writing talent, and *Story* achieved prominence by publishing some of the early works of William Saroyan, Truman Capote, Norman Mailer, Joseph Heller, and Mary O'Hara.

Recalls William Shirer, "John and I were always miffed. I think both of us gave Whit short stories, but he never published any of them. We never made it, although we helped him put out his first issue, which was printed on one of those mimeograph machines at the *Journalistenzimmer* (the press room at the telephone and telegraph office)."[6]

In 1932, John's publisher in London published *Bright Nemesis*, his fifth novel in six years. The reviews of this mystery, set in the arcane world of Balkans politics, murder, and intrigues, were mixed. While a reviewer for *The Spectator* commented that *Bright Nemesis* read as if an editor had badly combined "the crime report, the gossip paragraphs, and the foreign news of a go-ahead paper."[7] The critic from *The Times of London* praised the book for its vivid, realistic depiction of a "picturesque but uncomfortable area."[8]

At the same time he was driving himself to write, John's competitive urges found a non-literary outlet. During his youth, he had been sickly and sheltered; as an adult, he eschewed physical activity. But William Shirer recalls John's love of tennis. "He and I were about even as players," Shirer says. "Then, suddenly, he started getting better, and one day I asked him how come. He admitted that he'd been taking lessons from a pro. I looked into this, and found there was another pro who hated John's pro. They were great rivals, so this guy was eager to coach me.

"It was very funny because John and I often played at an indoor court, in one of Vienna's armories, and these two pros, who didn't speak to one another, would come and sit there urging us on, yelling about putting more spin on serves. We'd still play a five-set match absolutely equal. I had to give up tennis after I lost an eye in a skiing accident, and I don't think John continued playing."[9]

He did not. There simply was not enough time. When not working, John and Frances explored Vienna and its environs. Like many foreign residents, they fell in love with what John termed "the friendliest city in Europe."

Through good times and bad, the Viennese retained their zest for life—their famous *gemütlichkeit*. Marcel Fodor, who became John's mentor and friend (as he had become Dorothy Thompson's when she began her career in Vienna in 1922), explained the term in his 1937 book *South of Hitler* (for which John wrote a brief introduction.) "This strange word [*gemütlichkeit*] expresses the mentality of Vienna perfectly and has no equivalent in any other language on earth," he wrote. "[It] means a jolliness and gaiety, it spells carelessness and easy-going levity, but it also includes the ominous Viennese trait: laziness."[10]

Such an outlook on life seemed frivolous, even unreal, to John and other Americans weaned on the Protestant virtues of hard work and frugality. Yet *gemütlichkeit* was contagious. John succumbed; he reveled in Vienna's delights, and in the realization that being removed from Paris and the censorious eyes of Paul Scott Mowrer, he was his own boss. While this was an attractive proposition, it meant a lot of additional job pressure.

The reason was simple: by 1930, Vienna had become something of a bogus journalistic "beat." News gathering here had long been a matter of reporting the latest imperial fiats. After the fall of the Austro-Hungarian empire, habit dictated that foreign newspapers and news agencies maintain offices and assign correspondents here, as they had in the pre-war glory days. What most foreigners overlooked was how dramatically the reality of the situation in Vienna had changed.

With Austria's decline, all of Middle Europe had been devalued; the sum of its parts no longer equaled the previous whole. Vienna had become a distant second in importance to Berlin in the German-speaking world. Austria was now a tiny republic, and its capital a political backwater, remote from the true centers of European power—London was thirty hours away by rail, Paris more than twenty. If the foreign correspondents who gathered in Vienna to feast on the bones of empire found important news to report, they generally did so only by looking farther afield.

Thus, in addition to reporting the spot news in Vienna on a day-to-day basis, John regularly visited the other countries of the Danube basin: Czechoslovakia, Hungary, Yugoslavia, and Bulgaria, as well as Albania, Greece, and Turkey. To help with his news gathering, he maintained a network of paid contacts in each country. It also helped that John had learned his lessons well at the elbow of Henry Smith. He had a knack for spotting the obvious stories that others overlooked, and for finding fresh angles to old news.

In early 1933, for example, he went to the Turkish island of Prinkipo to interview Leon Trotsky, now a political pariah in Stalin's Soviet Union. John was surprised to discover that he liked, even admired, this architect of the 1917 Russian revolution; Trotsky was not the "monster" the western press had portrayed. John's profile of Trotsky, published in *Harper's* in April 1933, was unique for its depiction of the human side of Leon Trotsky, not simply dealing in the historical stereotype. "The skin of his face," John observed, "is as delicate and pink as a child's and his hands are glistening, shining. This is the man who nationalized women and ate their babies. It is odd, but I suppose you do not easily get over the stupidity of thinking of 'revolutionaries' as coarse-grained, dark, or rough; the thing that made an overwhelming first impression on me was Trotsky's lightness and cleanness. He was shining as if he had just emerged from an extremely happy Turkish bath."[11]

John reveled in the opportunity to meet famous figures like Trotsky, but he remained perplexed by the expectations of his editors in far-off Chicago. Writing in *The Lost City*, he lamented that "the incredible, idiotic thing about American journalism in Europe was that a man arriving in Belgrade or Warsaw, say, highly difficult and secretive capitals, where a story complex in the extreme had just broken, was expected to file an accurate interpretative dispatch about it within an hour or so of his arrival."[12]

John knew it was impossible to cover adequately such a vast, diverse territory as Eastern Europe. Like every other correspondent, John relied heavily on colleagues and friends. The art of "ear-biting"—pumping others for information—was a vital skill.

The American foreign correspondents in Europe at this time, almost all of whom were male, were by necessity *friendly* rivals. John's *CDN* colleague A.R. Decker put it this way, "Although we were all working for different papers, we generally cooperated and most of us thought the idea of scooping each other was pretty silly."[13]

An easy camaraderie developed among the Americans who, as John recalled, "traveled steadily, met constantly, exchanged information, caroused, took in each other's washing, and even when most fiercely competitive, were devoted friends."[14] Most of the time. At other times, this familiarity was fertile ground for bickering, jealousy, and soap-opera melodrama.

John recorded in his diary a heated exchange between his friends William Shirer and Jay Allen. "Bill, incredibly assaulted Jay with the demand that he answer yes or no to the question had he ever slept with [Shirer's wife] Tess," John wrote. "Jay was furious, so furious that he refused to answer, which increased Bill's discomfiture. 'If I did, it's my business and if I didn't, it's not yours.'"[15]

Despite such unpleasant incidents, John would always recall the years between the two great wars as "the bubbling, blazing days of American correspondence in Europe."[16] These were, he remembered in 1962 in his own abbreviated memoir, *A Fragment of an Autobiography*, the freewheeling days before journalism became institutionalized and sanitized. A reporter was only as good as his contacts and sources. "We avoided official handouts. We were scavengers, buzzards, out to get the news, no matter whose wings got clipped," John wrote.[17]

Radio was in its infancy, and television was still years in the future. It was the newspaper foreign correspondent who was America's eyes and ears overseas at the time the nation was reemerging from the isolationism of the 1920s. These 300 or so men—and a handful of women—wielded amazing influence, since it was they who shaped public opinion as they funneled into the United States the news from all of Europe, the Soviet Union, and the Middle East.

Only comprehensive, long-term coverage could build awareness of the complex events happening in Europe, yet most Americans regarded the continent's problems as insoluble. This made them less appealing as page one news than a story about the latest gangland slaying, a sex scandal, or even a sports story. In 1929, foreign news cables provided about twenty million words to American newspapers; that sounds impressive until compared to the two million words written for the same newspapers about the 1926 Gene Tunney-Jack Dempsey heavyweight fight.

That foreign news was still given a low priority in most newsrooms is further evidenced by the fact that just three American news agencies and seven newspapers had complete European news services. The expense involved had eliminated the others. It was estimated that the *Chicago Daily News* overseas service cost $1,000 per day to operate—a phenomenal sum at that time—and the *New York Times* service was even more expensive.

Because of the high cost of sending dispatches by cable, the regular mails were used for all but fast-breaking news stories. Cables that were sent were written in a skeletonized style known as "cablese." As John once explained, "This perhaps accounts for the singular similarity in style of most cable messages in most newspapers and also the standardized dullness of the style."[18]

In cablese, a man with a vandyke beard was "vandyked"; to be shot with a revolver was to be "revolverized"; and, writing a poem was "poetizing." Cablese was generally limited to dictionary words, and codes were seldom used because of the time needed to decipher them and because of the possibility of confusion. It had become legend how the Moscow correspondent of an American news agency had slyly arranged with his London office to send word of the death of Lenin, then gravely ill, by the coded message: "Send me 40 pounds." When Lenin died on January 21, 1924, the correspondent sent his prearranged cable, while censors prevented reporters of rival newspapers from filing their stories for nearly a day. Unfortunately for the enterprising reporter, the London bureau manager was out of the office at the time, and his assistant was unaware of the code. "Those Moscow men are too damned expensive," he muttered as he tossed the bulletin into the wastebasket.[19]

Newspapers, including the *CDN*, recouped much of the cost of operating an overseas service by syndicating foreign news reports to other smaller newspapers across the United States and Canada. The result was a kind of mass wholesaling of facts, opinions, and ideas. Given the relative paucity of foreign news coverage, when stories did appear, they were conspicuous. Thus the names of John Gunther and other foreign correspondents became familiar to millions of readers across North America because of their by-lined articles from far-flung corners of the globe. The correspondents took on a larger-than-life status, and wielded enormous influence. They became journalistic superstars. George Seldes has aptly described these people as America's "journalistic noblesse."[20]

In the popular imagination, fueled by countless B-Grade Hollywood films, the foreign correspondent was a typewriter-toting Phillip Marlowe, attired in the ubiquitous trenchcoat and wide-brimmed fedora. His was a shadowy, fog-shrouded world of midnight trains, wars, intrigues, deadlines, romance, and interviews with film stars and royalty, dictators and diplomats. That fictional caricature was only partially correct.

Reality included the mind-numbing drudgery of deadlines and low pay. That is not to mention the social, emotional, and physical toll of the travel and crazy, unpredictable hours. Traveling conditions in much of Europe at this time were still alarmingly primitive, particularly in Eastern Europe. Clean, comfortable hotels were scarce. There were no credit cards to pay bills (when a foreign correspondent was on the road his most precious possession was his letter of credit from the bank), and dining in local restaurants amounted to gastronomic roulette for anyone who loved to eat as much as did John Gunther.

In 1935, *Esquire* asked him to write a six-part series on Europe's best restaurants.[21] He was particularly fond of the food in the dining room of Sacher's, Vienna's once grand hotel, and he loved the *Heurigers*, the small, family-run wine bars and vineyards that dotted the hills around the city.

"John always had a taste for good living," William Shirer remembers. "If he could walk into a good restaurant and the head waiter came up to remember him and say some nice things, John loved it. His saving grace was that he admitted it. He wasn't pompous or anything. He'd say, 'Bill, I like to go to fancy restaurants and have the headwaiter make a fuss over me.'

"I think this developed fairly early in John's life. Often when you don't have much money in your youth, and then you get a bit of money, you like to spend it. H.R. Knickerbocker was a good friend of John's for many years, and he had those tastes, too. They were both very sociable."[22]

Because John enjoyed nothing more than a fine dinner or a gathering with friends, one of his fondest memories of his Vienna years was a lavish, crazy party given by Dorothy Thompson and husband Sinclair Lewis. They were visiting in late 1932, when Dorothy hit upon the idea of throwing a huge Christmas party to distract Lewis, who was in the midst a drinking binge. Dorothy rented the whole annex of a hotel in the Semmering, a vacation area about two hours north of Vienna. She set up a bar, and hired an orchestra. John and Frances attended, as did *CDN* Berlin correspondent Edgar Mowrer and his wife, Lilian, and many other friends and relatives, including at least one Austrian prince, and a baron and baroness. There were also five children with their nurses, assorted servants, and a dog. Jimmy Sheean, unable to get away from his job in Paris, quipped that the guests "may not all have been there at the same time, but at any given moment there must have been a horde."[23]

Unfortunately, the weather turned rainy and foggy, and so most guests drank too much and fell to arguing. When nerves frayed, the mood soon turned as foul as the weather. Sinclair Lewis, who loathed most of his wife's friends, slipped further into a drunken depression. Dorothy sought comfort in a traumatic lesbian encounter with Baroness Hatvany, an Austrian woman who wrote novels under the name Christa Winsloe. John was stricken by an attack of asthma, a lifelong ailment which was worsened by his heavy cigarette smoking. The Semmering party ended abruptly when Lewis departed for Italy, and Dorothy, Baroness Hatvany, and a group of the others dashed off to Budapest on the train. John enjoyed himself despite the sour ending to the celebration, even if he was ill most of the weekend.

John always loved a good party. He loved people, and he was profoundly curious about them. His humanism fueled an abiding faith in the theory that it is people more than ideas that drive history. Explains Shirer: "John would go to a country and he'd immediately want to know *who* had the power, *who* made the decisions, *who* had the money, those sorts of things. Wherever he went, he'd always want to interview the king, or the president, or the prime minister."[24]

John Gunther reduced everything, no matter how complex, to simple, human terms. He asked the sort of questions that the man on the street would have asked if thrust into the presence of the famous or the infamous. John was a sort of journalistic "everyman." It was a trait that served him well in Vienna, the beautiful, doomed city that he had grown to love.

CHAPTER FOURTEEN

John Gunther's fascination with people got him involved in Vienna's closely knit foreign journalistic community. He was elected president in 1932 of the correspondents' association founded by Whit Burnett and Martha Foley. One of his few duties was to arrange informal, "off-the-record" weekly luncheons for local and visiting celebrities and dignitaries. In this capacity John came to know many important people, including Dr. Engelbert Dollfuss, the diminutive Austrian chancellor—"the Flyweight Champion of Europe," as John dubbed him. Dollfuss, who "made a monkey out of Hitler" for a time, by steering a precarious middle course between Austria's warring Socialists and Nazis, attended cocktail parties at the Gunthers' flat.

John also entertained Oswald Garrison Villard, the editor of *The Nation*, the influential American liberal magazine; British socialite and gadabout Margot Asquith (better known as Lady Oxford), who was to become a close, lifelong friend and his *entree* into London high society; and H.G. Wells and his mistress, Baroness Moura Budberg, who, as William Shirer points out, had the "distinction" of being the mistress of two of the period's most famous writers—Wells and Russian novelist Maxim Gorki.[1] Rebecca West, Wells' former mistress, had by now married Henry Andrews, a Burmese-born, Oxford-educated banker.

Given John's own relationship with West, he was understandably curious to know more about Wells, whom he had previously encountered socially. He interviewed Wells at his hotel, and when the two of them hit it off, John and Frances gave a cocktail party for him. Years later, John recalled how he had also arranged for Wells to visit Dr. Darwin Lyon, the Austrian scientist who pioneered the development of modern rocketry. Wells, the author of the science fiction classic *War of the Worlds*, was fascinated by the potential of using rockets for interplanetary space travel. "Will your rocket ever be able to reach the moon?" he asked Lyon.

Lyon nodded.

"And when it reaches the moon will the rocket be able to return to earth?" Wells continued.

Lyon nodded again.

"If I have that assurance," Wells smiled, "I suggest we put G.B. Shaw on it."[2]

H.G. Wells, like many foreign visitors, assumed that John Gunther was the key figure in Vienna's foreign journalistic community, or if not him, then Marcel Fodor, who was one of the most highly respected foreign correspondents in Europe. But in the journalistic world it was well known that the real linchpin was amiable Robert (Bob) Best, the United Press (UP) news service's correspondent in Vienna since 1923.

The son of a Methodist preacher from Sumter, South Carolina, Best was rotund, boyish, and possessed a gracious southern charm. He was never too busy to do a good turn for a friend. Sadly, he also had a self-destructive darker side.

Best could be intense, and brooding. Despite the fact that many of his closest friends were Jews, he trumpeted pro-Nazi sympathies and a venomous hatred of Franklin D. Roosevelt's New Deal and of the Jews and communists he was convinced were behind it. Best, like most journalists, was perpetually short of money. For $5 a day, he covered for other reporters when they were out of town. Best lived with an aging, drug-addicted Austrian countess, whom the other Americans despised. John sarcastically remembered her in *The Lost City* as "not look[ing] more romantic than a pincushion."[3]

The woman was eventually locked away in an insane asylum, and Best married a German countess. He then moved to Berlin, where in 1942 he turned traitor, and became a Danubian version of the infamous British traitor Lord Haw Haw. Best made more than 300 pro-Nazi radio broadcasts in which he denounced the "Jew- nited States." When captured by the British at war's end, he was extradited to the United States to stand trial for treason. Unrepentant, he was sent to prison for the rest of his life. It was Best who served as the model for the main character in William Shirer's 1950 *roman-à-clef* called *The Traitor.*

In 1930 this was all years in the future. When John and Frances arrived in Vienna they found Best holding court daily at his favorite haunt—the Café Louvre, a coffee house that was a popular gathering place for Vienna's foreign correspondents.

To understand Vienna of the 1930s, is to know that it was a city of coffee houses. Coffee was Austria's national beverage, the drinking of which had been elevated to an event. Most Viennese lived in small, cramped apartments and, although they had little money to spend, they seldom stayed home in the evening. With coffee being relatively inexpensive, coffee houses proliferated. As John explained in a 1935 *Harper's* magazine article entitled "Dateline Vienna": "The coffee house is, of course, the inner soul of Vienna, the essential embodiment of the spirit of the town. It is, as everyone knows, much more than just a place to drink coffee in. Coffee you may have, in literally 40 different varieties, but you have also literature, conversation, and peace of soul and mind."[4]

Among Vienna's coffee houses, the Café Imperial was the haunt of Balkan spies and revolutionaries, the Café Louvre of foreign journalists, the Café Museum of painters and artists, the Café Pucher of politicians, and the Café Centrale of emigre intellectuals. The Centrale was also known to a generation of Viennese as the place where Leon Trotsky had left unpaid a tab of $4.80.

John described in his "Dateline Vienna" article the role of the coffee house in a foreign correspondent's "average day"—that is, if his own routine was typical. Never a morning person, he rose most days about nine o'clock. Still in his dressing gown, he would scan the most important of Vienna's twenty morning newspapers. Then he took telephone calls and visits from the anonymous informants, both men and women, who represented "different segments of surpressed opinion." Just before noon, John took the tram downtown, to the old *innere stadt*. Here, he usually stopped at the Café Imperial for coffee with a group that included Shirer, George Gedye of the *London Daily Telegraph* and the *New York Times*,[5] and Marcel Fodor of the *Manchester Guardian*.

Friends knew Fodor either as "Mike" or "Fodor," not Marcel, for as he once noted, "Marcel is a name for a tall, dark handsome chap, not a little roly-poly like me." Hungarian-born and English-educated, Fodor trained in metallurgical engineering, a profession in which he achieved distinction. During World War I, he was interned in England because of his nationality, and in 1919 changed careers. He convinced the *Guardian*'s editors that his ability to speak most of Europe's principal languages would make him a first-rate foreign correspondent.[6]

Fodor established himself in Vienna, and it was here, in early 1921, that he had met the young Dorothy Thompson. Pert and attractive, she was one of the very few women in a profession dominated by men. Fodor, who had an eye for feminine beauty as well as journalistic talent, took an instant liking to her. Their friendship proved mutually beneficial. Thompson introduced Fodor to the American contacts whose newspapers soon were publishing his dispatches. In return, Fodor took Thompson under his wing, and by April 1921, she was producing so many stories that *The Ledger* took her on staff at a salary of $50 dollars per week. While Thompson moved on to Berlin and much bigger things, Fodor, whose principal talents were languages and ideas, became a fixture in Vienna.

This is where a young J. William Fulbright encountered him in mid-1928. Fulbright, who went on to a long and distinguished career representing Arkansas in the U.S. Senate, had just completed studies as a Rhodes Scholar at Oxford University. Prior to returning home, he toured Europe, and one of his stops was Vienna. "It was a wonderful place for a young student," Fulbright still recalls, more than six decades later. "The city was beautiful, and the food was cheap."[7]

Like most visitors, Fulbright inevitably found his way to Vienna's coffee houses. In doing so, he encountered Fodor and his colleagues at the Café Louvre. "You could find a group of journalists there most evenings. I remember hearing Fodor hold forth, and he and I became friends," Fulbright says. "Fodor was a short, stocky man with a mustache, and it was obvious that he was very intelligent; he spoke with great authority on an astounding range of subjects.

"Fodor was going on a trip through the Balkans and Greece, and he suggested I go along with him as his aide. He'd made the trip many times and knew the routine well. For me, the most memorable part of the whole experience was visiting the Acropolis in Athens. Fodor explained to me its history in great detail; he had an insatiable curiosity about everything and was a natural teacher."[8]

Fodor related well to younger people, particularly Americans. When he and John Gunther met in 1930, they developed the same kind of student-teacher relationship that Fodor had engaged in with Thompson and Fulbright. It was said that Fodor taught more young foreign correspondents the business than any man alive. The professional relationship between John and Mike Fodor blossomed into a close friendship when they discovered that their mutual circle of friends included journalists Thompson, Raymond Gram Swing, and Hubert Renfro (H.R.) Knickerbocker.

Denis Fodor recalls that his father and John took to working and traveling together. "My father could do the legwork and move around easily because of his mastery of languages," Fodor says. "Languages were a problem for John, who spoke only some poor German. Through him, however, my father could plug into the American press and stay close to the newspaper business as it was practiced in that part of the world at the time. John brought that to the relationship."[9]

John and Mike Fodor combined their talents on many occasions. One of their most important scoops was one they had on the 1931 formation of the German-Austrian Customs Union, an economic pact that presaged the takeover of Austria by Hitler. John included a fictionalized account in his novel *Lost City*, recounting how he and Foder broke the story. Fodor also gave his version of events years later in an article. He recalled that after getting a telephone tip from Edgar Mowrer, the *Daily News'* Berlin correspondent, John had raced to the Café Imperial to tell him the rumor. When a call to a banking contact confirmed the news,the scratch for details started, as Fodor put it. The resulting story made headlines around the world.

Another big story that John Gunther and Marcel Fodor broke was written in the summer of 1934, when the two men visited Hitler's birthplace in the Austrian town of Braunau. They sought out and interviewed the Nazi dictator's surviving relatives, including a lame first cousin, an aged and poverty-stricken aunt, and his godfather. They even spoke to the midwife who had delivered the baby Adolf. This was the first time a foreign journalist, or anyone else, had bothered—or dared—to delve into Hitler's background. The inside story that John Gunther and Marcel Fodor revealed to the world painted a far less flattering picture than the image cultivated by Nazi propagandists. The Gunther-Fodor exposé appeared in different forms in *Vanity Fair* and *Harper's*.[10] It also got wide coverage in European newspapers, including some in Germany and Switzerland. When John made use of much of the same information in revised, expanded form in the writing of his 1936 bestseller *Inside Europe*, an irate Hitler banned the book in Germany. Even more menacing, however, was that following the outbreak of war, the names of John Gunther and Marcel Fodor were placed on the Gestapo's death list; the pair were to be hanged if they could be caught. John, who felt that he was not in any real danger, was fond of telling people this story at cocktail parties. Fodor, less fortunate, was forced to flee for his life when the Nazis invaded Austria.

Most mornings after coffee at the Café Imperial, Marcel Fodor and John Gunther went calling on various foreign diplomats. John was in the habit of visiting Czech, Italian, and Yugoslavian officials each week to learn the general line of policy and gossip, exchange information, and cultivate them as sources. As John pointed out, the value of any legation as a news source depends on how well you know the people in it.

Fast-breaking news had to be cabled each afternoon by half-past one Vienna time to make the *CDN*'s afternoon deadline in Chicago. That done, John often ate lunch at home before calling on more sources in the afternoon. Around five o'clock, he and many of his colleagues gathered at the Café Louvre, an undistinguished coffee house at the corner of the *Wipplingerstrasse* and *Renngasse* in central Vienna.

The interior was typical. It was spacious, with about forty marble-topped tables and violin-backed chairs in the center of the high-ceilinged room. Along one wall were booths, finished in dark brocades. Along another were a buffet of snacks and pastries and some rattan racks holding the day's newspapers. The latter were an attraction for impecunious journalists. The Café Louvre, like the Café Imperial, subscribed to most of Vienna's daily newspapers as well as fifty or so foreign ones. For the price of a coffee, one could sit all day, read the papers, talk, play chess, or simply pass time. It was here that Bob Best presided at his *Stammtisch*, the reserved table that was his home away from home. No one would ever have bothered trying to contact him at his apartment or office; he could be found at the Café Louvre day or night.

"The great advantage of the place, and the reason foreign correspondents made it their hangout, was its convenient location," Denis Fodor explains. "It was equally close to Radio Austria and maybe 100 feet or so from the main door of the telegraph office. A lot of correspondents, John Gunther, for example, usually dictated copy over the telephone to Paris. But if you filed stories by cable, that's where you had to go to do so."[11]

John's habit was to write at his office. Whatever news he had uncovered that day was phoned to Paris, from where it was cabled to New York, then on to Chicago; feature articles were mailed. After work, when he was not writing free-lance articles or novels, John and Frances entertained. As was customary in Vienna, they and their guests usually dined out, ending off the night sipping coffee and talking at the Café Louvre.

The coffee house took on a different atmosphere after dark, when it became a family social center. The married correspondents often brought their wives and children. Whit Burnett, who became a regular at the Café Louvre, recalled in his memoirs how at Bob Best's *Stammtisch* there was not a night that the regular table did not seat, along with the regulars, visiting playwrights, novelists, poets, short story writers, even spies.[12]

John remembered these smoky, conversation-filled nights and

the lifelong friendships that he forged there. In later years he often said that these years spent in Vienna were, in many ways, a golden period of his life. By 1934, however, it was increasingly clear that these carefree times were coming to an end. There was something ominous in the air—for Vienna, for Europe, and for John and Frances Gunther.

CHAPTER FIFTEEN

John Gunther felt that he had done the "right thing" in marrying Frances Fineman in 1927. But a nagging suspicion that the so-called "Act of God" that had induced him to propose was the product of Frances' scheming mind filled him with resentment. As a result, by the time they arrived in Vienna in the spring of 1930, the Gunther's marriage was badly strained.

They argued about everything, including Frances' writing. John could not fathom why his wife could not finish what she started. He accused her of lacking perseverance. She blamed her failures on the fact that she devoted so much of her time to helping with his work. While there was some truth in that claim, the reality was that Frances' problems were infinitely more complex. Even she knew it.

In Frances' troubled mind, her failings as a writer stemmed from hostilities she had developed as a school girl in Galveston. The root of her problems, she was convinced, had been a harsh high school teacher named Miss Knox, who had made her stay after class to write composition exercises; the memory of those hours spent in the deserted classroom stayed with Frances.

She regained some enthusiasm for writing at college, and during her 1924 trip to the Soviet Union she wrote freelance arts reports for the *New York Times*. Now Frances helped John with his bureau duties. She also worked as the Vienna correspondent for the *London News Chronicle*, approaching her duties with the same quirky intensity that she lived her life. Typically, on April 24, 1934, Frances had landed in jail while reporting on an anti-fascist labor rally. To prevent foreign journalists from interviewing Dr. Ernst Karl Winter, the right-wing dominated Vienna police surrounded the hall where the deputy mayor was speaking. Frances was one of fourteen people arrested for ignoring police orders, and for refusing to be searched.

As was the case for so many others, journalism was a means to an end for Frances. Her literary ambitions went beyond writing for newspapers and magazines. Frances' plans included novels, poetry, a semi-autobiographical play called *Mothers and Lovers*, and a political science treatise about history's great empires. This latter project, called *Empire*, became an obsession. It drove Frances mad with frustration.

She was a perfectionist with strong, but vague anti-imperialist views. Frances deplored British policy in Palestine, of that she was certain. The only problem was that her reasons kept changing; thus she rewrote and revised her manuscript perpetually. It took on a life of its own. Frances directed her resulting frustration at John, who was an easy target. Like Paula Jarret, the wife of the central character in John's 1964 novel, *The Lost City*, Frances accused her husband of "using" her as "a secretary, cook, manager, and occasional bedfellow." Such wifely devotions left her without the time or energy to complete her own writing projects.

While there was little merit in that argument during their first three years in Vienna—when the Gunthers had a housekeeper and, for a time, their landlord's young nephew as a secretary for Frances—the situation changed in early 1933. John's finances took a turn for the worse. In response to the worsening Depression, the *CDN* closed three of its overseas bureaus and slashed the salaries of all correspondents by 10 per cent. John, already disgruntled because the newspaper's tightfisted accountants forced him to keep meticulous financial records, could do nothing more than grumble. He increased his free-lance writing in an effort to maintain his income. This increased the demands on his time, and threw an even larger share of the *CDN* bureau work onto the shoulders of Frances. She responded by becoming depressed and withdrawn. The only hope that remained for the Gunthers' tattered marriage was for John and Frances to take the time to work out the differences between them. That was unlikely. The situation, and their personalities all but precluded it.

John, who had spent much of his youth in the company of his mother, sister, and aunts, was most at ease confiding in females. He was a man who had many female friends during his lifetime. One of the closest was an attractive young woman named Leonora Schinasi, whom he would meet in 1941 at a party at the New York home of publisher Bennett Cerf. Schinasi, a twenty-one-year-old native New Yorker, was working for *Liberty* magazine and dreaming of writing novels. She and John dated for a time, and then remained firm friends, even after Leonora wed prominent Hollywood producer Arthur Hornblow. She was someone in whom John confided for many years, often in long telephone conversation. She points out that he was simply "a man who needed and loved being with women."[1]

During the early days in Vienna, John was close to William Shirer's wife, Theresa—Tess, as she was known to her family and friends. Tess Stiberitz was native Viennese, dark-haired, beautiful, and just twenty when she and William Shirer married in January 1931. Like other Vienna-based American journalists, Shirer, then with the *Chicago Tribune*, was constantly traveling central Europe. Tess, a shy, quiet woman, sometimes spent a lot of time with John Gunther in her husband's absence. "He always had a *case* for Tess," Shirer says. "They had a relationship, and I think John sometimes confided more in her than he did in me."[2]

When Shirer was unceremoniously fired in October 1932, by Colonel Robert R. McCormick, the irascible owner of the *Chicago Tribune*, the Shirers left Vienna for Spain early the following year. It was during the two-year period between January 1931 and

February 1933 that John shared his innermost feelings with Tess Shirer.

His dilemma, he confided to her, was that he longed to be free of the miseries of both his marriage and his job. He lacked the resources or the resolve to quit either. Weighing on his mind, too, was a pact that he and William Shirer had pledged to be out of "the newspaper racket" and writing novels by age thirty. Shirer, unemployed, was inadvertently ahead of schedule. John was still mired in the grind of his bureau job. Compounding his frustrations was the fact that the allure of being a foreign correspondent had long since faded; it had become a job like any other.

Dreading the impact that a divorce would have on Frances and on his son Johnny, now five, John toughed it out in his marriage. It was not easy, for either partner. It was evident to John, and to anyone who knew Frances, that she was a very disturbed, angry woman. She alternately taunted and challenged her husband to divorce her, then pleaded with him to never leave her alone. When John agonized over how to react, she sarcastically observed, "I keep him from being obliged to marry other women."

As the Jekyll-and-Hyde nature of Frances' personality became evident, others in the Gunthers' circle of friends began to shun her. It was much easier to empathize with John, affable and extroverted, than with Frances, who had grown brooding and intense. Says Leonora Hornblow, who came to know Frances well in later years, "When you met her, you assumed she was a bright but shy person, and not very warm. It was only after you began to know Frances that you realized everything was on the *slant* with her. Nothing was head on; nothing was as it seemed."[3]

William Shirer gained a similar impression during those Vienna years. "Initially, most of us thought that she was good for John," he recalls. "Frances restrained his enthusiasms and seemed to be very concerned with advancing *his* career. She entertained rather nicely, particularly the local people whom it was advantageous to know—editors, politicians, and quite a few theatre people. But you could see that there was another side to her. She was moody and unpredictable. For example, she'd sometimes storm out of dinner parties for no apparent reason, leaving John to carry on as best he could. She did things like that. I think it was a fairly rocky marriage in those days. John, uncharacteristically, would say to me, 'You don't know the hell I'm living through.'"[4]

Marcel Fodor's son, Denis, just a boy in the early 1930s, often went with his parents to the Gunther apartment. Here he and Johnny played together. Fodor recalls Frances' "practiced kindness" and an intuition that she may not have been he person she seemed. "In retrospect, she was a very modern woman in some senses, with the same halations as a liberated woman of today," says Fodor. "In that way, she was before her time."[5]

To those who knew her well, it was clear that Frances was a woman whose hold on reality was tenuous. She had become an unhappy and frustrated—both professionally and sexually. In trapping John in marriage, Frances had herself become a prisoner.

Given the couple's unhappiness, John's long absences, and the libertine lifestyle of many foreign correspondents, it was inevitable that by 1934 the marriage had deteriorated to the point where both John and Frances had extramarital affairs. In John's novel, *The Lost City*, the protagonist Mason Jarrett sleeps with his landlord's niece and with a beautiful young sculptress. Were his experiences really John's? Most likely. Leonora Hornblow notes that John confided to her years later that the Jarret character was his "dream of himself." And John had always cannibalized his life for the raw material of his fiction, (as friends such as Emily and Helen Hahn, among others, have pointed out) to the extent that he "recycled" letters and even actual conversations.

William Shirer recalls how both he and John became infatuated with a popular young Vienna-born actress named Luise Rainer. Beautiful, petite, and just twenty years old, Rainer had appeared in a couple of German-language films, and by 1934 was the toast of Vienna as a result of her stage roles at the Max Reinhardt Theatre. The critics compared Rainer to Greta Garbo, and even then it was not so much a question of whether she would eventually go to Hollywood to make movies, but rather *when* she would do so.

"I don't know exactly how John met Luise Rainer," Shirer says. "I think *I* may have met her at a party at the Gunthers' apartment. My feeling was that Frances and John both liked her very much. He fell for her to an extent that I don't think Frances was pleased. John had a roving eye and liked to flirt."[6]

Shirer, by nature a reserved, introspective man, admits he was "somewhat intimidated" by Rainer, who was always surrounded by male admirers. He sensed, too, that she saw him and John mainly because of the opportunities it gave her to perfect her English.

John, always ebullient and bubbling with romantic notions, viewed the relationship differently, just as he had done while pursuing Helen Hahn a decade before.

"He was tall, husky, and blond," recalls Rainer, now retired and living in Switzerland. "He was, of course, very bright and had a great sense of humor. I thought he was a terribly nice fellow. I remember that he sometimes dressed in what are called knickerbockers. That was something very fancy in those days, in Vienna. He wasn't the best looking man that I'd ever met in my life, but he was good looking—what we girls used to call 'a good specimen!' However, I must say something simply and brusquely: I was *never* in love with him or anything of that kind. I don't know, of course, what he cared about me."[7]

John was despondent when Rainer, in 1935, left Vienna for Hollywood, where she had a brief, but glorious career. She won back-to-back Oscars as Best Actress—the only performer ever to do so—for her starring roles in *The Great Ziegfeld* (1936) and *The Good Earth* (1937). Her film career ended in 1943, as abruptly and spectacularly as it had begun. A woman of independent mind, she took exception to the sexual advances of Metro-Goldwyn-Mayer boss Louis B. Mayer. "Why don't you sit on my lap when we're discussing your contract, the way the other girls do?" Mayer once demanded of her. As long as she was making money for him, Mayer tolerated Rainer's feistiness. After a couple of ill-conceived and unsuccessful movies, however, the two exchanged angry words, and Rainer never made another Hollywood film.

"I didn't see John and Frances Gunther again for several years after I left Vienna, and when I did the memory is not a pleasant one," says Rainer. "I was married to John's friend [the playwright] Clifford Odets at the time, and we'd been having marital difficulties. I ran into John and Frances one day, and they said to me half joking and half serious, 'What did *you* do to our Clifford?' It was not what *I* had done to him, it was what he had done to me!"[8]

While John flirted with other women, Frances engaged in a series of sad little affairs. Moody and unpredictable, she was never as outgoing and personable as John. But she spoke German well enough to carry on a conversation, and knew many people in the Vienna journalistic and artistic communities. During John's long absences, she sought out lovers in the coffee houses and theatres, keeping a scorecard of the number of men with whom she slept—real or imagined is impossible to say. As she herself admitted, she derived no pleasure from her "sins." On the contrary, this self-destructive behavior devastated her emotionally. She was frigid, terrified by the prospect that lovers would reject her, as she felt her mother had.

In Frances' tortured mind, her life was a stage play in which she was acting as a "bad girl." It was a bizarre form of self-flagellation, a tragic, self-destructive role that involved suffering, guilt, and punishment. Frances, convinced that the 1929 death of the baby Judy had been a form of divine retribution for a lifetime of misdeeds, was haunted by fears that further tragedy would befall her and anyone close to her. Her twisted logic was that if she alienated those she loved most, it would somehow save them.

Sensing the precariousness of her mental state, Frances sought professional help. There was no shortage in Vienna, the birthplace of modern psychoanalysis. For a time both Frances and John tried to resolve their problems by placing themselves in the care of Dr. Wilhelm Stekel, a former disciple of Sigmund Freud. John would later describe Stekel as "one of the 10 most interesting people I have come to know."

Stekel had an undeniable flair for self-promotion, and reveled in his celebrity. It is said that over the course of his career he psychoanalyzed more than 10,000 people, many of whom sought him out solely because they had read or heard about him.

Stekel was also a prolific, and sometimes brilliant, writer, and after breaking with Freud he achieved a brief measure of fame beyond the bounds of psychoanalysis. He composed music, and wrote children's books, humorous stories, and theatrical plays.

Today, Stekel is remembered chiefly for his efforts to extend the Freudian theory of male-female relationships. In searching for a sexual basis for psychological disorders, he placed even *more* emphasis than did Freud on what he termed the "war of the sexes."

Amidst a blaze of publicity, Stekel established in Vienna in early 1935 the first "jealousy clinic." Here he set about treating the mental malady that "was more deadly than typhus or bullets."

Stekel claimed that "jealousy caused the death of someone, somewhere, every minute." His clinic was both busy and fashionable for a time.

John began a series of appointments with Stekel, ostensibly for his asthma—at least that is what he told William Shirer and other friends. "If somebody had a cat, for example, John would sneeze a lot if he was around it," Shirer says. "I think Stekel was trying to cure that. I don't know why Frances was going to him."[9]

In fact, John was intrigued by Stekel for another important reason: his Freudian analysis of what was called the "Authority Complex." Although Freud himself was not a political man and refrained from publicly discussing Hitler or other public figures of the day, his theories did provide a powerful analytical tool that was used by Stekel and others. Such diagnoses, Stekel's particularly, received a lot of public attention in the next few years, when it was hailed as a possible rationale for the rise of the European dictators.

Stekel's theory, as John Gunther interpreted it,[10] was that although people may resent authority, they cannot live without it. In that sense, the dictators were serving as surrogate father figures to many Europeans, who at heart were still peasants bewildered by the anomie of an urban, industrial society in the throes of economic depression. The Mussolinis, Stalins, Hitlers, and Francos of the world—like today's television evangelists—simplified life, and promised followers a sense of direction and security.

It was this aspect of dictatorship, so alien to America, that fascinated John. He and a growing number of liberals were alert to the rumble of distant thunder on both the right and the left. As the bright promise of the early years of the New Deal began to fade, those rumbles grew increasingly ominous on both sides of the Atlantic.

CHAPTER SIXTEEN

By 1935 there were ominous signs of political unrest in the United States. Roosevelt's New Deal reforms had sputtered in the face of growing conservative backlash. Ten million unemployed Americans were scratching out an existence on the dole, while millions more went hungry.

Some of these people abandoned hope. Others rallied behind the burgeoning union movement, which had been given its first real boost since World War I by Roosevelt's National Recovery Administration. Critics charged FDR's labor reforms fostered the growth of communism, yet membership in the American Communist Party remained at about 30,000, with about ten times as many sympathizers. This represented just 1 per cent of America's population. As historian Arthur M. Schlesinger, Jr., has observed, "Communism had a less enduring impact on the unemployed than it had on the conscience-stricken fugitives from the intellectual and professional classes."[1]

Far more Americans were attracted to the kind of radical solutions offered by right-wing social demagogues who grabbed the headlines with their promises to solve the nation's woes. There were fears that the most serious threat to democracy in America came not from the left, but rather from these messiahs of the middle class.

Sinclair Lewis ignited a lively debate among liberals with his 1935 novel *It Can't Happen Here*,[2] in which he explored how an indigenous fascist movement might take over the country. Another of John's friends, Raymond Gram Swing, concluded that political reality was already as chilling as fiction. *Forerunners of American Fascism*[3] was a collection of literary portraits of five Americans whom Swing, and many others, saw as would-be Hitlers: Father Charles E. Coughlin, the spellbinding "Radio Priest"; Louisiana's ambitious Senator Huey Long, the man one critic dubbed "a Mississippi valley rendering of Il Duce"; Mississippi Governor Theodore Bilbo; "gray-power" advocate Dr. Francis Townsend; and, newspaper publisher William Randolph Hearst.

Expatriate poet Ezra Pound approached matters from a different perspective. As an unabashed admirer of Mussolini, Pound added to the controversy with his book *Jefferson and/or Mussolini* (L'idea Statale; Fascism As I Have Seen It). The tract argued fascism was as American as apple pie, and drew its strength from the same populist impulses that had led the middle class to scorn big business, banks, and centralism. "The heritage of Jefferson," wrote Pound, "is HERE, NOW in the Italian peninsula, not in Massachusetts or Delaware."[4]

Ezra Pound was not alone in his admiration of the way in which Mussolini and Hitler had revived their ailing economies. A sizable body of American public opinion, led for a time by Charles Lindbergh, subscribed to the shrill message being preached by Roosevelt haters. Fortunately, for a variety of reasons that still fascinate historians, the nightmare scenarios visualized by Lewis and Swing never materialized. Fascism did not become a important force in national politics. America had no history of the kind of mass acquiescence to authority that is the hallmark of fascism. John Gunther understood this, and dismissed America's fascists as "a minor irritating scum at best."[5]

But he was fascinated by the growth of fascism, and sought to answer the most basic question of all: why had millions of presumably civilized and intelligent Europeans willingly followed the lead of brutal dictators?

As early as July 1926, John had discussed with Frances, and had even proposed to his editors, a series of articles entitled "The Rise of the Dictators." *Chicago Daily News* publisher Charles Dennis was initially enthusiastic, since Mussolini's Blackshirts were making headlines in Italy. Dennis suggested in a letter to John dated August 3, 1926, that stories "carefully picturing the various men, their origins and growth in power with their personal characteristics carefully set forth, would be a whale of a series."[6] Two weeks later, Dennis had followed up with another letter to John suggesting that *CDN* correspondents in the various European capitals could gather background material for the articles.[7]

It never came to pass. Work on the project was secondary to the needs of regular news-gathering, and several months passed before John found time to request a formal go-ahead. On November 12, 1926, he wrote Dennis another long letter trying to rekindle interest in such a series. Dennis and foreign editor Hal O'Flaherty discussed the idea again, and, as Dennis explained in another letter to John, "[we] found ourselves disposed to wonder whether the subject (of dictatorship) has not been crowded a bit into the background by the passage of time and the new interests that are stirring in Europe."[8]

For now, John shelved plans for the series. They were revived by events that occurred in Vienna on July 25, 1934. Members of four secret regiments of the banned Austrian version of the S.S. mounted a *putsch* aimed at toppling the government of Dr. Engelbert Dollfuss. The Austrian dictator had narrowly escaped assassination the previous October after thumbing his nose at Hitler. The Nazis were determined that he would not do so again. The rebels, led mostly by former noncommissioned Austrian army officers, planned on support from exiled fascists, sympathizers in Vienna, and from Dr. Anton Rintelen, Austria's pro-German ambassador to Rome.

John described the anatomy of a *putsch* in a breathless eyewitness account in the November 1934 issue of *Harper's* magazine.[9]

The day of the coup attempt had been hot and muggy. John had just finished his morning's work and was about to leave the office for a noon-hour swim when a few minutes after one o'clock, his telephone rang. "Have you heard the radio?" asked one of his tipsters. "The Vienna radio has just made this announcement: 'The government of [Chancellor] Dr. Dollfuss has resigned. Dr. Rintelen has assumed power.' It may be a joke; I don't know. I'll check it out and call you back in a minute."

John made some quick calls to the American legation, Marcel Fodor, the *CDN*'s Paris office, and then the Austrian chancellery, where there was no answer. Sensing that something was amiss, John and Fodor rushed downtown to the *Bundeskanzleramt*, the federal chancellery. Traffic was moving normally in the street in front of the building.

"The tawny oak doors were shut and a few policemen were outside, but otherwise nothing seemed wrong," John wrote. "I assumed that the government had locked itself in, preparing defense." That notion was quickly dispelled when from within came the muffled sounds of shooting and explosions. Police held back the crowd of reporters now straining for a better view, and demanding to know what was happening. John noticed that the only person allowed to enter the building was a white-jacketed waiter carrying a tray of beer steins; battling an attempted coup was obviously thirsty work.

He would later learn that 144 well-armed Austrian Nazis had stormed the chancellery just after lunch. A cabinet meeting was underway, and they had taken all of the ministers hostage. However, by five o'clock it was clear the ill-planned *putsch* had failed. With the chancellery surrounded by police and loyal elements of the Austrian army, the Nazi sympathizers lost heart. The rebels' morale cracked, and in a characteristically Viennese touch, one of the beseiged leaders rang the Café Eiles, a coffee house frequented by Austrian Nazis. He asked the waiter who answered if another of the *putsch* ringleaders was there to give him instructions. The man was not.

Faced with the prospect of surrendering or fighting to the death, the rebels laid down their arms in return for a promise of safe passage out of the building. As they were leaving, one of them shouted, "We've left one dead in the corner room upstairs." The man was Dollfuss. Shot in the throat at point blank range, he had bled to death.

Thirteen of the rebels eventually were hanged for their role in the murder. But the damage had been done. The bullet that had ended the life of Chancellor Dollfuss had also snuffed out the feeble hopes of Austrian democracy. The new chancellor was the plodding Dr. Kurt von Schuschnigg. A legal scholar by profession and an authoritarian by temperament, he was not up to the task of governing a country teetering on the brink of civil war.

John was shocked and saddened by the assassination. Despite his faults, Dollfuss had not been an unsympathetic figure. "[His] murder . . . marked the entrance of gangsterism into European politics on an international basis," he predicted in his *Harper's* article. "[It] is a heavy price to pay for temporary security, but [Dollfuss] died to keep anarchy out of Central Europe, and this is his best memorial."

Few observers realized at the time how flimsy a memorial it would be.

The aborted July revolt ultimately had the desired effect: Austria was destabilized and the way paved for the Nazi takeover that occurred three years later.

The events of July 25 spurred John again to begin plans for a series of profiles of Europe's dictators. He now decided to write them as free-lance submissions to *Harper's*, *The Nation*, and other American and British publications. As it turned out, he was unknowingly preparing himself to write the phenomenally successful book that in 1936 would cast him in the role of a modern-day Cassandra, and catapult him to worldwide fame and fortune.

CHAPTER SEVENTEEN

In 1932, a small New York publisher called Liveright Books published an irreverent, behind-the-scenes look at life in the American capital entitled, *Washington Merry-Go-Round*. The critic for the influential *Saturday Review of Literature* attacked the book, written anonymously by veteran political journalists Drew Pearson and Robert S. Allen, as "petty, malicious, inaccurate (and) biased."[1] A reviewer for the *New Republic* was kinder, pointing out that *Washington Merry-Go-Round* was alive with "the gossip the capital loves to whisper but hates to see in print."[2]

Predictably, the reading public was intrigued by the controversy, and by the prospect of juicy revelations about the underside of life among America's political elite. The book became a smash best-seller, going through some twenty-three reprintings.

Since nothing breeds imitation like success, other publishers soon began searching for variations on the *Washington Merry-Go-Round* theme. When Ray Long of the London publishing house Long & Smith put together an anonymously written symposium of European political gossip called *Not to Be Repeated: Merry-Go-Round of Europe*, he asked John Gunther to contribute five chapters on Central Europe. "The cash advance was small, $150 if my memory is right," John recalled in his book *A Fragment of Autobiography*, "but . . . I was hard up; besides, the idea was challenging."[3] The critics liked *Not to Be Repeated*, but the book was a commercial flop. Americans were not yet much interested in the European politics.

In New York meanwhile, Cass Canfield, president of Harper & Brothers, was not discouraged from pressing ahead with plans for a serious, comprehensive book about Europe.

"At about this time," he recalled many years later, "it occurred to me that if I could find someone to write about current international affairs in a way that would attract the non-specialized reader, the resulting book would be both useful and salable. What I had in mind was a book on Europe that would take the reader behind the scenes and present vivid portraits of the leading political figures. Of course, the problem was to find the right person to write such a book, which was not easy because of [its] great scope."[4]

Canfield knew John Gunther's writing. The two had met in London in 1925, and Harper & Brothers had published John's novels in the United States. Canfield also had read John's article about the Reichstag fire called, "Arson De Luxe," which had appeared in the October 1933 issue of *Harper's* magazine. Canfield chose John to write the Europe book, then had second thoughts. "It didn't seem to me that Gunther then had the necessary experience to write a book on the whole of contemporary Europe," he explained.[5]

Ironically, John and Frances had only recently discussed a similar book idea, which Frances had proposed. John rejected it for a couple of reasons, one being that, like Canfield, he did not feel that he had the expertise to carry it off. The other reason,—one that was even more important in his own mind—was the time commitment involved. "I was busy doing articles, and I dreaded cutting myself away from the old dreams of fiction for so long," he recalled.[6]

At the time, John was planning a long novel about Vienna. His agent saw the prospect of some easy money in a book about Asia, but John was adament. He was not yet ready to abandon his dream of becoming a novelist.

In Canfield's 1971 autobiography, *Up and Down and Around*, he recalled how he took his book idea to Hubert Renfro (H.R.) Knickerbocker. The celebrated correspondent for William Randolph Hearst's International News Service and the *Philadelphia Public Ledger* was at the height of his fame in the early 1930s. He had won the 1931 Pulitzer Prize for his reporting and had embarked on a hectic timetable that saw him write one successful book per year from 1931 to 1934.

Knickerbocker, "Nick" to friends, was a native of Yoakum, Texas. Born on January 31, 1898, he was red-haired, feisty, and at times priggish. Knickerbocker had briefly studied psychiatry and taught journalism at Southern Methodist University in Dallas before going to Germany in 1923 to continue his medical education. He had instead drifted back into journalism, serving for a time as Dorothy Thompson's assistant. Following Thompson's marriage to Sinclair Lewis, to whom he had introduced her, Nick stepped into Thompson's former job with the *Philadelphia Public Ledger*. It was through CDN Berlin correspondent Edgar A. Mowrer and his wife, Lilian, that Knickerbocker in 1929 met John Gunther. The two became fast friends.[7]

Knickerbocker declined to get involved in Canfield's project. He was too busy. "I'm not your man," Canfield recalls Knickerbocker telling him. "Try (John) Gunther. He's the only one with the brains, the brass, and the gusto to write the book you want."[8]

In late 1932 Canfield contacted John's New York agent, Bernice Baumgarten of the Brandt & Brandt agency. When John indicated that he still was not interested, the book was shelved for two years. Then, during the last week of September 1934, John left behind his marital woes and the grind of his bureau job when he traveled alone to the United States on leave. John and his agent met in New York with Canfield to discuss the proposed book; Canfield insisted it was worth doing. John continued to resist.

"I persisted in saying no to the project, and finally Miss Baumgarten asked me what, if any, financial advance would induce me to change my mind," John remembered in *A Fragment of Autobiography*. "To cut the whole matter off, I named the largest sum I had ever heard of—$5,000."[9]

He was shocked when Baumgarten said that she thought she could get the money, despite the fact that an advance of that size was far above average at the time. Her intuition proved right. Canfield agreed to the demand. Harper & Brothers would contribute $3,000, Hamish Hamilton (the company's British subsidiary) $1,000, and *Harper's* magazine the balance in return for three articles to be excerpted from the book. "I had the strong feeling that [the] book would not only sell but blaze a new trail," Canfield explained.[10]

Chagrined, John next tried to stall the signing of a contract. He announced that he would "further consider" the matter while he met his editors. He visited friends and a few relatives in Chicago, spoke about European events to a public affairs organization called the Foreign Relations Council (as all *Chicago Daily News* foreign correspondents were obliged to do when home on leave), and he met with publisher Charles Dennis and foreign editor Hal O'Flaherty. They had no objection to him doing the Europe book.

Nevertheless, back in New York in early December for the return voyage to Europe, John tried to evade a commitment. Cass Canfield, determined to see that he did not, paid him an unexpected—and unwelcome—early morning visit. A man of enormous personal charm and energy, Canfield could also be persuasive.

Born in New York City on April 26, 1897, he was a lean, heavy-boned man with a rough-hewn, yet sensitive face. He was ruddy cheeked, balding, with a prominent nose, bushy eyebrows and a mustache. Friends seldom saw him without his trademark pipe in hand. "His greatest quality was his openness and curiosity about everything," says his son, Cass, Jr.[11]

Canfield had served in the U.S. Army during the First World War, before graduating from Harvard in 1919. He then studied for a time at Oxford University and the Sorbonne in Paris, traveled around the world in 1923, helped found the magazine *Foreign Affairs*, and worked as a newspaper reporter for the *New York Evening Post*. Canfield joined Harper & Brothers in 1924, and was appointed manager of their office in London, where he did much to enhance the company's list of British authors, recruiting such talents as E.M. Delafield and J.B. Priestley.

It was also while he was in London that Canfield became friends with Hamish Hamilton, a wiry, erudite young Scotsman, who dressed immaculately, and had a passion for flying airplanes. When Hamilton started his own publishing house in London, Canfield backed him financially. Thus, Hamish (Jamie) Hamilton became John's publisher in England.

Following his return to New York, Canfield rose rapidly through the ranks at Harper & Brothers By 1929, he had become executive vice-president of the firm, and two years later was president. "I am a publisher," Canfield once quipped, "a hybrid creature, one part stargazer, one part gambler, one part businessman, one part midwife, and three parts optimist."[12] As such, he was always searching for new book ideas. He was certain that in the Europe book he had an idea for a bestseller, and he was determined to see it come to fruition.

Canfield called on John in his room at the Hotel Chatham early on the morning of his last day in town. Canfield's quarry was in a bad way; he was sitting on the edge of his bed with a cold towel wrapped around his head, "the personification of a man with an acute hangover," as Canfield described him.

Asked what he wanted, Canfield reminded John of the book project they had discussed. John moaned and fell back on the bed holding his head. Canfield smiled. He was prepared to sit there all day, he said, or until John signed a contract to do the book. "[John] had a late night; he hadn't done his packing, and I obviously was not at all welcome at that moment," Canfield remembered. "[He] finally burst out, 'I'll do anything you ask me if you'll just get out of this room and give me a chance to pack and get on that boat.' I replied that fortunately I happened to have a contract in my pocket, and that if he'd sign it, I'd leave immediately." John grudgingly agreed. "Oh, I'll sign—but," he growled, "it won't mean a thing."[13]

How wrong he was!

Looking back on the events of that morning a quarter-century later, John mused, "I wake up every once in a while wondering what on earth my life would have been like if Canfield, so quietly tenacious and persuasive, had not made his final approach that wintry morning so long ago."[14]

Faced now with the realization that he had contracted to write the Europe book, John had no choice but to begin work. Fortunately, his job in Vienna did not demand all his time. He wrote a trial chapter on Rumania, drawing upon his own knowledge of Central Europe, the voluminous newspaper clippings files he kept, and some information provided to him by Marcel Fodor. "It went like a dream," he noted. "I was basking in the relative contentment, even torpor, of Vienna."[15]

Work continued at a leisurely pace for a couple of months, with John writing the book in his off-hours. This idyllic situation came to an abrupt end one day in April 1935. John received news from Chicago that he had been promoted and reassigned to London. He was to succeed Negley Farson in what was the newspaper's most coveted bureau job. Tempering his delight was the stark realization that life for him, Frances, and Johnny had taken a decisive turn.

Despite the emotional pain of his marital woes and his discontent with his workaday routine, John had grown to love Vienna. For the rest of his life, he fondly referred to his time there as "green-lit silken days." In writing his 1964 novel, *The Lost City*, John struggled to capture on paper the mixed emotions that Mason and Paula Jarret felt on leaving their beloved Vienna. In so doing, he was relating what he and Frances had felt when faced with the same move.

"They would miss all their friends," he wrote, "but they would go away now; after five years they had had enough. Vienna, so much a part of them, would be behind them. They would say good-by to Mozart in the Musikvereinsall (concert hall) and Schlagobers in the cafes; they would say good-by to the . . . palaces with butterscotch coloring on lovely squares like the Josefplatz, to all the things they loved in Vienna, all the things their hearts remembered."[16]

The move to London also meant an increased workload—something John dreaded as he struggled to complete the Europe book.

CHAPTER EIGHTEEN

London was "a long jump" from far-off, sleepy Vienna, as John Gunther recalled in his book *A Fragment of Autobiography*. "I had to establish (new) relationships, since these are the basis of journalism. I had to learn my way about, although I knew London fairly well. I had, if possible, to get 'in.'"[1]

While based in Austria, John found it easy to contrive weekend trips which allowed him to research the Europe book. His *Chicago Daily News* editors expected him to informed, and doing so meant meeting regularly with his contacts throughout Central Europe. "I should equip myself to be able to *give* information, since it's always easier to ask for something if you offer something in exchange," he said. "Journalism is really a process of barter between two people who each know something and find it to their advantage to exchange or pool their knowledge."[2]

Following the move to England it proved impossible for John to travel to the Continent. The distances were too great, and the responsibilities of operating his new bureau left little opportunity for travel outside the British Isles. "Cemented firmly to a desk," as John put it, he was now on the job ten hours a day, six days a week.[3]

"Aside from a good deal of study, my major effort [in London] has been to meet people, all kinds of people," he recorded in his diary. "Most of what I have to get has to be obtained by telephone, since between reading the morning papers and sending in my [daily] story there is only an hour or so."[4]

John felt compelled to work on the Europe book every spare moment. Each evening after dinner, and early on Sunday mornings, he made his way from the small flat he, Frances, and Johnny had rented near the British Museum, to the *CDN* office in Bush House, a new office building on the Strand in central London. Given the perishable nature of the information he was working with, and the volatility of European political events, there was no alternative to the long crazy hours John worked on the book. The hectic schedule meant that there was little time to socialize, relax, or spend at home. This did not soothe the hurts or help to repair his damaged marriage.

The move to London had provided John and Frances with little more than a temporary respite from the cycle of self-destructive behavior into which they had fallen in Vienna. Yet, their "professional relationship" remained good; they still worked well together. Frances was enthusiastic about the Europe book. She prepared background notes on a variety of subjects. She read and commented on chapters. And when in 1935 John took a three-week summer vacation to catch up on his research with an exhausting 5,000-mile whirlwind tour of Paris, Rome, Berlin, Warsaw, and Moscow, Frances lightened the workload by accompanying him during the final two legs.

This ability to work while "living out of a suitcase" was a skill that John had honed to perfection over the course of a decade as a foreign correspondent. He had learned to utilize research time to the utmost advantage. Friends and colleagues in the cities he visited gave him detailed answers to a list of twenty-six key questions about the attitudes, habits, and lifestyle of Europe's major political figures. Jay Allen in Madrid, Ralph Forte in Rome, Morris Gilbert in Paris, and Marcel Fodor in Vienna briefed him, and even gave him background memoranda.

From London, John wrote scores of letters to his contacts in American embassies and consulates throughout Europe. He also entertained visiting journalists whenever the opportunity arose; sometimes these efforts paid handsome dividends. Over lunch one day, the Polish expatriate journalist Stephan Litauer "almost literally talked my chapter on [the late Polish dictator Josef] Pilsudski to me in three hours," John recalled. H.R. Knickerbocker, in from his posting in Berlin, shared his vast store of firsthand, "inside" knowledge about Hitler, Mussolini, and Stalin. John used all of the information to piece together the three personality profiles that formed the heart of *Inside Europe*.

One might wonder why other journalists, most of whom worked for rival publications, willingly provided John Gunther with information for his book. The reason was simple, really.

While dismissing any ideas that he was writing a "peep-hole" book full of "gossip for gossip's sake," John made it clear that he was concentrating on the human element of European politics in the same way that the authors of *Washington Merry-Go-Round* had in laying bare the tawdry realities of life on Capitol Hill. "Everybody likes gossip," John explained, "and I was treating gossip, as one British lady put it, 'in the grand manner.' Newsmen were delighted to have a colleague write things that, for various reasons, they themselves had to sit on."[5]

The same journalists who were "officially" the competition willingly shared this inside information with John for another reason: news and gossip were the stuff of normal conversation in the closely knit fraternity of foreign correspondents. Besides, at the time no one had any idea just how successful John's efforts would be. Previous books about the European political scene had sold poorly in the United States, and there was no reason to suppose that this book by this author would be any different. There was as yet no reason for any of the petty professional jealousies that arose in the wake of the phenomenal success of *Inside Europe*.

Some of John Gunther's colleagues later grumbled that he had "picked their brains" to write the book. Of course he had! That was how every American foreign correspondent in Europe worked. What stunned people most was how well John used the information he had been given; even his closest friends were taken aback by the extent of his success.

Marcel Fodor was an unlikely candidate to underestimate John's writing talents or ambition, yet like so many others he, too, was surprised when *Inside Europe* became a hit. "My father always figured John Gunther as a good journeyman-type journalist," says Fodor's son, Denis. "John always talked about finding the 'formula' to write a bestseller, but it still came as a surprise when he actually found it."[6]

George Seldes, who spent the twenty-one years between 1916 and 1937 in Europe working as a foreign correspondent, remembers his own reaction, and that of many of his colleagues to *Inside Europe*. "Everybody was envious of Gunther's success. We all asked ourselves why *we* hadn't thought of writing the same kind of book," he says. "I guess maybe many of us had, and that's why some people felt they could have done a better job than Gunther did. But the fact was that you really had to hand it to him—he did an excellent job."[7]

Human nature being what it is, H.R. Knickerbocker was among those who felt that John's success should have been his, if only fate had been kinder. Says his brother, Kenneth, "I guess when the book became an international bestseller, Hubert was bound to have been jealous. We never discussed it or anything like that; he never mentioned it at all. That was just my impression.

"My brother was an excellent writer, but, in retrospect, I don't think he could have done any better job with that book than Gunther did. It was really a significant book and a fascinating book because it moved into territory that no one else had ever explored."[8]

That blend of newsy candor and the freshness and immediacy that John Gunther worked so hard to inject into *Inside Europe* were at the heart of its popular appeal, and go a long way towards explaining just why the book caught the fancy of readers on both sides of the Atlantic. All of the information contained in *Inside Europe*—and such facts are the raw material of all reportage—were common property in the journalistic community. It was the book's organization and unique style that were his alone, as John was obliged to point out in later years.

The middlebrow, mass appeal of *Inside Europe* stemmed from its readability. John Gunther had never forgotten Henry J. Smith's dictum human interest is the stuff that breathes life into a news story. And so he structured the book around candid profiles of Europe's "big three"—Hitler, Mussolini, and Stalin, delving into the details of each dictator's personality and *how* it was that he wielded power. This approach, John confessed in a letter to Canfield, "derives from something deeper in me than political conviction; it comes from the fact, for good or ill, I instinctively think of myself as a novelist."[9]

It was this storyteller's leap of imagination, along with some prompting from Frances, that spurred John to resist the impulse to begin with a safe, conventional analysis of the English situation. Instead, he spotlighted Adolf Hitler. In 1935, the Nazi dictator was still an enigma to most North Americans. John's portrait of Hitler has stood the test of time. Even today, more than a half century later, it is still one of the best of the contemporary accounts of history's most bizarre and sinister personality.

In detailing Hitler's life, John recycled the material he and Marcel Fodor had uncovered on their 1934 visit to Hitler's birthplace at Brannau, Austria. Then, adding fresh information provided by H.R. Knickerbocker and others, he wrote an intimate 4,000-word profile of Hitler that examined the details of the fuhrer's personality as no one before had dared. The profile revealed in a matter-of-fact way the bizarre character of a man who eschewed friends, money, sex, religion, and physical activity in his Machiavellian quest for unbridled power; Hitler emerged as a dangerous, unpredictable ascetic, a peasant with insatiable drives and an "Oedipus complex as big as a house." The Nazis were outraged; *Inside Europe* was banned in Germany. News of the Nazi ban only served to increase public interest in the book. Like the rest of the world, America's fascination with the Nazi leader was growing. People thirsted for information on why this paunchy, ranting, Charlie Chaplin-like character was causing such turmoil in Europe. *Inside Europe* provided it in an entertaining fashion. John theorized in his introduction that "the accidents of personality play a great role in history."[10]

Even that idea certainly was not new. The Scottish historian Thomas Carlyle (1795-1881) had suggested it a half century before. But Carlyle's ideas took on a new relevance in the light of recent events in Europe. Combining a dash of Carlyle with a pinch of Stekel's theory of the authority complex was John Gunther's recipe for making sense of the incomprehensible. He speculated that Hitler, like Mussolini and Stalin, happened to be the *right* man in the *right* place at the *right* time—just as he was the *right* man to author a popular book on the European political scene. The pieces all fell into place. That was even the case with his choice of *Inside Europe* as a title.

While he was preoccupied with researching and writing, John had no time for the task of deciding on a suitable title. At first he called the manuscript "The New Europe." Then, successively, it became "The Age of Dictators," "Backstage Europe," "Doomed Europe," and finally, "Men Over Europe." None of these titles seemed quite right. Ever the perfectionist where his writing was concerned, John agonized in his search for a title that rang true.

He found himself pausing at dinner, while walking along the street, or in the middle of an interview, as he rummaged through his pockets for a scrap of paper upon which to scribble his latest idea. *Inside Europe*, the title he finally settled on and the one that brought him fame while adding a new expression to the English language, came to him one cold grey November day.

John was touring the Ebbw Vale, a coal mining district in Wales. He had gone there to write about former Labor Party Prime Minister J. Ramsay MacDonald, who was waging an unsuccessful fight to retain his parliamentary seat in the 1935 general election. On the train ride home to London, John sat alone in the dining car. The election and the landscape seemed a million miles away as he sipped a scotch to ease the chill of the autumn day, and gazed through the sooty, misted windows at an endless succession of gritty mining towns. He was preoccupied with titles for his Europe book.

"Suddenly I had it," he recalled years later in his book *A Fragment of An Autobiography*. "An Insider's Europe . . . Looking at Europe from the Inside . . . Inside Europe! I was terrified that I might forget this before reaching London, and scribbled the words in the margin of the *London Times*, while munching a cold, fatty lump of mutton."[11]

John was as excited as a cub reporter. Arriving in London, he immediately telephoned Jamie Hamilton, the Harper & Brothers representative in England. Hamilton, also enthused by the *Inside Europe* title, cabled the suggestion to Canfield in New York. When Canfield wired back word that he too liked it, John knew that the Europe book had the catchy title it needed. Thus was born the *Inside* series, one of the most succesful non-fiction series in the history of American publishing.

It was only later that John discovered he had not been the first to think of using the term "inside" in a title. *Variety*, the weekly show business newspaper, had long carried a column called, "Inside Stuff." And during the First World War the American journalist Herbert Bayard Swope had written a book about Germany entitled, *Inside the German Empire*. But neither the *Variety* column nor the Swope book had caught the public's fancy, nor popularized the term "inside" as would *Inside Europe*.

John recorded in his diary that he had "somehow" finished writing the massive, 190,000-word manuscript in just seven months. The final 8,500 words of a three-chapter section on England came tumbling out during a crazy all-night work session. The sun was still a rosy glow on the eastern horizon as he typed the last words at dawn on the morning of December 2, 1935. John was euphoric as he ran home through the still deserted streets. He awakened Frances for a brief celebration.

Jamie Hamilton, who was sailing for New York that morning, planned to take the completed manuscript with him. At eight o'clock John dispatched a messenger to the train station with the precious package, then he went to bed for a few hours. That evening, he and Frances attended a cocktail party for Hugh Baillie, the new London bureau chief for United Press, and later went to a ballet with friends. John unwound afterwards. "I had about a dozen beers," he noted in his diary.[12]

Within a matter of a few days, batches of galley proofs of the book (uncorrected pages of type) began arriving at the Gunther's door. To meet the tight production schedule, and to have *Inside Europe* on bookshop shelves ahead of any competition, Hamish Hamilton had begun typesetting the manuscript before it was even finished; Harper & Brothers in New York set the American edition from the British galleys.

Final checks were complicated by the fact that John, at Canfield's insistence, was rewriting and adding information right up till the last moment. The publisher wanted the book to be as current as possible. "By accident," John said, "I invented what has subsequently become known as 'book journalism'; a book became a kind of periodical."[13] For example, when Sir Samuel Hoare resigned from the British government, and was replaced by Anthony Eden, *Inside Europe* was between galley proofs and the production of page proofs (the actual pages of the book), Canfield had John rewrite the relevant chapter to reflect that fact. As a result, every word of revisions had to be checked and double checked. The task was tedious, given that the peculiarities of spelling, idiom, and the British and American libel laws necessitated that there be two distinct sets of galleys. It was the matter of libel that most concerned Hamilton.

A New York lawyer Cass Canfield hired to review the *Inside Europe* manuscript expressed an opinion that there was no problem with publishing the book in the United States. A statement that was considered libelous in Britain was not necessarily libelous in America, so Hamilton retained no fewer than three English lawyers to read the book; none knew that others were doing so. It was, John wryly observed, "a three-ring circus." Each of Hamilton's attorneys produced a lengthy memorandum detailing dozens of suggested changes and deletions. John was dumbfounded by many of their concerns.

One was that the details of the Hitler profile be scrupulously verified to lessen the possibility of the Nazi leader suing for libel in a British court. In retrospect, that would have been a fascinating spectacle! At the time, however, such a suit was a serious matter, given the delicate state of Anglo-German relations. These same concerns had inspired the barring of Winston Churchill, alienated from the pacifist mainstream of the Conservative Party, from appearing on British Broadcasting Corporation radio programs. It was feared that Churchill's hawkishness would insult Hitler and inflame the political situation.

Another problem with the *Inside Europe* manuscript was that in describing the German propaganda minister, John had noted that "(Joseph) Goebbels never kicks a man until he's down." Hamilton's lawyers excised that sentence, as they did this reference: "Even Communism cannot make the porter of the Hotel Metropole in Moscow efficient, or his telephone." This porter was an identifiable person, the lawyers pointed out, and he might sue. Also cut from the book was the statement that British Fascist leader Sir Oswald Mosley was the head of a "dwindling" movement. Hamilton's lawyers felt that John had left an opening for Mosley to sue, even if only for the publicity value in doing so.

While lamenting that such cuts were draining the lifeblood from his prose, John accommodated the lawyers concerns as best he could. He worked around the clock to correlate the British and American versions of the manuscript. What this involved was snipping apart the hundreds of pages of galleys and then pasting in typewritten inserts. On the morning of the day the task had to be completed, John recalled how a startled secretary had found him at the *CDN* office, "bent over the desk like a lobster claw, in the same crazed, concentrated position at 9:30 a.m. that I had been in when she left the night before."[14]

CHAPTER NINETEEN

As he was rushing to finish *Inside Europe* John Gunther was still obliged to send a daily news cable to Chicago, and to maintain his contacts in London. The former had become a chore, the latter a pleasure. John had immersed himself in the city's social and professional life. He also found time to head the London chapter of the American Correspondent's Association. As in Vienna, it was a duty that also put him at the hub of activity.

John's diaries for the period, portions of which were published as a two-part series in *Atlantic* magazine in early 1937, provide a vivid picture of life in the London of the day. The great city was the capital of a decaying empire, yet it remained a vibrant cultural mecca. The diaries are testimony to how John reveled in his relationships with the rich and famous who gathered here. A typical day's entry records encounters with any of a dazzling array of celebrities—it might have been anyone from Baroness Moura Budberg, violinist Jascha Heifetz or filmmaker Herman J. Mankiewicz, to dancer Agnes de Mille, actor Edward G. Robinson, political economist Harold Laski, Indian Congress dissident Jawaharlal Nehru, Zionist leader Chaim Weizmann, or American anarchist Emma Goldman. In one entry, John recorded how he and Frances had met H.G. Wells at a party. He seemed preoccupied, musing about a new novel or some thought-provoking work of history, one might have assumed. Not so.

The great man explained that he had just returned from Hollywood, where he had written a film script to help pay for a house that he was building in London. He had come back full of excitement and fresh ideas. After seeing the size and opulence of American bathrooms, Wells told Frances that he had immediately telegraphed his contractors: "Stop all work on the water closets until I return!"[1]

Meeting novelist Aldous Huxley, the idol of his student days, John observed that "Huxley is, as everyone knows, very tall and loose-limbed; his legs curl around a chair, his nose is short, almost pert, the nostrils alarmingly long. He looks somewhat like an extraordinarily elongated rabbit."[2]

While chatting with influential economist John Maynard Keynes at his club, John noted that "there are three colors of gray in his face; the mustache almost white, the eyebrows quite black, the hair medium. His voice is quiet, he lounges comfortably and his eyelids flutter."[3]

That John met such important people is testament to his impeccable contacts, for British society in 1936 was still tightly closed and acutely class conscious. One's social circle was determined largely by whom you *knew*. The famous have a way of meeting the famous, and John always had a knack for cultivating friendships with people who could open doors for him. Frances' brother, Bernie Fineman, now working in London as a film producer,[4] showed him around in the British entertainment industry. Rebecca West, Jamie Hamilton, and other friends introduced him to prominent people in publishing and letters. And a new friend, left-wing journalist Claud Cockburn, kept him informed of political gossip and events at Westminster.

But in London—as always—there was one influential, older patron and admirer who looked after John, seeing to it that he met all of the *right* people. That patron was Margaret (Margot) Asquith, the seventy-one-year-old widow of Herbert Asquith, the prime minister of England from 1908 to 1916.

When an earldom was conferred upon Asquith in 1925, he chose *Oxford* for his title. Unfortunately, there was a problem with that: objections from the descendants of an earlier holder of that same title. Asquith got around this difficulty by adding his family name; he became the first earl of Oxford and Asquith. Nonetheless, following his 1928 death, his widow was invariably referred to by friends and associates simply as Lady Oxford.

The sixth of the dozen children of Sir Charles Tennant, a successful businessman, Lady Oxford had been born to wealth and privilege. To paraphrase a line from W.S. Gilbert, of Gilbert and Sullivan fame, "she did nothing in particular, but she did it very well." Lady Oxford's great-grandfather, John Walter, had founded the prestigious *Times of London*, and, as a girl, Margot sat at the knee of Victorian England's poet laureate—Alfred Tennyson, a close family friend.

If England really was "for the few, and for the very few," as Disraeli once observed, it is fair to say that Lady Oxford was one of that select "few." Throughout her lifetime, she moved easily through the drawing rooms of the rich and powerful.

As a young woman, she had been a member of a social group who called themselves "the Souls." She counted among her circle a veritable *Who's Who* of London society, which included novelists John Morley and Virginia Woolf, the Archbishop of Canterbury, and politicians William Gladstone, Arthur Balfour, and Lord Haldane. When she died in 1946 at age eighty-one, the writer of Lady Oxford's obituary pointed out that she had been friends with every one of the eleven prime ministers who had governed Britain during her lifetime.

A large, big-boned woman, she had deep-set, searching eyes and a caustic wit. Her obituary in the *Times* referred to her as the longtime "*enfant terrible*" of British society. A "lifetime of audacities" included scribbling a note to Queen Victoria in pencil, declining a dinner invitation from King Edward VII, and staging a fashion show at Number 10 Downing Street during the eight years that she and her husband resided there.

It was said that Lady Oxford's personal and political loyalties—as well her animosities, which were many—were expressed with equal passion. A firm believer in the theory that reticence was symptomatic of a lack of imagination, not good manners, she was renowned for speaking her mind. "After fox hunting," she once quipped, "the greatest pleasure I have had in life has been intellectual and endearing conversation."[5]

George Bernard Shaw once asked Lady Oxford what she thought of his latest play. She touched a forefinger to her chin, and after a pregnant pause said, "I think it's perhaps a little long."

Shaw nodded his head sagely. "It's the only way I have of emptying the theatre," he replied.[6]

How and where John first met Lady Oxford is unknown. It may have been in London in 1924, or perhaps it was in 1934 when, as head of the Anglo-American Press Association in Vienna, he had arranged a luncheon for her when she visited. What is certain is that John and Lady Oxford became friends. She took him under her wing, and introduced him to people with whom few American journalists socialized.

It was through Lady Oxford that John became socially acquainted with the Prince of Wales and his American mistress, Mrs. Wallis Simpson. John had first met the prince in the summer of 1924, of course, during the midwestern portion of the royal's North American tour. They had met again that fall aboard the S.S. *Olympic* on the voyage to England. However, on both occasions, their meetings had been impromptu and impersonal, and so it is unlikely the prince remembered John a decade later. On the afternoon of December 6, 1935, the circumstances were markedly different.

John was invited to lunch at Lady Oxford's London home. It was a grand place filled with great, heavy furniture "that had been there a thousand years." In addition to John and the hostess, six other people were present, among them the prince and Mrs. Simpson. John, ignorant of etiquette, arrived dressed in a natty Savile Row suit. To his chagrin, he saw that the other men, including the prince, were attired in dark, pin-striped trousers—the "official" uniform of such events. Although nothing was said of his *faux pas*, eyebrows were raised, and John was suitably embarrassed. "I imagine it is better to be under- rather than over-dressed," he later consoled himself.[7]

As he related in his diary, "The Prince, whom I hadn't seen

close up for years, was smaller than I remembered him, blonder, and in better physical shape than his pictures show. He was extremely brisk, charming, and vivacious." The prince and Lady Oxford talked "incessantly" over lunch for twenty minutes. Then, almost as if she had been timing herself with a stopwatch, the hostess turned to John and brought him into the conversation. She asked if he skied. Seizing the cue, John and the prince then chatted about skiing in Austria, about Viennese restaurants, Chicago newspapers, and Mussolini's recent push into the African nation of Abyssinia. Exactly fifteen minutes later, Lady Oxford "perfect in such things," as John marveled, interrupted to rotate the conversation. The prince was introduced to another guest, and John talked with Mrs. Simpson, who struck him as "alert, sensible, and intelligent."

Lady Oxford invited John to such social events because she enjoyed his company, but she may also have had another motive, for on December 7, John wrote a letter on her behalf to Eugene Saxton. Cass Canfield's right-hand man at Harper & Brothers was in London on business. John explained to him that he had recently received a note from his friend Lady Oxford intimating that she was "desperately hard-up." That much was true. Following her husband's death, Lady Oxford was perpetually short of money. She had once told John that when she and her husband left Number 10 Downing Street in 1916, they were $250,000 in debt, a fantastic sum in those days.

It is unlikely that Lady Oxford actually wrote to John about such matters. Far more likely is that John, after tea and a few hints one afternoon, took it upon himself to speak with his publisher on her behalf. Such a gesture would have been typical of him. There were countless times during his lifetime that John quietly reached out to help friends and colleagues in need. Such was his nature, and given John's own spending habits, he always had considerable empathy.

John's letter to Eugene Saxton explained that Lady Oxford, who had already authored six books, "has an absolutely unparalleled intimate background of everything and anything, all persons, personages from about 1800 [sic] to the present day."[8] John pointed out—erroneously, as it happened—that it had been almost ten years since Lady Oxford's last volume of memoirs, and that perhaps she could be "tempted" to write a new book. "In any case, even if you aren't interested, would you, as a favor to me, write her that you would like to know if she is thinking of a book? Mention my name, say that you heard me say that she might be doing a book. Do not, of course, mention that I know she is desperately broke and so on."

Saxton did some checking and learned that Lady Oxford's last book, *More Memories* (1934), had sold poorly. So, while sympathetic to John's request, Saxton declined to write the requested letter; Canfield agreed that it would be unfair to raise Lady Oxford's hopes, only to then reject something she wrote.

If she was disturbed by John's inabilities to persuade Canfield to publish her next manuscript, Lady Oxford did not let it affect their friendship. They remained close during the rest of the time John was based in London, which, as it turned out, was not all that long.

John and Frances spent the 1935 holiday season in London, dining on Christmas night with Rebecca West and her husband, Henry Andrews. There were still strong feelings between John and Rebecca. They attended the same New Year's Eve party, and afterwards, in what were hardly the words of someone dispassionate, John wrote in his diary, "Rebecca looked gorgeous, and her talk was, as always, a golden, dusky flow, flawless in wit and rhythm."[9]

It was just one week later that John got his first look at *Inside Europe*. On January 7, an advance copy of the 510-page book arrived in London. "[It] burned my fingers," he confided to his diary. "I couldn't bear to be seen with it, so I carefully took the jacket off and folded and hid it in my pocket."[10] One of the few people to whom John showed the book was Lady Oxford. She was much impresssed. Over lunch, their talk turned to money. "Are you rich?" she asked suddenly. John, astonished, could only shake his head and laugh. "It never occurred to me that anyone who knew us well could have imagined that we were in anything but very moderate circumstances," he marveled.[11]

The reality was that like Lady Oxford, the Gunthers were perpetually short of cash. London was an expensive city, and they had difficulty making ends meet. In Vienna, John had set aside most of his monthly income from free-lance writing. Now there was little time for such extracurricular efforts. The result was that he and Frances were living off their savings. Faced with the reality that they would soon be broke, the Gunthers decided to give up parties, at least "for a while." That painful decision made at least one aspect of life easier for John: his doctor had advised him to lose twenty-five pounds. He had been enjoying far too much of the "good life." That, combined with his heavy smoking, odd hours, and an aversion to exercise, had taken a toll.

Unfortunately, the Gunthers' resolve to curtail their social lives soon weakened, especially after *Inside Europe* was published in England on Monday, January 13, 1936. The day was like any other working day for John. He had lunch with Jimmy Sheean, who was visiting London, then spent the afternoon at the foreign office seeking information on the Abyssinian crisis. By Friday the first reviews of *Inside Europe* began to appear in the London newspapers. It was only then that John got an inkling of how much his life was about to change.

He would forever recall how Frances had picked up a copy of that day's *Daily Telegraph*, and read aloud a review of the book by critic Harold Nicholson. At first, John thought she must be teasing when he heard the praise, capped off by the words "a serious contribution to contemporary knowledge."[12] But it was true.

Nicholson was warm in his praise of the book, as were most other British critics. Suddenly, everyone in London was talking about *Inside Europe*. The book became an overnight sensation. No one was more surprised at this turn of events than John. In his fondest dreams, he had never expected the book to receive such a reception. He was astounded when Jamie Hamilton informed him that *Inside Europe* was on its way to the top of the British bestseller list. It would eventually sell more copies than any other work of non-fiction by any American since Mark Twain. As offers began pouring in for foreign language rights, the dizzying prospects of the book's imminent American publication still loomed.

John, understandably euphoric, was forced to maintain his perspective by the fact that he still worked for the *Chicago Daily News*. In that capacity, on January 20, 1936, he joined the crush of journalists who thronged to Sandringham, the home of the royal family, to cover the death of King George V. Arriving at night, John relied on his newsman's instincts to search out his colleagues; he headed for the local pub. Gathered there were about fifty reporters from all around the globe. Given that the adjacent inn had just five bedrooms, this posed problems. It was one of those wild, sleepless nights that John did not soon forget.

He felt a certain smugness as he wrote a brief profile of the new monarch, Edward VIII. After all, it was not every newsman who had socialized with England's new king. The country would be different now, John pointed out in his article; stuffy tradition was out the window. He was right.

Among the first things that Edward did upon assuming the throne was to order the clocks at Sandringham set to the correct time. His father had always had them a half-hour fast to allow more light for shooting in the mornings.

While all of this was happening in England, back in New York, John's agent was busy cashing in on the success of *Inside Europe.* In addition to *Harper's* (as agreed to in John's original contract for the book), prior to the book's publication in the last week of January 1936, she sold excerpts from *Inside Europe* to *Esquire*, *Reader's Digest*, and *Cosmopolitan,* among others.

Despite this, and despite favorable North American reviews, initial sales were slower than in England, where the book had a much greater sense of immediacy.

John's mood was tempered, too, by news that he received from Chicago on February 12. Henry J. Smith, the *CDN*'s managing editor, had died of heart failure at age sixty-one. John had never lost his affection for Smith, the man who had given him his first newspaper job, and treated him like a son during his days as a cub reporter. Nothing brings a life into perspective like the death of a loved one or close friend, and so John now began taking stock of his own life. Despite his newly found success and fame, he was not entirely happy. The reasons were obvious.

Despite the five novels to his credit, he was still not the famous novelist he had always dreamed of being. What's more, his personal life was in tatters; and he was living on his savings, and his job had ceased to interest him. John had come to understood why in 1924 Hal O'Flaherty had been so eager to escape the grind of managing a news bureau.

Buoyed by the success of *Inside Europe*, and by Cass Canfield's request for chapters for a revised edition of the book, he decided the time had come to make his break. "I am going to get out," John mused in his diary. "I dislike so much the grind of daily cables. Work that you like never fatigues a person; the thing that's exhausting is work that you detest. And I have lost all flavor for daily journalism; the tang is out of it. It's time for me to do the work I like to do."[13]

John had lunch on May 2, with H.R. Knickerbocker and his wife Agnes, who were in town, and they discussed their mutual dissatisfaction with workaday journalism. John confided, too, that he was displeased at the prospect of having to pay British taxes on the royalties from *Inside Europe*. When Nick said nothing to dissuade him, John began to talk seriously about returning to New York. Here he hoped to make a living writing fiction.

On May 26, over dinner with Paul Scott Mowrer, his boss, John took the decisive step. He announced he was quitting the newspaper as of August 1. Mowrer, who was disappointed, tried his best to convince John that he was "letting the newspaper down." The two men talked until midnight, but John refused to change his mind. The discussion ended when John left for Paddington Station, where his sister, Jean, was arriving for a visit.

In a letter dated May 29, to Bernice Baumgarten, his agent, John said that "Frances, the governess, kid [Johnny] and me" would be returning home that fall.[14] He had already asked Cass Canfield to find him a small, inexpensive place in the country near New York, somewhere that he could write; John had plans for three books. The first, a 350-page project to be called *London Fog*, or maybe *Goodbye London*, would be the record of his "daily London doings." Since "everybody in England, from the King on down" would be in it, he felt it would be successful.

The second book was to be an ambitious novel set in Vienna. "This is a long and serious job and is where my heart most lies," he confided. As publisher of his earlier novels, John felt that *Secker* had first right of refusal in England. There was no question in his mind about that. However, he was not content with arrangements that his agent had made to allow Bobbs-Merrill the U.S. rights to his next novel. Reacting to her suggestion that he "whip up something" for Bobbs-Merrill, John was adamant. "If I publish anything at all it will be as good as I can make it, and I want a good publisher to put it out. So far, I have always written as an amateur because I have always had a job. Now that I am on the dole, I must pay serious attention to these things."[15]

The third book that John planned was an eastern version of *Inside Europe,* which he tentatively called *Inside Orient.* He hoped to get started on it by the late spring or early summer of 1937. The plan was to spend six months traveling and researching, and then to write the book. John estimated the cost of the trip to be at least $5,000—a considerable sum in the midst of the Depression, but one which he was certain Cass Canfield and Jamie Hamilton would assume. John left it to his agent to get the money.

Despite another of his bouts with asthma, John, Frances, and Johnny left London on June 3 for a one-month vacation in France and Spain. They stayed near Malaga as guests of Jay Allen, who was now working for the *Chicago Tribune.* It was here, while basking in the warmth of the Mediterranean sun, that John posted his letter of resignation to Chicago. It was effective August 1.

Although he bubbled with enthusiasm and confidence now that he would have the time to write what he pleased, John was not entirely certain of the course he had taken. Times were still tough. Eight million Americans were out of work, and tensions in Europe were on the rise. On July 20, less than a month after the Gunthers left Spain, the country erupted in civil war, and the rumor reached John in London that Jay Allen had been killed in the fighting. In despair, John cabled a Gibraltar hotel where he thought his friend might turn up, if he was still alive. A one-word reply from Allen brought a smile to his face; "Intact," it read.[16]

Bill Stoneman, the *CDN's* new man in London, arrived on July 24.[17] John showed him the routine. When Frances and Johnny departed two weeks later for a month at the seaside, he stayed behind to work on a revised edition of *Inside Europe.* "It's funny to be free," John wrote in his diary. "My daily routine is pretty much the same as when I had a job."[18]

The work went slowly—partly because of the large number of revisions and minor corrections needed, and partly because John was now worrying about friends. Edgar Mowrer had also been reported missing in Spain, and Jimmy Sheean was deathly ill in Ireland. Happily Mowrer, like Allen, would eventually resurface unharmed, and Sheean, being one stubborn Irishman, pulled through his illness.

With the *Inside Europe* revisions finally complete, John decided he, too, needed a holiday. He went to Berne to see his sister, Jean, who was vacationing there. From Switzerland, John went on to an Austrian lakeside resort at Velden. Here he worked on the London diary project, relaxed in the sun, slept late, and played some tennis again "after all these years." He was surprised to find that he missed Frances. "I try to work early in the morning and in the evening, when it is hard," John told her in a letter. "Wish you were here; why didn't I insist you come? Work on the diary has shown me, if I needed showing, what an enormous part of all my London life belonged oblongs [sic] particularly to you. Darling, I would be helpless without you and any kind of existence with you away is inconceivable. America is going to be such glory!"[19]

John's spirits were raised by word from New York that his agent had arranged an American lecture tour for him. It would pay him $500 a week. The news was good, too, from Berlin, where the 1936 Summer Olympic games were underway. "How marvelous that the Negroes won everything important at the Olympic games," John mused. Hitler's "master-race" Aryans were proving to be human, after all.

Following a quick visit to Yugoslavia, John arrived in Vienna on September 5. It was as if he was "home" again. He met Marcel Fodor at the Café Imperial, which was still a favorite haunt. They had coffee and talked a long while. Later they dined, and John was delighted when the waiters at the Grand Bar made a great fuss over him and promptly brought him platefuls of delicious *cerbabcici*, the small beef sausages that he so adored. John also had dinner with Bob Best at the Café Louvre. Best was now more enthusiastic than ever about the fascist tide that was engulfing Europe. "Best is one of the most complex—and attractive—characters I know," John noted, "violent, portentous, gentle, gullible, shrewd, all together."[21]

Walking alone through the streets of the Austrian capital, John revisited many of the people and places that had become so much a part of his memory. Somehow, he sensed that it would be a very long time before he would see Vienna again. The thought saddened him. "My God, I love this city," he mused in his diary.[22]

Back in London a week later, John and Frances made final preparations for their move to New York. John bought some new suits from his favorite tailor and wrapped up his personal business. Then there tearful good-byes to be said at a big farewell party thrown for them by Rebecca West, Jamie Hamilton, and other friends. Two days later, on September 23, John, Frances, and Johnny, Jr., caught the evening train out of Waterloo Station. Early the next morning, they sailed for New York on board the SS *Manhattan*.

Johnny, Paris-born and now six years old, was bubbling with excitement at the thought of living in New York. As their ship steamed out of Southampton harbor, he and Frances counted the stars on the Stars and Stripes flapping in the breeze at the ship's stern. John stood silently at the rail smoking as he reflected on the circuitous route that his life had taken. It was almost twelve years since the day he had left Chicago in search of fame and fortune. Now, he was bidding Europe good-bye; older and wiser, and in many ways sadder, he was going home to start all over again.

CHAPTER TWENTY

The SS *Manhattan* arrived at New York's West Twentieth Street pier shortly after eight o'clock on the morning of October 1, 1936.[1] On the pier that cool, overcast morning were John's agent, several friends, and a crowd of reporters and photographers eager to interview the author of *Inside Europe*. An initial North American press run of 5,000 copies had sold out quickly, and the book was already into a third printing. This caught everyone by surprise. "We figured that *Inside Europe* ought to sell just about 5,000 copies," Cass Canfield confided years later to an interviewer from *Time*. "That way, we'd have paid off our part of the advance and made a fairly decent profit."[2]

The timing of the book's American publication had been perfect. The ever-quickening pace of events in Europe sparked a surge of interest, and as had been the case in England, sales of the book were spurred by the excellent reviews. John's old friend Raymond Swing, writing in *The Nation*, pointed out that *Inside Europe* filled a real need at a time when America was reawakening from its self-imposed isolationism. "The vigor and almost impudent candor of this book mark it as distinctly American," Swing observed. "I cannot imagine a man of any other nationality writing it."[3]

Lewis Gannett of the *New York Herald Tribune*, echoed Swing, praising *Inside Europe* as "the liveliest, best-informed picture of Europe's chaotic politics that has come my way in years."[4]

Boosted by such plaudits and by its eventual selection as a Book of the Month Club alternate (March-April 1939), sales of *Inside Europe* soared, eventually topping the half million mark in the United States and England. This was phenomenal in an era when the sale of 100,000 copies of any book was still rare. All totaled, *Inside Europe* was published in seventeen languages, including a Dutch-produced German edition that was banned by the Nazis. These foreign sales amounted to at least another 100,000 copies; the exact numbers are uncertain. In 1936, international copyright laws were so lax that authors frequently did not receive the royalties due to them. That reality became a source of bittersweet amusement to John, particularly after he met some of the editors and translators who had produced pirated editions of his books.

But none of this much concerned John during his first few weeks in New York. He and Frances were busy getting resettled. Johnny stayed with Dorothy Thompson and Sinclair Lewis at their winter home at Bronxville, New York, while his parents searched for a suitable house in the country, within commuting distance of Manhattan. They found just what they were looking for at Chestnut Hill, Connecticut, a one-hour drive north of the city.

Frances was delighted. In her mind, this homecoming was a chance for a fresh start. Feeling intellectually revitalized, she plunged into work on her book about empires—the same one she had been working on for two years. Meanwhile, John resumed work on his novel about Vienna, and on his London diary project. Progress was slow because try as he might, he could not get down to work.

John was seized by a frustrating restlessness as he grappled with a host of problems, most of which were financial. The move home had been costly, and he was in debt. In mid-1937, in an effort to force himself to save, he began diverting some of his book royalties to pay for Harper & Brothers common stock. But while this promised a measure of long-term financial security, it did nothing to ease his short-term money woes. With that in mind, John began writing free-lance magazine articles about the subject that he knew best: European affairs, and his agent had sold a short story entitled "The Ambassador's Wife," to *Collier's* magazine for $750.

Raymond Swing and Whit Burnett, both of whom lived in nearby Westport, Connecticut, provided another diversion. They began dropping by on Sunday evenings to drink beer, and to teach John to play poker. He embraced both pastimes. "To land at John's is to encounter a great man at his work," Burnett mused in his 1939 memoir, *The Literary Life and the Hell with It.* "He is such a great man with such a charitable spirit that he never minds who encounters him at his work. He immediately stops it."[5]

All of this activity diverted John from work on the revised, updated American edition of *Inside Europe*. Altogether, six more editions of the book would be published over the next four years. The second edition, on sale in October 1936, was only slightly revised, while entire chapters were added to the third edition, which was published in mid-1937. John then reworked the manuscript completely for an October 1938 "Peace (Munich) Edition," and again for two 1940 "War Editions," and an illustrated edition. In the process, the original 180,000-word book grew by almost one-third. Cass Canfield, in an effort to spur sales of each successive edition, adopted an idea from the automakers. He offered buyers a fifty-cent rebate on trade-ins.

John was delighted by the longevity of *Inside Europe*. But he admitted that at times he had found himself "cringing with embarrassment at the multitude of verbal infelicities it contains—youthful overuse of exclamation points, clauses separated by commas instead of semi-colons, use of slang and journalese, too much quotation, slipshod paragraphing, and plain bad usage."[6] If others shared his evaluation it was not apparent.

Inside Europe won the Friends of American Writers Award for 1936, and sales which had initially been slow were now brisk. As a result, John was much in demand for promotional appearances, which he quickly found were more enjoyable than writing. On December 3, 1936, he appeared as a guest on Rudy Vallee's popular

Thursday evening network radio show. He talked about *Inside Europe*, and about developments in England, where events were about to take a startling turn.

Just one week later, on December 11, 1936, Edward VIII shocked the world by abdicating his throne to marry Wallis Warfield Simpson. John expressed his dismay in an article for *The Nation* (December 19) entitled "Notes on the Simpson Crisis." He lamented the King's decision as "an imperial as well as a personal tragedy." It had been instigated, he said, by Tory Prime Minister Stanley Baldwin, spurred on by his wife, and by sensational media coverage of the royal family.

The abdication crisis served John as a reminder of why he had been so ready to leave Europe that fall. Shortly after his return to the United States, he had conducted a brief, introspective "interview" with himself. It is unclear whether he wrote the unpublished article for public consumption, or merely as a bit of private fun.

In the article entitled "Myself and Europe," John reiterated how tired he had become of the workaday grind of running a newspaper bureau. Then, in response to the "interviewer's" question, he explained why he had returned to America after a dozen years abroad. Yes, he said, he would miss the genteel pleasures of old world life, and the excitement of having a ringside seat as history was made. He confided, too, that he would probably be ready "in a month or so, to take the next boat back."

Nevertheless, there were elements to life in Europe that John said he would not miss—what he termed the "spiritual niggardliness" of Europeans in political matters, for one. "I am grossly tired of the quarrelsomeness of European nationalism," he said. "Things may be bad in America, but you don't have the constant threat of Ohio, say, mobilizing against Illinois. Europe has not learned politically, to be a continent."

Politics, poverty, and propaganda, he argued, were at the root of Europe's troubles; sadly, the main impetus for peace was the high cost of modern war in dollars and cents. John felt that the Versailles Treaty, which had officially ended the First World War by dividing Europe along ethnic lines, had eased some of the traditional tensions. "Crude seizures of territory, in the manner of previous centuries, are very improbable."

Political developments in Europe were happening so quickly

that John had already lost touch. Just how misguided his analysis was would soon become apparent.

In a display of his old self-discipline, John finally succeeded in establishing a working routine. Doing so, he now devoted his attention to a Vienna novel about the events surrounding a 1931 financial scandal and crisis that had brought down the Credit Anstalt, the bank run by the wealthy Rothschild family. This was the same book John had already worked at for more than five years. By April 1937, he had written 250 pages, and still the story seemed to go nowhere. Cass Canfield urged John to hurry and finish the book. He had mixed motives for doing so; Canfield was eager to have any book by John Gunther on sale while *Inside Europe* was still selling briskly, and he wanted John to tackle a book about Asia. The thinking was that it would be called *Outside Orient* or *Outside Asia*, because John was a stranger to that area of the world and, therefore, he could not be "inside," as he had been in Europe.

But as yet John was having none of it. He insisted on finishing the novel first, and spent the summer of 1937 working on it. As he did so, his enthusiasm for the London diary project had waned, as did his bank account. Bernice Baumgarten sold portions of the manuscript to *Atlantic* magazine, where they appeared as a two-part series in the April and May issues.

It was mid-September when John sent Canfield a draft of the as-yet-unnamed Vienna novel. In a September 27 letter, John explained that he and Frances had decided to move back into Manhattan from Chestnut Hill, prior to leaving on an extended research trip for the Asia book. John instructed Canfield to follow the punctuation in his novel manuscript "exactly," and to see to it that copies were dispatched to various friends and colleagues for comment, among them Raymond G. Swing, Clifton Fadiman, William Shirer, Dorothy Thompson, and newspaper columnist Walter Duranty. "By the way," he added, "mention in the novel blurb, by all means, that I am a *novelist* by profession (not a beginner), have written several novels, but please do not give them titles."[7]

John posted a second copy of the manuscript to Hamish

Hamilton in London with a covering letter in which he dealt with the possibility of libel actions. His experiences in revising the British edition of *Inside Europe* to satisfy Hamilton's eagle-eyed lawyers were still fresh in his mind. "The hero and heroine (of the novel) are composites, not so much Frances and me as a lot of people will think," John assured Hamilton.[8]

John and Cass Canfield discussed possible titles for the novel at a *bon voyage* party, which friends threw in late October at the Gunther apartment on West 119th Street. When John rejected the titles "Red Danube" and "Ring Around Vienna," Canfield suggested "Lived on Earth." The matter was still unresolved when John and Frances sailed for the Middle East the last week in October, leaving Johnny in the care of a nanny and John's sister, Jean.

John departed armed with a bundle of letters of introduction and a list of contacts suggested by friends and colleagues. His plan was to visit as many of Asia's thirty countries as possible, and to learn as much about them as he could in a maximum of eight months of travel. Doing so was an expensive proposition. Even in 1937, with the world still struggling to escape the Great Depression, this kind of extended, pan-Asiatic odyssey was daunting. A first-class return ticket from New York to London on a ship such as the *Queen Mary* cost about 500 American dollars; at the time, an average factory worker only made about $20 a week.

Complicating matters was the fact that at this point in his career, John got no expense money from publishers, although Canfield and Hamilton allowed him generous advances on his royalty payments. Prior to leaving for Asia, he drew a total of $9,000 against the anticipated sales of planned books; $4,000 of that came from Harper & Brothers and $3,500 from Hamish Hamilton on the Asia book. John also borrowed $1,250 against royalties for the unpublished Vienna novel.

The problem with these arrangements was that they amounted to mortgaging the future to pay for the present. Much of John's advance money was spent on rent, food, taxes, and other basic living expenses, before the trip even began. The remainder paid for transportation and hotels. This left scant money for food and other travel expenses.

John's only solution to this dilemma was to contract to write newspaper and magazine articles as he traveled. For that reason, prior to leaving New York, he arranged to act as a correspondent for the North American Newspaper Alliance and a several magazines, notably the *Saturday Evening Post* and *Fortune*. The grueling precedent set on the Asia trip was one that John's financial troubles grudgingly forced him to follow throughout his career. "I still remember with acute anguish days I have had to spend grinding out articles when I should have been submerging myself in the atmosphere of a situation or a community," he lamented in *A Fragment of an Autobiography*.[9]

John's financial woes could not have been far from his mind when he and Frances arrived in Egypt the second week in November. A Cairo-based English-language magazine called *The Sphinx* and the newspaper *Egyptian Mail* sent reporters to interview John at the Continental-Savoy Hotel, where he and Frances were staying.[10] John was now seeing for himself the extent of the international fame *Inside Europe* had brought him. Even more importantly, he was discovering how his reputation now preceded him. Doors that once would have been closed were suddenly open; heads of state, prominent politicians, and generals were eager to grant him interviews.

It had been almost eight years since John had last visited the Middle East as a roving correspondent. This time around, he was determined to see the sights as well as to tend to business. John and Frances, who had never been to the region, shopped at the Cairo bazaar. Then they took a friend with them on a camel ride around the pyramids. The Arab drivers, pandering to American tourists, had nicknamed two of the beasts "Telephone Company" and "Baby New York City." Frances mailed Johnny a photo postcard dated November 11, 1937, showing the trio mounted on these "distinguished" camels, with the pyramids as a backdrop. "That is really Papa in the middle," she wrote. "I am on the right and a friend, Mrs. Eloni, is on the left. They are real live camels, and that is a real live Pyramid. It is about as tall as a 30-story skyscraper—but it is not so useful. All our love and kisses. Your loving Mutti and Papa."[11]

From Egypt, John and Frances traveled to Palestine. They saved time by flying from Cairo to Jerusalem. The trip, sixteen hours by train, was just two hours by air. Commercial air travel was still a novelty, and Frances described the flight in an amusing letter to Johnny. She noted how dismayed she and John had been upon arriving at Cairo Airport, and seeing the tiny de Havilland airplane in which they were about to fly. John wondered aloud if the craft was large enough to hold his 225-pound bulk, along with the pilot, Frances, four other passengers, and all their luggage. John and Frances, who were inexperienced air travelers, gripped their seats with white knuckles as the plane roared off down the runway and into a cloudless sky. Far below, Frances saw the Suez Canal looking "like a long, gray pencil in the sand." The English pilot, who had presumably flown the route many times before, read a newspaper while Frances, in the seat directly behind him, peered anxiously over his shoulder at "the speedometer."[12]

Following a touchdown in Jerusalem, the Gunthers toured the British-controlled Transjordan—where King Abdullah let John see his most treasured possession: a set of Coney Island distorting mirrors, Syria; and Iraq. In Baghdad, John hired a car for the drive to Tehran, the Iranian capital. The exhausting journey along mountain dirt roads took two long, dusty days and three sleepless nights. En route, they passed mud huts and ancient villages unchanged since biblical times. "They are desolate with squalor and poverty," John wrote, "but the petrol pump has become the center of the community."[13]

This was the reality of Iran, a land of contrasts. Its vain, iron-willed ruler, Reza Shah Pahlevi ("shah" being Persian for the word king), was an absolute ruler, who dragged his country into the modern age. By 1941, when after sixteen years on the throne he abdicated in favor of his son, he had angered conservatives with social and economic reforms which curbed the powers of the religious courts. He introduced co-education into the country's schools, raised the minimum legal marrying age for females from nine to fifteen, and allowed women to shed their veils when in parts of the city. He had also used petro-dollars to build railways, roads, and modern buildings. In 1937, central Tehran was dominated by a magnificent new train station and an opera house, even though the city as yet had neither rail links, nor an opera company.

Arriving in Tehran, John and Frances were relieved to discover that the city's main throughfares were paved. Their Arab driver explained that the shah had forbidden camels on Tehran's new streets, meaning that all caravans had to camp outside the city gates while the hawkers proceeded on foot to the central marketplace. This had caused much resentment. Curious whether such fiats caused similar problems elsewhere, the driver asked, "Have you got rid of the camels yet in Paris and New York?"[14]

The shah was one of the few heads of state with whom John failed to secure an interview during his Asia trip. He was a ruler who did not tolerate any kind of criticism; his diplomats around the world were under standing orders to send to Tehran copies of all printed references to the shah. Once, when a French newspaper made a disrespectful joke, the shah recalled his ambassador to Paris and severed diplomatic relations.

John used information from local sources (which he prudently did not identify), to write a candid portrait of the shah. In light of the subsequent history of that troubled land, some of his 1937 observations proved to be intriguing, especially his analysis of the Iranian leader's relationship with his subjects. "They are mostly Muslims of the Shia variety, fanatically backward. All through his career, the Shah has had to fight the mullahs, priests." That battle was one the shah's son continued, and ultimately lost, with disastrous consequences for Iran—and the rest of the world.

John and Frances were back in Jerusalem by December 3, 1937, for dinner at Government House with Sir Arthur Wauchope, the British High Commissioner. Four days later, on their last day in the Middle East, they dined with Zionist leader Chaim Weizmann, whom John had met two years earlier in London.

Weizmann was living at the town of Rehovoth, outside Tel Aviv. His home, filled with exquisite Ming porcelain and surrounded by lush citrus groves, was near the Daniel Sieff Research Laboratory, a facility he'd set up to conduct crop experiments. John and Frances toured the operation, then had lunch with Weizmann and his wife, Vera.

In view of their family backgrounds, Weizmann, destined to become the first president of the Republic of Israel in 1949, was witty, gregarious, and charming. Like John, he appreciated the finer things in life, and so the two men got along well, despite their twenty-seven-year age difference.

It was ironic that John, a gentile, was more sympathetic toward the Zionist cause than was Frances, who was Jewish. The Gunthers often argued politics during the early years of their marriage, with the Middle East situation being a regular topic. John summarized his own feelings in a June 1930 article for *Harper's* magazine entitled "The Realities of Zionism." While he was sympathetic to the cause, he concluded that while "Zionism is an emotional necessity to certain Jews . . . it is an economic and political failure."[16]

A decade later, John's views had evolved. He had considerable sympathy for the cause of a Jewish homeland, and did what he could to further it. Alexander Rafaeli, who headed the Paris office of the Irgun Zvai Leumi (known popularly as the Irgun), the Jewish underground, in 1938-39 recalls that John referred to him a prominent journalist who had some ideas about organizing the Jewish underground in Nazi Europe. John helped in other ways, too.

While he was reluctant to be publicly associated with lobby efforts organized in the U.S. in the 1940s by the Irgun, for fear of the effect on his journalism career, John was ready to provide strong moral support. Says Rafaeli, "He was always behind us, arranging contacts and meetings, and introducing us to important figures."[17]

When Rafaeli, now a Jersualem doctor, was dispatched to America in 1940, to rally support for the Jewish cause, John made some quiet representations on his behalf. "Gunther's experience and information as a man who knew well foreign governments and foreign lands was quite important for us," says Rafaeli.

John arranged meetings for him with an official of the War Information Office (or the Office of Strategic Services, he cannot recall which) who was receptive to Irgun plans to establish a radio station to broadcast to the Jews in Europe via a transmitter in London.

In 1940, Frances was still lukewarm to the Irgun's cause, and to the idea of a Jewish state. She favored an ethnically-mixed Palestine, one where Jews and Arabs would co-exist in peace. That is a theme that comes across forcefully in her writings from this period. Typical is a nine-page poem called "Message to Islam," which was found among her papers when she died in 1964. Written in a mixture of English, Hebrew, and Arabic, the unpublished poem is an impassioned plea for harmony in a anguished land. It concludes, "Come, in the name of the merciful and compassionate god of all mankind: let us stand united in friendship, let us live united in peace."[18]

Such quixotic sentiments did not sit well with Frances' brother, Bernie, who was a staunch Zionist. Nor were they well received when voiced to Weizmann, David Ben-Gurion, Moshe Shertok, and other Jewish leaders whom the Gunthers met in Palestine.

John breathed a sigh of relief when he left behind the Middle East and all of its problems. He and Frances sailed on December 9, 1937, out of Port Said, Egypt, aboard the SS *Conte Verde*. Ahead of them was India, a vast subcontinent in the throes of turmoil.

Also ahead of them was a chance encounter with the charismatic nationalist leader Jawaharlal Nehru, an encounter that would add fuel to the fires of the already troubled marriage of John and Frances Gunther.

CHAPTER TWENTY-ONE

During the voyage to India, John was busy reading page proofs for his new novel, now called *Ring Around Vienna*; Canfield had airmailed the pages to Jerusalem. John explained his tardiness in returning the proofs by claiming that he had been in Iran when they arrived. In truth, he was unhappy with the book, and was rewriting portions of it. "You will agree, I think, that all of the changes I have made, and there are many, improve not only the texture and free flow of the narrative, but they fill out several important gaps," he told Canfield in a December 14 letter, written while he was at sea.[1]

The rewriting was difficult because of the competition for John's attentions during the voyage. The mix of people traveling first class was intriguing. Among the passengers with whom the Gunthers became friends was a young Indian Maharijie (the brother of the

Maharajah) from the principality of Mysore, in southern India. Would John and Frances, he inquired, honor him with their presence as guests at his palace?

The Maharijie was met at the Bombay wharf by servants, who whisked him away in a carriage pulled by a team of white bulls. Before bidding him good-bye, the Gunthers agreed to visit Mysore after Christmas. They remained in Bombay for now. John had an appointment to interview the Aga Khan. The spiritual leader of ten million Khoja Muslims in India, and the Middle East, was one of the world's wealthiest men. John described him as the "bon-vivant of several continents."[2] The rotund holy man delighted in his stable of racing horses and in his love of good food and drink. Asked once by a follower about his fondness for alcohol, which is strictly forbidden to most orthodox Moslems, he reportedly replied, "Ah, you forget that wine turns to water as soon as it touches my mouth."[3]

Frances described their luncheon with the Aga Khan in a letter to Johnny. She noted that their host had eaten so much "that Papa [John] said 'compared to him, I eat like a canary bird.'"[4]

The Gunthers spent a quiet Christmas 1937 at their Bombay hotel where they fashioned a tiny paper Christmas tree, decorated their room with pictures of snowy scenes, and exchanged gifts. Frances gave John an Indian silk dressing gown, a tie, and handkerchief. John gave her a pair of bracelets decorated with rubies and white sapphires.[5] He was soothing the disappointment Frances had suffered on a pre-Christmas jewelry shopping expedition. At one shop in which she had gone searching for rubies, Frances noticed the gems were not of prime quality.

"What's happened to all of the good rubies?" she asked the shopkeeper.

"Oh, we've put them away," came the reply. "We're saving them because Barbara Hutton (the Woolworth's department store heiress) is coming soon."[6]

A few days after Christmas, John and Frances departed on the 500-mile train ride from Bombay to the Maharajie's home at Bangalore. The trip, a grueling twenty-seven hours, was an eye-opening experience. Indian trains were not the sleek, fast models of efficiency that John was accustomed to in Europe. They were slow, crowded, and hot, even for first-class passengers. There were no interior corridors. Thus, to get to the dining car it was necessary to wait until the train stopped, then jump down, and run along the tracks. Likewise, there were no sleeping cars. John and Frances carried their own blankets on the trip, and they hired native porters to make up their beds each night. Happily, accommodations at the Maharijie's palace were more comfortable. Their host provided them with a lavish suite of five rooms for their private use, and servants to tend to their every whim.

Bangalore, nestled in the Eastern Ghat Mountains of southern India, is blessed with hot, dry days, and cool nights, and John and Frances found this a relief after sweltering, frenetic Bombay. Feeling rejuvenated, they asked their host for a car and driver for an excursion to Mysore, the state capital. Here they were given a guided tour by the Maharajah's British-born private secretary, who recommended that they visit Hindupor, in the neighboring state of Pradesh. Upon doing so, they paid a long-haired little man, who lived in a jungle hut, to show them some wildlife. They saw a sambar (a large Indian deer), exotic birds and monkeys, but no tigers. Frances was not surprised. She wrote to Johnny, Jr., that part of the "jungle" was not dense or lush. "It looked very much like Connecticut," she said.[7]

Upon his return to Bombay in early January, John found a long letter from Cass Canfield awaiting him. There was good news, and bad news. The good news was that the revised edition of *Inside Europe* was selling briskly in the United States—at a rate of more than 1,000 copies per week. The bad news was that although everything was ready for an April 6 publication in New York of *Ring Around Vienna*, both the Book of the Month Club and the Literary Guild had declined to recommend the novel to members. And what's more, Canfield reported that Hamish Hamilton was having second thoughts about publishing the book in England. Lawyers there had advised against it. Canfield admitted that he, too, was "considerably disturbed" about the danger of a libel suit. "Our lawyers, who are most reasonable people, point out that the story is libelous from beginning to end from a technical point of view," he said.[8]

John had based characters on people he had known in Vienna.

One of them was Robert Best, the pro-Nazi, United Press correspondent; another was Best's lover, a neurotic, aging German baroness with a drug addiction and a malevolent disposition.

A few days after receiving that disturbing letter, John got a postcard from Canfield, informing him that a lewd phrase uttered by a prostitute character in the novel had been deleted, at the urging of lawyers.[9] John was livid. He dashed off an uncharacteristically harsh letter telling both Canfield and Hamilton that he refused to make or allow any further cuts to the novel.

Hamilton responded with a conciliatory letter in which he said he had taken the liberty of sending a copy of the proofs to Marcel Fodor in Vienna to get his comments. Nonetheless, he was blunt in saying that he had spent many hours "reading and re-reading every sentence with an eye on the libel possibilities," and after doing so had concluded that "fairly drastic alterations" were needed. Hamilton, sensitive to John's frustrations, allowed that at the time of his previous letter John had "probably (been) tired out . . . and fed-up with the whole thing." But he appealed to John's common sense as well, and offered a veiled reminder of his precarious financial position. "From your point of view," Hamilton said, "it would be tragic to throw away the result of several years work."[10]

Enclosed in the package Hamilton sent was another set of uncorrected galley proofs with all "potentially libelous portions" marked. Hamilton suggested John rewrite those parts of the novel, removing the baroness character, and deleting all references to the Best character "living in sin" or being tainted with even a hint of involvement in the Credit Anstalt banking scandal.

Hamilton's letter did nothing to soothe John's wounded ego. He was having none of rewriting the novel. John flatly refused to make further cuts. He was content to leave the whole matter in the hands of Fodor, whom he trusted and respected. If Marcel Fodor felt that publication of *Ring Around Vienna* would lead to legal action by Best or his lover, John said that he was willing to let the book sit until he returned home and had time to rewrite it properly. Having made that decision, John and Frances left on a nine-day trip to the Punjab and the North West Frontier.

If John hoped that in traveling he would escape his troubles, he was mistaken. The trip north gave fresh impetus to smoldering emotions which for ten years had burned away at the fabric of his marriage to Frances. Ironically, John confided to his friend

Leonora Hornblow many years later that he felt relations between himself and Frances were never closer than while they were traveling in Asia. "He felt that was the only time they ever got along really well," Hornblow recalls.[12]

Frances apparently did not share those sentiments. True, she and John had temporarily reconciled after Vienna, where their spiteful mutual infidelities had strained the marriage to the breaking point. However, Frances was still groping for an elusive *something* that she felt John was unwilling—or incapable—of giving her. She found what she thought she was seeking in the person of the romantic, strikingly handsome Indian dissident named Jawaharlal Nehru.

Born in Allahbad on November 14, 1889, the future prime minister of India was a member of one of the country's most distinguished families. His great-grandfather and grandfather had held posts under India's last Mogul emperor. His uncle was the Dewan (prime minister) of one of the small native states. Perpetuating the family's tradition of success, in the early decades of this century Nehru's father, Motilal, had been one of India's best-known lawyers. As John explained, "When one says that [Nehru] is a Kashmiri Brahman and the son of Motilal Nehru, it is as if one were to say that a man was a Boston Cabot or Lowell whose father was like Mr. Justice Holmes. He comes not only from the bluest blood in India, with a tremendous pride of race and heritage, but of a family with a deep tradition of public service and utility to the community."[13]

Nehru had an English tutor from his earliest youth; in 1905, at age sixteen, he went off to England, where he attended Harrow and Cambridge and read for the bar. A shy, introspective young man, he burned with inner passions that found their outlet in India's fight for independence from England. In 1912, Nehru returned home, where he fell under the spell of Mohandas Karamchand Ghandi, twenty years his elder and already one of the leading figures of the Indian nationalist movement. Nehru drifted into socialism and revolutionary extremism. By 1938, he had already been sentenced to seven prison terms totaling more than fourteen years. Several of these sentences were commuted, but Nehru still spent more than nine years behind bars. These wasted years were filled with agony. While he was in jail, his wife Kamala was in declining health. In 1936, she died. Nehru, still just forty-seven, was left alone to care for their daughter, Indira. (Two years after her father's 1964 death, she followed in his footsteps, and became prime minister of India.)

At five-feet-seven, Nehru moved with a dancer's grace. Courtly in his bearing and speech, he cut an impressive figure. Women of all races, married and single, young and old alike, found him irresistible. As B.N. Pandy, one of his biographers, has noted, "Women were instantly drawn to (Nehru) by the image he effortlessly projected of a persecuted man, loved by all but understood by none, deprived of all worldly blessings, and dedicated to fighting nobly for a just cause." According to Pandy, Nehru "had a clear preference for tender and romantic relationships with married women who, by virtue of their distinguished position, came in close contact with him."[14] His romances with Edwina Mountbatten and Madame Chiang Kai-shek have been widely discussed. Considerably less has come to light about Nehru's relationship with Frances Gunther, one of the first of the wives of prominent foreigners with whom he became involved.

John and Frances had met Nehru during their years in London. In 1938, they chanced to encounter him once again at Juhu, while attending an audience with Mahatma Gandhi. John, like William Shirer and Jimmy Sheean, was fascinated by the bespectacled, rubbery little man who was challenging the mighty British Empire by the sheer force of his will. "Mr. Gandhi, who is an incredible combination of Jesus Christ, Tammany Hall, and your father, is the greatest Indian since Buddha," John wrote. "This man, who is at once a saint and a politician, a prophet, and a superb opportunist, defies ordinary categories."[15]

John was astounded to find that Gandhi was a multidimensional character, anything but the single-minded "fakir," as Winston Churchill had labeled him. The saintly little man in the loincloth had a mischievous, yet gentle sense of humor, which John saw one day as they ate lunch together. Conversation got around to the subject of the Aga Khan. John mentioned to Gandhi how in their recent meeting the Aga Khan had boasted of being the "only man in the world who could eat mangoes out of season."

"Did he really say that?" Gandhi chuckled. When John nodded, Gandhi waved to one of his aides who brought him a fresh mango.

"I have a refrigerator," said Gandhi, giggling with boyish delight.[16]

Although he admired Gandhi, John was at a loss to understand the little man's mass appeal. Hitler, Mussolini, or Stalin, he could comprehend; Gandhi was a different matter. He did not fit the Stekel theory about political leaders as patriarchs. A mystic and a man of seemingly endless contradictions, Gandhi defied easy categorization. All that John could decide about him was that, "Mr. Gandhi adds up to a great deal."[17]

Like most westerners, John and Frances found it easier to relate to Gandhi's associate Nehru, who was western-educated, well-read, and refined. *Inside Europe* had found a wide audience in India, and even Nehru, only recently released from prison, had heard of the book. When John spoke on January 6, 1938, to a national radio audience about the deteriorating European situation, Nehru was asked to introduce him. It was the Indian leader's first time on radio, John noted.

The two men talked following the lecture. When Nehru learned that Frances was scheduled to give a speech a few days later. He readily agreed when asked to introduce her. By chance, John and Frances had planned their visit to the North West Frontier the third week in January, the same time that Nehru was traveling to the area. He volunteered to act as their guide for a few days. Nehru, who dismissed most Americans as obvious and superficial, found John and Frances agreeable company, and vice versa. He also realized that John was someone who could be a valuable ally in the fight to promote the Indian nationalist cause in America and England. When Nehru offered to provide John with background notes on Indian personalities and politics, John accepted eagerly.

Having grown impatient with the irritating, endless debate over his novel, John sought refuge in northern India. He was sure that no one from New York or London would be able to reach him there. John went off, leaving Frances in the company of Nehru. The relationship between the two, which had begun in Bombay, continued during John's absence. It is not clear whether the passions between Frances and Nehru that had stirred in Bombay, and which now flourished during John's absence was physical, although that seems likely, for Nehru was irresistibly fascinating to many women. Frances began writing him passionate love poems, and showering him with letters.

John certainly knew about her infatuation—and may even have condoned it. John assumed that Frances had fallen in love with an ideal, not a man. Both he and Frances had indulged in affairs during the course of their troubled marriage; there was no reason to believe this was not just another passing fancy, likely to fade as quickly as it had blossomed. If it did not, it was meant to be.

Back in Bombay on January 27, John read the latest mail from Canfield and Hamilton. One letter had actually reached him in northern India. While flying over the Khyber Pass, one of the plane's crew had rummaged in a Royal mail bag, and found an envelope with his name on it. It was from Cass Canfield.

John responded to it with a long, baleful letter in which he admitted that Frances shared the fears of Hamilton's lawyers that the Baroness would sue over the novel. Still, he stubbornly reiterated his faith in the book. And he remained adamant: there would be no more cuts. "I am, frankly, so fed up with this whole goddamned [sic] business as to be, at times, willing for the novel to be unpublished," he wrote. "I simply cannot take on the task of rewriting it to suit Hamilton's neurotic lawyers . . . I don't give a damn whether you publish it or not."[18]

John was preoccupied with the matter for several days. It played upon his mind during a January 31 visit with the viceroy, the Marquess of Linlithgow, who cast aside protocol to invite the Gunthers to spend a night at the Viceregal palace. It preoccupied him, too, during a trip to Jaipur, where the Maharajah of Rajasthan staged an elephant fight in his honor. "[The elephants] do not hurt each other, I am glad to say," Frances was quick to point out in a letter to Johnny.[19]

The Gunthers ended the Indian portion of their trip on February 9 with lunch at Government House with His Excellency and Lady Brabourne. Then they departed by plane for brief stopovers in Burma, Malaya, and Bangkok. They arrived in steamy Singapore on the evening of February 20, after an exhausting twelve-hour flight. Awaiting them were a conciliatory letter from Hamish Hamilton[20] as well as a letter from Marcel Fodor warning John that he felt a libel action was a certainty if *Ring Around Vienna* was published.

John wrote Hamilton another long letter, in which he said that he accepted Fodor's advice, but he would not—indeed, *could* not—rewrite the novel until he returned home. "I can't tell you how inexpressibly fed up I am with all these letters and cables," he wrote, "I must explicitly ask that you and Harper follow me in this and defer publication until I return."[21]

Canfield grudgingly accepted that decision. He was more concerned with recouping the money he had invested in the Asia book, since he had already wired John another advance in India, and a further $4,000 when John ran out once again in Java.

Next stop on the grand tour was the Philippines. While en route there by ship, John and Frances met the president of the Manila telephone company, who like many other people on board had read *Inside Europe*. The man arranged for a free, long-distance call to Johnny in New York, half a world away. Such a call was still a rarity, and John and Frances marveled at the clarity of the line.

The conversation with New York reminded them that they had already been on the road four months. Both of them were feeling homesick, weary, and drained by the tropical heat. "I have enough (notes) for about five books already," John told Hamilton in one of his letters. "It has been by far the hardest work I have ever done—meeting people, 10 or 12 hours a day, research and reading incessantly, gathering every kind of information, trying to check and classify and annotate it."[22] But the Asia trip was still a long way from complete.

John met with R.C. Wilson, the head of the United Press bureau in Manila on March 8, 1938, and interviewed General Douglas MacArthur, who at the time was serving as an advisor to the Philippine army. John was much impressed by the young American officer who met him at the door and ushered him into MacArthur's penthouse suite in the Manila Hotel. The young soldier's name was Dwight D. Eisenhower. He and John would meet again in 1943, when Ike was Supreme Commander of the Allied armies battling Hitler.

The following day John interviewed Manuel Quezon, the first president of the Commonwealth of the Philippines. The event was front page news in local newspapers. A photo in the *Manila Trib-*

une showed John sitting in Quezon's office; the two men sat smoking and chatting amicably for photographers, like visiting heads of state.[23] Quezon, who could be an "extraordinarily engaging little man," as John put it, got on well with foreign journalists, whom he courted shamelessly. Quezon—"the Beau Brummel among dictators"[24]—and his wife hosted a private dinner for the Gunthers aboard the presidential yacht. John, who was well aware that Quezon was attempting to buy his goodwill, relished the flattery all the same.

From Manila, John and Frances moved on to Hong Kong, their base for a planned two-month visit to China. They were here on March 11, 1938, that they heard news of the Nazi invasion of Austria. John spent several anxious days worrying about cherished friends in Europe. He breathed a sigh of relief only after word that Marcel Fodor and his family had been rescued by Jimmy Sheean in a breakneck drive from Vienna to Prague just hours ahead of Hitler's advancing armies. The Fodors were brought to the United States shortly thereafter by friends, and housed temporarily at Twin Farms, the Vermont home of Dorothy Thompson and Sinclair Lewis. They resettled later in Chicago, where John and Dorothy helped to finance a lecturer's chair for Fodor at Lewis Institute, (now part of the Illinois Institute of Technology.)

Cass Canfield, sensing that events in Europe had created a perfect backdrop for publication of *Ring Around Vienna*, cabled John in an effort to convince him to pause in Hong Kong long enough to rewrite the book. But John refused. He was still adamant. He had "other plans" that he would not change. They included a trip to the cities of Shanghai and Hankow the first two weeks of April.

At the time, Hankow was under ferocious attack by the invading Japanese, and John and Frances witnessed an air raid from the safety of the roof of the American consulate. John also scored a journalistic coup when he interviewed the leader of China's Kuomintang nationalist forces. Generalissimo Chiang Kai-shek, a brusque, humorless man, seldom met with foreign journalists.

Born in 1887 in Chekiang province, near Shanghai, Chiang had gone to Japan to study as a young man. It was here that he came under the influence of Dr. Sun Yat-sen, the Chinese intellectual who in 1911 had founded the nationalist People's Revolutionary Party (popularly known as the Kuomintang.) Following Sun Yat-sen's death in 1925, Chiang emerged as his successor. It was Chiang who led the nationalist armies which routed the warlords and reunited China.

On December 1, 1927, with political gain in mind, Chiang had wed for the second time in his life. His bride, Soong Mei-ling, was the youngest of the three daughters of one of China's most influential families. Charlie Soong, the family patriarch, had made his fortune on returning home from the United States by selling Bibles door-to-door. All three Soong sisters were beautiful, intelligent, and American educated. All married wisely. Ai-ling, the eldest, wed Dr. H.H. Kung, a direct descendant of Confucius, who during the 1930s, was the prime minister of China. Ching-ling, the second eldest, married Sun Yat-sen—a happenstance that was to have a profound impact on thirty years of postwar Sino-American relations.

It happened that Emily Hahn, to whom John had been so close during his youth in Chicago, became the China correspondent for the *New Yorker* magazine in 1935. When she fell in love with Sinmay Zau, a Chinese intellectual and nationalist, she also became friends with many of the key figures in the Chinese nationalist movement, among them the three Soong sisters. In 1938, when John arrived in China, he found Emily teaching English in Shanghai. They had a joyful reunion, and she organized a dinner party for him. It was at this party that John met his Chinese "publisher, editor, agent, and translator."

Until that moment, John had no idea these people even existed. These were, he instantly realized, the pirates who had produced Chinese and English bootleg editions of *Inside Europe*, which sold in the Far East for twenty cents each, rather than the five dollars the genuine article fetched. The humor of the situation was not lost on John, who years later remembered the evening's conversation as pleasant and the food excellent. "Of course not one word was uttered by them [the pirates] in regard to rights, contract, payment of royalties, or the like," John recalled in *A Fragment of Autobiography*, "nor was I so crude or commercial-minded as to bring up such indelicate topics."[25]

Having these local "contacts" paid off in another way, however.

One of the people he met at Emily Hahn's dinner party arranged the interview with the reclusive Chiang Kai-shek. It helped, too, that Madame Chiang had read *Inside Europe* and suggested that her husband agree to grant John an interview. Emily Hahn points out that Chiang cared little for the foreign press. "He was first and last a military man," she says.[26]

The only pre-condition to the interview was that John had to submit in advance a list of questions, which were "as comprehensive and pungent" as he dared to make them. The April 6 interview, which John recounted in a lengthy article he wrote for the next day's *New York Times*, took place on the Chiang's home at Wuchang, across the Yangtse River from Hankow. Madame Chiang acted as interpreter and served tea for John, Frances, and Chiang's aides W.H. Donald, who was his Australian advisor, and for Hollington K. Tong, his American-educated chief of information.[27]

John, who saw Chiang as "certainly a reformer (and) almost a missionary," described him as being of medium height, "slight, straight, wiry, with delicate features" and restless dark gray eyes. The generalissimo handed John written answers to each of his dozen questions. He then turned the tables, and began quizzing his interviewer. Chiang was a man who got to the point quickly; he asked John for a summary of the "European situation" in "one or two sentences."

Unlike Nehru and Quezon, whom John had genuinely admired, there was little rapport between he and Chiang. Yet when a severe attack of asthma, landed him in a Hankow hospital, Chiang visited him. The fact that Chinese forces had defeated the invading Japanese in a major battle near Taierschwang that very week no doubt contributed to the generalissimo's sociability; he was eager for news of the victory to reach the west. Chiang offered John and Frances the use of his private plane, a shiny Douglas with an American pilot. They declined, however, knowing that the Japanese air force were gunning for the aircraft.

Frances related her own impressions of Chiang and his wife in a letter to "My dear Nehru," dated April 14. There was, she observed, "Methodism in his madness"—a wry reference to the fact that Chiang had converted to the Methodist religion as a condition of marrying Mei-ling Soong, whose mother's family had been Christian for 300 years—"he believes in himself: destined, the chosen one."[28]

Frances was decidedly less impressed by some of the people around Chiang. In 1938, the Kuomintang and the Chinese Communists, with Russian prompting, had formed a United Front to battle the invading Japanese; the Communist representative at Chiang's headquarters was a personable, well-spoken young man who talked freely with John about Chiang and about the muddled Chinese political situation. The western-educated son of a Mandarin (government official), that young man was Chou En-lai—Mao Tse-tung's chief aide and the future Premier of Communist China. John thought Chou "shrewd and competent . . . a good man for the job" as the Kuomintang-Communists liaison officer. Somewhat less impressed, Frances described Chou as "admirable, intelligent, honest," yet "he doesn't seem destined."[29]

The Gunthers completed their visit to China with stops in Peking and Shanghai, a teeming city of four million that was jointly administered by American, British, Italian, French, and Japanese. Shanghai was a wide-open frontier town. Sinophobia was rampant, as was evidenced by the sign in a Shanghai park that read: "NO DOGS OR CHINESE ALLOWED." The city, the center of more than half of all of China's industry and trade, was also a study in contrasts. Home to the world's finest night life,and its poshest private clubs, it was also the site of some of Asia's most wretched slums. This was a city with no taxes of any kind, leading Jimmy Sheean to observe that Shanghai was the city "par excellence" for two things: money and the fear of losing it.

It was said that work crews picked up 29,000 bodies off the streets each year. Some of these unfortunate wretches were the victims of poverty or drugs, others of racially motivated violence, many of crime. Shanghai was a city dominated by ruthless underworld gangs, particularly the notorious Green Circle, which controlled the lucrative opium trade, smuggling, extortion, and prostitution. A persistent rumor had it that the gang's leaders had even inducted Chiang Kai-shek into their inner circle. "We will be glad to leave Shanghai as we do not like it very much," Frances told her son Johnny in a letter. "It is full of foreigners who are only here to make money out of the poor Chinese . . . and full of Japanese who have beaten the Chinese and are getting ready to beat all the foreigners too."

The last stop of the Gunthers' eight-month Asian odyssey was Japan, where they saw firsthand an ancient culture marching inexorably towards a twentieth century war. John and Frances were astounded by the stark contrast between the bustling chaos of the Chinese cities they had just visited, and the orderly spaciousness of Tokyo—modern, dignified and antiseptically clean.

As a people, the Japanese were unfathomable to John, who shamelessly subscribed to all of the Western racist stereotypes of the day. In China, he had met with and come to know many of the country's political leaders. In Japan, on the other hand, his contacts with politicians and military men were limited; hence, his impressions of the Japanese were generally superficial and unfavorable, especially when he compared them with the Chinese. The Japanese were, he reported, physically short and squat, lacking in humor and fanatically zenophobic. "If you ask a Japanese to choose between spending the rest of his life on an island with either a Chinese or an Englishman, he will pick the Chinese, who will presumably become his slave," John wrote. "The Chinese confronted with a similar choice, would almost certainly pick the Englishman, who he assumed might be educated to become his equal."[31]

In John's mind, Japan was personified by the exalted, divine emperor who ruled the nation. It was forbidden for the Japanese people to look directly at or to even mention the name of Emperor Hirohito, the 124th emperor in an unbroken dynasty that traced its roots back to 600 years before the birth of Christ. On those rare occasions when Hirohito traveled, police and soldiers made sure that every window shade along the route was drawn. It was said that the royal tailor, who was not allowed to actually touch the emperor, took his measurements by eye. Similarly, court doctors were obliged to wear silk gloves during physical examinations.

Hirohito, who died in early 1988, had formally assumed the throne in 1928, and in his first decade of rule he granted just three interviews with foreign journalists. In fact, American news agencies in Tokyo had a standing offer of a $100 bonus to any correspondent who interviewed the Emperor; the money was never collected. When John's efforts likewise proved unsuccessful, he made do with information gleaned from a variety of sources, including Japanese Prime Minister Prince Fumimaro Konoye, western diplomats and correspondents, and a small number of Japanese intellectuals and dissidents. Like many westerners who visited Japan about this time, John came away from these conversations convinced that a Pacific war was imminent. Japanese expansionism, fueled by an insatiable hunger for raw materials and living room, dictated it. "The Japanese push south, west, southwest. They will sooner or later encounter, first the Russians, who sit somberly and wait, second what is left of the British Empire—which is quite a lot," warned John, once more playing the Cassandra role. "If they turn east, they may meet the United States."[32]

It was with such dark forebodings in mind that John and Frances set out for Los Angeles aboard the SS *Empress of Japan.* Following a brief stopover in Hawaii on June 10, they arrived back on American soil six days later. All together, they had traveled more than 30,000 miles, visited twenty-four of Asia's thirty countries, conducted more than 200 interviews, and John had already written dozens of newspaper and magazine articles. With him, he carried several suitcases bulging with clippings, books, and research notes. Frances carried with her baggage of a very different kind—memories of Nehru, the man with whom she had fallen in love.

CHAPTER TWENTY-TWO

Franklin D. Roosevelt sensed early in his first presidential term that Germany, Italy and Japan were "bandit nations" that America would one day have to deal with. But foreign policy did not have a high priority in the early years of the New Deal. In fact, Mrs. Roosevelt once invited foreign correspondent Anne O'Hare McCormick of the *New York Times* to dinner at the White House with the request, "I wonder if you could try to get the president more interested in foreign affairs."

With the exception of one unsuccessful attempt to secure American membership in the World Court, FDR made no effort to change the country's pacifist and isolationist mood. Thus, the transition from isolationism to interventionism was long and tortuous—especially for America's friends. British Prime Minister Neville Chamberlain voiced the cynicism that many nations felt when in 1937 he scoffed, "It is always best and safest to count on nothing from the Americans but words."[2] Chamberlain then dedicated himself to placating Hitler through a disastrous policy of appeasement.

That not everyone accepted isolationism as a basis for American foreign policy was clear. John Gunther and many other liberals sympathized with the anti-fascist Popular Front that had been forged in 1935 by the world's socialists and communists. One of the first commitments John and Frances kept after arriving home from Asia was to attend the 1938 League of American Writers' Congress, held June 4 to 6 at Carnegie Hall in New York. The civil war being fought in Spain—"a political battlefield between democracy and reaction," as poet Archibald MacLeish described it—had become the rallying cause of the liberals-left coalition.

The cavernous New York concert hall was stiflingly hot, and filled with a haze of tobacco smoke on opening night. The orchestra and all the balconies and boxes were jammed by a capacity audience of 3,500, while another thousand persons were turned away at the doors. In addition to Writers' League President Donald Ogden Stewart, the speakers that night included Ernest Hemingway, American Communist Party leader Earl Browder, Dutch leftist film director Joris Ivens (who was working with Hemingway on a film about the Spanish civil war called *The Spanish Earth*), and chairman and master of ceremonies Archibald MacLeish. All five spoke about the war in Spain.[3]

In the wake of the success of *Inside Europe*, John was among a group of prominent writers invited to sit on the stage. Before the meeting, he dined with his long-time friend Walter Duranty of the *New York Times*, Ernest Hemingway, and F. Scott Fitzgerald, now working in Hollywood as a screenwriter at Metro-Goldwyn-Mayer. John recalled that Hemingway, who was always nervous before he spoke in public, fidgeted like a schoolboy during dinner. He had no last line for his speech. Duranty did nothing to soothe Hemingway's fears when he cautioned him, "You should know that the last line of a speech is the most important." As it turned out, Hemingway ended his seven-minute talk with an eloquent reminder about the writer's duty to "write truly" about war. Duranty's own speech was more sincere than polished. Each time he wanted to emphasize a point he could only think to shout, "See!"[4]

John and Frances stayed in New York for a few days after the conference. He partied with friends at the 21 Club, the Stork Club, and various other nightspots, while she spent her days with Johnny and combed the newspapers for news of Nehru and India. During the first week of July, the family moved back to the house at Chestnut Hill. John planned to spend the summer here working on the Asia book. Before plunging in, he took time to answer the stack of mail that had accumulated during his absence. Among the correspondence was a cable from Hamish Hamilton pleading that the time was right for a revised edition of *Inside Europe*. Inspired by the energy of the Writers' Congress, as well as by his need for money, John agreed. His 1937 income had been $24,000—a princely sum in those days,[5] when the average factory worker only made about $1,200 a year—and so his income tax had been "something terrific," as he put it. In addition, John was faced with bills for the Asian trip totaling more than $13,000, all of which had to be repaid out of his future book royalties.

John set out his planned work schedule in a letter to Hamilton, and explained that the Asia book had priority, given the fact that he anticipated it would run to at least 550 pages, and had to be completed by Christmas. In the back of his mind was his commitment to do a five-week cross-country lecture tour starting January 25, 1939. Since the contract called for him to be paid as much as $750 for each of the seventeen scheduled lectures, he was reluctant to do anything that would jeopardize or postpone the tour. What this meant, of course, was that although he was keen to begin work, any revision of the Europe book, and of the novel *Ring Around Vienna* would have to wait.

All of John's plans changed in the face of the quickening pace of events in Europe. On September 29, 1938, British Prime Minister Neville Chamberlain and French leader Edouard Daladier met Hitler and Mussolini in Munich. That conference ended with Allied capitulation to German demands for the annexation of a large chunk of Czechoslovakia. Chamberlain predicted that the Munich agreement meant "peace in our time;" Cass Canfield surmised that events in Europe had reached a critical juncture. If *Inside Europe* was to be revised, it should be done immediately. John agreed, and so work on the Asia book came to a halt while he worked on a new edition of *Inside Europe*.

As the Christmas 1938 deadline came and went, John still had six chapters to write. On January 11, he sent Canfield some painful news: "What I have to say is that I have taken a final accurate check of time, space, and energy at my disposal and do not see how I can finish the manuscript before the beginning of the lecture tour."[6]

Canfield and John's agent, Bernice Baumgarten, had convinced Harry Scherman, the founder and president of the Book of the Month Club, to offer *Inside Europe* as its March-April 1939 diviary. Scherman was also interested in seeing the Asia book. But when the postponement in the scheduled completion date delayed any final decision, John grew impatient. He considered a contract offer from the Literary Guild, the BOMC's competitor. Tempting though the prospect of instant advance money may have been, he heeded the counsel of both his agent and Canfield in rejecting the Guild's offer. The problem was that the Guild regularly undercut the price that retail bookstores charged. When that happened, store owners refused to stock the publisher's full-price edition. The publisher as well as the author lost money.

While John had hoped to write as he traveled on his lecture tour, doing so proved impossible. It was early March 1939 by the time he returned to his typewriter, and public interest in the Asia book was growing. It had been heightened by the appearance of chapters from the book in *Reader's Digest*. The *Inside Asia* excerpts marked the beginning of John's long and mutually rewarding association with the *Digest*.

Upon his arrival back in New York after the Asia trip John's agent had arranged a meeting for him with DeWitt (Wally) Wallace and his life, Lila, the magazine's founders.[7] John visited them at their home at Pleasantville, a rustic New York town a half-hour drive north of Manhattan.

Wallace, a forty-eight-year-old native of St. Paul, Minnesota, had been out of work and broke when he started the magazine in February 1922. The Wallaces put together the first issue on the kitchen table of their Greenwich Village apartment. When all 1,500 copies were sold, they got busy on a second issue. Lila Wallace worked to support them, while her husband rummaged through the magazine racks at the New York Public Library for material. The Wallaces relocated to Pleasantville in September 1922. Here, they produced the *Digest* first in a garage, then in an abandoned bank building.

DeWitt Wallace had originally set himself a goal of a circulation of 5,000 copies, but the magazine caught on with the reading public to an extent that no one had dreamed. There was something quintessentially American, and middle brow about *Reader's Digest*. For the start, there was a heavy emphasis on miracle and achievement stories, and some critics charged that it oversimplified issues. If it did, the public did not seem to mind; *Reader's Digest* became one of the most amazing rags-to-riches stories in the history of magazine publishing. By 1926, U.S. circulation had reached 20,000; a decade later it had skyrocketed to an astounding 1.8 million, and the Wallaces became multi-millionaires. Foreign language editions they started were no less successful. Through it all, the Wallaces always regarded themselves as "average" people, with an innate feel for the values and interests that had made America great.

DeWitt Wallace, shy and unassuming in public, was a human bulldozer with a razor-sharp business mind and a knack for knowing what people wanted to read. The Wallaces had long admired John Gunther's work; his unaffacted style seemed perfectly suited to the *Digest*, and so a deal was struck. The magazine agreed to feature the chief personality chapters from John's forthcoming book at a rate of $1,500 per article. This arrangement was sweetened still further because *Digest* editors sometimes offered articles to other magazines. Thus, material from the Asia book found wide readership in *Harper's*, *Current History*, *Asia*, and the *Atlantic*. When John's profile of Philippines dictator Manuel Quezon appeared in the January 1939 edition of the *Atlantic*, it sparked street demonstrations in Manila. "It seems that some of the people near Quezon are very unhappy about my remarks concerning his financial position and the help that rich people have given him," John quipped in a letter to Jamie Hamilton.[8]

The deal with the Wallaces eased John's immediate financial troubles, but it also made additional work for him. He was now compelled to write the personality profiles before writing the rest of the book. It proved especially difficult to organize the mass of research material on China and India. Doing so, left John awed by the scope of the task he had undertaken. He confided that he "felt like a mouse nibbling on an elephant" when writing about India, a nation so vast that it seemed like a continent unto itself.

Nevertheless, the writing of *Inside Asia* went quickly. John decided that this was because he was "so passionately interested" in his material. In reality, it may also have been more due to the reality that he was not nearly as knowledgeable about Asia as he was about Europe. Based largely on his experiences during his trip, the book was a series of personality sketches of Asia's leaders. John's friends Stuart Chase and Archibald MacLeish, as well as Walter Mallory, the executive director of the Council on Foreign Relations in New York, read the manuscript and offered comment and criticism.

The *Inside Asia* manuscript was delivered to Cass Canfield the second week of April, and Harpers planned to dispatch a copy to London on the first ship sailing, which happened to be a German-registered freighter called the *Bremen*. Upon learning this, John telephoned Harper & Brothers with a request that the package instead be sent via the Cunard Lines' *Aquitania*. "The Bremen gets there first," John was told by a puzzled secretary. "Yes," came his reply, "but my books have been banned in Germany, and this manuscript tells something about war. The first thing ships do when war is declared is scoot for home. My publisher is in London—not Berlin!"[9]

When the book was safely in the hands of his publishers on both sides of the Atlantic, John took some time off. He visited relatives on the West Coast, and spent a few days in Hollywood talking with officials of Twentieth Century Fox studios about writing a film screenplay, and he attended several parties. At one, on May 25, John encountered Tallulah Bankhead, the gravel-voiced leading lady, who as much a character off stage as she was on it.

"I'm in a helluva fix, because I think you're a writer, yet you look like a football player," Bankhead sighed after being introduced to John.

"Why should that matter?" he asked.

"Because I don't know whether to be witty or sexy," she replied.[10]

John began packing for a June trip to Europe. He planned to finance it by writing a series of articles for the North American Newspaper Alliance and *Reader's Digest* and by doing a series of live radio broadcasts for the Red Network of the National Broadcasting Corporation (NBC). With the political crisis in Europe deepening, American interest in events there had mushroomed. John Gunther and other foreign correspondents familiar with the European situation became instant "experts" whom other reporters consulted; newsmen were themselves becoming newsmakers.

The April 11 issue of *Look* magazine featured a photograph of broadcaster Walter Winchell interviewing John. The nasal-toned Winchell, who was often described as "the greatest town gossip in the greatest town in the world [Manhattan]," had never been abroad himself. John was also interviewed when he and Frances vacationed in Florida. A reporter for the *Miami Herald* sought John's opinion on whether or not America should become more involved internationally. Repeating views that he had expressed in a widely read article the previous October in *The Nation* and had echoed in *Inside Asia*, John left no doubts where he stood on the matter. "I would be the greatest isolationist in the country, if isolation were possible, but it isn't," he insisted. "We have to negotiate with these dictators, and to do that we have to have some shoulders and muscles to show that we have to be listened to."[11]

Inside Asia was published in the United States on June 8, 1939. Critic Clifton Fadiman, writing in the *New Yorker*, praised the book as "a corker" and an even better read than *Inside Europe*. "I deem it the plain duty of all anti-parish-pump citizens to ship east of Suez at once with John Gunther as their dragoman," he bubbled.[12] The *New York Times'* reviewer agreed, terming the book "a vivid panorama."[13] A critic for *Time* called it "a lively, gossipy, not too profound but interesting encyclopedia of present-day Asia."[14]

Cass Canfield reported to John that early orders in the U.S. totaled more than 28,000 copies—five times as many as for the first printing of *Inside Europe*. John was buoyant as he sailed from New York on June 21 aboard the *Ile de France* for a six-week tour of Europe. Leaving Frances and Johnny at home in Connecticut, he planned to visit London, Paris, Berlin (despite the angry Nazi reaction to *Inside Europe*), Danzig, Warsaw, Moscow, and other neutral capitals. His intention was to gather material for a series of articles to be called, "Inside Europe Revisited." But what John termed "the tremendous hammer of events" disrupted that notion, and "knocked my pace, my itinerary, into a cocked hat."[15]

John arrived in Paris on June 28, aboard the noon train. He spent the next week working and visiting with friends, then addressed the American Club on July 6.[16] Three days later, he made the first of a dozen live radio broadcasts on NBC.

"How did I sound?" John asked Frances in a letter dated July 9. He went on to say that *Inside Asia* had been published in England to mixed reviews. (In Japan, the book's reception was markedly less kind. Censors had used pen knives to cut out entire passages of text that were considered "detrimental to the national peace and order.") The London critics savaged the book figuratively rather than literally, attacking John for what they regarded as his "anti-British Empire sentiments." John seems to have been unconcerned; he apologized to Frances for his shoddy penmanship in his latest letter, explaining, "I have an awful hangover."[17]

That letter was not the only indication that John's trip to Europe was not all work. *New York Evening Post* gossip columnist Leonard Lyons reported in his "Lyons Den" column that John had been the subject of an investigation by Scotland Yard and the Belgian secret police during a visit to Brussels. Several cables with the following cryptic message had arrived at his hotel: "Be on your guard. The man who says he is Gunther is an impostor." The cables were signed "Knickerbocker." John's friend, H. R. Knickerbocker, was enjoying a practical joke.

Not to be outdone, John cabled a reply that read, "Uncle Joe not at station to meet me. Advise. (Signed) Trotsky." It was this reply that caught the eye of a telegraph operator and brought John some unexpected police attention.[18]

John did his second radio broadcast on July 23 from Geneva, having just returned from a hurried, anxious visit to Berlin. The "shadow of the Gestapo" had been everywhere in Germany, he reported, and the tension was palpable—for John, it may have had something to do with Hitler's anger over *Inside Europe*. While noting that Germany was readying for war, John still felt that it was "all but impossible for (the Nazis) to make war this summer."[19] He was not the only foreign correspondent who held that opinion.

On July 28, he got together in Geneva with his old friends Mike Fodor and William Shirer, both of whom were visiting Switzerland on assignments. It was like old times; the three of them sat in Shirer's hotel room drinking wine and arguing politics most of the night. Fodor agreed with John: Germany was not yet ready for war. Hitler, he speculated, was short of iron ore, one commodity vital to any war effort. Shirer was less certain.

The mood was darker two weeks later when John and Shirer met in the Baltic port of Danzig, the Polish-controlled "Free City" that had become one of the focal points of Hitler's demands. Although predominantly German, Danzig had been taken from the Reich by the terms of the 1919 Versailles Treaty, formally ending the First World War. "It is not part of Germany," John explained in a broadcast a few days later, "but it is more German than Germany. Danzig is full of smoke—emotional smoke; it is full of shirts—brown and black; it is full of (German) trucks and cannon; it is full of officers in Reichswehr uniform; it is full of nerves, spy fever, uneasiness."

John told his radio audience how he had just come from an interview with Joseph Beck, the Polish foreign minister. In a grim mood, Beck had told him that while his nation did not want war, Poles were ready for it. "We have a line from which we cannot retreat," he declared.[20]

John and Shirer discussed the situation over lunch on the afternoon of August 11. Then they took a taxi to Zoppot, the nearby Baltic summer resort, where they talked and whiled away the rest of the day on the pier, the beach, and in a local casino. At midnight, John was in a carefree mood as he dashed off to catch a train to Warsaw. He informed Frances in another of his letters that *Inside Asia* was selling strongly, and if that trend continued the book would earn him $40,000 by Christmas. "What I want to do with it is build a small house. Do you?" he asked.[21]

John was still mulling over the possibility of becoming a homeowner, when he traveled on to Moscow. He was there on August 24, the day the Nazi-Soviet pact was announced. Sensing that war was now imminent, John flew back to London via Stockholm and Copenhagen. An hour after arriving in England as "the last passenger on the last plane to leave Sweden" before the outbreak of the that war everyone now agreed was inevitable, he made his first NBC broadcast in two weeks. He had been unable to report on conditions in Eastern Europe or the Soviet Union since leaving Warsaw two weeks before; all lines had been cut. He described for listeners how the airports he had passed through that day, while en route to London, had been jammed with thousands of Polish refugees.

As his plane had flown into London, the airplane stewardess

had pointed out an ominous sight—"what seemed to be big silver beetles in almost every park and green space in the city. They were, in fact, anti-aircraft balloons, being readied for action." On the ground, John observed that all public buildings were being reinforced with piles of protective sand-bags; in his favorite bookshop the proprietor had shored up the building with huge timbers and buttressed the windows with hundreds of copies of Margaret Mitchell's popular novel *Gone with the Wind.* In typical British "stiff-upper-lip" fashion, the hall porter at John's hotel told him, "Well sir, we got through the last war all right. We'll get through this one."[22]

The situation was out of control. Of that much, John was certain. "The Continent resembles some gigantic sealed train, a railway train, with some 350 million people on it, plunging recklessly towards some destination—no one knows what," he said. "The window shades are drawn. The doors are locked. No one can see outside these days."[23]

Caught up in the drama of the momentous events being played out around him, John postponed his return home. Although he had rejected a chance to return to the *Chicago Daily News* foreign service, he was by now following developments with the eagerness of a cub reporter.

In another NBC broadcast on September 1, John announced: "It's a strange face that London wears tonight. It's a dark face. We're having a blackout here. The streets are black, the houses are black."[24] So was the mood. John was among the grim-faced crowd that packed the House of Commons press gallery on September 3, 1939, to watch as Prime Minister Chamberlain officially declared war on Germany, and her Axis allies. Winston Churchill spoke for the British people when he declared on the floor of the House of Commons, "In our hearts this Sunday morning, there is peace. Our hands may be active; our consciences are at rest."[25]

Sensing the vital role that Churchill, rejuvenated after a decade in the political wilderness, was about to play in the coming conflict, John used his contacts in London to arrange an interview. His efforts paid off quickly. The war was just ten days old when a government information officer called John's hotel to tell him that he could meet with Churchill that afternoon at Admiralty House. As always, Churchill was hospitable towards the press.

"[He] looked like an extraordinary kewpie doll made of iron and shiny pink leather," John recalled. "I noticed that his powerful body rose atop thin legs." Churchill, an ever-present cigar clenched tightly in the corner of his mouth, asked John to have a "highball" with him. The two men then spent a few minutes examining a large folding wooden chart behind Churchill's desk in the Admiralty Room. Constructed in 1911, when he had become First Lord of the Admiralty for the first time, Churchill had resurrected the map on his 1939 return to the office. He used it to keep track of the daily positions of the ships in the British and German navies. Casting his eyes westward across the miniature ocean, he growled that American aid would be vital since the war promised to be long and bloody. "The German," he noted, was always "a tough creature to beat."[26]

Churchill, who at age sixty-five had emerged as the grand old man of British politics, patiently answered John's questions about the differences between the conflict that began in 1914 and the one that was now underway. The former had been a war of politicians and generals, he said. This new war threatened to be a "war of peoples, a conflict of ideologies."

Then, growing pensive, Churchill slipped into the role of interviewer. He began to question John about his recent trip to Eastern Europe, and the Soviet Union. "There were not many observers in London then who had been in Moscow a fortnight before and who could give a firsthand account of Russian moods and challenges," John noted. He surmised that this was why Churchill had granted him an interview.

As their conversation was about to end, Churchill sat "brooding aloud" about the Soviet Union and its unfathomable nature; Soviet policies were "a mystery in a mystery in a mystery," he said. The key to this mystery, he explained, was Russian national interest. Churchill's words echoed in John's mind a few weeks later, when the prime minister made his first wartime broadcast to the British people, describing Russia as "a riddle wrapped in a mystery inside an enigma."

Years later, recalling the day that he had heard the unpolished version of that now-famous Churchillian remark, John mused: "To this day I do not know whether he had thought of this bit of language during our talk and automatically filed it away for later use, or had invented it earlier and was trying it out on me."

The Churchill interview concluded John's work in London, and so he booked passage to New York on the liner *Normandie*, due to sail September 20. John had received a cable with the shocking news that Frances had fallen ill while vacationing at Lake Placid in upstate New York.[27] She was in the hospital, and her doctors were doubtful that she would live. John left for home convinced that if he was not already, he soon would be a widower.

CHAPTER TWENTY-THREE

Alone through the long, hot summer of 1939, Frances had grown increasingly restless. She did not drive an automobile, and so she relied on trains or on friends to take her places. Living in rural Connecticut, she felt abandoned and sought escape in her writing, and in corresponding with Nehru.

Frances had written to him ever since their involvement in India the previous January. She viewed the relationship much differently than he did. While her letters smoldered with passion, his replies were curiously detached, although he did sign many of them "love Jawaharlal." Responding to one of her missives and to a picture postcard from Lake Placid, Nehru commented that while Frances was "real enough," the subject of her correspondence seemed as distant as news from "another world."[1] Undeterred, she continued showering him with adulation; Frances was entranced by Nehru, and by the romance of India's struggle for independence.

Meanwhile, she was still grappling with two projects she had begun during her years in Vienna: a semi-autobiographical play called *Mothers and Lovers*, and the manuscript of the political science treatise she called *Empire*. By 1939, the latter had grown to several hundred pages. It was muddled and incomplete, but interesting reading. *Empire* was a project on which Frances would work for more than twenty years without success. She was, John sometimes chided, "a Penelope writer who by night unwove what she'd woven by day." At the time of her death the incompleted manuscript was found among her papers, along with dozens of cartons containing thousands of meticulously filed newspaper clippings and scraps of paper upon which Frances had scribbled notes and ideas.[2]

One chapter, headed "Empire," discussed the nature of the British Empire. Although England's imperial glory was already in the past and the empire in decline, Frances seems to have been oblivious to any of this. It did not fit neatly with her theory. Applying the unwieldy principles of Freudian psychoanalysis, she described the English dread of foreign invasion as those "of a grown-up based on the subconscious memories of actual and frequent rape in childhood and the fear that these may be repeated." One cannot help but wonder whether Frances was trying to analogize England's history with the events of her own troubled childhood, when she had been sexually abused by her stepfather.

Elsewhere in the manuscript, Frances compared Cromwell's England to Germany under Hitler. Frances, still unaware of the Holocaust underway in Europe, commented that perhaps Hitler was not as bad as John and some other commentators maintained; after all, "many of the great leaders in history have been dictators, including George Washington!"

Frances sent Nehru these chapters of the *Empire* book, requesting his comments. But his response could not have been what she had anticipated.

"What do you mean by going off the deep end and trying to impress upon me the virtues of . . . Hitler and (the) like?" Nehru chided.[3]

His anger did not diminish Frances' ardor. On the contrary, the scolding only reinforced her devotion to him. Like a sinner intent on self-flagellation, her reply praised his inner strength. "You write like an angel . . . your words shine, burn, sear, illuminate and heal," she said. "Reading you I always feel impure and unworthy but not depressed. I always get a lift. I feel now I must pull myself together and be good and strong and disciplined and worthy to partake of Jawaharlal's god-like prose."[4]

Knowing Frances' precarious mental condition, John was filled with dread during his week at sea. He was still haunted by having been absent when his mother died ten years earlier; he sensed that history had repeated itself. He was certain that by the time he arrived in New York he would be a widower. He left England feeling depressed, and very alone.

His attentions were diverted during the voyage by the presence of Agnes Knickerbocker, the wife of his friend and colleague H.R. Knickerbocker. The two men had become close after they were introduced several years earlier by their mutual friend Dorothy Thompson. John and "Nick"—as colleagues called Knickerbocker—had worked, wined, and dined together.

Knickerbocker, who in 1939 was working for the Hearst newspaper chain, had decided to remain in Europe to report on the war while Agnes departed for home with the couple's children, and their Danish governess. John and Agnes spent a lot of the time together during the seven-day voyage. They strolled the deck, dined, and talked about their lives. Agnes, like John, confided that she was miserable in her marriage. She complained that Nick was insanely jealous, that he drank too much, chased other women, and neglected her for his work. It was the classic litany of complaints from the wife of a foreign correspondent.

Montana born, Agnes was several years younger than her husband, whom she had met in the late 1920s while touring Europe with her mother. Knickerbocker, once-divorced, was attracted to her instantly. Most men were.

Being petite, with flowing chestnut-colored hair, and passionate dark eyes, Agnes exuded a none too subtle sensuality. She loved to flirt and enjoyed the attention that she attracted.

"Agnes was not what you'd call good looking in the conventional sense. She was dark, with a smoky complexion, and she was very stylish," says John's friend Leonora Hornblow. "As [playwright-producer] Moss Hart used to say, 'She had *lady juice*.'"[5]

H.R. Knickerbocker's younger brother, Kenneth, has similar recollections of his sister-in-law. "Agnes was really pretty, a gorgeous gal," he says. "She had a perky way about her. I remember the first time I saw her. The whole family (from Dallas) was in New York on a holiday. Agnes got off a plane, and she had on a panama hat, cocked a little bit to the side. She looked fetching—that's the word for it. She embarrassed my brother a good deal because she liked to turn heads. *Everybody* liked Agnes."[6]

Kenneth Knickerbocker recalls how at one point in the early 1930s, his brother was touring South America, and Agnes stayed in Dallas, at the home of another brother named Ronald. "Agnes had an affair with Ronald," says Kenneth Knickerbocker. "She just had a way of tempting intimacy, if you understand what I mean by that. In fact, it nearly caused a real tragedy because she got drunk when my brother Hubert came back, and she told him that Ronald had raped her. That was a bunch of bull. Ronald burst and nearly tried to kill himself over that."[7]

Agnes Knickerbocker cast the same amorous spell on John. What happened next was inevitable: they became lovers during the week they were together at sea. While Agnes seems to have been content to engage in a brief shipboard fling as a diversion from the aching loneliness and boredom of her life, John longed for something more. He was frustrated by years of unhappy marriage, and convinced that he would be a widower by the time he reached New York—if he was not already.

Just as he had done years before, when as a young man in Chicago, he had pursued Helen Hahn, John fantasized about a relationship with Agnes. "I think his falling in love with her was unplanned. I really do," says Leonora Hornblow. "It just happened."[8]

Years later, in a sad little novel called *The Indian Sign* (1970), which was the last book John wrote before he died, he tried to explain his emotions. "I felt that my love for her justified and excused all my failures and dishonesties. I was exculpated by the phrase, 'God is love.'" he wrote. "Now I understood why honorable men in the total embrace of passion, became spies or criminals, cheated friends, sold out countries, betrayed the most sacrosanct of trusts. My physical passion for her remained fixed, dogged, and absolute."[9]

Although Agnes and John went their separate ways when the *Normandie* arrived in New York on September 27, 1939, he was determined to continue seeing her. Agnes departed for Dallas, where she planned to live with the Knickerbocker family, and John set about making travel plans to go to Lake Placid. Miraculously, Frances was still clinging to life. She had undergone emergency surgery on September 19. No one expected her to live, but she did. By the time John visited her at the hospital where she was convalescing, Frances had recovered her acerbic tongue.

The drainage tubes protruding from her abdomen, her doctor told John all was not well. When Frances had fallen ill, she had refused medical attention until she was moribund. Even then, she was uncooperative, ignoring all pleas to reveal where her husband could be contacted in Europe. In the end, someone noted the London address of John's bank on a canceled check; that was how he was located.

John was astounded. Did Frances hope to die to spite him? Did she view death as some sort of bizarre revenge, or an act of liberation? John did not know. He had long since ceased to understand Frances' motivations.

John and Frances sat for a long time on a hospital porch, gazing at the scarlet, orange, and russet patchwork of fall colors. At first, the talk was of London and Paris and their friends in Europe. Then John mentioned that he had crossed the Atlantic on the same ship as Agnes Knickerbocker and the mood darkened.

Frances despised Hubert and Agnes Knickerbocker. She loathed Agnes for her demure femininity and attractiveness. At the same time, she resented the close friendship between John and Nick. Her animosity towards Nick went back to the mid-1930s in Vienna. The pair had argued bitterly about the Soviet Union, which Frances described as "a political democracy." Knickerbocker thought that such an opinion was ill-informed prattle, and he said as much. But it was not just a difference of opinion that soured relations between. Petty personal insults flew like poisoned darts whenever they got together.

Such petulance was not unusual for Frances. Early on in the Gunthers' marriage, she reveled in the effect that her quarrelsomeness and unpredictability produced. It attracted attention, and even more importantly, it embarrassed John, whose success she had grown to envy. Frances had desperately wanted a journalism career of her own, and when for a variety of reasons she found that she could not have one, she became bitter and frustrated; Frances was a complex, enigmatic woman.

She was an intellectual, a woman at home in the world of ideas and theoretical concepts. She was bright, perceptive, and shrewd. She was also capable of a kind of sustained systematic thought that John envied. Frances could be warm, generous, and passionate—to the point of being obsessive. She possessed a tremendous inner resilence, and an intuitive knack for grasping the essence of a person or a situation. Those who knew her well recall her wit and sharp tongue, which she could use with devastating effect.

Sadly, the legacy of an unhappy childhood dogged Frances all her life. She trod the thin line between mental instability and rationality. Bizarre swings of mood were characteristic; one moment she could be wallowing in depression, the next she radiated happiness and goodwill. Frances craved love and security, both of which eluded her. Time and time again, her cries echoed unheard, like those of an child alone in the night.

Such were the tenor of the times, and the nature of Frances' own flawed personality that when all was said and done, her fate was one of loneliness, heartbreak, and ultimately the tragedy of wasted potential. Sometimes she was her own worst enemy, for Frances had a way of alienating even those who loved her.

In Vienna, when John began playing tennis regularly with William Shirer, Frances smashed his racket. He was spending too much on the tennis court, she said.

Friends of the Gunthers recall that one of her favorite antics was to lock herself either in the bedroom or bathroom, where she would remain totally silent, sometimes for hours at a time. When at last the commotion and confusion on the other side of the door became too frantic, she would suddenly emerge as if nothing had happened.[10]

The cumulative effect of such behavior was disastrous. It underscored and even reinforced the fragility of Frances' mental condition. It also poisoned John's feelings for her and left him feeling distressed and ashamed at how bitter their relationship had become. "John told me something once that I never forgot. It chilled me," recalls his friend Leonora Hornblow. "He came to hate Frances. One summer, when they were living in that rented house up in Connecticut, John said that he'd sometimes wake up in the middle of the night and lie there listening to Frances breathe. He said he sometimes wished that she'd stop breathing.

"He would have left her a lot sooner, but he always said he just didn't know what would happen if he did. Frances was *that* unstable."[11]

Now, on that September day in 1939, as John and Frances sat talking on the porch of the Lake Placid hospital, the tension between them became palpable. When he could take no more, John went to speak with the doctor about transferring Frances to hospital in Manhattan.

John's mood was brightened by news that his books were selling well. The 1938 "Peace Edition" of *Inside Europe* had been given fresh life by the rush of world events, and *Inside Asia* was selling at the pace of 1,500 copies a day.

With the war in Europe apparently heating up, Cass Canfield was eager to update *Inside Europe* yet again. John agreed, reluctantly. After almost five years of writing and revising the same material, even he had grown weary of it. "One can carry a thing too far," he cautioned Hamish Hamilton.[12]

Thus, when John had sailed for Europe in June, he had done so with plans for a new book about events there. The theme was one that he had voiced often in recent years—namely that a key impetus against war in Europe was its staggering financial cost at a time when almost every country was suffering from the lingering economic malaise of the Great Depression. By the late summer of 1939, however, it seemed that war might actually revive the ailing European economy, in a perverse way.

Faced with six months work to revise *Inside Europe*, John's enthusiasm for other projects dimmed. His original intention had been to publish expanded versions of his broadcast scripts under the title *The High Cost of Hitler.* When events moved too quickly for that, John conceded in a letter to Canfield that any Hitler book would be short and not terribly interesting. "On the whole, I don't care much whether you do it on your side or not. I leave it entirely up to you," he wrote.[13]

The slender manuscript was completed the first week of October. Upon reading it, Canfield decided against publication. But Hamish Hamilton produced a limited edition in England. By the time it appeared, the book's message had been superseded by events in Europe, and so the book died quickly.

John was unconcerned. He was preoccupied with his marital problems, and with plans for another *Inside* book. At the urging of the poet Archibald MacLeish, who had recently returned from Argentina and Chile, John suggested to Cass Canfield that he write about Latin America. Like many American liberals, John feared the area was a prime target for Nazi Fifth Column activities.

As Canfield considered the Latin America book, John departed in mid-November on a quick trip to Turkey and Yugoslavia after a sharp disagreement with Frances. She lamented the fact that although she had reached a "make-or-break" point in her life, she simply could not do what she so longed to do—write. She continued to blame John, who was unsympathetic.

In a long, uncharacteristically blunt letter written on November 20, 1939, from Belgrade, he vented his anger while also trying to inspire Frances to get on with her writing. There was no reason for her not to do so, he said. He warned her he would be "bitingly disappointed" if she had not finished her play by the time he returned home.

There is no record of Frances' reaction to John's letter, which did not have the desired effect. Frances in frustration turned her attentions to politics. Having had a change of heart about a Jewish state, she was the guest speaker on November 14 at a New York membership rally for Hadassah, the women's Zionist organization.[14]

John arrived home a few days before Christmas 1939 to find Frances still bogged down in her writing, and still wallowing in self-pity and anger. That John neither empathized nor understood is not surprising. By now, he was numb to Frances' pain.

In his heart, John was convinced that if only he could end his marriage he would find everlasting happiness in the arms of Agnes Knickerbocker.

CHAPTER TWENTY-FOUR

The poet Keats might well have had John and Frances Gunther in mind when he mused that when a love dies it "to nothingness . . . sink[s]." The Gunthers' marriage continued to exist in name only in the months following Frances' stay in hospital. They continued to share an apartment at 300 Central Park West in Manhattan, but John and Frances had become strangers. Inevitably, the topic of divorce came up more and more in the course of their arguments these days. Each time it did Frances insisted that she would agree to end the marriage only when John told her whom he was in love with. Although he suspected that she already knew, John stubbornly refused to comply with the demand.

His feelings for Agnes Knickerbocker were bittersweet. On the one hand, he was wracked by guilt at having fallen for the wife of a close friend. On the other hand, he was as giddy as a schoolboy in love for the first time, and convinced that he and Agnes would marry once they had sorted out their lives. This furtive romance continued on a long-distance basis throughout much of 1940. Agnes lived near the Knickerbocker family in Dallas while Nick remained overseas covering the war. Agnes rented a postal box, and she and John wrote passionate letters. They met secretly in New York.

In the face of this, John and Frances had arrived at a largely unspoken, undefined "agreement." He was free to spend his days in any way he pleased, as long as he came home for dinner. Evenings were reserved for Johnny. This suited John. He fell into a routine of sleeping late in the mornings, lunching with friends, and working on magazine articles at a small two-room office he had rented at 40 East Forty-ninth Street.

Nancy Barnett, John's secretary at the time, recalls his erratic work schedule. "He appeared some days. Some days he didn't come in at all, or he'd call to say that he'd be in later. I knew that his home life wasn't very happy. Frances seldom called the office, and John was careless about leaving little notes about his social life around his desk. When I was cleaning up, I'd see them and say to myself, 'Oh, oh. This is something that goes no farther than here.'"[1]

John, who had gone to Venezuela briefly in July 1940 to begin work on the next *Inside* book, left from New York in late September to do the bulk of the research. He confided to friends that the trip's timing was a mixed blessing. While he was relieved to be immersed in his writing and freed from the stress of coping with Frances, he agonized over being so far away from Agnes. John forced himself to board a flight for Mexico City, the first stop on a planned five-month tour of Central and South America.

Prior to his departure, Cass Canfield had introduced him to Sumner Welles, the U.S. undersecretary of state. Welles had once courted Canfield's sister, and so he responded generously to the request for help. As John recalled later, when he had gone to Washington in June 1939 to meet with Welles, "it took [the undersecretary] about 30 seconds to grasp what I was after."[2] Welles provided letters of introduction to most of the heads of state in the region, and sent messages on John's behalf to American diplomats in Latin America. The effect was instantaneous; John was given a red carpet reception everywhere he went. "This was something quite new for me," he marveled. "I had started out for Asia with exactly three letters of introduction, all informal, but now I had virtually a semi-official status."[3]

This arrangement allowed John to persuade *Reader's Digest* to buy advance chapters of the coming book. NBC's Blue Network provided additional money when it commissioned a series of broadcasts. And Pan American Airways, eager to promote its expanding services in Central and South America, gave John free transportation on the trip, during which he was to fly more than 19,000 miles—the equivalent of five flights between New York and Los Angeles—in Pan Am's new DC-3s and giant clippers.

Writing to Frances shortly after his arrival in Mexico City, John reported how he had fortified himself at the New York airport with a couple of mint juleps bought for him by author-critic Clifton Fadiman, who had driven him to the terminal. With his nerves thus calmed, the 1,850-mile morning flight to Brownsville, Texas, had been grand. That afternoon's shorter second leg of the journey, from Brownsville to Mexico City, had been another matter.

The aircraft was buffeted by air currents much of the way. Making matters worse, the radio went dead for a time, the pilot simply shrugged his shoulders and as John recounted, "He went off course a little to fly me very low over some Mexican pyramids."[4]

John's already busy Mexico City itinerary became even more hectic after he dined with U.S. Ambassador Josephus Daniels. The ambassador pulled diplomatic strings to arrange interviews with both Mexico's newly elected President General Avila Camacho, and the outgoing President General Lázaro Cárdenas. John's interview with Camacho on October 5 was typical of meetings he had with Latin American *politicos* over the years. He reported the conversation in a lengthy dispatch to the *New York Times*.

It had been dusk as he and two companions arrived at Camacho's door. An aide scrutinized them through a peephole. Inside the white stucco-walled courtyard they were met by the president's adopted son, his personal physician, and "some of the toughest-looking bodyguards . . . outside the movies." A few minutes later, they were escorted across a lawn to a terrace, where Camacho awaited them. One look at their host and John understood why he had been nicknamed *El Buchudo*—the Double-Chinned. Hefty, big-shouldered, and middle-aged, with bulldog jowls, Camacho was an imposing figure. In a natty brown tweed suit and blue sports shoes, he looked more like a man-about-town than the career military man that he was.[5]

From Mexico, John worked his way south through the five nations of Central America, and then traveled counterclockwise around South America, beginning in Columbia and ending in Brazil. He stopped briefly on the way home in Trinidad, Cuba, Puerto Rico, and Palm Beach, Florida.

Welles' letters of introduction had smoothed the way everywhere, except Argentina. Suspicious border guards there had searched John and his luggage, on suspicion that he was a cocaine smuggler. It was the only time that this ever happened to John in a lifetime of travel.

In Buenos Aires, the American Embassy held a luncheon for him. It was "a splendid occasion," John recalled, "except for the fact that I wasn't there."[6]

In Lima, Peru, he and Paul Gallico, a well-known New York sportswriter, showed up at the airport together for a flight to Columbia. The agent at the Pan Am check-in counter warily eyed the two of them; each man weighed over 200 pounds. "You'll go to Bogota," he said, "but not together."[7]

In Nicaragua, dictator Anastasio Somoza (who was an admirer of FDR) was almost *too* cheerful, and too charming. The "cleverest politician between the Rio Grande and the Panama Canal," as John described him, Somoza feted his guest and staged a military parade in honor. John, bemused by this display of respect, was also aware of the flimsiness of Somoza's civility. During their conversation, the Nicaraguan dictator repeatedly referred to American Ambassador Meredith Nicholson as "boy."

This was just the sort of information with which John filled his notebooks. By the time that he arrived back in New York, he was lugging several large suitcases that bulged with research material, and copies of *Reader's Digest* articles he had been obliged to write along the way. Altogether, John had interviewed more than 400 people, including the heads of eighteen of the twenty nations he had visited. The expedition had been an eye-opener for him. Trite

John Gunther in 1937, one year after finishing *Inside Europe*.

Joseph Anton Schoeninger, John Gunther's maternal grandfather. Circa 1900. (*Courtesy Gretchen Corazzo*)

John Gunther with his grandmother, sister, and cousins. Pictured here are John's sister, Jean (front); (middle row, left to right) Margaret Vladimiroff, Joseph Schoeninger, Gretchen Schoeninger; (back row, left to right) Boris Vladimiroff, Hester Schoeninger, John Gunther, and Lizette Schoeninger, John's maternal grandmother. Circa 1914. (*Courtesy Gretchen Corazzo*)

John Gunther's graduation picture that appeared in the University of Chicago's *Cap & Gown* in 1922. (*Courtesy University of Chicago Archives*)

In the spring of 1929, John and Frances visited his maternal cousins, the Schoeningers, in Carmel, California. (*Courtesy Gretchen Corazzo*)

Frances in Vienna, 1935. (*Courtesy Frances Gunther's estate*)

John Gunther in front of the Wailing Wall, Jerusalem, in 1937. (*Courtesy Chicago Sun-Times*)

Paul Scott Mowrer (1887-1971), chief of the *Chicago Daily News* overseas service. (*Courtesy Richard Mowrer*)

Edgar Ansel Mowrer (1892-1977), was Berlin bureau chief for the *Chicago Daily News* in the 1930s, and brother of the newspaper's overseas service chief. (*Courtesy Richard Mowrer*)

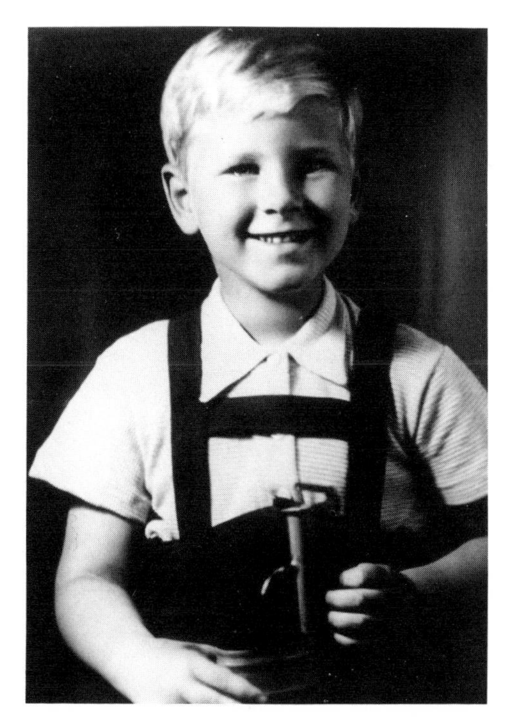

Johnny, circa 1935. (*Courtesy Frances Gunther's estate*)

Advertisement for *Inside Europe*, published by Harper and Brothers, 1936.

JOHN GUNTHER

INSIDE EUROPE TODAY

A brand new book about Europe —not in any way a revision of Mr. Gunther's classic "Inside Europe," but a *totally* new work, which describes vividly the personalities, problems and tensions that distinguish the new, exciting postwar Europe of today.

How Europe Has Changed
Adenauer
U. S. Army on the Rhine
Crisis in Berlin
De Gaulle
Tragic Conflict in Algeria
Italy— What's Going On
Macmillan & the Establishment
Struggle in NATO
Common Market— at Sixes and Sevens
Khrushchev

Inside Europe Today was published in April 1962 by Harper and Row, in both hardcover and mass market paperback—the first time ever for a new Gunther book. (*Courtesy Chicago Sun-Times*)

Pulitzer Prize-winning journalist H.R. Knickerbocker and his wife Agnes, circa 1936. (*Courtesy Kenneth Knickerbocker*)

John and Frances on their pan-Asian tour in late 1937. (*Courtesy Frances Gunther's estate*)

Though known as a print journalist and author, Gunther, like many of his colleagues, also reported for radio. (*Courtesy Chicago Sun-Times*)

Left to right: John Gunther, M. W. Fodor, Mrs. Fodor, Frances Gunther, Dorothy Thompson, and Sinclair Lewis in a Viennese cabaret.

Marcel Fodor, circa 1939.
(*Courtesy Denis Fodor*)

Egypt was the site for this postcard photo of John (atop center camel), Frances (right), and an unidentified friend. Taken in November 1937, it was sent by Frances to Johnny. *(Courtesy Frances Gunther's estate)*

John Gunther and his new bride, the former Jane Perry Vandercook, relax at the Ambassador Hotel in Chicago. The couple was married in a quiet ceremony in Chicago on March 5, 1948. *(Courtesy Chicago Sun-Times)*

After WWII Marcel Fodor returned to Europe and became editor of *Die Neue Zeitung*, a West Berlin newspaper. Here (circa 1955) he is checking page proofs from the typesetter. (*Courtesy Denis Fodor*)

Frances Gunther became involved with the Emergency Committee to Save the Jewish People of Europe in 1943. (*Courtesy Frances Gunther's estate*)

Martha Maria Fodor and Marcel Fodor at their Berlin home in the late 1940s. (*Courtesy Denis Fodor*)

John Gunther visits with Thomas V. Sayers, head of the *Chicago Daily News* library in 1959. Gunther was in Chicago to receive an award as "Communicator of the Year" from the University of Chicago Alumni Association. (*Courtesy Chicago Sun-Times*)

Dr. Alexander Rafaeli (right), a member of the Jewish underground, became one of Frances' closest friends following her emigration to Israel. (*Courtesy Dr. Alexander Rafaeli*)

John Gunther's books were translated into eighty-seven languages and published underground behind the Iron Curtain in Europe and in Asia. (*Courtesy Chicago Sun-Times*)

John Gunther with University of Chicago President George W. Beadle (standing) and Provost Edward H. Levi. Gunther wrote *Chicago Revisited*, a tribute to his alma mater, which was published by the university in 1965. (*Courtesy Chicago Sun-Times*)

John Gunther (circa 1965) lecturing at the University of Chicago. (*Courtesy Chicago Sun-Times*)

In August 1961, Frances returned to the U.S. from Israel for a cancer operation. The illness had taken its toll by this point in her life. (*Courtesy Mary von Euler*)

though it may sound, what he found surprising was the realization that America's "backyard"—an area that the foreign policy makers in successive administrations had treated either with benign neglect or contempt, depending upon the circumstances—was anything but the homogeneous whole that most Americans assumed. John decided that Roman Catholicism, the climate, and the divisive effects of the mixing of the European and native races had been important factors in the historical development of a region that did not conform to the outsider's preconceptions.

Barely one-sixth of the 120 million people in Central and South America in 1940 were of European origin. The rest were black or *mestizo*, the offspring of natives and white immigrants. "By and large those countries which are purest white—Costa Rica, Chile, Argentina, Uruguay—are those which are the healthiest politically, and which are nearest to democracy," John wrote. "It would be misleading to assert that race is a dominant issue in Latin America, (but) it is an important issue."[8]

Despite his liberalism, and his sympathy for the cause of blacks and other ethnic minorities, John unwittingly—and shamelessly—subscribed to most of the racial stereotyping that pervaded the American popular culture of the day.

It was natural that John Gunther, who came of age in the early 1920s, was exposed to such prejudices on a daily basis. There had been a strongly anti-Semitic flavor to campus life at the University of Chicago, and white antagonism towards the Windy City's large black population was no secret. As an educated, liberal-thinking young man, John had quietly rejected the rabid racism and xenophobia that he encountered. Yet his values were inescapably those of white middle class America—the same conservative values that De Witt Wallace of *Reader's Digest* espoused as "promoting a better America, with capital letters."

Optimism and an absolute faith in the virtues of the American way were hallmarks of this vision. Part and parcel with it were the competitive ethic and the timeless and universal suspicion of anyone different.

These were the same values that shaped John's interpretation of all that he encountered during a lifetime of travel. And these were the same values that he unconsciously promoted in his writing. As Clifton Fadiman once noted, "[Gunther] taught us a hell of a lot about our world, in primer terms. He's drawn the maps for us."[9]

The map of Latin America that John Gunther sketched was markedly different from the one that had customarily been drawn by most other American writers. American trade with Latin American in 1939 amounted to more than one billion dollars annually, and U.S.-based multinationals had invested almost three times that amount there. Even so, most Americans remained blissfully ignorant about Latin American affairs. What alarmed John was the realization that Nazi Fifth Columnists were active in virtually every country that he visited; Hitler had boasted that he would create a new Germany in Brazil. Like a modern-day conquistador, the Fuehrer dreamed of exploiting the vast mineral wealth of Mexico, and of the other underdeveloped nations in the region.

The U.S. Army in 1940 had prepared a list of fourteen "strategic materials" which were vital to a wartime economy and which America could not produce for herself. All could be had in abundance in the nations of Latin America. John Gunther risked stating the obvious when he predicted that, "If the Germans win the war and turn their attention to the United States, it is almost certain that Latin America will be their avenue of attack."[10]

In Washington, President Roosevelt shared those concerns. Thus, John had only been back in New York a few days when Sumner Welles telephoned to ask him to come to Washington to brief the president on political conditions in Latin America. He was flattered to do so.

Often during his years in Europe as a *Chicago Daily News* correspondent, he had met with state department officials to report what he had seen and heard on his travels. Never before had he been called upon to share his knowledge with the White House. The invitation was a measure of his growing international reputation.

John's only previous encounter with Franklin Roosevelt had been seven years earlier, in 1934. While home on Christmas leave from Vienna, he had visited Washington, and colleagues had taken him along to a presidential press conference. "I was startled and amazed," he recalled. "I'd been used to the stuffy, useless kind of press conferences we got in Budapest or Paris; this was something new to my experience." What was striking was the fact that Roosevelt sat at his desk, with a broad window behind him. "At once I knew I was home," John marveled. "No European dictator would ever possibly sit with his back to a window."[11]

John was excited about the prospect of a personal audience with FDR. His spirits flagged when upon arriving at the White House at the appointed hour on the morning of April 7, 1941, he was informed by presidential secretary General Edwin (Pa) Watson that he could not possibly have more than five minutes with the president. FDR was scheduled to meet before lunch with the Commissioners from the District of Columbia, and with a cabinet member. Further dimming John's chance of spending much time in the Oval Office was the fact that Hitler's armies had invaded Yugoslavia the day before, and the mood in Washington was grim. State Department officials scurried in and out of the White House all morning with the latest reports on the fighting. Seeing this, John was crushed when, after a couple of hours of waiting, Watson told him to go away and come back after lunch.

When he did so, John was surprised to be immediately ushered into FDR's office. He found the president leaning back in the big chair behind his desk; Marguerite (Missy) LeHand, his private secretary, scooped up Roosevelt's dog, Fala, and exited, leaving John and FDR alone.

"Hello! How are you?" Roosevelt said as he hitched himself up in his chair, and extended his hand.

John was convinced that the president did not "know him from Adam," nonetheless the two men began chatting. Presently, FDR turned to the subject of foreign affairs. He then proceeded to talk non-stop for the next forty-five minutes! John tried to listen closely, but his mind wandered.

He studied Roosevelt's face—the best-known face in the world at that time, except possibly for Hitler's. "I kept thinking that (FDR) looked like a caricature of himself, with the long jaw tilting upward, the V-shaped opening of the mouth when he laughed, the two long deep parentheses that closed the ends of his lips," he later wrote.[12]

Embarrassed that he was taking so much of the president's time, John jumped in at the first opportunity to mention that he had just returned from visiting every one of the countries in Latin America. The president seemed amused.

"What? All twenty?" he said with a laugh. "Even Paraguay?" When John nodded, Roosevelt asked, "What are the bad spots?"

John mentioned Panama, whose dictatorial ruler, Dr. Arnulfo Arias, like Roosevelt was a Harvard graduate. That bit of information surprised FDR, who launched a second monologue. A half-hour later, it was still going, and John was becoming acutely uneasy. He was embarrassed by the candor of the president's comments and by the fact that their meeting was continuing so long, while more important matters were kept waiting. When John leaned forward in his chair as if to rise, the president patted him back into place with a wave of the hand; Roosevelt was enjoying himself.

He was analyzing the European situation in detail when the ringing of the desk telephone interrupted him. John surmised that the caller was Secretary of War Henry Stimson. The president became absorbed in a heated discussion of the secretary's policy on Manchuria. Stimson, angered by something that Roosevelt said, abruptly ended the conversation by hanging up. In an unguarded moment, the president looked wounded. In John's words, "He (then) turned, saw me, looked at me with some surprise, stretched out his great hand, and ended the interview with one of the most startling single remarks I have ever heard:'So long! I've got to run along now!' And all the time I had been having a hard time keeping my eyes off his wasted legs."[13]

CHAPTER TWENTY-FIVE

The visit to the White House boosted John's spirits at a time when he was downcast both about his marriage and his writing. The meeting with the president helped him to organize his thoughts. Writing *Inside Latin America* was torturous, even though John now had the apartment to himself. Frances had gone to Los Angeles to spend the summer with her brother, Bernie. Johnny was visiting with friends.

Still John could not settle down to work, for his mind was abuzz with thoughts of Agnes. "I see thousands of people," he told Frances in one of his letters.[1] In fact, the hyperbole was only a slight exaggeration. Marcel Fodor had been in town for a visit, as had Dorothy Thompson, Edgar Snow, and William and Tess Shirer. John reported that he had lunch or dinner with friends almost every day, and each Saturday he hosted a cocktail party or went out to one. He was at Cass Canfield's apartment one night when he lamented aloud that he was running out of continents to write about.

"What will I do?" he asked Clifton Fadiman.

"Try incontinence," came the reply.[2]

Weighing heavily on John's mind, too, were his on-going financial problems. Despite the fact that his income for 1940 was more than $65,000, a phenomenal sum in those days, he had trouble making ends meet. The reason was obvious: he loved to spend money. At one point in the spring of 1941, John wrote to share with Frances the exciting news that he and Johnny had just bought "the damnedest, most stunning black and red leather convertible." In the next sentence he bemoaned the sorry condition of his bank account. "At the moment, I'm practically dead broke, but some *Reader's Digest* money will be coming in, enough for current expenses," he said. "I think we definitely have to face the necessity of cutting down the well known Gunther scale of life. I know. I know. It's what we always say and never do, largely because of my personal extravagances."[3]

The solution he proposed was simple: spend $20,000 to buy a house in the country. That way Frances and Johnny would always have "a roof, no matter what happens." He was still struggling with the decision of how to make the final break with Frances, and the suggestion may have been his way of lessening his feelings of guilt about "abandoning" her.

By mid-May of 1941, John knew that he could not meet his deadline for delivery of the *Inside Latin America* manuscript. Cass Canfield, Bernice Baumgarten, and Harry Scherman of the Book of the Month Club had grown impatient with his lack of progress and were pressuring him. John finally threw himself into the task, working long hours, seven days a week for three solid months. He completed a 600-page manuscript before Labor Day. Despite the speed with which he had worked, this was the first *Inside* book in which John deviated from the formula that he had developed; he did *not* begin with a personality profile.

"I found that I had to start out with a general explanation of the subject, if only because I had to explain it to myself," he admitted years later in *A Fragment of Autobiography*. "I suppose, to be honest, that I was not particularly interested in [my subject]."[4]

Inside Latin America was published in early October 1941. Sales were strong, and the book was praised by Undersecretary of State Sumner Welles and other administration officials. Meanwhile, it was promptly banned in Panama, and the Dominican Republic. In Brazil, a pro-Nazi newspaper columnist took exception with John's discussion of German espionage activity in the region, and accused him of being an American spy.

In Washington, Federal Bureau of Investigation agents studied *Inside Latin America* after a special agent in Oklahoma pointed out in a memo to headquarters that the book mentioned the bureau's counterespionage activities "in several countries."[5] All of this publicity, plus the fact that Harry Scherman selected the book as a Book of the Month Club title for November ensured bestseller status. Book club sales alone totaled 320,000 copies, which was more than club sales of *Inside Europe*. What's more, total sales exceeded those for *Inside Asia*, which in retrospect proved to be the more significant book.

Most reviewers praised the readability and the vividness of *Inside Latin America*. Others attacked it for over simplifying the issues. Typical was Joseph McSorley of *Catholic World*, who blasted John for what he termed, "superficial, exaggerated, and inaccurate" reporting.[6] The criticisms were ones that John heard each time a new *Inside* book appeared. Each time he did, he responded angrily.

Thus, when Eleanor Roosevelt in her syndicated newspaper column quoted a "South American friend" who dismissed *Inside Latin America* as misleading and intellectually dishonest, John wrote the first lady a long letter. "May I make a quiet protest?" he inquired.

Explaining that he had spent five months traveling in Latin America, and then seven months writing the book, John continued, "I should have been delighted to have spent five years (there) instead of five months, but my theory was and is that five months is better than nothing. It's amazing how much one can do in five months when one knows how."[7] John picked up on that theme again in *A Fragment of Autobiography* when he pointed out, "My kind of book would never get done at all if I allowed myself unlimited time."[8]

With the success of *Inside Latin America* assured, John turned his attentions once more to his personal life. Frances had returned to New York, resigned to the inevitability of divorce. As John had traveled in Latin America, she had slipped ever deeper into her own fantasy world. Frances took a perverse delight in writing sarcastic, taunting letters to John.

One can well imagine John's discomfort as he read Frances' letters. Several questions gnawed at him. How much did Frances know about his relationship with Agnes? Was she deliberately mocking him?

John had contemplated cutting short his South American tour to return home and end the charade by announcing to the world that he and Agnes were in love. But were they really?

John was both frustrated and puzzled by Agnes' behavior. He could not fathom her unwillingness to leave her husband. "John told me that he read Agnes' letters, and he never could figure out what she wanted," says Leonora Hornblow. "He didn't know if she really loved him, whether she was simply bored and having an affair, whether she was trying to spite her husband, or what. That's the reason John vacillated so much about their relationship."[9]

While John agonized, Frances was preoccupied with her own romantic dreams. She continued to correspond with, and send book parcels to Nehru, whom she had not seen for two years. In a letter she wrote to him in the spring of 1940, while John was in Venezuela, Frances told Nehru of her recent illness. "I didn't seem to mind dying as [much as] I thought I would," she said. "I wanted very much to leave a will and testament as that seemed the proper thing to do when dying. But I was too tired to dictate one, so I said it in my mind and hoped that would do. I asked John to finish my book. I left my journals to Johnny for his daughter and to India . . . I told you I had wanted to know you and cherish you and bear you a son, that I was sorry to leave you without having done any of those things."[10]

Nehru, who was immersed in events in India, took the time to answer Frances' letters. Nevertheless, his replies are coy and circumspect in tone. In one, dated August 27, 1941, written from jail in Dehra Dun in the Uttar Pradesh province of northern India, he confided that he had never understood the opposite sex. "Because of this lack of understanding I've always been a little afraid of women," he said. "For really imaginative people it is difficult to draw the line between fact and fancy, especially for women who have suffered through more imagination than men."[11] If Nehru was dropping a none-too-subtle hint about the nature of their relationship, it fell on deaf ears. Frances clung doggedly to the dream that Nehru, so unattainable and distant, would one day be hers.

Against that mental backdrop, Frances became depressed and angry about the life she and Johnny led in Connecticut. One evening in early October she sat down at the typewriter to vent her feelings. She rehashed longstanding complaints about John's lack of interest in her and in his son. She accused him of trying to assuage his guilt at not spending more time with Johnny by coddling him when they were together. "You are a rotten father," Frances chided. "Your child is deficient and inferior in everything that only a father can teach him. Your excessive petting can only make him a pansy."[12]

Having opened the floodgates of her emotions, Frances held nothing back. All of the disaffection, hostility, and fear that had been building within her came out in a torrent. She was tired of the dark charade that their life together had become, tired of John's obsession with his writing, tired of their marriage. "I give up. I give up. Let's call it a day. I really can't go on with it—I really can't," Frances pleaded. "You see, it's much worse than living alone—everything [sic] thinks I'm living with somebody, but the joke's on me; I'm living with nobody, with somebody who's the life of the party, but nobody to me."

She continued, "I've felt as dead as an emptied potato sack—acting like an automaton or a robot in a vacuum. You have every right to think and act as you need to—if you feel that being a writer and an artist is incompatible with being a human being and a husband, and if you feel that you must choose the former and renounce the latter, well and good, that's your choice and good luck to you . . . I didn't begin this letter with the intention of saying anything so drastic as separation and divorce—I really didn't—but that seems to be the unavoidable conclusion."[13]

There is no record of John's reaction to Frances's letter. However, the fact that he had taken a room in a midtown hotel speaks volumes. He had accepted that the break was final. One Saturday afternoon in late October, he and Frances met at the apartment to divide up their possessions. Frances declined the suggestion that she take most of their furniture and belongings. They spent an agonizing day culling through the detritus and the memories of fourteen years of marriage. Frances took most of their huge record collection, John the many books he had bought over the years; they divided the furniture, and John hired a moving van to haul away his things to storage.

John could take no more. Whether out of guilt or anger, he knew that he had to get away. On October 22, 1941, he flew to London to do a series of broadcasts from the besieged British capital. He was only too willing to escape his troubles by losing himself in work, and in the war that was now raging in Europe.

CHAPTER TWENTY-SIX

Transatlantic commercial air service was in its infancy in 1941. The flight that carried John Gunther from New York to Europe that autumn was a grueling twenty-two hours. The Pan American Airlines' "Yankee Clipper" flying boat touched down in the Azores before going on to neutral Lisbon. Here, in the Portuguese capital, John changed to a plane of KLM, the Dutch airlines, for the final leg of the flight to London. There was a tacit agreement between Germany and England that passenger traffic along the Iberian air corridor would not be attacked.

By today's supersonic standards, the twenty-two-passenger, four-engine Boeing B314s used on these early transatlantic routes traveled at a snail's pace. However, at the time, this "luxury" air service inaugurated by Pan Am two years earlier, was considered one of the marvels of modern technology—the 1940s equivalent the Concord airliner. After all, the New York-to-London trip by sea usually took seven days, and with the Battle of the Atlantic still raging in late 1941, such crossings were a risky proposition, even for American ships.

Having taken off from the Marine Terminal at New York's LaGuardia Airport at 9:30 a.m., on Wednesday, October 22, John and his fellow passengers arrived in London late the following afternoon. Flying into this beleaguered city of seven million persons, John pressed his nose to the window and surveyed the city below. What he saw was a chilling, almost unbelievable sight.

The east end of this hub of the British empire, where much of England's heavy industry was located, had been flattened. By now the worst of the blitz had ended, as Hitler unleashed his war machine on the Soviet Union. This gave Londoners a chance to begin the massive task of clearing away the rubble caused by the bombing. In the days following his arrival, John could scarcely believe that this devastated city was the same one he had once called home.

For fifty-seven consecutive nights, from September 7 through to November 3, 1940, an average of 200 German bombers had swooped down on London. In the crowded skies above the city the rag-tag Royal Air Force had faced the fury of the mighty Luftwaffe. Victory in this life-and-death battle for air superiority had not come cheaply. British losses during the two-month period totaled 497 planes, while the Germans lost 808.

On the ground below, entire city blocks of homes, schools, factories, and historic buildings were razed. More than 14,000 persons were killed, another 18,000 wounded. Most of the dead and maimed were civilians, giving rise to a black humor that aptly summarized Londoners feelings about suddenly being unwilling front-line observers. "Join the Army and escape the war!" advised one bit of street wisdom.

Compounding Londoners' misery was rationing of food, clothing, and many other consumer goods. Bloodied though they might have been, the British people remained unbowed. "Grim and gay, dogged and serviceable, with the confidence of an unconquered people in their bones," wrote Winston Churchill, "they adopted themselves to this strange new life, with all its terrors, with all its jolts and jars."[1]

The Roosevelt administration, fearful that the fall of England would have grave implications for America's overseas interests, on March 11, 1941, had passed the "lend-lease" bill. The measure extended military and humanitarian aid to England and "the government of any country whose defense the President deems vital to the defense of the United States." By implication, this necessitated an increased role for the U.S. Navy in efforts to keep the North Atlantic sea lanes open. By the last week of October 1941, marauding German U-Boats has sunk ten American merchant ships. Then, on October 30, tensions between Washington and Berlin escalated dramatically when the destroyer *Reuben James* was torpedoed with the loss of ninety-six American lives while on convoy duty off Ireland.

In this tense atmosphere, radio reports from London by John Gunther, and other American correspondents, found an eager audience back home. John stayed for two months, doing a series of eyewitness broadcasts for NBC, and writing articles for the North American Newspaper Alliance. With each passing day, however, he found it more difficult to concentrate. He struggled to rationalize his relationship with Agnes Knickerbocker.

Nick's presence in London did not make things any easier, nor did the fact that Nick boasted to John about an affair he was supposedly having with a young woman who worked for the British Broadcasting Corporation. While Nick complained that Agnes did not write him often enough, he apparently had no inkling that she and John were involved in dangerous liaisons of their own.

John was awash with conflicting emotions, and oblivious to the irony of his situation. On the one hand, he despised Nick for cheating on Agnes and bragging about it; on the other, he was excited by the thought that here was the excuse that Agnes needed to divorce her husband and marry him. The more he reflected on the situation, the more John was convinced that the time had come to propose marriage to Agnes. It was now or never. Taking stock of his life, as in 1936 when he quit the *Chicago Daily News*, John was not content with his lot.

A few days before leaving New York "on vacation," as he had explained it, he had been interviewed by reporter Robert van Gelder of the *New York Times*. Van Gelder's literary snapshot recorded that, "Gunther looks bigger than his 218 lbs. (He is) a tall man with shoulders like those of Lorna Doone's brothers—big enough to block a wide doorway. His features are Byronic, set in too heavy a frame."[2]

Standing before a mirror, John saw staring back at him a robust forty-year-old, a man who had achieved fame as "the world's foremost political reporter"—as the newspaper ads for his book *Inside Latin America* so grandiloquently described him. It was not a public image that disturbed him. In fact, he was keen to play the role to the hilt.

John continued to be acutely conscious of status and wealth. In March 1941, he recorded in his diary, "Income tax—$12,683.24—on an income of about $65,000—highest yet."[3] Even with an income more than sixty times the average annual industrial wage of the day, John was still hard pressed to make ends meet. While he provided Frances with about $800 per month to support herself and Johnny, he made no effort to curb his own spending. John traveled freely. He bought gifts for his friends. He dressed smartly. He drank only the best liquor, and lots of it. He maintained an office with a secretary. He was a regular at Manhattan's best night clubs, and he rented a smart apartment at 530 Park Avenue. John was fond of inviting people "to come to 530 at 5:30" for drinks and food. Like his father, he was never one to save for a rainy day. John delighted in lavishing money on himself, and on his friends.

Helen Hahn, John's college sweetheart, recalled sharing a cab with him one day in New York around this time. When she happened to admire an expensive Leica camera that he was carrying, John insisted she take it as a gift. "That was typical of him," she recalls. "He was extremely generous, and liked to spend money and give gifts."[4]

Nancy Barnett, John's secretary at the time, has similar memories. "He was a big spender and lived up to the very limit of his income. There was no doubt about that. You could tell by looking at him that he spent a lot on clothing. His apartment was very expensive; he had a gorgeous phonograph with a tremendous record collection, and a nice collection of modern paintings. I always had the impression that here was a man who'd come from a background that was not distinctive socially or otherwise, who'd gotten into the big time and deservedly was making the most of it. He enjoyed every minute of life."[5]

John confided to William Shirer and other friends that he longed for just two things: success as a novelist, and the hand of the woman he loved—Agnes Knickerbocker. John Gunther was Victorian in many of his attitudes. His romanticized view of male-female relationships today seems quaint, or chauvinistic—depending upon your viewpoint. But at that time there was nothing atypical in his adherence to the notion of man as the pursuer, and woman the pursued. John fantasized about flying home, sweeping Agnes off her feet and marrying her. It would have been the romantic thing to do.

Only it was not that easy. There were too many complicating factors, the pain of John's nagging confusion about Agnes' true intentions was one. While professing to love him, she refused to divorce her husband. Agnes reacted angrily when she learned that John had saved each and every one of her letters like cherished treasures. "Please destroy them!" Agnes had insisted. He refused.

John was wrestling with his emotions. Did Agnes really love him, or was she merely using him to spite her husband?

Did he really *love* her or was her appeal the fact she was the wife of another man, the wife of Pulitzer Prize-winning journalist H.R. Knickerbocker? He could not decide.

Then there were John's problems with Frances.

The two of them were no longer living or sleeping together as man and wife, but Frances still clung to her husband with an emotional desperation that was terrifying. She refused to consider ending their marriage. Like John, she was trapped in a world of wistful dreams and tortured realities. Among her papers found after her death was a scribbled note dated "1941," which set out her priorities in life. It read, "What I want: 1) to finish this book [the "Empire" manuscript over which she was still agonizing]; 2) to go to Nehru, to go to Jay [a pet nickname for John]; 3) to have two children; 4) to write four more books; 5) to live usefully."

Frances fantasized about being at Nehru's side, where she would take up the fight for Indian's independence. That struggle was not going well. In November 1940, Nehru had been sentenced to four years in prison for his revolutionary activities. The British authorities ignored pleas from supporters of the Indian Congress (the nationalist movement led by Nehru and Gandhi) that he be spared the harshness of life of an ordinary criminal behind bars. Nehru was imprisoned in the Indian city of Dahra Dun. Although Nehru and Frances continued to regard their relationship in markedly different ways, he corresponded with her when his jailers permitted it. Frances sent him parcels of books, and samples of her poetry—some of which dealt with the war or pacifist themes. Others were long, baleful proclamations of her undying love for him.

Typical of the latter was a poem entitled, "Life Has a Rendezvous With Us." In it, Frances related how in the darkness before dawn she sometimes awakened with a terrible, aching loneliness, only to reach in vain across her pillow in search of Nehru's hand. She went on to repeat her oft-stated desire to one day bear his child. "On your birthday, I am gay and devout," she wrote. "I thank God privately for having created/ the universe and life and you./ I thank your mother for having borne you/ and your father for the love that bred you./ I bow to our ancestors./ I dream of our son."

Writing to Nehru on November 14, 1942, Frances described a party she had thrown in New York to celebrate his birthday. Later, alone in her hotel room, she sat thinking of him. "I want to be with you," she wrote. "It is not possible that anyone can want to be with you as much as I want to be with you and not be with you and live."[6]

Meanwhile in London, John was attempting to cope with his inner turmoil in his own way. He immersed himself in work, and spent his free time at his London club, or he socialized. Hamish Hamilton, doing wartime service in the American Division of the British Information Ministry, entertained John often. So did Lady Oxford, now a spry seventy-seven years old, and Rebecca West, who by late 1941 had married and was basking in the popular success of her latest book, *Black Lamb and Gray Falcon*, a two-volume account of pre-war travels in Yugoslavia.

On December 7, 1941, John was still struggling to sort out his emotions. "Wild, savage, lonely, unbelievable thoughts of X

[Agnes]. Can't endure it," he wrote in his diary at one point in late 1941.[7] It was nothing in London that stirred John to action, but rather the momentous events that unfolded half a world away.

News reached the British capital that Sunday evening, shortly after the dinner hour, that Japanese fighter planes and bombers had attacked the U.S. Navy's Pacific fleet at its base at Pearl Harbor, Hawaii. The following morning, President Roosevelt appeared before an emergency joint session of Congress. In a speech that would echo down through history, Roosevelt declared that December 7, 1941, was "a day that will live in infamy." He called for a declaration of war against Japan. Within hours the Senate voted approval 82-0, the House of Representatives 388-1 (the lone dissenter being Montana Republican Jeannette Rankin, the first elected woman representative, who had also voted against U.S. entry into the First World War.) That same day, England and its allies declared war on Japan. Three days later, Germany and Italy entered the fray, declaring war on the United States. Europe's conflict had engulfed the world.

John, like many other Americans, was stunned by this dramatic turn of events. Like almost everyone else, he had sensed that war with the Axis powers was inevitable, yet the reality of its outbreak came as a shock. Whatever the outcome, the world had was changed forever.

It was with a awful sense of foreboding that John departed England for New York on December 16, 1941, aboard what was to be, for the next four years, the last regularly scheduled American transatlantic passenger ship. It was a tense, subdued voyage for John and for the 189 other passengers on board. The ship was painted a muted camouflage gray, with its name blotted out, and portholes papered over to black out its running lights at night. The captain zigzagged his way across the North Atlantic, as a precaution against attack by the U-Boat packs that prowled the shipping lanes to such deadly effect. To everyone's relief, the voyage proved uneventful, the only real excitement being the birth two days out of New York of a baby girl to a French refugee woman. The ship arrived in New York harbor on December 24, a cool, overcast day.[8]

John spoke briefly with the reporters who had crowded the dock to question passengers about conditions in Europe. He then carted his bags to his apartment and dashed out to do some last-minute Christmas shopping for Johnny and his sister Jean, who was now living in New York and working for an organization called the Foreign Policy Association.

While he was window shopping along chic Fifth Avenue, some jewelry caught John's eye. In a moment of impetuosity he bought it as a gift for Frances. Reflecting on his behavior many years later, John acknowledged that in the midst of his confusion and guilt, his motives had not been entirely unselfish. In John's 1970 *roman a clef, The Indian Sign*, protagonist and narrator Nelson A. Nelson also buys some jewelry as a Christmas present for his estranged wife. "It pleased my ego to be kind," Nelson explains, "but of course it wasn't kindness at all. I didn't want to hurt myself by hurting her."

Whatever John's subconscious motives may have been, Frances frustrated them, for when presented with the gift, she began weeping. John retreated in confusion. It was not a very merry Christmas for him, or for Frances.

CHAPTER TWENTY-SEVEN

Throughout his life, John Gunther sought relief from his troubles in one of two ways: working or socializing. In early 1942, he found that he could not work, and so his life began to revolve around New York's illustrious cafe society. Many of the old Vienna crowd, including William Shirer and Jimmy Sheean were now living in New York. Like John, they became part of a hard-drinking social circle which included members from old New York families, show business, the sports world, writers, Europeans who had fled their homelands, and even a few military figures. "If in some ways it was the New York equivalent of Evelyn Waugh's Bright Young Things in London before the war," noted British travel writer Jan Morris in her 1987 book *Manhattan '45*, "in others it was a foretaste of Jet Sets yet to come."[1]

Walter Winchell, Leonard Lyons, Ed Sullivan, and the other

New York gossip columnists became celebrities themselves by reporting the comings and goings of New York society. Its members idled away the nights, eating and drinking at plush hotels and expensive night spots. Like John's beloved Vienna coffee houses, each establishment catered to a slice of the city's social life. Sardi's was popular with the theatre people and visiting Hollywood celebrities. El Morocco was an expensive supper club frequented by "old money" (prompting the *New Yorker* to quip that it was here that "the dress-for-dinner contingent is making its last stand."); Toots Shor's (owned by a Runyonesque character of the same name who subscribed to the theory "a bum who ain't drunk by midnight ain't trying") was popular with baseball players and other sportsmen. The 21 Club ("21" to regulars), a one-time speakeasy, was an "in" place for movie stars and writers. Another was the famous Stork Club, which became one of John's favorite haunts because he was given red carpet treatment here.

Like 21, the Stork Club had begun life as an upscale speakeasy. Following the repeal of Prohibition, owner and resident host Sherman Billingsley—"Sherm" to the regulars—turned it into Manhattan's trendiest nightspot. Billingsley, who grew up as a dirt poor Oklahoma farm boy, considered the restaurant to be "his place," and he treated the more celebrated patrons as his personal guests.

Walter Winchell had his own private table at the Stork Club, and was on hand most nights to see and be seen. It was Winchell who dubbed the restaurant "the New Yorkiest place in town," and it was his syndicated *Daily Mirror* newspaper gossip column and network radio broadcasts that created the night club's aura of mystery and glamour. Winchell, like other favored patrons, dined in the exclusive Cub Room, an inner sanctum isolated from the rest of the establishment by a red velvet rope and an imperious maitre d'. Even for those privileged enough to be invited inside there was a pecking order; Sherm Billingsley tended to those celebrities who were personal friends, or rated special treatment. Those chosen few usually received complimentary Arpege or French champagne, and Billingsley, himself, personally saw to their bills.

Everyone who was *anyone* frequented the Stork Club, if they were deemed acceptable by the management, for Billingsley was an unabashed racist. He let it be known that blacks were not welcome at the Stork Club. Nor were Jews, despite the fact that "resident publicist" Walter Winchell, the grandson of a rabbi, spoke fluent Yiddish, and had grown up in Harlem when the neighborhood was Jewish. However, his network radio show and syndicated column reached an audience of fifty million people.

Black singer Muriel Rahn, who starred in a 1944 Broadway production of *Carmen Jones*, was turned away at the door when she tried to enter the Stork Club for a guild-sponsored party. The maitre d' curtly informed her that she "had not been invited." When Rahn produced her invitation, the maitre d' sniffed that the restaurant was full. He then turned heel, and walked away.

A similar incident occurred in 1951, when the famous black dancer Josephine Baker was shabbily treated by the the Stork Club staff. Rather than let the humiliation pass, she complained to the National Association for the Advancement of Colored People (NAACP), pressed the matter in the courts, and loudly denounced Winchell, who had witnessed the ugly incident without intervening—despite his frequent pronouncements about being a liberal, and opposing racial discrimination.

The ensuing public controversy received front page coverage in all the the New York papers, and Winchell's many enemies were quick to denounce him. Rival columnist Ed Sullivan of the *New York Daily News* called Winchell "a small-time Hitler;" others called him a lot worse. Winchell, who was more used to talking about other people than being talked about, reacted angrily. It was the beginning of the end for his career when the tide of public opinion turned against him.[2]

Like many radio personalities, Winchell tried without success to make the transition to television. His frenetic, machine-gun manner of speaking was ill-suited to the new medium (apart from a stint as the narrator on the 1920s gangster series, *The Untouchables*). Thus when Winchell resigned from the American Broadcasting Corporation (ABC) television over a contract dispute, the network was quick to accept. By 1960, syndication of Winchell's column had dropped from 1,000 newspapers to 150; three years later, the *Daily Mirror* closed after a fourteen-day printers' strike. The Stork Club, too, fell on hard times, closing its doors in 1965. Owner Sherman Billingsley died broke. But all that was years in the future.

In the early 1940s, the Stork Club reached its zenith. Such was the allure of the club, and the nature of celebrity that even the most famous willingly suffered indignities for the "privilege" of gaining admittance. On one occasion, Nobel Prize-winning writer Sinclair Lewis was stopped by a surly doorman who did not recognize him. Thinking quickly, Lewis explained that he wanted to talk to a newspaperman.

"Give me a summary of what you want to tell him," the doorman demanded.

Once inside, Lewis was escorted over to a table in the Cub Room where John Gunther was having a drink. John vouched for Lewis, then quizzed him on what he had told the doorman to gain admittance.

"I can't remember," Lewis said. "I can't even remember the first line of any lecture I've made. I'll bet you can't either."

"It's a bet," said John. He then began, "Ladies and Gentlemen, we're here tonight . . . "

"Okay, okay," Lewis said. "You win. What are you drinking?"[3]

It was to the Stork Club that John often took the beautiful women he was seen escorting around town. Gossip columnists spotted him there with of Broadway and Hollywood actresses, singers, and writers. On one occasion Leonard Lyons reported that producer Michael Todd encountered John sitting at a favorite Cub Room table having dinner with a stunning brunette. Todd had noticed the woman in his own office a few days earlier. Assuming that she was there for the usual reason, he told his staff to offer her a spot in the chorus line of one of his shows. The woman had laughed, and walked out. Todd was curious. He stopped to say hello to John, and to be introduced to his date. John introduced him to Kathleen Winsor, the author of a best-selling historical novel entitled, *Forever Amber.* She could not dance.[4]

Apart from an ability to get a good table at the Stork Club, 21, and other New York night spots, John's celebrity status had other implications. For one, President Roosevelt invited him on April 23, 1942, for tea and a chat about *Inside Latin America*, which was still selling well six months after its publication. Upon arriving at the White House, John was startled to find FDR and the first lady waiting at the front door. There were embarrassed smiles all around. Mrs. Roosevelt explained that the White House staff had scrambled the president's calendar with the unfortunate result that he had two appointments scheduled for the same time—one with John, the other with Prince Bernard and Princess Juliana of the Netherlands.

Mrs. Roosevelt made the best of an unfortunate situation by suggesting that John join them for the meeting with the Dutch royals. "What he (the prince) thought of my being there, I have no idea," John wrote later. As it turned out, the prince recalled having met John in London during the mid 1930s, and so the tea quickly turned informal. They gossiped about events in Europe, and about John's upcoming trip to Hollywood. He planned to spend July and all of August working on three movie screenplays.

In the wake of Pearl Harbor, John pondered his role in the war effort. "What am I, a coward?" he asked of himself in his diary.[5] Dealing with his uncertainties in the same way that many other writers and entertainers did, he opted to do his part by working on films that supported the Allied cause. On a trip to Washington in the spring of 1942, he met director Frank Capra, who was making films for the Office of War Information. Capra invited John to come to Hollywood to write some scripts about the Army. Not long afterwards, he did so on a four-week guarantee at $1,500 per week.

Producer Darryl Zanuck of Twentieth Century Fox asked John and Mickey Uris to co-author a documentary about the United States Signal Corps. John also wrote a commentary for a film about Air Force pilots called *Thunder Birds*, which starred Gene Tierney and Preston Foster. And he worked on a script for *The Battle of China*, a documentary being co-directed by Capra and Russian emigre Anatole Litvak as part of a series of propaganda films called *Why We Fight*.

John enjoyed the work. He was well suited to the frenetic pace of Hollywood, where during the early 1940s the studios turned out films with machine-like precision. Hollywood "gasped" at the speed with which he wrote, as a *New York Post* entertainment reporter noted. John was fascinated by the complexity of the movie-making process—"Cooperative creativity as a fine art . . . " he described it in his diary.[6]

Adding to his enjoyment at being in southern California was the social life. John's name soon began appearing in the Hollywood gossip columns. Louella Parsons reported that he dined with the Rathbones, and that he attended a birthday party that Anne Warner threw for her husband Jack. Another columnist reported that John had been seen with actress Patricia Dane, who told friends that she liked "to hear Gunther talk about the war." John also met John Huston, Geraldine Fitzgerald, Marlene Dietrich, Miriam Hopkins, and Greta Garbo, among other stars. Garbo, in particular, would become a close friend, while Hopkins and John had a brief romance.

John began dating the former Paramount film starlet in late 1942, when Hopkins moved to New York. She was starring on Broadway at the time, and traveling in the same social circles John. Her attraction for him was understandable. A native of Georgia, Hopkins was a dazzling blond. She had occasionally dated publisher Bennett Cerf early in her career. Cerf recalled in his memoirs what it was that made Miriam Hopkins's so alluring. On one occasion he had taken her to a Yale-Princeton football game, and within minutes of taking a seat, she "had twenty Yale boys explaining football to her . . . she was irresistible."[7]

Hopkins had originally studied ballet, but had instead settled for work as a chorus girl after she broke an ankle. She eventually turned to acting, and for a time in the 1930s became a popular film star, mostly playing sharp-tongued characters. In 1939 she engaged in a publicity-inspired feud with Bette Davis, her co-star on several occasions. By the time that Hopkins met John Gunther she was middle-aged, and her years as a leading lady were past, as were three (of her four) marriages. For a time, some people seriously wondered if John Gunther might become her fourth husband. He might have, had he not been still in love with Agnes Knickerbocker.

Throughout this period, John and Agnes continued writing and calling, and from time to time they met in New York. Always the script was the same: furtive nights or weekends followed by the inevitable tearful partings. Always in the back of John's mind were fears of being found out before he was in a position to ask Agnes to marry him. Always there were uncertainties about Frances. Some days she steadfastly refused to agree to a divorce; others, she appeared to waver.

All of this emotional turmoil took its toll on John, who was still not working, apart from the Hollywood junket. Plans for another *Inside* book, this one about the United States, were shelved when he could not decide how to begin the massive project. About the only work that he was doing regularly was his radio broadcasting, which he did not consider to be serious work.

Beginning in 1939, John began doing some work for NBC,

which asked him to hold forth on a range of subjects. At times, he appeared as a panelist on "Town Meeting of the Air," a current affairs program that featured journalists, diplomats, and academics. John was usually interviewed in his capacity as "a famed foreign correspondent," or as "one of America's foremost authorities on foreign affairs."[8]

At other times, John took part in other NBC news shows. Typical was a December 4, 1939, show that dealt with the question, "What are the Real Issues of the European War?" Appearing along with John were his old friend Jay Allen, now a freelance newspaper reporter, and Anne O'Hare McCormick, of the *New York Times*. In John's comments, written in advance, he painted a vivid picture of the scene in London at the time of his recent visit. He described being awakened one morning by the sound of a brass band playing martial music. "It occurred to me that this is a very strange war indeed . . . a war without parades, without banners, without heroics, without romanticism," he said. John continued on to make the point that the war in Europe was a complex tangle of competing causes: England versus Germany, democracy versus dictatorship, and conservatism versus revolution.

Throughout this period, depending upon his own schedule and the course of the war, John's voice was heard on radio regularly. He served as a guest commentator when Raymond Gram Swing was away. He sometimes filled in for Walter Winchell, and sometimes appeared on a question-and-answer program called "Information, Please." The latter show was a lot of fun, and puns flew thick and fast. Once the panelists were asked to identify a certain Middle Eastern potentate. When John quickly volunteered the answer, emcee Clifton Fadiman demanded, "Are you Shah?" Without missing a beat, John replied, "Sultanly."[9]

Radio broadcasting was easy work for John. Like most old newspapermen, he regarded the medium more as a form of entertainment than as a serious news vehicle. There were a number of reasons. One was was the technological limitations of radio. At one point, John mused in his diary, "Problem of a radio man: to get near a mike. My job should be to report, not merely to see. But from the point of view of a book, to see is best. To hell with radio."[10]

Another problem with news broadcasting from John's perspective was that while network radio had come of age during the war, the medium still had a long way to go before reaching its true potential. In good part, this was due to restrictions placed on reporters in the field by their bosses.

Until October 1945, the networks operated under a bizarre self-imposed rule that all news reports had to be done live. The use of recordings was forbidden. As a result, correspondents were obliged to call in eyewitness reports by telephone. While this sometimes made for dramatic radio—as in 1940 when Edward R. Murrow described the Nazi bombing of London as it happened—it seriously impeded the ability of correspondents to do their jobs. Such a restriction would not pose any problem in these days of cellular telephones, but in the 1940s it was virtually impossible to report a war in which often there was no real "front"; armies attacked or retreated with lightning speed.

This ridiculous policy against the use of recording in news broadcasts had another significant consequence. Correspondents sometimes reported to America via shortwave radio, and because of prevailing atmospheric conditions the quality of the signals received in New York (where the networks were headquartered) usually seemed better during daylight hours, than at night. Yet because of the restrictions it was forbidden to tape the reports. As a result, the quality of live network broadcasts from Europe varied greatly. Sometimes the signal could not be received at all. And, of course, the time difference between New York and Europe meant a long night for anyone who was reporting live during prime time evening hours.

What all this amounted to was frustration for network correspondents, and a lessening of the respect accorded radio by print journalists—John Gunther among them. He often wrote scripts off the top of his head. Typically, his diary entry for October 24, 1939, reads: "Did my broadcast about India—in two hours and 10 minutes of actual writing time. And the research was not difficult. All out of my head, except for a few bits of current news, in fact."[11]

In February 1943, John and John Vandercook, the explorer-adventurer, launched a half-hour radio show on Sunday evenings on NBC's Blue network. Although the show provided John with a focus and gave him a high profile, he was growing restless. He longed to return to writing. "I can never remember what I say in a broadcast . . . but I know every line of every story I have ever written," he mused in his diary.[12]

On the rare occasions when radio did spark his interest, it only made him long for the old days when he had been a newspaper reporter. On November 7, 1942, he was eating dinner with his son Johnny when Nancy Barnett, his secretary, called to say that the Allies had landed in North Africa. John raced to the office with Johnny in tow, to rewrite his radio script for that evening. He dashed off six pages on the implications of the invasion, all in forty minutes. "I think I wrote that the biggest and best news since Pearl Harbor had happened, or something of the sort," John recalled in his diary. "This was very good going and reminded me of newspaper days again. It is a pure joy to work under pressure."[13]

In the spring of 1943, John decided that the time had come return to reporting. Doing so would be his real contribution to the war effort. Cass Canfield and Carl Brandt were enthusiastic. So John arranged with the North American Newspaper Alliance (NANA) syndicate, and NBC radio's Blue Network to serve as a war correspondent at the headquarters of Allied commander Dwight D. Eisenhower.

John had some difficulty in arranging clearance. Ike, headquartered in Algiers, was reluctant to allow journalists to join him at this crucial time in the war. It was only at the intercession of John McCloy, undersecretary of war, that the general made an exception for John.

On the evening of June 25, Miriam Hopkins threw a small farewell party for John, and for Jimmy Sheean, who was also going overseas. What began as an intimate Saturday night gathering of a dozen people grew until a crowd of more than sixty of the "regulars" were jammed into Hopkins' Sutton Place apartment. Photographer Margaret Bourke-White was there, so were writers Dorothy Parker, Jay Allen, and gossip columnist Elsa Maxwell. It was a memorable send-off.

CHAPTER TWENTY-EIGHT

Early on the morning of Sunday, June 27, 1943, John Gunther showered, shaved, and donned a fresh, new United States Army uniform. Accompanied by Miriam Hopkins, who had decided to see him off to war, he departed for LaGuardia Airport by cab.

As he reported to the departures area John was lugging Miriam's portable typewriter, which he had borrowed, and a bulky officer's kit bag—"55 pounds, to the ounce," he would recall.[1] Most war correspondents had low travel priority, and went overseas by ship. John was more fortunate. Friends in high places had appealed to Major General Harold L. George, the chief of Air Transport Command (ATC), to get him on a flight to the front. Ignoring the fact that John lacked a visa for a stopover in England, the clerk issued him a plane ticket for Marrakesh, Morocco, the "end of the line" for ATC flights.

During the war the ATC, the army air fleet used civilian aircraft to carry men and supplies to U.S. bases around the globe. The service logged a staggering three million miles a day. Despite being able to fly the long transoceanic routes only in fair weather, during the crucial 1942-43 flying "season" the ATC carried 50,000 passengers, and cargoes of everything from rope and refrigerators to ammunition and Coca Cola.

In at least one sense, the ATC was on a par with many commercial airlines: its flights were invariably late; sometimes they did not appear at all. John spent a long, tiring day waiting and wondering if his plane would ever arrive from Washington, D.C., where it had been delayed. It was not an encouraging start to a trip already fraught with uncertainty. In the heat of the midday sun the thermometer in the makeshift passenger lounge rose as did the level of the passengers' impatience. John wrote in his diary (which was later published as the book *D-Day*), "By noon, I looked as if I had been dragged heels first through a Turkish bath, and then bounced up and down in a fountain."[2]

The DC-4 Skymaster that was to carry him on his journey finally appeared out of the darkness at nine o'clock that night. When it did, twenty-eight weary passengers were jammed in around a load of spare parts for military aircraft in Europe. Shortly afterwards the plane roared down the runway and off into the northeastern sky. John fell asleep listening to the drone of the engines, and craving a cigarette.

The next thing he knew, it was five hours later. Someone shouted above the roar that they were about to land at Gander, Newfoundland. At that time the town was an American air base that had been included as part of the 1940 Lend-Lease deal by which Great Britain traded eight military bases to the U.S. for fifty old destroyers. (It was not until four years after the war, in 1949, that Newfoundlanders voted in a referendum to become the Canada's tenth province.)

John's memories of Gander were vivid. He recalled it in *D-Day* as "prunes for breakfast and a thin soup of chopped beef; barracks on stilts; a thin icing of frost on mud; a couple of Royal Air Force ferry planes; a ping-pong table and the Encyclopaedia Britannica in the officers' mess; broad wooden walks over slimy puddles; the atmosphere of a western frontier town still in construction . . . ."[3]

Feeling rejuvenated, John crawled back into his makeshift seat on the plane shortly after breakfast for the ten-hour transatlantic flight to the United Kingdom. Peering out the window at the sun dappled ocean far below, he saw what he at first thought were huge white caps on the waves. Then he realized what he was seeing: icebergs. It was with a renewed sense of purpose that he and several of the other passengers examined the plane's arctic survival gear, and the Mae West lifejackets stowed in the overhead luggage racks. "Almost useless, I'd say," sniffed a colonel who was a medical officer. "In water this cold nobody could survive for more than thirty minutes."

Spurred on by this revelation, John began reading in earnest the emergency instructions painted in heavy block letters on the wall next to his seat. They explained the procedure for "ditching"—crash landing in the sea. "I had not known before that you must loosen your collar, otherwise your neck will be broken," he noted.[5]

Fortunately, the instructions for ditching were not needed; their plane arrived after a routine flight at an airport near the town of St. Andrews, Scotland. Head winds had slowed them, however; they had missed the scheduled connecting flight to Morocco. John stayed over until the next night. He slept, telephoned friends in London, and sat on a terrace watching the comings and goings of military aircraft. He flew on to Marrakesh on June 29, landing in time for breakfast. There was a brief stopover before he went on to Algiers aboard a Royal Air Force flight that arrived early that afternoon. John marveled about the speed of modern air travel. "We had come from New York to Africa, via Scotland, in less than three days overall, and in an elapsed flying time of 30 hours, 58 minutes—without a bump."[6]

John encountered several friends, Richard Mowrer of the *Chicago Daily News* and Irwin Shaw, the novelist-playwright, in Algiers. The city was as busy as a ticking clock. John did the first of what was to be an irregular series of radio for NBC radio on Friday, July 2. The combination of the time difference between North Africa and New York, military censorship, and a lack of equipment prevented him from fulfilling his original tri-weekly broadcasting schedule. In fact, events were such that it soon became impossible for John to make any reports at all for several weeks.

Noticing that the port was jammed with ships and troops, John sensed that something significant was in the works. When he asked for an explanation, Lieutenant Colonel Joseph P. Phillips, the military public relations officer, sent him to Harry Butcher, the chief aide to Allied Commander in Chief (C in C) General Dwight D. Eisenhower. Butcher, who was cordial, instructed John to go to the stores, and withdraw a field kit. It contained a mosquito net, some blankets, a helmet and gas mask, a canteen, a flashlight and various gadgets "which I did not understand,"[7] as John noted. He had no inkling of why he needed this gear, or of where he was going. Then a British officer assigned to help him prepare mentioned that his destination was the island of Malta, in the strait between Sicily and Tunisia. As both John and the enemy would subsequently learn, Eisenhower was about to move his headquarters there to prepare for Operation HUSKY—the invasion of Sicily, the vulnerable underbelly of the Axis powers.

Malta, the main supply base for British armies in North Africa battling General Erwin Rommel, the infamous Desert Fox, was considered strategically vital. Thus German and Italian forces besieged the island. Despite losing more than 1,000 planes in the battle, the Luftwaffe bombed mercilessly; in January 1942, alone, Nazi bombers pounded Malta 262 times. Yet the Allies somehow held the island—this "Stalingrad of the Mediterranean," as a visiting Russian journalist dubbed it. The cost in men and equipment was terrible. The Allied high command survived by taking refuge in an elaborate system of underground tunnels that provided haven from the bombing and welcome relief from the relentless sun.

General Eisenhower, who eschewed publicity, had initially wanted no correspondents along when he went to Malta. It was Phillips and Butcher persuaded him that someone should be there to record for posterity what was about to unfold. John and British journalist Ted Gilling, a former exchange telegraph operator at Buckingham Palace, were allowed to join Ike's staff; John was to file stories to the War Department in Washington for use by a "pool" of eighty-six North American papers, while Gilling's dispatches were fed to the British Ministry of Information for use by papers in the United Kingdom.

John, along with most of Eisenhower's staff, left Algiers for Tunis, the Tunisian capital, on the afternoon of July 3. They flew on a stripped down, bullet scarred DC-3 of the Troop Carrier Command. After spending the night in Tunis, John and Ted Gilling made the dangerous two-hour flight to Malta early on the morning of July 5. Upon their arrival they wandered aimlessly in the scorching heat for most of the day. No one they met had the faintest idea where they were to report. As John subsequently learned, General Eisenhower's plans were such a closely guarded secret that only a small handful of people on the island even knew of his imminent arrival.

After finally contacting the C in C's advance organizers, John and Ted found a room on the fourth floor of a tumbledown hotel called the Phoenicia, where many Allied officers were being billeted. "One cannot tell, however, what parts (of the hotel) had been demolished and what the bombing has obliterated," John noted. "About one-quarter of the structure is in ruins, and every inch is permeated with heavy white limestone dust. There are no elevators, of course; the stairs are crumbling, half worn or bombed away, and dangerous in the dark. You can climb right up to the roof where most of the top has been blown off."[8]

The room accommodations were primitive. John slept on an iron bed frame surrounded by sand fly net, and used his coat for a pillow. The hotel's water supply was turned on for only a few hours per day, and all bathing was forbidden. In the stifling heat John, who had not showered in four days, felt as grimy as he looked. His shoe laces were broken; his pants belt was broken; his sunglasses were broken. And he was bedeviled by sand fleas. When John encountered British Field Marshal Bernard Montgomery ("Monty") for the first time, Monty shook his head and observed, "You look hot. Very hot. I must say, you look *very* hot."[9]

Despite his discomfort, John made do. In fact, he confided to his diary that he savored the hardship. It had pushed his personal anguish out of his mind; life in New York, and his troubles with Frances and Agnes indeed seemed a long way off. "What I have enjoyed most so far is the aloneness," he wrote. "Before long this emotion will change, of course. Not a soul knows where I am; it is inconceivable that I should get a letter; I have no impulse at all to write anybody."[10]

Despite the daily air raids, the grim realities of the war still seemed remote. In John's mind, the severest hardship was the shortage of everyday items such as toothpaste, razor blades, soap, shoelaces, and matches. The night of July 7, he managed to sleep through a German air raid. It was a dangerous thing to do. "The most extraordinary thing in the world is the way you get used to things," he wrote. "I feel as if I have been in this hotel for months, and I wouldn't trade a minute of it for anything on earth."[11]

John and Ted Gilling toured Malta on July 8, and had lunch with the British governor, Field Marshal Lord Gort, at his residence in the Verdala palace. Built in 1586 by the Knights of St. John, the palace had enormous, thick stone walls and roof. The defenses, which had been built to withstand bombardment by sixteenth century Turkish cannons, proved less effective against the might of high-explosive Nazi bombs; parts of the palace were badly damaged. Even so, Eisenhower's staff was hurriedly turning the building into a makeshift command post. Ike was billeted in a small clay-floored room that was so damp that the general complained he could not even light a cigarette.

The same afternoon they toured the palace, John and Ted wandered across the road to explore a labyrinth of caves and tunnels which served as a makeshift air raid shelter. There, in the cool, shadowy gloom, John was surprised by a familiar figure in a spotless white British naval uniform. "We were deep down; surrounding us was slimy rock. I have seldom felt so entirely encased by walls. I recognized the approaching figure at about the same moment he recognized me," John later recalled; it was Lord Louis Mountbatten, a cousin of England's King George VI. "Well, you certainly are *inside* Malta," Mountbatten chuckled.[12]

John, who by this point in his career had already grown weary of "inside" jokes (they would continue the rest of his life), laughed in spite of himself. It was a matter of much pride with him that he has been recognized by someone as eminent as Mountbatten. John could not resist sharing the story with others, including General Eisenhower when he arrived on the island.

John, Ted, and three other reporters, who were part of Field Marshal Bernard Montgomery's contingent (Ned Russell of the United Press, Evelyn Montague of the Manchester *Guardian*, and Frank Gillard of the BBC), sat down with Ike on the morning of July 9. This informal "press conference" went on for over an hour. They discussed news coverage of the impending military operation, and Ike listened to suggestions from the newsmen about how they could do their jobs more efficiently. As John recalled, the conversation was frank, yet the atmosphere was cordial. The general promised to reconsider the details of the censorship under which news reports were written.

"This was the first glimpse I had of the commander-in-chief," John wrote. "(He is) medium height with a nice solid build; a hard friendly handshake; sandy hair, widely set bright blue eyes under a fine broad forehead; a wide mobile grin; an impression of modesty, directness, and common sense." But beneath the easy charm, John detected "a note of essential toughness, even ruthlessness." And there was another quality that John recalled long after: Ike's modesty. "I never saw him wear more than two decorations, although many of his men are bedecked like awnings."[13]

Ike had informed the newsmen that they were to consider themselves part of his staff; they would be treated as such—and held responsible as such. True to his word, he arranged for them to dine that evening with General Sir Harold Alexander, the British officer who would command ground operations in Sicily; Alexander, said to have been the last British soldier to leave the beach at Dunkirk, was candid in outlining for them the details of Operation HUSKY. "He looks a little like W. Somerset Maugham, with an uplifted chin, a beautifully poised head, neat brown mustache," wrote John.[14]

After dinner, John and Ted Gilling were again summoned to Eisenhower's quarters. The C in C announced that he would see to it that they were *fed* at least one hard news story per day, and they were free to report it, providing the pair agreed to observe a few basic rules. Having no real choice, they agreed with Ike's request that they be "moderate" in their reporting ("Don't call it a *big* attack," he cautioned them. "Maybe it's going to fail. Then where would we be, if we had claimed it was something very big?"),[15] that they avoid detailing the specifics of military operations, and above all, that they write nothing about him *personally*.

Although Eisenhower was the supreme commander of five separate military forces—including the American Army and Air Force, the American Navy, the British Army, the Royal Navy, and the Royal Air Force—he wanted no mention of himself in dispatches, unless it was essential. Even then, it was only to be in connection with the names of other officers of the Allied high command. For security reasons, stories could not be datelined as being from "General Eisenhower's headquarters," but rather "Allied headquarters." All communiques would be marked "MOST SECRET," and air mailed to both Algiers and Tunis. From there, they were to be wired directly to New York.

Satisfied they could work under those restrictions, John and Ted returned to their hotel, where they climbed up to the roof to watch preparations for Operation HUSKY. The invasion was scheduled to begin at first light, but Alexander and Eisenhower had been concerned about the weather. It was apparent why. The prevailing wind, which usually dropped at dusk, had continued to blow stiffly all night. It swayed the trees and whipped up foamy whitecaps on the sea. No matter, the decision was made to proceed with the invasion. And so a few minutes after nine o'clock John peered up into the moonlit sky at the first wave of fighters and transport planes carrying parachutists and glider troops. The aircraft skimmed low over the harbor and winged their way northeast on the seventy-five-mile flight to the beaches of Sicily. The shock troops of Operation HUSKY, the largest amphibious invasion ever to that time, were on their way in. At dawn on the morning of July 10 more than 160,000 Allied troops and 600 tanks were put ashore under the cover of an intense naval bombardment. The battle for Europe had begun.

Malta was alive with rumors, speculation, doubt, and finally jubilation the next day, as the first sketchy reports of the fighting reached Ike's headquarters. Montgomery's landings were thought to be successful, but there was no word for several hours from the General George Patton. "Just like [him] not to let us know a darned thing," commented one of Eisenhower's aides.[16]

At four o'clock that afternoon John and Ted went to the Verdala Palace to speak with the C in C. He was jubilant. "By golly," he muttered. "I don't understand it! By golly, to think we've done it again!" The Allied forces had caught the German and Italian defenders by surprise. Ike grinned as he rocked back in a wicker chair, his heels hooked on the lower rung. "Every once in a while I like to tell you fellows something like this, because you might hear it from somebody else, and if *I* tell you, it shuts you up!" he said with a laugh.[17]

It was not until two days later that John and Ted saw firsthand the success of the invasion. They accompanied Ike and a couple of his aides on a running visit to General Patton at the Sicilian beachhead; an impatient Ike could wait no longer to find out how his unpredictable general was faring. At one point, the Royal Navy destroyer carrying Eisenhower's party came under shelling from a German shore battery. "The last time I came under fire . . . the shots fell 300 yards away, but now they're missing by 400. I guess we're doing better," Ike quipped. Rejecting a steel helmet offered to him, he whispered to John, "They treat me like a bird in a gilded cage."[18]

That comment was echoing in John's mind, as the ship passed Cape Passaro, a quiet beach on the southeast coast of Sicily, John impulsively suggested to Ike that he should go ashore.

"Why?" came the puzzled response.

John replied that a news story about the Allied C in C visiting occupied Europe would have great propaganda value. He did not mention that such an event would be a news scoop for him. Ike liked the idea. He barked some orders, and the ship promptly halted. Eisenhower and a few aides boarded a duck—one of the amphibious vehicles used to transport men and equipment to the beach—for an impromptu landing. John, touting a movie camera, was at the elbow of the C in C of Allied forces as he waded through the surf to set foot in occupied Europe for the first time. A glance at the uniforms of the soldiers unloading supplies, erecting tents, and building signal boxes, told Ike they were Canadian, not American troops. Approaching the first officer he spotted, he said, "My name is Eisenhower. I want to talk to the senior Canadian officer of this beachhead." Informed by the startled soldier that headquarters was already several miles inland, they borrowed a couple of jeeps and set off. The ride through the hot, dusty Sicilian countryside was bumpy and fast. There were German snipers everywhere. Otherwise, the visit uneventful, and when Ike returned to his ship he was in a buoyant mood. "I kept thinking that this man might be a four-star general and all that," John wrote, "but what I would always remember about him was that he was such a splendid human being."[19]

That experience on the beach intrigued John. It also inspired him to gain a fresh perspective on the fighting, one that could not be found at Ike's headquarters. "I have been bursting with ideas for stories these crowded days. I go to bed happy, and wake up feeling wonderful," he wrote in his diary. "Yet I feel that I have so much still to learn, and that every year there are fewer years left to learn in."[20]

John and Ted Gilling left for Montgomery's headquarters in Sicily a few days later. This flamboyant, brash Irishman had become a legend among the Allied troops to whom he was known as "General Alex." Only a handful of close aides, and other generals dared to call him "Monty" to his face. "[He] looks something like a hawk, something—I don't mean this disparagingly—like a fox," John wrote. "He has the most piercing and luminous blue eyes I have ever seen. He is very alert and clipped in conversation, and his most striking verbal mannerism is the way he repeats himself. When he talks, he puts the second finger of his right hand on the little finger of his left, and ticks off his points with mathematical precision."[21]

Upon meeting the General for the first time on Malta, John had presented him with a letter of introduction from Wendell Willkie, the prominent Indiana Republican who would be the GOP's candidate in the 1944 presidential election. Willkie had promised John a series of letters, but being busy he had suggested that John write them. As John later told *New York Post* gossip columnist Elsa Maxwell, he then had the pleasure of describing himself as "My old friend Gunther . . . " Willkie signed the letters without even reading them; some were addressed to people whom, it turned out, he had not even met.

When handed Willkie's letter, Montgomery was puzzled for a moment. Then, suddenly, it came to him. "Ah, ah!" he exclaimed. "Willkie, Willkie . . . of course I know Willkie. He was my guest at Alamein (in late 1942). Ha, Willkie! Why, I showed him a great battle once!" Turning his attention to John, the general said, "Oh yes, you're Gunther," he chuckled. "Inside or outside of what, I can't remember."[22]

At one point during their rambling conversation, Montgomery mentioned to John that he had kept a diary for many of his thirty-three years in the army. It would "blow off everybody's head between Alamein and London," he laughed. Intrigued by John's comment—which had been prompted by a request from Cass

Canfield—that he should allow others access to the information since the true history of the war in North Africa "could never be written without it," Montgomery asked, "Tell me, would I get any money for my diary?"

"About $100,000, General," John speculated.

"A hundred thousand dollars? How much is that?" Montgomery asked an aide. Informed that it amounted to about 25,000 pounds British, he smiled to himself. "Well, guess I won't die in poorhouse after all," he said.[23]

Unlike the intimate situation at Ike's headquarters, in Sicily John and Ted were thrown into an Eighth Army press pool made up of fifteen journalists and six "conducting officers" whose job it was to oversee and guard them. The senior officer, Major Nigel Dugdale, had a wonderfully dry sense of humor, and on one occasion encountered John wandering about the camp in pajamas. "Where's your necktie?" he demanded.[24]

One of the conducting officers did not drive, so he could not transport the journalists. As a result, some dispatches took a week to reach North America. But on the whole, conditions were better in Sicily than on Malta. Censorship was less stringent, and for the first time in several weeks John was able to send a cable to NBC. Accommodations were improved, food was better, and with the front just two miles distant, there was no shortage of combat news. On the morning of July 21, John and Ted witnessed a furious battle for Simeto Bridge, a key point on the main road to the town of Catania, where crack units of the German army were dug in. The dead from both sides lay where they had fallen. Wrote John, "The shelling had been so intense . . . that there had been no opportunity for burial parties. We saw charred lumps of men, bodies without faces, a heap of old clothes with a leg protruding upward like a signpost, and bloated corpses melting blackly into the earth. The smell was sharp and obscene."[25]

John had experienced the horrors of modern war in Syria in 1926, when he had accompanied the French army sent to crush Druse rebels, but that had been nothing compared to the carnage he encountered in Sicily. Everywhere along the roadsides were the shallow graves of fallen soldiers, their helmets hanging forlornly from makeshift wooden crosses. Piles of empty petrol cans littered the ditches. Camouflaged tanks, looking like grazing elephants, rolled across the sloping, brownish-green countryside. The unmistakable, pungent smell of death was on the wind.

Convinced that the battle for Sicily had bogged down, John returned to Malta. He did some live radio broadcasts for NBC, and wrote a couple of articles about Eisenhower for *Reader's Digest*. Ike, too, was back on the island after returning from the front, and John was given a room in the same house as the C in C and his chief aide, Harry Butcher, were staying. For several days, John saw a lot of Eisenhower, and was able to gather additional information for his articles. They were among the first to provide the American public with a close-up glimpse of Ike at war, and helped to foster the war hero image that later served Ike so well during two terms in the White House.

John left Malta on August 3, 1943, bound for neutral Cairo. Here he interviewed Allied commanders, including Major General Lewis H. Brereton, the head of the U.S. army and air force in the Middle East. The Egyptian capital seemed strange indeed after the rigors of life on Malta; John was dazzled by the lights at night, and by the city's relaxed atmosphere. Although imports of consumer goods had been reduced slightly, the resulting shortages were insignificant. Only a year earlier, the German army had camped at Alamein, just forty miles distant. So certain was Rommel of taking the city that he had actually reserved a suite of rooms at Shepheard's, Cairo's finest hotel. By now, the panic that had gripped the city in those dark days was long forgotten. The hotels, restaurants, and clubs again were packed with the well- to-do, and apart from the fact that the telephones seldom worked—as was normal in Cairo—Egyptians seemed oblivious to the war, and to the cloak-and-dagger intrigues swirling about them. "Heaven knows I have not been away from New York long, but the normality here, all the rather febrile gaiety, seems odd," John wrote.[26]

He ran into several journalist friends from New York, and encountered comedian Jack Benny, of all people, on the terrace at Shepheard's. John and Frank Gervasi of *Collier's* magazine went out on the town. At the Club de Chasse, a busy open-air cafe in the shadow of the pyramids, they spotted a smartly dressed, powerfully built young man. It was King Farouk, the Egyptian monarch.

Gervasi, who knew Farouk, introduced John. The king was in a jovial mood, and treated them to a couple of bottles of champagne. John wisely did not mention that in his pocket he carried a letter of introduction to Farouk from Wendell Willkie.

After his recent visit to Eypyt, Willkie had written a book entitled *One World.* In it, he had suggested that it was Lord Killearn, the British governor, and not King Farouk who was the country's real ruler. Neither Farouk nor the British were pleased. The book had been banned and the mere mention of Willkie's name elicited hostility from Egyptian nationalists. Later, John learned that the Farouk letter was one of those that had been addressed to someone Willkie had never met.

From Egypt, John flew to Turkey, another neutral country. He interviewed Turkish officials in Istanbul, wrote some articles for the North American Newspaper Alliance, tried without luck to do some radio broadcasts for NBC radio, and revisited many of his old haunts from the days when had been based in Vienna. John found no shortage of companions. George Earle, a former American diplomat in Vienna and Sofia who had also been governor of Pennsylvania, was now in the Navy and stationed in Istanbul as assistant naval attache; Cyrus Sulzberger and Eric Gedye of the *New York Times* were there covering the war. So, too, were a number of other American reporters. Gedye, whom John had known in Vienna, mentioned that their mutual friend Bob Best was also in Turkey. The long-time United Press correspondent in Vienna, was working now for the Nazi news agency. John and Best had been close friends and regulars at the Café Louvre, the popular gathering spot for Vienna's foreign correspondents. John could not bear—nor did he dare—to contact Best.

Following brief stops in Beirut, Cairo, and Cyprus, John departed for New York aboard an ATC plane, which flew a circuitous southern route via central Africa to Brazil on its way home. As the aircraft neared the coast of southern Florida in the early evening of September 11, John stared out the window and daydreamed about the events of the last eleven weeks.

He had traveled thousands of miles, written a total of fifty-three articles, and done a dozen radio broadcasts. He had seen the war up close; he had smelled death, and more than once thought he had felt its clammy grip closing on him. "I reflected a little on this journey," John wrote in his diary, " . . . it had made me love Europe again, it had taught me a little about politics and the war and much about myself . . . ."[27] That newly found self awareness would prove invaluable in the trying days that lay ahead.

CHAPTER TWENTY-NINE

Back in New York after his eleven-week trip to the front, John Gunther knew that his perspective on life had changed. When confronted by the death and suffering that he had witnessed, his own problems had seemed insignificant. John examined his life, and resolved to start anew. To do so, he reconciled himself to the realization that he had to confront the demons which had haunted him for so long. That meant sorting out his tangled relationships with his wife Frances, and with Agnes Knickerbocker.

Following their separation, neither Frances nor John had begun divorce proceedings. The marriage had settled into an uneasy truce. By 1943, Frances no longer agreed to a divorce. She was content to let John take the initiative. When he was slow to do so, Frances taunted that she was his "excuse" for not having to marry any of the other women in his life. An element of truth was in that, but there were other reasons, too.

Apart from the trauma that he imagined the final break would have on Johnny, now fourteen, the reason John had not sought a divorce two years before—and still hesitated to do so—was his uncertainty about Frances's reaction. A decade earlier, when in Vienna, he had seriously contemplated divorce. He had been dissuaded by fears that Frances would harm herself, him, or Johnny. That had ceased to be a major concern. What John now dreaded most was Frances causing an uproar. He was not eager to have the gossip columnists delve into the details of a messy divorce, particularly his love affair with the wife of a friend and colleague. While John knew that the whole story would come out, he did not want it to do so until he was free to ask Agnes to marry him. Recalls Leonora Hornblow, "He knew Frances, and he knew it wasn't going to be easy getting out of the marriage . . . Frances made him incredibly angry sometimes, and irritated most of the time. She drove him wild."[1]

In the fall of 1943, Frances Gunther was dividing her time between a house that John had bought for her in Wilton, Connecticut, and an apartment he had rented for her in Manhattan. Nancy Barnett, John's secretary, recalls Frances as "having a very difficult time of it."[2] To fill the void in her life, she enrolled in courses on American diplomatic history and foreign policy at Yale University. In August 1943, she took part in a British Broadcasting Corporation transatlantic radio panel discussion on the future of the British Empire, which was moderated by Alistair Cooke. She was also active in an group called the Emergency Committee to save the Jewish People of Europe, and on November 23, 1943, she appeared on Capitol Hill along with New York Mayor Fiorello La Guardia to lobby the House Foreign Affairs Committee in support of a resolution to aid Jewish refugees.[3]

Frances had discovered the Zionist underground movement—the Irgun—in 1940, and embraced the group's militancy, which she felt could be adapted to the situation in India. She urged as much in her letters to Indian nationalist leader Jawaharlal Nehru. Achingly lonely, brooding, and passionate, Frances continued to be obsessed with Nehru, and with all that he represented. In a war-weary world filled with darkness and destruction, he had become her beacon of stability and hope;

she fantasized about going to him, and about becoming part of his life.

A letter that Frances wrote to Nehru dated September 19, 1943, hints at the fragility of her emotional state. "The sun is up calm and warm, but before dawn, when it was still dark, I had to turn on the bed light and took out your letters that lie in my bed table drawer," she wrote. "There were letters in your own hand. I have made typed copies of your letters that I read for everyday reading and the real letters lie in a special envelope for special, state, or desperate occasions, like dark, blue dawns like this dawn. I took them and read them—you'd think I'd know them by heart by this time—I do know them in my heart, but my slow mind needs them again anyway. I can't tell you what they do to me. They warm me like the sun. They dispel the wickedness and weariness in me and make me feel strong."[4]

When Nehru's nieces visited New York, Frances took them in, entertained them, and introduced them to American society from Eleanor Roosevelt down. Nancy Barnett recalls helping with arrangements for a party that Frances gave for the girls at her apartment. It was attended by many celebrities; Oswald Garrison Villard, the editor of *The Nation* magazine came. So, too, did Random House publisher Bennett Cerf, and many other members of the New York literary and theatre communities; John was not among them. Recalls Barnett: "Nehru's nieces rather took over to see that everyone had enough to drink and all that. They were having a ball. They were attractive, beautiful girls in their saris. I think they'd arrived in the U.S. on a troop ship, and they were full of tales about that."[5]

With the war still raging, most American liberals were preoccupied with issues other than India's fight for independence. Frances Gunther was one of the few who continued to be an outspoken proponent of the cause. In early 1944, she wrote a curious little softcover book on the subject entitled *Revolution in India* (Island Press).[6] It is a measure of her dedication to Indian nationalism, and to Nehru (who praised the book, while adding, "My sole grievance is that you boost me too much."[7]) that this highly personalized and partisan analysis of the situation was the only book that she ever completed. For all her intellectual brilliance and seething ambition, Frances remained incapable of the sustained effort needed to complete her literary projects. Thus all of her grand plans came to naught.

Frances intimated to friends that she was writing several books, one of which was to be titled *Inside Gunther.* In fact, in December 1940, she had written an article for the *Chicago Daily News* called "Inside Gunther's Interesting Library."[8] The article consisted of a list of books that John Gunther, "the famous journalist," was reading during the Christmas season. Despite the precedent, an *Inside Gunther* book was either a product of Frances's imagination, or it may have been another of the taunts that she so delighted in tossing her husband's way. If it was the latter, she achieved her purpose.

Given Frances's precarious mental state, the mere threat of her writing an *Inside Gunther* "tell-all" account of their marriage, and revealing the intimate details of John's personal life was enough to make him uneasy. It is not difficult to imagine his reaction, even a couple of years later, when Frances casually mentioned the possibility of such a book to a Minneapolis gossip columnist named Virginia Safford, who was visiting New York. When Safford reported the news, it spread quickly. "Of all the journalists who roam the world [Gunther] is perhaps the most colorful," Safford wrote.[9] Others evidently agreed, because several publishers called to express interest in such a book. Cass Canfield of Harper & Brothers had already suggested the same idea to John. He would continue doing so, without success.

Inside Gunther was never written, either by John or Frances. He was too busy with other concerns, and her desk remained heaped with uncompleted plays, articles, and manuscripts. Among them was the *Empire* book, which Frances had been writing for eight years. Verse was the sole literary vehicle that suited her passionate temperament, and emotional urges.

Frances was writing several long, introspective poems that dealt with the themes of life, love, and war. She was groping for some higher meaning in life, a philosophical anchor. The humanistic poetry Frances labored over in the empty sleepless nights which had become her bane, reflects the angst of the times, as well as her own unfulfilled ambitions and sexual urges. There were poems written to her beloved Nehru, who languished in a British prison in India until July 1945. Others expressed broader concerns, mostly Frances's doubts and fears about humanity's future.

In one series of haunting, tragic poems called "Earth,"[10] she gave voice to the lamentations of a tired planet wracked by war, evil, and barbarity. And she wondered how mankind could be so destructive. In another group of poems entitled, "What, Victory?" Frances wrote of, "The loneliness/the desolateness/the sickness to the heart/of all of us all over the earth . . . ." She mused about the docility of the women who looked on in silence as their men engaged in an orgy of bloodletting. "During the whole ritualistic procedure,/this is what we are thinking:/Your [sic] poor bloody crazy crackbrained stark staring/raving mad suicidal lunatic blathering beloved/infantile idiots/all of you/everywhere."

Frances mailed copies of these poems to Nehru. She also submitted them to popular magazines such as *Atlantic*, *Saturday Night* and *Ladies Home Journal*, all of which rejected them. Having been asked for comments on one of the war poems, Dorothy Thompson scribbled a note to Frances with the observation that America was "not ready for this poetry."[11] She was right.

For obvious reasons, Frances did not show the poems to her estranged husband. Even if she had done so, it is unlikely that he would have offered any worthwhile criticism. John had an expansive capacity for work, yet he had fallen into a creative lethargy. He was writing little, and merely "going through the motions," even with his evening radio show on WJZ, the NBC affiliate in New York. As he admitted in his 1962 memoir, *A Fragment of Autobiography*, "my heart and backsides were not in it."[12] His diary entries from this period, often one-liners, note that he had a "dopey day" or lost the day to a hangover.[13]

John drank when he thought about Agnes; he was preoccupied with her. She dominated his life. It frustrated him that he was no closer to understanding Agnes's intentions than he had been before his overseas trip. While she continued to plead for time to deal with her emotions, it seemed that she lacked the will—or was it desire?—to leave her husband. Like John, she had become enmeshed in a bittersweet affair from which there was no easy way out.

Deep down inside, John was like a vain, lovesick school boy who refused to confront with that reality, or to let go. Years earlier, as a young reporter at the *Chicago Daily News*, he had pursued Helen Hahn, his first true love, long after their relationship was cold. Two decades later, he was a successful forty-three-year-old journalist approaching the height of his fame. He had traveled the globe, witnessed wars and revolutions, dined with presidents and kings, and had written books and countless articles that had been read by millions of people. But where matters of the heart were concerned, John remained vulnerable. He could still be a fool for what the poet Tennyson called "the cruel madness of love."

In his autobiographical novel, *The Indian Sign* (1970), the protagonist, Nelson, receives a note from his lover, Karen, that could well have been directed to John—and probably was, for Leonora Hornblow says that the novel is an accurate reflection of what happened. "I mean, that's the way he described it to me," she notes.[14] Says John's old friend William Shirer, "I urged him not to publish the book. I asked him why he wanted to open those old wounds. But he said it was something he *had* to do."[15]

That letter from Karen to Nelson in *The Indian Sign* reads, in part: "I feel that there must not be the slightest possibility of a misunderstanding between us, and so I must repeat what I found is so mournful to have to say, that is, the deep conviction that we can never be married. I do not want to be cruel, but, dear heart, the obstacles are insurmountable. You have to take me as I am."[16]

That was something John was not prepared to do. Nor was he ready to break off the relationship. Instead, he decided the time had come to take a dramatic step that would prove to Agnes just how much he loved her. In 1924, John had run away to Europe in a melodramatic gesture at least partly intended to impress Helen Hahn. Now, he opted to prove his love to Agnes by seeking a divorce.

John was surprised when Frances agreed to comply quietly with his request for a divorce. She had no fight left in her, and so the end of their troubled marriage came with a whimper, not a bang.

On the advice of his lawyer, John traveled to Las Vegas to seek the divorce. A brief item on page nineteen of the March 9, 1944, edition of the *New York Times* announced, "Gunther Obtains Divorce." Beneath the subhead, "Foreign Correspondent Says Wife Deserted Him in 1941," was a brief story datelined the previous day from Las Vegas. It read: "John Gunther, author and foreign correspondent, obtained a divorce today from Frances Gunther. He charged that she deserted him in 1941. Judge George E. Marshall awarded to Mrs. Gunther custody of their child, John, Jr., 15, together with $200 a month for his support and $600 monthly allowance."

The ease with which he had gotten the divorce came as a relief to John, who now was eager to propose to Agnes. Although in conversations with friends he expressed no regrets about how his marriage had ended, in his heart John must have felt remorse. After all, Frances had shared his life and his thoughts for seventeen stormy, eventful years. It had been she who had borne his two children. It had been she who encouraged his early efforts to write novels. It had been she who spurred him to create the first two *Inside* books; Frances had helped with the research and editing. In some ways, the literary success that she had so desperately wanted for *him*—and which he had achieved—was at the root of their troubles. When it came, she had envied him, even loathed him.

The letters between John and Frances over the years made it clear that they really had cared for one another. At times, they had loved one another. At other times, they had hurt one another. But when all of the tears had dried, and the echo of the angry words had died away, the memories of Paris, Vienna, and London lingered. Those would never fade. To their dying days, although they could never again live under the same roof, John and Frances still had a special place in their hearts for one another. They remained friends. Says Leonora Hornblow, "I think she loved him to the day she died. And he loved her, but he was never really *in love* with her, if you understand what I mean; that's a woman writer's distinction."[17]

At the conclusion of *The Indian Sign*, Nelson reflects upon his relationship with his estranged wife. Those words also seem to capture the essence of John's feelings towards Frances. He wrote: "My respect for her sense of fundamentals had never declined, nor my delight in her wit and brightness, her unexpectedness and capacity to extract pleasure from the harshest texture of the philosopher's stone to the powdery glitter of a moth's wing."[18]

Just what happened in the wake of the divorce is not entirely clear; only the outcome is. Hot on the heels of the final break with Frances, John wrote Agnes a long, passionate letter reviewing their relationship, and proposing marriage. As she was reading it, Agnes was surprised by her husband. On impulse, she stuffed the letter into the pocket of an old tweed walking jacket that was close by. Unfortunately, the jacket belonged to Nick, who later found and read the letter. His reaction to it was predictable, and emotional.

In John's novel, *The Indian Sign*, when the aggrieved husband Mac reads Nelson's love letter he flies into a rage and humiliates Karen in front of a succession of family members, dragging her like a penitent, pilloried felon from house to house. Finally, the tension explodes in a flurry of flying fists, broken glass, and verbal venom.

Not long afterwards, Mac sends Nelson an angry, threatening letter that reads, "I consider you to be a person without honor, a moral imbecile. I will follow you to the end of your days and shoot you down like a dog."[19] The missive ends with the news that Mac and Karen intend to divorce. However, when Nelson promptly responds with a note of his own stating that he still hopes to marry Karen, her husband does an abrupt about face; he announces that he never wants to see Nelson again, and that he has forbidden his wife from seeing or communicating with him.

Leonora Hornblow says that this "fictionalized" account of what happened reflects the reality, as John related it to her.[20] However, many years later Hubert Knickerbocker's brother Kenneth said he had no recollection of the fracas that is described in *The Indian Sign*.[21] About all that can be said for certain is that the affair between John and Agnes came crashing to an end in early 1944. When a terse note to that effect from her to him arrived in the mail a few days after the letter incident John was devastated.

"We discussed it often, and John could not believe that Agnes had shown Nick the letter, or left it where he would find it," says Leonora Hornblow. "His reaction was that it was the dumbest thing he had ever heard of. It was all so silly, but it was almost as if Agnes had wanted to be found out."[22]

While Hubert Knickerbocker raged, and Agnes begged his forgiveness, John collapsed in emotional and physical despair. As Hornblow says, "He was not a man to harbor ill feelings."[23] Instead, he internalized his grief. The Nelson character in *The Indian Sign* relates how, "For a time I felt that my brain was being drawn out by a needle; the grief and sense of irrevocable loss left me unutterably drained, destitute . . . My yearning, heartbreak, desolation, blotted out every other aspect of my existence."[24]

What lifted John out of his depression was not so much acceptance of his lot as a realization that he faced ruin if he did not begin to earn a living. He was spending his savings, and his whole life was in danger of unraveling. John's financial situation had started to deteriorate in late 1943. He had proposed to publish the diary that he kept during his trip to the front to earn some quick money. When Cass Canfield agreed, John set about readying the manuscript, which ran to about 90,000 words. He was sustained in these efforts in November 1943, by checks from his agents, totaling more than $13,000.[25] Included were some advances from his publisher, royalty payments on books, fees for magazine articles he had written while traveling, and his salary from NBC. While such a sum was a lot of money at the time (when more than half of all American households existed on less than $122 per month) it barely paid the monthly bills which John incurred in maintaining the house in Connecticut, two apartments, an office, and his footloose lifestyle. And in the wake of the divorce, he needed an additional $800 per month to meet court-ordered child support and maintenance payments, even though Frances never pressed him for the money. She received help from her brother and mother.

As always, John sought to forget his troubles by throwing himself into his work. He was encouraged in that regard when his war book, published under the title *D-Day*, began selling briskly on both sides of the Atlantic. Canfield sent John a note reporting advance sales of 20,000 copies, with the result that upon publication *D-Day* leaped into ninth spot on the *New York Times*' bestseller list.[26] Reviewers generally praised the book's personalized, anecdotal style. One of the few exceptions to this trend was a review in the March 14 edition of the *Chicago Daily News* by Howard Vincent O'Brien, one of John's old friends. O'Brien's main criticism was the book's blandness. He observed that John was so good-natured, so affable, that he had managed to sanitize the war. "He must have met fatheads and stuffed shirts wearing stars on their shoulders. He does not mention them," O'Brien chided.[27]

What O'Brien apparently overlooked was that with the war in Europe a long way from being won, military censorship was still very much in effect. Every word that John had written for public consumption while at the front had been vetted; the same was true of *D-Day*. In fact, during production of the book, Cass Canfield had issued a memo to his editors and other staff alerting them that the book's contents were subject to the rules of military censorship. In recent years, with the experiences of Watergate and the Vietnam War era behind them, American journalists have become much less willing to comply with such restrictions. Media accounts of the American-led invasion of Grenada in 1983, and of the Gulf War eight years later, sparked sharp controversies about the nature of journalism in a democratic society. But in 1944, any such debate was muted by jingoistic fervor. Few journalists cared or dared to challenge the government. To do so was considered disloyal at best, treasonous at worst.

Ironically, these same war time dictates served to relax some traditional common law restrictions on journalists and novelists. In 1936, Harper & Brothers lawyers had made John rewrite portions of *Inside Europe* to avoid libel actions. With the outbreak of war such concerns were forgotten. For that reason, and because in 1937 he had advanced John $1,250 on the book, Cass Canfield now encouraged John to resume work on his novel *Ring Around Vienna*. Six years earlier, after what John termed "frenzied agonies and disappointments," Harper & Brothers had shelved the book over concerns about libel.

That novel, set against a backdrop of Viennese mystery and intrigue in the early 1930s, contained disparaging references to United Press correspondent Robert Best, whose pro-Nazi leanings and virulent anti-Semitism had been well known to the foreign journalistic community. During the war, Best made German propaganda broadcasts and worked for a German news agency in Turkey, and he was wanted by the U.S. government on treason charges.

Best's status as a traitor removed the reservations Cass Canfield or Hamish Hamilton, John's British publisher, had about *Ring Around Vienna*. But John was still not enthusiastic about resurrecting the Vienna novel. Instead, he spent the summer of 1944 crafting what he intended as "a serious political novel." In a letter to Hamish Hamilton dated July 25, 1944, John explained, "The atmosphere and background is all fancy junk about spies and such, but don't let that deceive you. It is just something bright on which to hang the story."[28]

Originally titled *A Love of Country*, the novel was published in November 1944 as *The Troubled Midnight*. This was the first

Gunther novel since 1932. In the intervening fifteen years, John had become so well-known as the author of the *Inside* books that most people had forgotten—if they had even known—of the existence of his earlier novels. That was the case with author Thomas Mann.

John had sent the winner of the 1929 Nobel Prize for Literature a copy of *The Troubled Midnight* in the hope that he would provide an endorsement to be used on the book's dust jacket and in advertisements. In a letter to John dated November 28, 1944, Mann applauded him for having the "courage to take steps into the world of the novel."[29] It was hardly the sort of praise that John could have hoped for, or that would help sell books.

British novelist Somerset Maugham, who had also received an advance copy of *The Troubled Midnight*, was no more encouraging. "I was glad to see that you had drawn two recognizable Englishmen, which is just as difficult a thing for an American writer to do as it is for an English writer to describe Americans," Maugham wrote in a letter dated December 10, 1944. After adding that he "looked forward" to the next John Gunther novel, Maugham ended with the caustic observation, "You are too clever not to know that you have still got a good deal to learn about the technique of novel writing. We have all got to go through the mill."[30]

Unfortunately for John, although *The Troubled Midnight* was a moderate success, with sales of about 37,000 copies, most critics shared Maugham's assessment. A *New York Times* reviewer praised the book for its readability.[31] Other reviewers were less positive. Typical was a brief, anonymous review that ran in the *Chicago Daily News* on January 31, 1945. Under the headline, "John Gunther Tries a Novel," the writer—who should have known better—observed, "John Gunther apparently could not resist doing a novel despite the success of his 'inside' formula, and *The Troubled Midnight* is the unfortunate result."

Despite the tepid reviews, Hollywood came calling. John's agent sold screen rights to the novel to Paramount Studios for $5,000, and gossip columnist Hedda Hopper reported that critic-writer Gilbert Seldes (the brother of foreign correspondent George Seldes) was doing the screenplay as a vehicle for Ginger Rogers.[32] The film version of *The Troubled Midnight* was to be called *The Ambassador's Wife*. For the usual Hollywood reasons, Seldes' script never made it before the cameras, it went through several reincarnations before finally being shelved.

None of these developments were of serious concern to John. In mid-1944 he had at last turned his attentions to the writing of another *Inside* book. This one, the fourth in the popular series, would be John's most daunting undertaking ever: a sprawling, lavishly-detailed portrait of America, the world's mightiest and most prosperous nation "in the first gaunt years of the atomic age," as John put it.[33]

When he had conceived the project in 1936, John's original plan was for a single volume in two parts. The first would focus on the inner workings of the Washington power structure; the second would be a snapshot of America in all its richness and diversity, a study of democracy in action. De Tocqueville, the eighteenth century French historian, had profiled the America of Andrew Jackson in a classic study entitled *Democracy in America, 1835-1839*. No one in the 100 years since had attempted to repeat the exercise, and though John Gunther was too modest to ever compare himself to De Tocqueville, such comparisons were inevitable.

To touch the soul of a great, sprawling nation, as De Tocqueville had, was no small task. On several occasions John had announced he intended to begin work on the books, only to reconsider as the magnitude of the task became clear. In recent years, John twice had gone to Washington to begin research. Each time, circumstances had convinced him to abandon the project, which he felt would take two or three years to complete. With that in mind, in October 1941, John had asked Cass Canfield to register the title *Inside U.S.A.* with the Authors' League of America.[34] That was as far as things went because John, beset with personal problems, had departed for Europe.

In August 1942, Eugene Saxton, Cass Canfield's right-hand man, had written to urge John to get on with "Uncle Sam's portrait."[35] John balked at the suggestion, arguing that it would be impossible to write honestly about politics with the war raging. He also argued that the book would most likely be rendered obsolete by the outcome of the upcoming presidential election. By late

1944, there were no such fears, since it was obvious Roosevelt would be returned to the White House. The only question in most people's minds was whether or not FDR would live long enough to complete his unprecedented fourth term. John doubted it.

He, along with film star Orson Welles, writer Quentin Reynolds, and critic Mark Van Doren, had done a radio broadcast that Roosevelt liked, and so the four men were invited to attend FDR's inauguration celebrations on January 19, 1945. John, who had not seen Roosevelt in person for almost two years, was shocked by the changes in him. During a reception at the White House, the president sat slumped in his wheelchair, limply shaking hands with guests who filed past. History records that Roosevelt had a scant few weeks to live; John and a great many other people sensed as much. "I was terrified when I saw his face. I felt certain he was going to die. All the light had gone out underneath the skin. It was like a parchment shade on a bulb that had been dimmed," he recalled. "I could not get over the ravaged expression on his face. It was gray, gaunt, and sagging, and the muscles controlling the lips seemed to have lost part of their function."[36]

Knowing that Roosevelt's life was nearing an end, and the situation in Washington was in flux, John altered his plans for *Inside U.S.A.*. He resolved to write two books. The first would be a survey of all forty-eight states, the second a companion volume to be called *Inside Washington*. So eager was Cass Canfield to publish both books that he advanced John $25,000 to help cover his living expenses while he was researching and writing the first book, with a pledge of a further $25,000 for the second. Canfield also acceded to a demand by John's agent that Harper & Brothers increase author royalties on the books from the standard 15 per cent to 17.5 per cent. In return, John agreed to the insertion in the contract of a penalty clause limiting the manuscript to 300,000 words—approximately 600 pages. With rationing in effect, Hamish Hamilton in London was concerned about finding enough paper to print anything longer.

John was confident he could deliver both books as promised. With that goal in mind, he asked his lawyer to find him a country home to use as a writing retreat, and which would at the same time provide Frances and Johnny with a comfortable place to live. On June 15, the *New York Times* reported that John had purchased an attractive twenty-three-acre ocean front estate at Madison, Connecticut. He had borrowed some money from Cass Canfield, and signed a contract for $8,000 in advance expense money to provide *Reader's Digest* with excerpts from *Inside U.S.A.* as it was being written. The property, formerly owned by candy manufacturer William F. Hoops, boasted a rambling eleven-room residence with an airy front porch and a scallop of private sandy beach. There were also a boat house, stables, a workshop, and servants' cottages. "The house itself is nothing much, but the thing as a whole has enormous possibilities," John told Hamilton in a letter dated July 25, 1944.[37]

With Johnny now attending Deerfield Academy, a private boarding school in Massachusetts, the house at Madison was more than Frances needed. But John had fallen in love with the property, and felt that he owed it to Frances to see that she was well taken care of. It gave him peace of mind. Like a boxer in training for a big bout, John was readying himself for the battle to come.

During his years as a reporter, he had developed an astounding ability to focus himself when there was a deadline to be met; it was a self-discipline that he never lost. Now that he was committed to writing *Inside U.S.A.*, John resigned from NBC Radio ("Most of the radio money went into income tax anyway," John quipped in the letter to Hamilton[38]) and prepared a seven-page summary of the book, copies of which he sent off to Canfield, Hamilton, and to other friends around the country, including poet Archibald MacLeish and broadcaster Edward R. Murrow. John received back letters outlining detailed suggestions. Henry Seidel Canby, chairman of the Book of the Month Club, urged him to bear in mind "the prominent influence of the Protestant sects" on life in the United States.[39] Author-critic Clifton Fadiman opined that American culture was headed "for suicide, largely as a result of anti-cultural elements [*Time* magazine founder Henry Luce] masquerading as civilization."[40] Mark Van Doren suggested a stronger "literary" content to the next Gunther book. "Our education has never grown up . . . at least since the days when Jefferson could serve his country because he knew Greece and Rome, and Lincoln because he knew the New Testament."[41]

Bearing all this advice in mind, John went knocking on the doors of prominent senators, congressmen, and public officials in Washington to sound them out on whom they felt he should interview. Armed with a list of key people in every state, he put Nancy

Barnett, his secretary, to work dispatching hundreds of letters requesting interviews.

During the summer of 1944, when he was not working on his novel, John gathered background material. "I am fine, so far as anyone can be fine these days, and working hard and well," John told Hamish Hamilton.[42]

By day he worked, by night he sought distraction. He remained a familiar figure at Manhattan's night spots. Everyone knew which ones; Leonard Lyons, Elsa Maxwell, Walter Winchell, and other gossip columnists took care of that.

Most nights John dined and drank at the clubby Cub Room in back of the Stork Club, at 21, or some other restaurant or night club. After hours, he was sometimes among a group who piled into Walter Winchell's car to cruise the streets listening to the car's police radio. These were crazy, fun nights, and almost always, John was accompanied by a beautiful woman. He was spotted at various times with novelist Kathleen Winsor, actress Marianne O'Brien, "concert piano improviser" Grace Castagneta, or Leonora Hornblow—who was then Leonora Schinasi. Other times, John dated dancer Tilly Losch, or actresses Joan Thorsen or Simone Simon. "He was always fun to be with," says Hornblow. "He loved to laugh, and what made him irresistible company was that he was always absolutely interested in the person he was with. Nothing is more seductive."[43]

Also still very much in the picture at this time was Miriam Hopkins, the tempestuous blonde actress. Elsa Maxwell reported in her *New York Post* column on October 23, 1943, that she, Winchell, Dorothy Parker, and dozens of other people had gone to a crowded, noisy birthday party John had thrown for Miriam Hopkins at her apartment, since his place was too small. Likewise, the *Chicago Daily News* reported that upon arriving home from the front the previous September, John, still attired in his soiled uniform, had gone by cab from the airport to visit Miriam (ironically, at the time she was starring in a Broadway play called "The Perfect Marriage"), and invite her to dine with him.

"You have time to change," Hopkins advised after surveying his dirty uniform.

"Oh, but I'd rather not change—yet," John replied. "This is the first uniform I've ever had. I never had a uniform. Not even a Boy Scout's."[44]

John's friends from those days knew how deceptive were reports of such a carefree lifestyle. Beneath the frivolity, these were difficult days for Gunther, who was struggling to reconcile the success of his career with the failures of his personal life. Leonora Hornblow feels that he did not have "intentions of anything long term" with any of the women that he was dating, although he and Miriam Hopkins were serious for a time. "I think he felt—and he would deny this if he were here, and say, 'Don't listen to that woman'—I really think that he expected to pick things up again with Agnes Knickerbocker."[45]

CHAPTER THIRTY

The writing of *Inside U.S.A.*, the longest and most complex of the *Inside* series, was a stark example of what Ernest Hemingway meant when he talked of "grace under pressure."

John Gunther always recalled the book as "the hardest task I ever undertook."[1] It stands as a testament to his professionalism and talent. Few writers would—or could—have finished such an ambitious task when faced with the kind of pressures which for fifteen months turned John's life into a living hell.

Three previous *Inside* books had dealt with people and places that had still seemed exotic to most Americans. *Inside U.S.A.* was a departure from that pattern. Here was a book in which there could be no room for naivete or "innocence." As John told Hamish Hamilton in one of his letters, "It is always more difficult to write about your own country than a strange land."[2]

Inside U.S.A. was intended as a national self-portrait, one written by an American who had gained an outsider's perspective after more than a decade abroad. John maintained that aside from his curiosity, the only real virtue he brought to the task was his ignorance of the country. "Not only was I writing for the man from Mars; I was one," he quipped.[3]

His approach was simple. John set out to look at each state through the eyes of prominent politicians, business and civic leaders, academics, and writers. Of course, in focusing on such a select group, he exposed himself to charges that he ignored the lives of ordinary people in favor of the influential and powerful. It was a criticism of the *Inside* books that had been made before. By now, John had formulated a valid defense, namely that journalism is history on the run; there was a limit to the number of interviews he could do and still meet a deadline.

John Gunther never claimed that the *Inside* books were definitive history. He always maintained that they were book-length journalism which made sense of an increasingly complex world for the average reader. In writing *Inside U.S.A.*, his goal was no different. He set out to present Americans with a warts-and-all literary portrait of themselves, and their nation.

In the 100 years since de Tocqueville had written *Democracy in America, 1835-39* no one had even attempted a book the likes of *Inside U.S.A.* In 1945, the time seemed right.

The Allied victory over the Axis powers had given Americans an uncritical pride in the prowess of their armed forces, in the productivity of their economy, in the rectitude of their motives, and in the strength of democratic ideals. As John noted in the introduction to *Inside U.S.A.*, America was a nation "more favored by man and nature than any . . . in history, now for the first time attempting with somewhat faltering steps to justify its new station as a mature world power."[4]

Here was a country of 140 million persons, one widely hailed as the greatest democracy and the greatest republic on earth. However, to examine the essence of that republic was to confront the daunting gap between myth and reality.

John began his research by reading the Declaration of Independence and the Constitution. He was astounded to discover that nowhere in either document does the word "democracy" appear.

One of the cornerstones of the American political system has always been, "One person, one vote." Yet in 1945 many of the nation's thirteen million blacks—fully 10 per cent of the population—had been disenfranchised by the political process, and they would continue to be until the great civil rights movement two decades later.

Even more startling, in 1945 residents of the District of Columbia legally had no vote at all! Until November 3, 1967, the District was administered by three commissioners who were appointed by the president. On that day, a government consisting of a mayor-commissioner and a nine-member council, all appointed by the president and approved by the Senate, took office. It was not until May 7, 1974, the citizens of the District of Columbia approved the Home Rule Charter, giving them for the first time an elected mayor and a thirteen-member council.

America's public education system was widely regarded at home as being one of the world's finest. But statistics indicated that almost 15 per cent of military draftees in 1943 could neither read nor write. In a land where the average age was just twenty-nine, almost three million adult Americans had never gone to school a day in their lives.

And any illusions about enlightened public opinion were dispelled by a post-war poll, indicating that 51 per cent of GIs in occupied Germany felt Adolf Hitler had done "a lot of good" for his country in the years from 1933 to 1939, while 22 per cent actually felt that the Nazi dictator had been justified in persecuting Jews.

These "might is right" sentiments had manifested themselves in some disturbing ways back home. Statistics that John uncovered showed that in Mississippi in the sixty-two years between 1882 and 1944 there had been 573 lynchings; in Georgia during that same period there had been 521. Most of the unfortunate victims were black people strung up by whites for crimes real or imagined.

First in production of coal, oil, steel, electricity, copper, cotton, and scores of other vital raw materials, the U.S. economy was the world's strongest and richest. The country boasted of having four-fifths of the world's automobiles, and half of all its telephones. Nonetheless, statistics showed that just one family in ten had an annual income above $4,000, with the annual per capita income of the residents of New York State—at that time, the most populous in the union—being just $595.

Americans were smug in the assumption that they enjoyed the world's highest standards of public health. Yet with no national health insurance program, 40 per cent of all draftees in the Second World War had been rejected as physically unfit for military service. Of the GIs stationed in occupied Germany in 1946, one in four had been afflicted with venereal disease. Fully 40 per cent of American homes had no bathtub or shower; 35 per cent had no indoor toilet; 30 per cent had no running water.

With file folders bulging with such preposterous, fascinating information, John set out in November 1944 to discover America for himself. He began an exhausting thirteen-month tour of the country with a "dry run" through New England, an area he had never before visited. This was followed by a long swing through the South, up the Pacific coast, through the mountain states, and the Midwest, and then finally by a trip down the Atlantic seaboard. Somehow, John managed to visit all forty-eight states, and all but five cities with a population of more than 200,000.

The experiences confirmed his suspicions that the task he had set for himself was far more ambitious than anything he had ever envisioned. Writing in his 1962 memoir, *A Fragment of Autobiography*, he recalled, "Never before had I taken a project so seriously, although I know now that I did not take it seriously enough; my activity was always subject to indulgences and interrupted by bouts of confusion or apathy."[5]

At first, John found it difficult to concentrate. He faced too many distractions. During his initial stop in Boston, John spent precious days holed up in his hotel room reading page proofs for his novel, *The Troubled Midnight*. Not long afterwards, he received word of the death of Dorothy Thompson's stepson. Wells Lewis (the son of Thompson's second husband, author Sinclair Lewis), had been shot dead by a sniper while serving in Europe with the U.S. Army. John did his best to console his old friend from afar. Doing so was especially difficult just then, given the upheaval in own life at the time.

The wounds of his ill-fated love affair with Agnes were not yet fully healed, and never one for formal religion, John was struggling to make sense of the strange turns that his life had taken. "My generation grew up in an atmosphere of destruction and revolt," he explained many years later in a statement of beliefs that he wrote for a book compiled by his friend and colleague Edward R. Murrow. "I believe that we are all part of a universe that has certain forms, patters, interrelations, and compensations, even for the worst of personal tragedies. But I do not know enough to know why I think this."[6]

The one thing that John did know was travel. It became his salvation.

Nothing is more distinctively American than the urge to go for the sake of going, to discover what is inside oneself by wandering the vastness of the American landscape. It is a legacy bequeathed to us by the restless men and women who rolled back the frontiers. It was a legacy bequeathed to John by his father, Eugene, who like so many others had succumbed to the irresistible lure of the open road. So, too, had John. It is no coincidence that much of *Inside U.S.A.* deals with the theme of belief in oneself, or lack of it. John Gunther, like America in 1945, was searching for a renewed sense of identity.

His travels became as much an odyssey of self-discovery, a search for meaning, as a journalistic expedition to discover the heartbeat of America. Alone for long hours aboard trains, waiting in terminals and airports, and during the long nights in lonely hotel rooms, he thought about his life and about world events. Doing so, he gradually settled into the kind of peripatetic routine that had been so familiar to him during his years as a roving correspondent in Europe.

Keeping busy was always a form of self-therapy that helped John cope with his despair. "I've tried to the utmost to get everything organized in every city in advance because my time is so short and I don't want to waste it," he told his agent, Carl Brandt, in a note written from a hotel room in Omaha, Nebraska.[7]

This urge to plan ahead meant losing a half day in every three to travel or simply in making long distance phone calls, sending telegrams, and writing letters. With the war still winding down, transportation and lodgings were not always easily arranged.

Prior to leaving New York, John had written to every state governor posing three basic questions: 1) How does your state differ from all the rest? 2) What does your state contribute to the Union as a whole? and, 3) What led you to public life, and what do you consider to be your chief accomplishment? Out of forty-eight governors, all but one responded with an invitation to visit. John realized that doors closed to most other journalists were open to him.

His visits were front page news in many local newspapers, particularly in the Midwest, the mountain states, and the South. In Texas, he was asked to address a joint session of the Texas legislature. Everywhere he went people wanted to talk, curious about the book he was writing. "I had no idea how well known I was, unbecoming as it is for me to say this myself, until this journey," John noted.[8]

He had sent a telegram to Kansas governor Alf Landon, the GOP presidential candidate in 1936, stating, "Am author *Inside Europe* etc., can I see you Topeka Friday." Landon's reply was swift and pointed: "We are not hicks in Kansas and know perfectly well who you are. Come to dinner six o'clock." Landon graciously had him to dinner two consecutive nights, one with a table full of conservatives, the other with liberals.[9]

In Memphis, John had not bothered to contact E.H. (Ed) Crump, the last of the great city political bosses. "I did not want to see him, because it was my gentle intention to make him a villain and I did not wish to be under any obligation to him," he explained. For that reason, John was astonished when Crump called his hotel room. After complimenting him on his books, the bossman went on to say that John could not possibly get a "fair picture" of Tennessee without the "advantage" of a conversation with him—especially after John had been rebuked by the state's irrascible old Democratic senator, Kenneth McKellar. The senator had taken offence with one of John's questions and curtly asked him to leave his office. "So I went over to call on [Crump], with his steaming pyramid of cotton-white hair and cheeks like three hard red apples, and had an illuminating hour," John recalled.[10]

He had a similar experience in Minneapolis. When a brief story about his visit appeared in the morning paper, a man who had seen it rang to announce that he would drop by John's hotel room at five o'clock that afternoon. John did his best to dissuade the unidentified caller. The man was insistent, and so in desperation John said he would call him back. When he asked for a name and number, the response came back: "Why I'm Hubert Humphrey. I'm the mayor!"[11] Humphrey rose to national prominence not long afterwards, of course, when he was elected to the U.S. Senate. Later, he served as Lyndon Johnson's vice-president, and in 1968 was the Democratic presidential candidate who lost out to Richard Nixon.

In Cincinnati, John attended a dinner party given in his honor by a well-heeled resident. John was puzzled by the embarrassed silence that greeted him when he asked, "Who runs thic city?" As the conversation proceeded, he realized why his question had elicited such a muted reaction: everybody who ran Cincinnati was at the table, although they were too modest to admit it. As the dinner party was breaking up a few hours later, one of the guests turned to John and said, "I don't know about you, But I've learned more about Cincinnati tonight that I've learned in 20 years!"[12]

Such sessions yielded a wealth of information, all of which John dutifully recorded in his notebooks. He informed Carl Brandt that by mid-August 1945, he was just two-thirds of the way through his trip and had already amassed half a million words of notes from almost 700 interviews. To lighten the load he was carrying, John dispatched bundles of notes and reference materials by registered mail to Nancy Barnett in his New York office. "I have such a mass of stuff as will stagger you," John told Canfield in a July 14, 1945, letter from Seattle. "I have a kind of sneaking hunch it may be two books."[13]

The work was wearisome, but gratifying. John reveled in it. The people he met were mostly friendly, the travel varied, and interesting. John saw many old friends, and made some new ones. He visited Sinclair Lewis in Minnesota, and had lunch in Baltimore with H.L. Mencken, whom he had not seen in eighteen years. "It was a delight to find him a sweet old softie," John noted in a letter to Frances.[14] He also became acquainted with David E. Lilienthal, head of the Tennessee Valley Authority (TVA), Paul Hoffman, president of Studebaker car company, and legendary newspaper publisher Joseph Pulitzer.

Meeting such a varied group of people helped to brighten John's mood, of that there can be no doubt. By now, he was even regaining his sense of humor. In the April 30 letter to Frances, he poked good natured fun at her unabashed idealism. "The South has been a whole new world to me. I've been up to my neck and will be for some time in our brown brethren," he wrote. "I have wondered a lot what would have happened—not without amusement—if you had been with me these past few weeks, whether you would have had the same feeling you did in Palestine and India discovering a new minority disciminated against and oppressed, and going into it full-blast to try to help."[15]

John confided to Carl Brandt, "I have never enjoyed anything more in my life . . . Mr. Justice [Oliver Wendell] Holmes said that the test of a person's love for his job was his willingness to deal with the drudgery it involves. I am thinking of writing a nice piece when this is all over, 'The fun of writing *Inside U.S.A.*'"[16]

Life was looking up in other ways, too. Cass Canfield wrote on November 14, 1945, with news that Grosset & Dunlop, a New York publisher, had paid $1,500 for the right to print 15,000 copies of a $1 paperback edition of *The Troubled Midnight.*[17] Foreign language editions had also been published in Swedish, Dutch, and Spanish. A few days later, Canfield wrote again to inform John that his name was back in the headlines in Europe. While Hitler may have raged over what John had written about him in *Inside Europe*, other top Nazis were less hostile. Canfield reported that Wilhelm Frick, Hitler's minister of the interior, had cited passages from *Inside Europe* as part of his defense at the Nuremberg war crimes trials. "Mr. Frick must be slightly cuckoo in as much as your reference to him as 'a tool of Hitler' is anything but flattering," a bemused Canfield said.[18]

The Frick anecdote reminded John that the war in Europe was finally over, after six terrible years. Although he had been on the road in the south on VE day, May 8, 1945, John had followed the war news keenly. It was impossible for him to work on the book while traveling, and so he was occupied his off time writing letters, keeping his notebooks, and writing an article for *Liberty* magazine in which he lamented the cooling of East-West relations. John felt strongly that if Washington and Moscow did not find a way to peacefully co-exist, Hitler would have won the war even in death. "This had nothing whatever to do with my book, but my disappointment and apprehension about rising tensions in American-Soviet affairs was so acute that I had to express myself somehow," John explained later.[19]

John regretted that in April he had declined an invitation to fly to Europe as a guest of the U.S. Air Force, to "see at first hand the final act of the *Götterdämmerung* I had watched build up for more than 20 years."[20] The trip had been organized by the Association of Radio News Analysts in New York, and Canfield had urged John to go. He had declined, saying he could not in good conscience interrupt his road work for *Inside U.S.A.*

John finished that portion of his research in early December

1945. After taking Christmas off, he began writing early in the New Year. "Periods of dogged endeavor, joy, and despair alternated," John recalled in *A Fragment of Autobiography*.[21] At first, the work went smoothly. Then progress came to an unexpected halt late on the afternoon of April 25, 1946. That afternoon, John received word of his son's illness in that fateful phone call from the school doctor at Deerfield Academy.

CHAPTER THIRTY-ONE

In the split second it took the doctor to utter those dreaded words, "brain tumor," John Gunther's world was turned topsy turvy. His son was gravely ill, the one person in his life who had always been there, the one person he loved with all his heart and soul.

As the implications of the neuroligist's diagnosis became clear, John was swept with a powerful sense of déjà vu. The mysterious crib death of the baby Judith in January 1929, had left both John and Frances wondering where they had failed as parents, and as human beings. Frances had fallen into a depression, which was fueled by an irresistible sense that something in her own behavior had brought on this terrible occurrence. Now, John was seized by the same crazy, irrational fear.

Was news of Johnny's illness a punishment for his own human

frailties—for his affair with Agnes perhaps? Why Johnny, he wondered?

His thoughts drifted back fifteen years to November 4, 1929, the day of Johnny's birth at the American Hospital in Paris. Frances, obsessed by the death of her daughter barely ten months earlier, had smothered Johnny with attention; John, too, had doted on the boy.

Born three weeks premature, Johnny had been jaundiced, and slept through much of the first few weeks of life. Frances meticulously recorded every detail of his physical development in her diary. It was as if in doing so, she hoped to atone for the laxity that she feared had contributed to Judith's death.

Johnny was two weeks old when Frances had his thymus checked for the first time, since an undiagnosed thymus ailment is what she believed had killed her daughter.

The Gunthers had moved to Vienna when Johnny was just a few months old. He attended kindergarten here, spent his formative years playing with the children of other foreign correspondents, and whiled away many an evening on his father's knee at the Café Louvre coffee house. Johnny was six when John was transferred to London in 1935. He spent eighteen months in the British capital, then his father quit the *Chicago Daily News* to return home to the United States. Johnny then went to public schools in Wilton, Connecticut, and Manhattan before enrolling in the fall of 1943 at Deerfield Academy, a private boarding school for boys about twenty-five miles north of Springfield, Massachussets.

Teachers here quickly recognized Johnny as "a very unusual boy . . . whose future is almost unlimited."[1] He was keenly interested in science, particularly physics and chemistry, and early on announced his intention to one day study at Harvard. His marks, which were mostly A's, indicated he would have no trouble doing just that. In January 1946, the headmaster at Deerfield reported to his parents that Johnny had scored 134 on an IQ test, it was the highest mark ever recorded at the school.[2]

In most other ways, Johnny Gunther appeared to be a normal, healthy teenager. Despite being pudgy and overweight as a boy, he had sprouted to almost six feet in height, was lean as a sapling, and fair-haired, with gentle blue eyes that mirrored an insatiable curiosity, and an easy good humor.

The picture of Johnny that emerges from school reports, and the memories of those who knew him is one of a shy, sensitive young man. He shared his father's geniality and quickness of mind, as well as some of his mother's quirkiness. One of Johnny's teachers once told John and Frances, "You know, your son lives in a world altogether his own."[3]

Henry Eisner, a classmate of Johnny's at Deerfield, had that same impression. "Johnny was very funny and well liked. He was easy going and could laugh at himself, and I never saw him lose his temper," Eisner recalls. "But there was another aspect to him, an introspective side. Johnny was always kind of phlegmatic."[4]

Johnny was imbued with an undefinable kind of helplessness, an emotional sensitivity that friends sensed. Bertha Brenner, the mother of one of Johnny's chums from his elementary school days, recalls how her son Edgar "sort of adopted him and became protective." The two boys grew to be close friends, and when they swam together in the school swimming pool, Johnny's weight sometimes posed a problem when he was climbing out. "Edgar would hold out his hands to help him, without ever looking look into Johnny's eyes as he was doing so."[5]

Johnny, as had his father when he was young, spent many hours alone in his room. Where John had read and composed stories, Johnny tinkered with a chemistry set. But his intellect remained raw and largely unchanneled. In that sense, and some others, too, Johnny was not unlike his father.

A counsellor at Treetops Summer Camp in the Adirondacks, where Johnny spent several summers, noted in a 1938 report that Johnny, then nine years old, was "not competitive, not athletic, but]was still[popular with the other boys."[6] That he could not hit a home run or win a foot race never seemed to bother him. Two years later, another Treetops counsellor observed that Johnny had a "slight problem" with bed wetting, which may have been a result of his emotional insecurities about the state of his parents' marriage. He also had a irritating tendency to forget, and to misplace his things. However, the counsellor's report suggested that Johnny's worst trait was his "indifference to ordinary tasks, and a willingness to allow others to do jobs for him."[7] John did little to remedy this laziness.

Because he traveled so much, John was away from home a lot of the time when Johnny was a child. Frances had raised him. It was she who loved him; she who disciplined him. Mother and son were close. Temperamentally, they were kindred spirits; they shared a love of abstract concepts and ideas. "From Frances he got a tremendous lot," John wrote, "his gift for fantasy, the realism and long view of his intelligence, his delicacy of perception, his creative curiosity."[8]

John, who had grown up longing for the love and companionship of his father, was determined not to be guilty of the same omissions where his own son was concerned. Thus, even after John and Frances split, Johnny saw a lot of both his parents. Before going away to school in the fall of 1943, he spent summers with his mother in Connecticut, and winters in New York with his father. John arranged his schedule so he could be home for most holidays. Even so, there were occasions over the years when John was not there when his son needed him.

Typically, John had been been traveling in the spring of 1940, and he called New York to say that he could not be back in time for a concert in which the school band was to play some music that Johnny had composed. "You could certainly get here if you hired an airplane," Johnny protested, knowing that John sometimes did just that when he had to be somewhere in a hurry.[9]

It was because of incidents like this, and because of the memories of his own childhood that John showered his son with affection whenever they were together. When she was angry, Frances sometimes accused her husband of "excessive petting," of raising "a pansy." While such barbs stung John, he struggled not to let them affect his relationship with Johnny. He loved the boy much too deeply for that. In fact, it was a concern about how a divorce would affect Johnny that had stayed John's hand in that regard for so many years.

With all of this, and much more racing through his mind, John sat staring into the icy darkness on the night of April 25, 1946, as he, Frances, and Dr. Putnam drove to Deerfield. By the time they arrived at the school it was almost ten o'clock, and their mood matched the weather. Within minutes of their arrival, John was seized by an unshakable premonition that Johnny's illness would kill him. It was nothing that was verbalized. It did not need to be; the averted eyes of one of the doctors spoke the words that his lips did not. The pall of death was palpable to John as he entered the infirmary room where Johnny lay. The boy suspected that he had contracted polio, but the instant that John saw his son's right eye drooping limply on his cheek, he knew Johnny had not been that lucky.

The doctors advised the Gunthers that Johnny needed an operation immediately to relieve the pressure that was building inside his head; the tumor was pressing on Johnny's right optic nerve. Putnam had the boy transferred the next morning to the Neurological Institute of Columbia-Presbyterian Hospital in New York. "That building!" John wrote. "It became the citadel of our hopes and fears for more than a year, the prison of our dreams."[10]

On April 29, just four days after the tumor was diagnosed, Johnny went into the operating room for six hours of exploratory surgery. Afterwards, Putnam told John that when he had cut open Johnny's skull, he had found a tumor the size of an orange growing in the right occipital parietal lobe. "I got half of it," he said.[11]

Johnny's face was the size and color of a football when he returned from the operating room, the result of edema, the swelling caused by the shock of brain surgery. His eyes were swollen shut, and upon awakening, he could barely speak through a fiercely swollen mouth. Johnny suffered unimaginably. Nevertheless, with youth was on his side, his recovery was rapid.

John and Frances were astounded to discover that Johnny was depressed not about his condition—which had still not been fully explained to him, but rather about school work he had missed. For that reason, when Johnny announced on May 10 that he wanted to write a letter, Frances persuaded him to dictate it to her on the assumption that it was a message for his Deerfield teachers or classmates. It was a letter to Albert Einstein querying an aspect of the renowned physicist's Theory of Relativity. Johnny had read about it, and during the long hours he lay in bed, his mind fixed upon a point he felt he had to share with Einstein. John was incredulous, nevertheless he posted the letter with a brief covering note. Much to his surprise, Einstein responded promptly, and graciously. What's more, he invited Johnny to discuss his idea in person when he was out of hospital and healthy again. Sadly, it was an invitation that Johnny never got to accept. "I guess Dr. Einstein saw through my letter, but it really was a pretty good job of bull slinging," Johnny playfully wrote in his diary on May 31, 1946. "What a man he must be to reply anyway."[12]

Doctors were initially optimistic that the tumor inside Johnny's brain was a type that could be eliminated by X-ray treatment. However, because it was still growing, Putnam had left the boy's skull open, covering the incision in the bone with a bandaged flap of scalp. This technique was intended to give the tumor room to "decompress"—to bulge outwards without exerting killing pressure on the rest of Johnny's brain, particularly on the area of that controlled his eyesight.

But always the tumor was there, a frightful lump on the side of the boy's shaven head. Sometimes it was dormant for weeks on end; sometimes it grew madly, and split open, oozing frightful fluid. There seemed to be no pattern, no rhyme or reason to its growth. This irrational parasitic lump was slowly sucking the life out of its young victim. "All that goes into a brain—the goodness, the wit, the sum total of enchantment in a personality, the very will, indeed the ego itself—[was] being killed inexorably, remoselessly, by an evil growth," John wrote.[13]

In the face of it all, he and Frances continued to pray for a miracle. They dreamed that the tumor might somehow disappear as mysteriously, and as quickly as it seemed to them to have appeared. That it would not was made painfully clear to John the day he chanced to see an X-ray technician's report that mentioned that Johnny's tumor was "undergoing glioblastomatous transformation." John, who had read everything about tumors that he could find, had dreaded hearing mention of the prefix "glio." He knew that any tumor bearing that fearful description was invariably fatal.

To this point, Johnny had remained in surprisingly good spirits. Although his parents and doctors avoided telling him too much about his illness, he knew more than they suspected. One days when he was being visited by Bertha Brenner, the mother of his friend Edgar, he told her, "You know, the thing (the tumor) is inside me, and it's getting bigger and bigger. It's going to get me."[14]

Johnny felt well enough to go home in June 1946, although he continued visiting the hospital each afternoon for radiation treatments. He even spent a few precious weeks that summer with Frances in the big house at Madison. It was here that he was visited by Henry Eisner, one of his Deerfield classmates. The boys played chess, which Johnny loved to do. "It was very frustrating for him," Eisner says, "because the tumor had affected his vision and he said that couldn't see all of the pieces on the board."[15]

After dinner on Sunday evenings, the boys, along with Frances and

John, who sometimes came out from New York, would sit on the porch watching the sea, and listening to radio broadcasts of the Boston Symphony. These were idyllic, warm family times, and gave Eisner a chance to know the Gunthers, whom Johnny seldom talked about. He was certainly aware of his parents' discord, but he had never openly discussed it with either of them, until later that year when Johnny's curiosity finally got the better of him. His diary entry for November 16, 1946, reads: "... resolved to ask father about divorce." The following day he wrote: "... got father's and mother's side of divorce all straightened out. What wonderful parents!"[16]

The reality was that by the time Johnny fell gravely ill, John and Frances had largely resolved their differences, and were behaving cordially towards one another. Recalls Henry Eisner, "I liked them both very much. If I hadn't been told, I'd never have known there'd been trouble between them. They'd patched over their differences, and they were always on good behavior when I saw them at Madison. The only sign that things weren't right was that they slept in separate bedrooms." Henry Eisner recalls.[17]

On one occasion, he remembers Frances spontaneously hugging him, and giving him a kiss him on the forehead. "She thanked me for spending time with Johnny," he says. "I think she liked me because I'm Jewish. She was, too."

Eisner's memories of John are equally warm. "Physically, he was a big man, and I remember being struck by how big and soft his hands were when he shook hands," says Eisner. "John Gunther had a gentleness, and a geniality about him that made him likable. And he had a quick mind. His knowledge of world affairs was astounding. I remember that sometimes the neighbors would come over to sit on the porch. They would talk about events in post-war Europe, and I'd listen to the conversation, which went way over my head."

Sadly, these good times were shortlived. The tumor that was sapping Johnny's life inevitably began growing again. When it did, he returned to hospital, where his youthful optimism slowly unraveled. John noticed it for the first time one day when Johnny grew agitated as he waited for his therapy. He began repeating that surely the X-rays he was getting were "just for pictures." The amount of time he was spending under the machine had evidently raised the notion in his mind that something infinitely more serious was going on, that this must be some kind of medical treatment. "Does this mean that I have cancer?" he asked John. Later, he whispered to Frances, "I have so much to do! And there's so little time!"[18]

That prediction was confirmed, when Putnam consulted with Dr. Wilder Penfield, a world renowned neurosurgeon from Montreal, Canada. Penfield came to New York the third week of July. He studied Johnny's charts and X-rays, looking for any hint that Putnam's diagnosis was incorrect, as well as for any possibility that the tumor might have changed, for better or worse. When he was done, Penfield could only confirm the earlier diagnosis. He explained to John and Frances in calm words stripped bare of rosy euphemisms, "Your child has a malignant glioma. It will kill him."[19]

When the doctors gave Johnny the same grim news, he listened carefully, then looked the doctor in the eye and asked calmly, "How shall we break it to my parents?"

To this point, John and Frances had placed their faith in the expertise of the doctors treating Johnny. Now, as the finality of Johnny's illness became undeniable, they were seized by a growing desperation. They began the search for a miracle cure, or at least for something to halt the cancer's inexorable advance. "The thought never left us that if only we could defer somehow what everybody said was inevitable, if only we could stave off Death for a few weeks or months, something totally new might turn up. What we sought above all was time," John wrote.[20]

Theirs was a search driven more by frustration, and helplessness than by conviction. John wrote or telephoned doctors all over the country in his search for answers. Then, one day Frances chanced to read a newspaper article about an experimental tumor treatment involving intravenous dosages of mustard gas, the same toxic substance that is used as a chemical weapon. "If it were my son, I'd try it," one prominent physician advised. When John tracked down the doctors involved in the research, they agreed to make Johnny a human guinea pig.

He got his first injections of mustard gas in early August. The initial signs were positive, but that glimmer of hope was shortlived. The tumor began to grow again after just a few weeks. John and Frances were downcast, but they were still not willing to give up. They simply took another tack.

Raymond Swing had told John about a revolutionary "naturopathic" diet said to work wonders in controlling the growth of cancerous tumors. With nothing to lose, in September 1946, Johnny went on this strange saltless, fatless diet. Again, the initial indications were encouraging. The tumor's growth was arrested, Johnny's over-all condition improved markedly, and for a few weeks it seemed as if the impossible had come to pass: Johnny Gunther's life had been saved. In a letter to his friend Henry Eisner dated November 3, 1946, Johnny joked that while he was was still "interned," the peculiar diet that he had been place on seemed to be working; the only problem, he confided, was that he "suspected" that all of the unsalted squash, turnips, and other vegetables he was obliged to eat "all are laxatives."[21]

Throughout the period of Johnny's illness, John continued trying to work on *Inside U.S.A*, but progress was slow. It was not easy for John to write, given his emotional state, and knowing how much depended upon the book's success.

With Johnny's health apparently stabilized, John wrote like a man possessed. He was under enormous pressure to finish the book, for he desperately needed money to pay Johnny's medical bills. His original $25,000 advance was long since been spent; in February 1947, he had to ask Cass Canfield for another $10,000.

Canfield and Hamish Hamilton were understandably impatient to get *Inside U.S.A.* into bookshops in time for the spring of 1947, as planned. With wartime rationing still in effect in England, Hamilton had put off publishing several other books in order to have enough paper for the latest *Inside*.

Adding to everyone's impatience was the Book of the Month Club's (BOMC) interest in making *Inside U.S.A.* its main selection for June 1947. However, as 1946 drew to a close, the time frame for the Club to make a decision grew perilously short. At stake was an advance royalty payment to John and his publishers of about $100,000—one of the largest ever by the BOMC to that time.

John sent the first thirty-two chapters of *Inside U.S.A.* to BOMC president Harry Scherman on October 28. To provide the Club's five-member editorial board with a varied sampling, John wrote several isolated chapters, rather than doing everything in the logical sequence it would appear in the book. "I have had a good deal of experience with this seemingly mixed-up technique since it is one I followed with all the *Inside* books," John explained in a letter to Scherman. "There was always some pressure on time at the last moment. Without trying to draw too fine a line, I've always tried to keep them as up-to-date as possible."[22]

Based on the material in those thirty-two chapters, Scherman announced in November that the club had chosen *Inside U.S.A* as its main selection for the following June. The first two *Insides* had been BOMC "dividends," while *Inside Latin America* had been a dual selection. *Inside U.S.A.* was the first Gunther book to be chosen as the Club's main selection; it was an honor, and meant a tremendous boost to the book's sales. "This [also] produced fantastic complications. I have faced many deadlines, but never any so formidably ironclad as this one now pending," John wrote in *A Fragment of Autobiography*.[23] The implications of failure were frightening. If John did not finish the book, BOMC would have no main selection for the first time ever; the consequences would be disastrous. March 15, 1947, was set as the absolute deadline for John to deliver his manuscript.

Except in the final days, when chapters went directly from typewriter to being typeset, everything that he wrote was retyped by his secretary, Nancy Barnett. Five copies were made. John kept one copy; another went to Canfield; one to a historian who had been hired to check facts; one was perused by a libel lawyer; and the other went to John's friends for their comments. Some chapters were rewritten over and over. Nancy Barnett estimates that she retyped the entire 482,000-word manuscript—two-thirds the length of the Bible—at least three times.[24]

All of this checking, correcting, and retyping took precious time, and with each passing day everyone involved in the project grew increasingly tense. Harper & Brothers revised the book's production schedule four times, as delay followed delay and the manuscript grew longer and longer. "He just has not been able to deliver [the book] at all in the time he originally planned," Canfield lamented in a January 24, 1947, letter to Hamish Hamilton. "I don't think even Gunther himself had any idea how long a book it would turn out to be."[25] Even so, Canfield had absolute faith in John's ability to meet his deadline; at one point, he even returned a chapter to him with a note suggesting that it was a "little short," and perhaps he "could add a few more words."

John worked best at night and on weekends, when the building where he kept his office on East Forty-ninth Street was quiet. "Sometimes it seemed that I was the only person still there, with a light burning, in our entire building as 11 p.m. became midnight, and then one o'clock, two o'clock, three o'clock in the morning," John wrote in *A Fragment of Autobiography*. "I ached with frustration and self-pity. But weariness was compensated for by exhilaration."[26]

Despite the interruptions and the ache in his heart, John somehow met his March 15 deadline. In early May, just seven weeks later, *Inside U.S.A.* was published with a first printing of more than a half million copies. The first press run of 125,000 copies was the largest for any book Harper & Brothers had ever published. The BOMC ordered 380,000 more copies for its members, while Hamish Hamilton ordered 35,000 from the U.S. when the shortage of paper in England scuttled printing plans there. The 979-page book sold for five dollars, which was two dollars more than the usual price tag on most hardcover books in 1947.

Despite its cost, *Inside U.S.A.* became an instant best-seller. One day not long after the book's publication, Macy's department store in New York did 90 per cent of its book business with *Inside U.S.A.* Pre-publication orders spurred by a massive publicity blitz put the book into the number one spot all across the nation, and reprint rights were sold to at least nine foreign-language publishers, including Russian and Japanese. Sales were given a boost, too, by the hundreds of news stories about reactions to the book. "Boston Most Charming City in America, Says Gunther," read a headline in one newspaper; others noted, "Author Gunther Appalled at Drinking and Sexual Habits in South," and, "Executive Denies *Inside U.S.A.* Charges on Georgia Mills." Politicians and editorial writers everywhere thundered or crowed about the book, depending on what had been written about their states, of course. *Inside U.S.A.* was boycotted in many stores in Salt Lake City, while civic leaders in Tulsa, Houston, Indianapolis, and Concord, New Hampshire (" . . . the ugliest [state capital] I have ever seen") were indignant about what John had written about their cities. On the other hand, civic leaders in Phoenix ("the cleanest city in America") were long in their praise, while one newspaper editor in the West went so far as to suggest that John Gunther should be appointed to the U.S. Senate as an "extra" senator, representing all of the states. In Washington, President Truman and no fewer than fifty senators—Canfield's promotions people actually kept track of such things—had alluded to *Inside U.S.A.* by year's end.

Readers reacted, too. Letters poured in containing the proverbial bricks, bats, and bouquets. So many letters were received that Canfield considered the idea of making a booklet out of them. One man from Florida complained that *Inside U.S.A.* insulted "every woman in the South," and that John had placed himself beyond the pale of human decency." He concluded by stating, "If you have a shred of common decency you will refund my money." They did.

Another reader wrote to congratulate John, but added that "on page 509 the comma after *Who's Who* is not needed and should be deleted." Others sent leters dealing with everything from the choice of materials used to bind the thick book, to the state of their personal lives. There were requests for autographed photos, pleas for advice or money, and one British serviceman even wrote to ask John for help in emigrating to the U.S.[27]

Critical reaction to *Inside U.S.A.* was no less lively. The reviewer for *Time* predicted the book would by forgotten by year's end;[28] other reviews were among the best ever for any of the *Inside* series. Orville Prescott in the *New York Times* described *Inside U.S.A.* as "consistently intelligent and . . . unfailingly good reading."[29] John was delighted. "Authors can wait all their lives for a review like Prescott's," he said.[30]

Almost as important, and certainly every bit as satisfying to John as these critical plaudits, were the laudatory letters and cables from friends and colleagues. A few were from unlikely sources, among them a note from Sinclair Lewis. After reading an advance copy of *Inside U.S.A.* sent along by Canfield, Lewis obligingly wrote a brief endorsement, which was prominently featured on the dust jacket. What surprised John was that in the twenty years they had been friends, Lewis had never been warm towards him; it was not in his nature. Nor did Lewis often praise the work of other authors.

John always recalled how in 1935, Lewis had predicted that *Inside Europe* would not sell more than 3,000 copies. A decade later, as John was researching *Inside U.S.A.*, Lewis had chided him for wasting time on an "impossible" project. Now, a few weeks after publication of *Inside U.S.A.* John was a week end guest at the Lewis home in Thorvale, Massachusetts. Lewis' latest book, *Kingsblood Royal* was number one on the fiction best-seller list at the time, while *Inside U.S.A.* was number one on the non-fiction list. The two authors had fun joking about it.

John's elation was tempered only by his exhaustion from the strain of writing the book, and by his concerns about his son's health. The success of *Inside U.S.A.* ensured that he could pay all of his bills for now. But he could not afford to rest. John intended to immediately begin work on *Inside Washington.*

He took a few days off to travel to Deerfield, where he and Frances attended Johnny's graduation ceremony. Despite all of his pain and suffering, Johnny had insisted on trying to keep up with his school work. John hired a private tutor who worked with the boy several hours each day. The effort paid off. Johnny had passed a rigorous six-hour entrance examination for Harvard in early April, and his reports cards from the Tutoring School of New York showed that he was maintaining a daily average of ninety. It was an emotional moment as John and Frances joined the parents, family and friends who crowded into the historic Deerfield Church on June 4 for the graduation ceremonies of the Deerfield Academy Class of 1947. Incredibly, there was Johnny, looking frail and tired, his head swatched in white bandages as he took his place among his classmates.

"Johnny was a hero to the class," recalls Henry Eisner. "We admired his courage, but we were mystified at what had happened to him."

Even then, few of Johnny's classmates realized how seriously ill he was. "I guess that we deceived ourselves into believing that he was on the road to recovery," Eisner says.[31]

As Johnny's name was called that day, he made his way forward to the pulpit ever so slowly. He grasped his diploma, shook hands with the head of the school's board of trustees, and then smiled weakly. The applause that greeted him was thunderous.

"Everything that Johnny had suffered was in a sense repaid by the few heroic moments of that walk down the center aisle of that church," John wrote. "This was his triumph and indomitable summation. Nobody who saw it will ever forget it, or be able to forget the sublime strength of will and character it took."[32]

Many of Johnny's classmates had already received acceptance notices from Harvard, and Johnny was impatient to know if he had been accepted, too. John contacted officials at Harvard, and after he explained the situation to them an arrangement was worked out to tell Johnny he had been admitted, even though it was obvious that he would never be able to attend. Sadly, the letter announcing this good news arrived too late for Johnny.

He seems to have sensed that his time was drawing short when in early May doctors had operated yet again. This time they cut into Johnny's brain to a depth of four inches to remove cancerous tissue. Still they had not gotten all the tumor. Now it was growing again. None of the therapies being tried and retried seemed to have any effect. "People may ask if it would not have been better if we had had fewer doctors and less treatment. Perhaps we tried to do too much," John wrote later. "But Johnny loved life desperately and we loved him desperately and it was our duty to try absolutely everything to keep him alive as long as possible."[33]

They were able to do so until the end of June 1947. When death came, it was mercifully quick. Dr. Cornelius Traeger, one of Johnny's doctors, had been visiting author Sinclair Lewis, when he was seized by the unshakable sense that the end was near for Johnny. Suddenly taking leave of his host, Traeger explained, "I have a feeling that Johnny Gunther will die this weekend."[34]

He did not. But on the morning of Monday, June 30, Johnny seemed unusually tired and disoriented. About eleven o'clock he complained of a severe headache, and his skin color was deathly pale. An ambulance rushed him to hospital, where Traeger surmised that the pounding headache was the result of a cerebral hemorrhage. The tumor had eroded a blood vessel inside Johnny's head. Nothing more could be done for him except to pray, as everyone waited for the inevitable.

John and Frances were alone in the room with Johnny when he died that night. The doctors and nurses were all tending to an emergency elsewhere when Johnny suddenly began to fight for breath. He gasped, and trembled. Then he was still.

Johnny's suffering had ended.

All of those long months of operations, all of the suffering, and of the doctors' examinations were over. At the moment of death, none of Johnny's doctors were at hand, not that there was anything they could have done anyway. "All the doctors!—helpless flies now, climbing across the granite face of death," John would write later.[35]

Frances, weeping uncontrollably, reached out for Johnny through the transparent plastic curtain of the oxygen tent. John grasped his son's arms for the last time, and he felt the warmth and energy of life draining away. The color slowly faded from Johnny's face, replaced by the icy blue pallor of death.

The Borough of Manhattan death certificate shows that Johnny Gunther's suffering ended at 11:05 p.m., June 30, 1947. He was only seventeen years, seven months, and twenty-six days old.[36]

CHAPTER THIRTY-TWO

Johnny's funeral was held at noon on July 2, 1947, at a Unitarian chapel at the corner of Eighty-first Street and Madison Avenue in Manhattan. Many family friends were away for the summer, and while John and Frances received an avalanche of telegrams and calls, few could get back to the city in time to attend the service. With classes having ended at Deerfield for the year, Johnny's classmate Henry Eisner was at home in South Orange, New Jersey, when he received a phone call from John informing him of Johnny's death. John asked Henry if he wanted to attend the funeral. He did.

Frances being Jewish and John not, the service was conducted by a rabbi, who was a family friend, and by a Unitarian minister. It was the rabbi who read a poem that Johnny had written in May 1946, "The Unbeliever's Prayer." It went: "Almighty God/ forgive me for my agnosticism;/ for I shall try to keep it gentle, not cynical, nor a bad influence./ And O!/ if Thou are truly in the heavens,/ accept my gratitude/ for all Thy gifts/ and I shall try/ to fight the good fight. Amen."[1]

Eisner recalls the scene that day: the church filled to overflowing with the flowers which surrounded Johnny, laid out in his best tweed suit, and looking so young and peaceful. At last he was free of the incredible pain that he had endured for so many months. "It was a very small, very sad service," Eisner recalls, his voice growing soft with emotion even now, more than four decades later. "It was pathetic, it really was."[2]

Eisner was the only one of Johnny's classmates who made it to the service. The school's headmaster and one of Johnny's teachers were there, however, as were a few of the Gunthers' friends and neighbors, some of the doctors who had treated Johnny, and even one of the nurses who had cared for him in hospital. The woman, Anna Parmelee, wrote a heartfelt account of the funeral, which appeared in a New York newspaper. "Shining down on [Johnny's] coffin was a single bright light—as bright and brilliant as the boy himself," she wrote. "Following the eulogy the doors of the church were thrown wide open. When the bright sun poured through those open doors, throwing the rest of the church in semi-darkness, it was as if a pathway to Heaven had opened for Johnny. I knew then he would live forever."[3]

After the service John and Frances went to Ferncliff Crematorium, where Johnny's body was cremated. They drove back home along the Hudson River in silence, watching as a rising wind whipped the water into whitecaps. There was nothing more for either John or Frances to say, nothing more for them to do but grieve.

Johnny's death tore the heart out of Frances. Through all of the unhappiness and emotional turmoil that had dogged her, she had always loved and devoted herself to her son. He was gone now, and she had no one left. There was an aching void in her life. For a time she withdrew into herself. At one point during Johnny's long illness, when she could take it no more, she had run off for a couple of weeks. No one knew where she had gone, and she never said. What sustained Frances through these dark days was her faith, and her intellect. "The impending death of one's child raises many questions in one's mind and heart and soul," Frances wrote later.

"It raises all the infinite questions, and each answer ending in another question."[4]

During those final days, on occasions when there were no visitors at the house in Madison, Frances and Johnny had spent the lazy summer days talking about these "infinite questions." They had sat on the beach in front of the house reading aloud everything from the Bible to the Koran, to Buddha and Confucius. Sometimes they read Somerset Maugham, G.B. Shaw, Spinoza, or Einstein. Other times, they discussed world events, particularly what was happening in India and Palestine. They talked, too, of love, marriage, and careers as they planned the future both of them knew Johnny would never have. At other times, they just played games or sailed.

It was a precious time for mother and son. Yet always lurking in the shadows which intruded into their lives even on the brightest of summer days were life's brutal realities—Johnny's imminent death, the pain of the Gunthers' failed marriage, and the kind of hatred and bigotry that was everywhere in a world still nursing the wounds from six years of war. There was no escape, even in a sleepy town like Madison (pop. 2,000).

Bertha Brenner, the mother of Johnny's boyhood friend Edgar, recalls a disturbing incident that occurred during one of her weekend visits to Madison. Because Frances was having lunch with journalist Edgar Snow, who was an old friend, the boys met Mrs. Brenner at the train station. The three of them went for lunch at a private social club at which Frances was a member. Afterwards, they swam in the club's pool.

The next day, Frances, Johnny, and their guests returned to the club for lunch. This time, they were met at the door by the manager. He asked for a word with Frances. The two disappeared into his office for several minutes. When Frances emerged, she was fuming. She and her party left the club without eating lunch. Later, Frances recounted for Bertha Brenner her conversation with the club manager.

"Mrs. Gunther, that woman and boy who are with you *appear* to be Jewish," he said. "We have a strict policy here. No Jew has ever crossed the threshold of this club."

"Well, I've done so many times!" Frances snapped, as she rose from her chair. "And *I* am Jewish. But don't worry, I will never enter this club again!"[5]

It had never occurred to the man that Frances might be Jewish, and the revelation that she was had clearly shocked him. "Frances told me that the manager had turned pale, and his hands began to shake," Bertha Brenner says. "This wasn't the first time that this kind of thing had happened to Frances. She had blond hair and blue eyes, and people didn't know that she was Jewish. Sometimes she heard remarks that hurt her deeply."

Such incidents highlighted the glaring contradictions in Frances' character. Life's travails sometimes reduced her to an inconsolable wreck. This happened on countless occasions during her marriage to John, and at the final break she had been so devastated emotionally that she seemed to lose all self control. At other times, Frances displayed an inner strength and resiliency that surprised everyone, even her closest friends.

Says Bertha Brenner, who came to know Frances well during the time that Johnny was ill, "There's no question that she could be moody. But [in 1947] she had just gone through the divorce, and that was very painful. She seemed to have accepted it, and even to be relieved that it had finally happened.

"Frances wasn't very outgoing. She didn't like having to meet people. She would sometimes say to me, 'You know, I prefer being with you.'"[6]

Brenner's comments echo those of Helen Hahn, one of John's girl friends from his days at the University of Chicago. Hahn once observed that, "Frances was not always the helpless little thing that she pretended to be."[7]

Indeed, Frances maintained her composure surprisingly well in the wake of Johnny's death. She and John drove up to Madison, where they spent several days at the house talking, and consoling one another. It was here, after a few drinks too many one night, that John decided that there was only one way for him to purge his grief: he would write a personal memoir of Johnny's life, illness, and death. The book would stand as a memorial to Johnny for everyone who had known, and loved him.

While researching *Inside U.S.A.*, John's intention had been to write two books: one about the country as a whole, the other about the Washington political scene, its personalities and power structure. By mid-1947, he had serious doubts about the latter project, despite the urgings of his new agent, Harold Ober (he had reluctantly left the Carl Brandt agency after more than twenty years after a disagreement over the fees[8]), and publisher Cass Canfield. Harper & Brothers wanted to publish *Inside Washington* in the spring of 1949, while the memory of *Inside U.S.A.* was still fresh in people's minds. American sales of that book were boosted in early 1948 by the publicity surrounding the opening of a Broadway musical review of the same name.

Inside U.S.A., the musical, featured sixteen original songs plus overture and finale, all by the well-known team of lyricist Howard Dietz and composer Arthur Schwartz. The show, which cost more than $250,000 to produce (a lot of money in 1948), premiered with a three-week tryout in Philadelphia. Critic Edwin Schloss of the *Philadelphia Inquirer* pronounced it, "the season's most brilliant and entertaining review."[9] When both *Life* and *Look* magazines published photo spreads on *Inside U.S.A.*, expectations for the show were high in New York. The *New York Times* reported advance ticket sales of $408,000.[10]

People were drawn by the Gunther name, and by the show's thirteen-member cast, and a "Stars and Stripes" chorus headlined by co-stars Jack Haley, best known for his role as the Tin Man in the 1939 film classic *The Wizard of Oz*, and by Beatrice Lillie, the Canadian-born actress. The day that Lillie signed to do the show she was appearing in a play in London, and she telephoned Arthur Schwartz to ask, "What have you gotten me into? I went to a book shop and bought *Inside U.S.A.* this morning. Lots of maps fell out. Where are the lyrics?"[11]

Inside U.S.A. opened on Broadway on April 30, 1948, at the New Century Theatre. The glittery opening-night performance was attended by the Duke and Duchess of Windsor, playwrights Moss Hart (who along with Arnold Howitt had written the sketches for the show) and George S. Kaufman, Billy Rose, the screenwriter, and William Randolph Hearst, Jr. Critic Brooks Atkinson of the *Times* praised *Inside U.S.A.* as "keen and impeccable. As musical shows go, it is a thoroughbred that represents the best brains in our showshop."[12] Robert Coleman of the *Daily Mirror* pronounced the show "a handsome hit."[13]

Despite such promising reviews, *Inside U.S.A.* failed to live up to expectations. The only tune to emerge from the score as a hit was a stiff, somewhat overblown number called, "Haunted Heart." A strike by the American Society of Composers and Publishers (ASCAP), which delayed the recording and radio play of music from *Inside U.S.A.*, may have had something to do with that. By the time that Bea Lillie was able to record an album of songs for RCA, the show's momentum had died. It closed after a steady, albeit unspectacular, two-year run. Arthur Schwartz had plans to take *Inside U.S.A.* to CBS television, doing a half-hour musical revue every other Thursday evening, however, the idea never worked out.

John had been bemused by all of this. The experience was a bit of fun for him, nothing more, even though he had invested a small amount of money in the show. Leonard Lyons reported in his *New York Post* gossip column on March 21, 1948, an anecdote that illustrates the reason for his attitude. He had been at the theatre watching rehearsals for *Inside U.S.A.* one day when a press photographer was taking pictures of the cast. Someone suggested a picture of John.

"What have you got to do with the show?" the man asked him.

"*I* am the author of the title," he announced solemnly.[14]

John was out of his element in the theatre; he had no illusions to the contrary. He still derived his livelihood—and a very good one it was—from books and journalism. By 1947, John had all but abandoned radio. His enthusiasm for any return to the medium had been stifled by the way in which his old friend Bill Shirer was dumped by CBS.

The onset of the Cold War gave rise to a paranoia that by the late 1940s had begun began to permeate all aspects of American life. Led by a congressional body called the House Un-American Activities Committee (HUAC), and by an ambitious junior senator from Wisconsin named Joseph McCarthy, the hunt for Reds and so-called "fellow travelers" was off and running. Shirer was only one of the unfortunate innocents who got caught up in the web of suspicion when he dared speak out. Ironically, Shirer became a victim of a mindset that had inadvertently been created by himself, John Gunther, and the others in what news commentator Eric Sevareid would describe as "that extraordinary band of American journalists, some with Midwest hayseed still in their hair . . . ."[15]

It was a vision of the world that was rooted in the parochial,

WASPish values of turn-of-the-century rural, and small town America—the America of Norman Rockwell paintings. The hallmarks of this vision of the world were an unwavering faith in God, flag, and country. America, a nation borne of revolution and nurtured on diversity, became uneasy when confronted with forces and ideas that it could not understand or control. Those suspicions were strong in 1945, in the wake of a bloody war that had ended with the defeat of two enemies—Japan and Germany, and the emergence of a dangerous new one in the form of the Soviet Union.

Upon his return to the U.S. from Europe after the war, William Shirer had settled in New York. Here he began working as a freelance journalist, and doing a news commentary show on Sunday evenings for CBS. Shirer brought an unabashedly liberal Democratic perspective to the news, one to which John Gunther also subscribed. The difference between the two men was more one of temperament than substance. William Shirer, cerebral, enormously talented, and volatile, had never been reluctant to speak his mind. That tendency had got him fired from his job with the *Chicago Tribune* in 1932, and it landed him in hot water many other times.

John Gunther was a different character entirely. Amicable, self-effacing, and slow to anger, he was from the old school of journalism that stressed objectivity; telling all sides of a story was important, as was maintaining a sense of detachment. Although his non-fiction books were certainly political, he rarely used them as a platform for his own opinions. That is not to say that his politics did not show through, only that his message was subtle and understated.

John Gunther focused on people, and he conveyed a vast amount of information—and opinion—by weaving into his narrative the sort of anecdotes and gossip that educated readers while entertaining them. That was the essence of his genius. Literary critic Malcolm Cowley had noted as much back in 1936. Reviewing *Inside Europe* in the *New Republic*, Cowley talked about John Gunther's "greedy appetite for curious and apparently trivial bits of information that acquire a sudden meaning when pieced together."[16] It was not that John hesitated to make his political views known, as Cowley astutely pointed out, only that he usually did it so skillfully and subtly that most people did not even realize it. Some did, of course.

The vigilant eyes of Federal Bureau of Investigation agents fell upon John on several occasions because of things he wrote or said. Founded in 1908 as the investigative arm of the Department of Justice, the FBI was given the task of enforcing federal criminal statutes. As such, its two principal jobs were general investigations, and domestic security operations. Director J. Edgar Hoover built an anti-radical division that was shaped by his own fanaticism about radicals, communists, liberals, and socialists—who were one in the same in his mind.

John Gunther had first come to the bureau's attention in 1937, when a story in the American communist paper *The Daily Worker* mentioned in passing that John Gunther was a supporter of the Abraham Lincoln Battalion, the American volunteers who had gone to Spain to fight the fascists.[17]

In 1942, agents had checked him out again after a sharp-eyed agent noticed an innocuous reference in his book *Inside Latin America* to the FBI's counterespionage work.[18] The following year, on September 26, 1943, John on his weekly radio show with John Vandercook said that, "In a way we should be thankful to the Japanese for having made Pearl Harbor and for having given us the realities of war."[19] In context, as part of a discussion of America's involvement in the war, the observation was hardly shocking. However, as one more piece of what was regarded as a pattern of suspicious behavior, FBI agents made a transcript of the broadcast and deposited it in the Gunther file. Like sharks drawn by the minutest scent of blood in the water, they began circling lazily, relentlessly.

Under J. Edgar Hoover the FBI kept watch on hundreds of prominent American journalists and writers, particularly in the late 1940s and early 1950s, when Cold War paranoia was at its peak. *New York Times* reporter Herbert Mitgang delved into this little-known aspect of American history in a 1988 book entitled, *Dangerous Dossiers: Exposing the Secret War Against America's Greatest Authors.*[20]

John Gunther was among those whom agents suspected of subversive activities. Despite the fact that he had always maintained a good relationship with the State Department (much to the dismay of colleagues such as George Seldes), both the HUAC and the FBI compiled files on John Gunther.[21] For that reason, while he was researching *Inside U.S.A.*, John had visited Washington several times. On each occasion, his requests to meet with Hoover were turned down. In early December 1947, John was in town again for an interview with President Truman at the White House, and prior to his arrival he again wired Hoover asking for an interview.

Hoover's official response was that his schedule for the week John was planning to be in Washington was "uncertain," so an interview was unlikely. But the handwritten comment that Hoover scribbled on the bottom of John's telegram indicates the real reason that he was reluctant to grant an interview. "I am not keen about it as [Gunther] is far, far left of center," he had written.[22]

At the urging of his aides, Hoover reconsidered. He met with John on December 6. It is open to conjecture who gained the most information from that interview. The conversation was general and cordial, and John left FBI headquarters that day little suspecting that the only reason he had been allowed into Hoover's office was because the FBI wanted to find out more about him.

It was not really necessary to be devious about discovering John Gunther's politics. After all, he was not shy about his views, which he stated both publicly and privately. Fortunately, John had a keen sense of discretion, and knew where and how to voice his opinions. He was particularly vocal in criticizing what he and many other liberals regarded as the growing danger of a war with the U.S.S.R. William Shirer was no less critical of this hawkish mentality which pervaded a powerful segment of American public opinion. But, unlike John, he paid the price for his candor.

Although Shirer's news show was among the most popular on the airwaves on Sunday evenings, he was informed on March 10, 1947, that the J.B. William Shaving Cream Company was withdrawing its sponsorship. The company supposedly wanted to back a show that reached a younger audience. Shirer suspected more sinister reasons. He and other liberal broadcast commentators—including Raymond Swing, John Vandercook and Bob St. John, whose shows had already been cancelled—had come under fire from conservatives.

Shirer had heard rumors that he would be the next to go, but he believed that CBS head William Paley and news chief Edward R. Murrow, both of whom were long-time friends, would protect him. He was wrong.

Paley announced that March 30 would be Shirer's last show. The ensuing public outcry failed to convince the CBS boss to reconsider.

So did a telegram of protest from a liberal-oriented media watchdog group called the Voice of Freedom Committee. That group, chaired by writer Dorothy Parker, included several dozen well-known writers, and Hollywood film stars, including Gregory Peck, Ring Lardner, Edward G. Robinson, Arthur Miller, Judy Holliday, and John Gunther. All signed the telegram to CBS.[23]

As the date for Shirer's last broadcast neared, relations between him and Paley became increasingly bitter. There were fears that the CBS chief would simply cancel Shirer's show outright, rather than risk allowing him to vent his anger publicly. John was aware of the situation, and offered to do Shirer's last show for him in order to spare everyone embarrassment. Shirer was having none of it; he insisted on appearing himself. Ever the professional, he did so without incident. But his broadcast career was ruined, and the market for his free-lance newspaper and magazine articles suddenly dried up, too. For several years, it was difficult for Shirer to earn a living. He was effectively blacklisted. The experience understandably left him embittered, cynical, and frustrated.[24]

Having witnessed the fate of his friend, John was leery of having anything more to do with radio broadcasting. All of his worst suspicions about the medium had been verified. Thus, he was content to stick to what he did best—write. And there was a lot of writing to be done.

The memoir of Johnny that he had in mind was a project that he felt he undertake to exorcise the demons which haunted him. "He had loved Johnny very much, doted on him," says John's friend Leonora Hornblow. "He once told me that his son's death was the most terrible thing that ever happened to him. It was something John just couldn't get out of his mind."[25]

On one occasion not long after Johnny's death, he was strolling along Sixty-second Street just as Phyllis Cerf, the wife of Random House publisher Bennett Cerf, was coming out of her house. Mrs. Cerf spotted her son John about to run out into traffic. "Johnny!" she shrieked. At that instant, she saw John Gunther. His startled face was so contorted in pain that the scene was forever seared into her memory.[26]

Because of such incidents John began research for the memoir of Johnny a few days after the funeral. It was a task unlike any other that he had ever undertaken. He gathered Johnny's school and camp reports, medical records, letters, and excerpts from his own diary, as well as from those of Frances and Johnny. In doing so, he was delving into his own life and emotions, examining his beliefs and values as he never had before. It was a difficult, sometimes painful process, but John was determined to see it through. Once he began writing, the story came tumbling out.

"I am working hard on the memoir about Johnny and should have a draft complete by this time next week," John told Cass Canfield in a letter dated August 1, 1947. "I think the title will be from a quotation by John Donne [1572-1631]—"Death Be Not Proud," don't you rather like that?"[27]

In lesser hands such a book could easily have become a trite or melodramatic account of suffering and grief, or simply a father's eulogy for his lost son. But John recounted the story of Johnny's life and death simply and honestly. The book is a remarkable amalgam of reportage and personal memory. There is no calculated pathos, no straining for sympathy, only the inspiring story of Johnny's couragous battle against an unbeatable foe—Death. "I write . . . because many children are afflicted by disease, though few ever have to endure what Johnny had," John explained in a foreword to the book, "and perhaps they and their parents may derive some modicum of succor from the unflinching fortitude and detachment with which he rode through his ordeal to the end."[28]

John sent copies of the finished manuscript to Frances, as well as to several friends. William Shirer, Dorothy Thompson, Cass Canfield, and the others who read *Death Be Not Proud* were deeply moved; Thompson hailed it as "a true love story on the purest level." Frances called to volunteer a brief afterword consisting of a mother's memories of her son, as well as her thoughts on some of the philosophical questions that she and Johnny had wrestled that last summer at Madison. John agreed, somewhat reluctantly; he was unsure of just what Frances had in mind.

Nonetheless, he was pleased with reaction to the book. He was even more pleased with Cass Canfield's decision to donate the profits to children's cancer research. The book, which John asked Canfield to make "slim and dignified," was scheduled for publication in late 1948 by both Harper & Brothers in New York, and

Hamish Hamilton in London. Meanwhile, *Ladies Home Journal* paid $7,500 for an an excerpt, and *Reader's Digest* $4,000.

Once the arrangements for publication of *Death Be Not Proud* were sorted out, Canfield urged John to complete the *Inside Washington* book, and then to do a revised edition of *Inside U.S.A.* that incorporated the fresh information in the thousands of letters which had been received from readers. John had discussed with Canfield a $25,000 advance for the Washington book, however, his enthusiasm ebbed in the wake of Johnny's death. John had already used much of his material in *Inside U.S.A.*, and Franklin Roosevelt's death on April 12, 1945, had changed the Washington political scene dramatically.

John had twice met President Harry S. Truman. The first time was in November 1945, when the two men were introduced; the second was on December 8, 1947, when John had gone to Washington to interview Truman. Like just about everyone else, John had underestimated the new president. He had written a short profile of him called, "The Man from Missouri" for the June 1945 edition of *Reader's Digest*, but John did not feel that he *really* knew much about Truman. The prospect of plunging into research on the Washington scene anew, and of researching the new president's life and career was daunting just then. John felt emotionally and physically drained after the events of recent months; he was not up to the two years of intensive effort that he knew would be necessary to complete another *Inside* book.

Besides, there was another even more compelling personal reason for his reluctance: at the age of forty-six, he was about to remarry. John Gunther had fallen head over heels in love.

CHAPTER THIRTY-THREE

John Gunther's friend Leonora Hornblow has observed that "John loved Frances, but he was never really *in love* with her."[1] The difference was subtle but important. While John may have married in 1927 for reasons that even he did not entirely understand, there was no mistaking his motives the second time around. This time, he really was in love.

The object of John's affection was an attractive young brunette named Jane Perry. She was the former wife of explorer, author, and broadcaster John Vandercook. John had first met Jane in late 1943, when he and Vandercook acted as co-hosts of a weekly radio show on NBC It was easy to understand why John was drawn to her. She was attractive, bright, outgoing, and vitally interested in writing, publishing, and the arts. All were interests that she came by naturally.

Jane Perry, the only child of Hilda (née Hedley) and Reginald Perry, had been born in 1917 in New York City. Her mother was of English ancestory, but had come from Montreal, Canada. She attended Barnard College in New York and was very musical; she taught piano. Like John Gunther's mother, Hilda Perry was a strong, vibrant woman, and it was she who ran the family

Reginald Perry was a man of great charm. His dream in life was to become a writer. When things did not work out for him in that regard, he turned to a job in advertising to support his family. Like millions of other Americans, he was thrown out of work by the Depression. Luckily, he found another job in Washington with the Department of Labor.

Jane Perry received her early education at Birch Wathem, an experimental school for gifted children on Manhattan's lower West Side. When her parents temporarily relocated to Washington, she stayed behind in New York to attend Brille School, and later went to Vassar, the well-known women's college in Poughkeepsie, New York. The day she graduated in 1938, Jane married John Vandercook, whose first wife had died of cancer three years earlier. Vandercook was a distant relative of her father Perry, and Jane had met him when he visited the family's summer home in Vermont.

Lean and bearded, Vandercook cut a dashing, romantic figure. He hailed from a distinguished family. His father was one of the founders of the United Press Association, while his mother was a novelist, and the author of many books for girls. Vandercook followed in his parents' footsteps. He was a member of the Explorer's Club, a popular author, sometimes painter, would-be actor, and accomplished *bon vivant*. He had achieved fame at the tender age of twenty-three by writing a best selling biography of King Henry Christophe of Haiti entitled, *Black Majesty* (1928). At the time Vandercook and Jane Perry wed in 1938, he was thirty-six and had written six more books.

From the beginning, the Vandercooks traveled widely. On their honeymoon they set off on a six-month trip to Hawaii and the South Pacific. From there, they journeyed to France, where they had a front-row seat for the outbreak of the Second World War. That experience stood Vandercook in good stead when in September 1940 he went to work for NBC as a news commentator.[2]

Vandercook was restless, moody man, and when his second marriage crumbled, he and Jane divorced. Jane took a job as an editorial assistant at Duell, Sloan & Pearce, a small New York publishing house. This is where she was working when she and John began dating. At first, the relationship was casual. In the wake of his separation, and the end of his affair with Agnes Knickerbocker, John had savored his life as a footloose bachelor. For a time, he dated many beautiful women.

Leonora Hornblow, who met John in 1941 at an after-theater party at the home of publisher Bennett Cerf, recalls the strong first impression he made on people, women especially. "You see, John was incredibly famous at that time. It's something that will never come around again. Foreign correspondents were the glamour figures of journalism," she says.

"Jane and I used to laugh at John. He had such an appetite for life. He enjoyed everything, and was so engaged by people. He was a big, burly teddy bear. Women found him attractive in an odd sort of way."[3]

Jane Perry certainly enjoyed his company, and she found herself drawn to him. During the time that Johnny was ill, their relationship blossomed. When John felt down, Jane was there. In those dark days when he needed all the encouragement that he could to get to continue writing *Inside U.S.A.*, Jane was there. By early 1948, John had fallen in love with her. Only his closest friends knew of the couple's plans to marry.

After delivering the final manuscript of *Death Be Not Proud* to Cass Canfield on February 12, 1948, John left for a vacation in California. He visited his relatives at Carmel, then rendezvoused with Jane in Chicago the first weekend in March. They were married on March 5 in a quiet ceremoney performed by a prominent judge who was a friend of the Perry family. When news of the wedding leaked out a few days later, it was carried by newspapers across the country. The *Chicago Tribune* ran a photo of the newlyweds on March 8; the rival *Sun-Times* carried a brief report, as did the *New York Times*, and many other papers.[4]

John and his bride took up residence in New York, and John began work on a several writing projects. Gardner Cowles, the editor of *Look* magazine, had approached him to write a series of articles on Eastern Europe and the Soviet Union. John and Jane began making preparations for a May departure for a long trip to

Europe. It would be his first visit to the Continent in more than five years. John also began work on a short biography of Franklin Roosevelt which made use of the mass of information he had gathered for *Inside U.S.A.*. John hoped to deliver the manuscript to Cass Canfield by mid-May 1948 for publication early the next year. That plan did not work out. The writing was more difficult than he anticipated, and there were too many other distractions.

It was proving difficult for him to erase the memory of Johnny from his mind. He was also busy closing his office in anticipation of the upcoming European trip and the uncertainty of his new life; John planned to stay abroad at least six months. On March 17, he wrote a glowing letter of recommendation to Cass Canfield on behalf of Nancy Barnett, who had been "much more than a secretary" to him for seven years. Barnett had typed the final copy of almost every book, article, and radio script that John had written during that time. She had also kept his office books, helped with research, maintained his morgue of several hundred thousand newspaper and magazine clippings, and generally kept his life—personal as well as professional—in order. John was grateful for her loyalty, and more than a little sad to bid her goodbye. "Really, she is a find, and I think I am doing you a favor in writing this letter rather than the opposite," John told Canfield.[5]

For her part, Barnett took with her only fond memories of her years in John Gunther's employ. "He was always very nice to me, and very considerate," she says. "I think I started out in 1941 at thirty-five dollars per week, and I was making sixty-five dollars per week when I left. That was good money in those days. And John raised my salary just before I left so I'd be able to tell people I was making that much more."[6]

John's attentions were also diverted these days from work on the Roosevelt book by press reports about the trial of Bob Best, his good friend from his Vienna years. Best's table at the Café Louvre had been the hub of the foreign journalistic community in the Austrian capital in the early 1930s. In addition, for five dollars per day, Best had often covered for other American reporters when they were out of town; he had written under the pseudonym Eugene Crawford.

Best had married a German woman, and during the war made more than 300 propaganda broadcasts for the Nazis. Thus, when he was captured by the British after the war, he was returned to the

U.S., where he went on trial in Boston for treason in April 1948. As he was being indicted, Best ranted that the proceedings were part of a worldwide Bolshevik conspiracy.

The trial's outcome was never in doubt: an unrepentant Best was found guilty. On April 16 he was sentenced to life in Leavonworth Prison, where he died four years later, in 1952, broken and disgraced.[7]

John and other Americans who had known Bob Best as a friend were saddened. But few were surprised by the court's decision. John was only grateful that he had not been subpoenaed as a witness, as had William Shirer. It was Shirer who in 1942 had broken the news that Best had turned traitor. Now, on April 5, 1948, Shirer was called to testify against him. Shirer took no pleasure so doing. The irony of him bearing witness against an old friend was not lost on him, nor was Best's assertion that he had been the victim of a leftist conspiracy. After all, William Shirer had been unofficially blacklisted because of the mere suspicion that *he* was a communist fellow traveler or dupe. Shirer mused for a long while about what had driven Bob Best to work for Hitler. Out of this came a novel called *The Traitor* (1950), which is based on a character who closely resembles Best.[8]

Meanwhile, John and Jane continued making plans for their Europe trip. John had decided to make it a working holiday. He planned to take along his notes, so he could work on the Roosevelt book in Europe. He also hoped that his travels in Eastern Europe would yield material for a book about life behind the Iron Curtain. In addition to the money he had received from *Look*, the *New York Herald-Tribune* had joined in to underwrite the costs of the trip in return for some newspaper articles.

John and Jane left New York in mid-May bound for the Italian island of Capri. They spent three carefree weeks here sitting in the sun, swimming, and enjoying each other's company. John read the galley proofs of *Death Be Not Proud*, which he approved, and returned to New York the second week of June. He was somewhat uneasy about doing so after he received a letter dealing with a paragraph about Johnny's "German and Hebrew heritage," which

Frances wanted to insert in her portion of the manuscript.

"I guess I am just . . . bored by too much ancestory, but never mind. Print it as it is," John told Frances in a letter dated June 24 from Naples. He continued, "I was much moved by your chapter, seeing it in proof."[9]

Frances, too, was still finding it difficult to forget the pain. Her torment is evident in the eleven-page afterword she wrote for *Death Be Not Proud*. Frances was still wrestling with some of the philosophical questions that she and Johnny had talked about that last summer at Madison. She lamented the days, months, and years of her life that she now realized had been wasted. "Yet at the end . . . when one has put away all the books, and all the words, when one is alone with oneself, when one is alone with God, what is left in one's heart? Just this: "I wish we had loved Johnny more."[10]

Seeking to atone for some of what she perceived of as her "sins," Frances decided to got to Israel, which had come into existence as a country on May 14, 1948, following the withdrawal of British forces from Palestine. Frances told Bertha Brenner and other friends that she hoped to work to improve relations between Arabs and Jews. Those plans were thrown into disarray when her application for a visitor's visa was turned down. She wrote John asking if he could help in any way with an appeal. John suggested that Frances reapply for a visa as a journalist, or that she appeal directly to Israeli leaders, some of whom she had met during the Gunthers' 1937 visit to Palestine. Beyond that, John was reluctant to get involved; he was too busy attempting to put his own life back together.

His writing was going slowly. John worked on the Roosevelt book in a desultory way during the stay on Capri. His original plan for a short quick biography had been revised in the face of a growing realization that there was a lot more to tell than he had at first thought. The lengthy outline that John developed suggested a book of 80,000 to 90,000 words. With that in mind, he wrote Canfield to say that publication would have to be put off until the spring of 1949, "for the simple, complete, and devastating reason that I haven't got the damned thing done, and see no possibility of finishing it until we return in October."[11]

Having resolved the issue, John and Jane proceeded with the rest of the trip. They made their way to Rome for a June 30 private audience at the Vatican with Pope Pius XII. The experience was "moving and beautiful," John told Frances in a letter.[12]

According to protocol, John was not allowed to quote anything that the pope said, however he could not resist jotting down one remark. John dared to ask His Holiness his thoughts about the news that day that Marshal Tito of Yugoslavia had split with the Kremlin, and been "ex-communicated" from the Soviet-led world communist movement. The pope stared at John a moment then intoned, "I have not heard from my informants in Belgrade yet."[13]

John got a chance to apprise himself of the situation there on August 26, when he and Jane interviewed the Yugoslavian dictator at his summer villa on the outskirts of Zagreb. At the time, the western media was filled with reports of Tito's differences with Moscow. Unlike other Eastern European leaders, he stubbornly refused to fall into line with Soviet policies, much to Stalin's displeasure. There had been much discussion of Tito, and of the future of his nation, yet the Yugoslavian leader remained very much a shadow man. Most people in the west knew little more about him other than the fact that during the war he had led a ferocious and deadly campaign of guerilla warfare against the invading Germans. Josip Broz—Tito was his revolutionary name—did not grant many interviews to American reporters. Thus John was uncertain of just what to expect when he went calling.

John and Jane sat down with the Tito on a terrace surrounded by quiet gardens. An interpreter and a secretary were positioned about ten feet away. As John observed, "It isn't easy to have an informal chat with a dictator when you have to talk through people who are kept off at such a respectful distance." It turned out that communicating only seemed to be difficult. Tito actually understood more English than he admitted; John noted how on a couple of points, he corrected the translator.

One of the conditions of the interview was that John was not to ask any political questions, and certainly nothing about the recent break with Moscow. Following introductions there were a few moments of awkward silence. Then John asked Tito an innocuous question that seemed to interest him. Things were off and running in a freewheeling conversation. John was struck by Tito's quiet self-confidence. He was anything but the blustering bully that many media reports pictured him to be.

John was impressed, too, by Tito's physical presence. At fifty-five, his hair was greying, but he still exuded an aura of strength.

He was heavy set, short, and handsome. He dressed that day in a smart white suit with red polka-dot tie and just one small medal pinned to his lapel. Throughout the interview he laughed a good deal as he puffed contentedly on his cigarettes, which he smoked in a small holder shaped like a pipe. Only Tito's eyes gave a clue to the man's ruthless temperament; they were icy blue, small, and cold. It was clear that here was someone used to getting his own way, and that he was unafraid of speaking his mind.

The conversation touched upon everything from the 1948 American presidential campaign to the place of Yugolslavia in post-war Europe, and whether or not the U.S. and the Soviet Union would go to war—as many people in Washington feared. Tito expressed confidence that such fears were groundless. State Department officials were keen to hear this, and when John visited Budapest he met with officials at the American Embassy to give them a full account of his conversation with Tito. The details were passed along to Washington.[15]

John and Jane visited almost every country in Eastern Europe, and in each they interviewed either the leader, or high-ranking government officials. It seemed like old times to John—in some ways, at least. Nowhere was that more so than in Vienna, where at the Hotel Bristol the hall porter greeted him as a long-lost friend, and kissed Jane's hand.

Vienna was still occupied by the Allies at the time. The soldiers who were everywhere, and the shattered buildings in many parts of the city served as a reminder of the indignities that this beautiful old city had suffered since John last set foot there. He was saddened to see how haggard and poor the inhabitants looked. Even during the 1930s, when he had been the *Chicago Daily News'* resident correspondent, life had not been so lean. In 1948, there were severe shortages of consumer goods of all kinds, and the drabness of the streets reminded John of Moscow when he had visited twenty years before.

John and Jane toured Vienna, and sought out some of John's friends. Few of them were to be found. John learned that three of his closest friends, all Jewish, were gone: one had committed suicide when the Nazis took the city in 1938; one had been murdered in an extermination camp; and one had simply disappeared without a trace. John and Jane visited the house in the suburban Dobling district where John, Frances, and Johnny had once lived.

The grand old house was pock-marked with bullet scars, and its windows had been blasted out. The surrounding neighborhood had been the scene of heavy fighting when the Red Army took the city from the Germans in April 1945. The same struggle had devastated portions of the historic downtown area.

The Café Louvre, where John had spent so many happy hours, was just a memory; the building itself had been destroyed by a bomb, and a bank now occupied the site. The building in which the *Daily News* office had been located was now occupied by a strip club, and the local offices of the Communist Party.

John's shared his thoughts on Vienna, his experiences in meeting Tito, and his observations on the situation in Eastern Europe in a series of articles that he wrote for *Look* and the *New York Herald Tribune*. Some were written en route, others were written in London. On the way home to New York, John and Jane spent several days in the city in the company of Leonora Hornblow and her husband Arthur, who was in England to produce a movie. John introduced Jane to Leonora, and took the two of them to lunch. Afterwards they accompanied him to his favorite tailor, Anderson & Shepherd on Savile Row. He had not shopped there for almost five years.

When Arthur Hornblow chanced to drop in at the same shop later that day, one of the clerks approached him and announced very earnestly, "Mr. Hornblow, Mr. John Gunther was in the shop earlier today with *two* ladies. One of them was your wife."

Hornblow laughed as he explained the situation to the chagrined clerk.[16]

CHAPTER THIRTY-FOUR

John Gunther's book about his travels in Eastern Europe was published by Harper & Brothers in the spring of 1949. *Behind the Curtain* was an expanded and revised version of the articles that he had written about the trip. With Jane's help, the book was completed in a rush following the Gunther's return to New York in mid-September. Jane had assumed the role of John's editorial assistant, personal critic, and muse; it was a role that she would fill for the rest of her husband's life, and it was to her that he dedicated this book.

With publication of *Behind the Curtain*, John had two new books in stores. *Death Be Not Proud* had appeared in February 1949 to laudatory reviews; one by John's friend Walter Duranty in the *New York Herald-Tribune* on February 6, 1949 was typical. "To read [the book] is to grasp the meaning of man's power to defy

Death's hurt, to be filled with confidence and emptied of despair," Duranty wrote. "It will bring fresh spirit to the weary, and new confidence and light to those who walk in shadow."

Initial sales of *Death Be Not Proud* were slower than they might have been for an *Inside* book. As of early March, Cass Canfield reported to John that about 17,300 copies had been sold.[1] The subject matter no doubt frightened off many readers. But John was not concerned. His motivation for writing *Death Be Not Proud* had not been to make a lot of money, but rather to create a memorial to Johnny, as well as a message of hope to anyone, anywhere who was suffering with illness or nursing a loved one who was.

That being the case, Cass Canfield surmised that the book had what in the argot of the publishing world is known as "legs"—a long shelf life. He was right. *Death Be Not Proud* would continue to be in demand long after any other John Gunther book, and long after its author's death. The book is still in print as a paperback, more than four decades after it was first published. From time to time Jane Gunther still hears from readers. So, too, does Johnny's friend Henry Eisner, who is mentioned. Eisner says that he is never surprised by the calls or letters, most of which come from young people eager to interview him for school essays.[2]

A whole new generation of readers was introduced to *Death Be Not Proud* when in February 1975, nearly five years after John's death, ABC-TV did a made-for-television movie based on the book. The film was written, directed, and produced by Donald Wrye, and it starred Robby Benson as Johnny. Unfortunately, the critics were not enthusiastic about the adaptation; *New York Times* television writer John O'Connor chided Wrye for "fudging" the unhappy details of the Gunthers' marriage breakdown.[3]

From the beginning, *Death Be Not Proud* struck a responsive chord in readers. In the first few months after publication John heard from hundreds of people around the world who had been moved by the story of Johnny's courageous struggle. A woman from California sent money to start a Johnny Gunther scholarship in chemistry; someone from a small town in Pennsylvania mailed John a donation for children's cancer research. Whitelaw Reid, the vice-president of the *New York Herald-Tribune* contacted Cass Canfield with word that he planned to nominate John for a Pulitzer Prize in 1949.[4]

While all of this attention was welcome, what John found most satisfying was a growing sense that Johnny's death had not been in vain. John donated chemistry lab equipment to Deerfield Academy in his son's memory, and in September 1948, he gave Columbia Neurological Institute $6,500 for children's cancer research. The money came from advance sales of the book. Thousands of dollars more would follow. John derived much satisfaction from doing so because the president of the university at the time was Dwight D. Eisenhower, who had accepted the job after retiring from the army in June. John had not forgotten the kindness and concern of the Institute staff who had cared for Johnny to the end, nor that Ike had taken time to write him a letter of sympathy when Johnny died.

Reader reaction to John's other new book, *Behind the Curtain*, was likewise strong, albeit for different reasons. While some critics chided him for not saying anything that was new, others praised him for summarizing the situation in Eastern Europe, and for creating such a vibrant picture of the reality of everyday life there. *Behind the Curtain* was an important book in the sense that it was one of few accounts at the time by a western journalist who preached tolerance and common sense as a counter to Stalin. There was none of the ugly Cold War rhetoric that had become such a prominent feature of life in post-war America. Instead, John took a long, sober look at the realities of what was happening in the nations which had fallen under Soviet domination.

Behind the Curtain served to galvanize American public opinion in that it confirmed people's suspicions: life in Eastern Europe was difficult and dangerous. One brand of totalitarianism—Nazism—had given way to another—Stalinism. Yet John warned against anti-communist hysteria, and militarism. He argued forcefully and intelligently that the best way to meet the Soviet challenge was to understand it, and to prove to the world the superiority of the American way of life. John cautioned that any war between the U.S. and the Soviet Union would be a bloody signal "that Hitler, even in death, will have won the war."[5] It was a warning that John had sounded before; it was one that he would repeat again, and again, to anyone who would listen.

"Despite many faults, this book has two immense virtues: objectivity and intellectual honesty," reviewer Alexander Werth of the British publication *New Statesman* wrote. "These qualities no longer exist in Eastern journalism, where everything is 'party line'; but they are also very far today from being universal in Western journalism . . . [*Behind the Curtain*] belongs to a great journalistic tradition, which is, unfortunately, today in danger of dying."[6]

John's cautious optimism was a welcome antidote to the doom-and-gloom scenarios being painted by many American observers. For that reason, *Behind the Curtain* sold briskly. And sales were given a major boost when *Reader's Digest* published an excerpt, and the Book of the Month Club named *Behind the Curtain* one of its Dual Selections for June 1949. The other book chosen that month was George Orwell's anti-totalitarian novel, *1984*.

The royalty money was most welcome since John and Jane had decided that his Park Avenue apartment was too small for the two of them. John used some of the money that he earned from *Behind the Curtain* as a down-payment on a four-story, eighty-year-old brownstone at 216 East Sixty-second Street in New York. The house had a beautiful two-level garden at the back, and in 1949 it was included in tours by the New York City Gardens Club.[7] Thus, at age 48, John purchased his first house. Not long afterwards, he and Jane bought a small dog, a poodle. The man that some critics had dubbed "the Marco Polo of the Book Club" was finally putting down roots.

The house on Sixty-second Street became the home that John had always wanted. For the next twelve years it became the center of his life. It was here that he found the peace of mind to write, and to put his life back together again, as the memory of Johnny lingered with him. The Gunthers became a familiar couple at New York night spots, and social events. They also loved to entertain, and their home became a literary salon of sorts. There was a constant stream of people—well-known writers, artists, musicians, actors, and politicians—dropping by for parties and dinners, or simply for drinks and conversation. When Nehru (who had become India's first prime minister when that country achieved its independence from Great Britain in 1947) visited the U.S. for the first time, he came to tea. And the Duke and Duchess of Windsor came to dinner when they were in town. On one such occasion, John introduced another guest, Paul Auriol, to the duke, who murmured, "Don't I know something about your father?"

"Possibly," came Auriol's reply. "He's the president of France."[8]

Unlike Frances, who was uncomfortable in the company of such personages, and at best merely tolerated the whirl of social activity in which John reveled, Jane delighted in opening her front door to famous guests. That was one of the reasons that these were the best of times for John Gunther, who had never lost his wide-eyed sense of wonderment at meeting a celebrity—even though he was by now as famous as many of the people who came through the door of his home.

"People were *always* coming and going," says Leonora Hornblow. "It's a wonder that John got as much work done as he did. The Gunther house was what my husband used to call an 'up house'—you always felt good there, and you were glad to be asked back. The food was always excellent, the people were interesting, and you enjoyed yourself.

"The Gunther's parties weren't sedate, but they weren't rowdy either. They were merry. People mixed, and they moved around."[9]

John recounted in a letter to Frances the events of a boisterous 1951 Christmas party. It was evidently a typical evening. The house had been jammed with people, and the merriment went on all night. "A nice man named Eddie Albert sang songs on a guitar. Truman Capote looked on with the visage of an ancient maiden aunt (he is a full twenty-six)," and a "drunken Irish cop" crashed the party in the early hours of the morning. When John threw the man out, there was a commotion. No sooner had it died down than the Gunther's garbage man entered unannounced. "This was a shock to the elegant Mr. Capote, who was wearing a velvet dinner suit, embroidered smock, and (maybe I am making this up) sandals," John wrote.[10]

On any given evening at 216 East Sixty-second Street one might have encountered John's old friends Jimmy Sheean, William Shirer, Edward R. Murrow, or Dorothy Thompson; publisher Bennett Cerf sometimes came by, as did writers John Steinbeck, Irwin Shaw, Anthony West (Rebecca West's son), Joseph Mankiewicz, and Merle Miller; concert pianist Arthur Rubinstein; cartoonist Al Capp; movie producer David Selznik, and stars Rex Harrison, Montgomery Clift, Marlene Dietrich, Frederic March,

Myrna Loy (who had been married to Arthur Hornblow), Audrey Hepburn, and occasionally even Greta Garbo.

For reasons she never publicly explained, the enigmatic Swedish film star had walked away from her career in 1941, at the age of thirty-six. Garbo lived the last four decades of her life as a semi-recluse, dividing her time between the French Riviera and an apartment in Manhattan, not all that far from the Gunther's house on East Sixty-second Street.

Since her death on April 8, 1990, accounts by those who knew her during the last four decades of her life suggest that while Garbo may have been out of the public eye, she maintained an active social life among a select circle of friends. She loved to walk each day, and to visit antique shops. Because so few people knew what she looked like, or expected to encounter Garbo on the streets of New York, her privacy was maintained.

Garbo evidently felt comfortable at the Gunther home, for she visited on many occasions. Jane and John first met her in 1949 at a Russian Easter party at the home of mutual friend George Schlee, the husband of *haute couture* designer Valentina Nicolaevna Sanina—better known to the world as Valentina. The Gunthers, Schlee, Valentina, and Garbo began to socialize, and they spent Christmas Eve 1949 together.[11]

John was much intrigued by Garbo, and about this time he sometimes began accompanying her on her daily strolls through the streets of New York. "She is a very odd woman indeed," John told Frances in one of his letters.[12]

William Shirer has a theory about why John and Garbo became friends. "John could be very charming. I think he flattered her, and that's why she liked him," he says. "Like every young man of my day, I admired her. But when I met her, I wasn't as impressed as some people were. I don't think she had any fondness for me."

Shirer recalls John telling him that he had been working in the study of his house on Sixty-second Street one day (probably on the Roosevelt book) when about noon there came a knock on the front door. It was Garbo, out for her daily stroll. John, of course, invited her in even though he was writing. "She sat down [in John's study] and ate a sandwich she had with her. And then she wanted to talk. It drove John nuts," Shirer says.

Jane Gunther recalls no such incident. She says that although Garbo may have dropped by once or twice unannounced, they usually knew when she was coming. However, she does recall that several times in the late 1940s and early 1950s there was speculation Garbo would make a return to the screen. Garbo and John discussed the possibility of him writing a script for her about a romance between a foreign correspondent and a beautiful German spy. The story was based on the true adventures of a mysterious countess named Rosie Waldek, who was a friend of Dorothy Thompson's. MGM production head Dore Schary was keen to produce the picture, and though John thought the plot "corny in the extreme," he went to Hollywood in May 1951 to develop it. He spent a month there in the Bel Air Hotel writing a script. Garbo remained uncommitted for a time. But in the end, both John and Schary were disappointed; Garbo changed her mind about a comeback.[14]

Garbo sometimes spent time with the Gunthers at the summer home of Jane's family in Vermont. She was there in August 1949, and again a couple of years later. On that occasion, John left the Waldek script on a night stand when Garbo came for the weekend. He hoped that she would read it. "Garbo never mentioned it, and after she left he discovered that she'd never even opened it," Shirer recalls John telling him.[15]

John was far too busy to dwell on the disappointment. His hectic social life obscured the fact that he was working with renewed energy these days. He had to because he needed the income. His frenetic lifestyle dictated it. As he told Frances, he was "living on a book a year." The problem, as always, was that John spent his money before he made it. He once quipped, "I've eaten every book before it's written." There was more truth to that statement than even John cared to admit.

William Shirer recalls dropping by the Gunther house one evening to find John and Cass Canfield pacing the floor as they awaited a phone call from the Book of the Month Club. "John was saying, 'My God, if we don't get this [endorsement], I'll have to sell the house.' Canfield was a bundle of nerves, too."[16]

The essence of the problem, as always, was John's love of the good life, and his delight in spending money on others. He provided his sister, Jean, who was now working in New York, with a small stipend. He bought gifts for friends. He traveled. He would often call the bank, check the balance, and then buy whatever it was that had caught his fancy.

John had paid $33,000 for the house in New York; at the time new houses in the burgeoning suburbs springing up all across America were selling for $3,000 to $4,000. He told Frances in one of his letters that the mortgage, property taxes, insurance, and other basic living expenses amounted to more than $20,000 per year. When the cost of maintaining a lavish lifestyle was added in, it was not easy to make ends meet. "We have to earn an appalling lot of money in order to maintain this darned house (forgive me, House; you are extremely close to my heart and very charming) and live in what is doubtless an extravagent style."[17]

Included in John's monthly expenses, of course, was the $800 per month alimony payment that John sent to his ex-wife. Even after Frances finally succeeded in getting a visa, and moved to Israel in early 1949, he continued sending her the money. On her own, Frances lived quietly and frugally, and after selling the house at Madison, she gave John some of the proceeds. On one occasion, when things were particularly tight for the Gunthers, Frances loaned them $10,000. Other times, she suggested that John suspend alimony payments until he could afford to make them again.

Gossip columnist Louis Sobol of the *New York Journal-American* would have been shocked to learn just how wrong he was when he speculated that, "John Gunther, unless Uncle Sam has taken too heavy a bite, certainly must have earned close to a million from the royalties of his books.

"Like Ernest Hemingway, he is a big man physically. But unlike the Fisherman of Cuba, he seems to have no inkling for the outdoor sports and is more of a 21 or Stork Club man and is an amiable guest at parties, also a confirmed first nighter. It is a toss-up as to who among our literary men is a heavier earner, Gunther or Hemingway. But they'll never have to toss a benefit for either."[18]

Such rumors amused John, who never tired of seeing his name in the columns. Publicity helped to sell books, and books were his bread-and-butter.

As 1949 drew to a close John was working hard to finish another book. What had started out as a short character study of FDR had grown into a full-length biography that was causing John no end of agony and frustration. He told Frances in a letter dated January 20, 1950, that he had been working hard on the manuscript for more than three months, and still had several more weeks of writing ahead of him. "The book is pretty good in spots, a kind of synthesis," he explained.[19]

It was a difficult book to write. John had never been a Roosevelt intimate, but over the years he had spent time with the president on several occasions. And in the course of his research, he had also interviewed Eleanor Roosevelt, as well as more than eighty of FDR's closest friends and associates, including Bernard Baruch, Sumner Welles, and Robert Sherwood. Doing so had given John a relatively balanced sense of Roosevelt, the man.

That was no mean feat given the intense emotions that FDR evoked in people. It is generally forgotten today that in 1933 an assassin in Miami had narrowly missed ending Roosevelt's life. The shots missed the president, but killed the visiting Mayor Anton Cermak of Chicago, and wounded several bystanders. Even in 1949, four years after his death, the momentous events which had shaped his thirteen years in the White House were still too recent for most observers to view dispassionately. John tried his best to do so, yet even he found it difficult. He could not hide his admiration for Franklin or Eleanor Roosevelt.

For their part, the Roosevelts—Eleanor in particular—admired John's work and found him to be good company. FDR was a master when it came to pampering egos and charming friendly reporters and commentators. Given that most editorial writers began vilifying Roosevelt, and the New Deal early on in his first term, the president knew full well that he needed all of the help that he could muster to retain the support of the American people.

Eleanor remembered the many kindnesses that John Gunther had extended to her over the years. On May 1, 1940, she had been touched when the liberal journal *The Nation* honored her "distinguished service in the cause of American social progress." More than 1,000 people had attended a gala dinner in her honor at the Hotel Astor in New York. John had been one of the speakers who paid tribute to the first lady. In subsequent years, Eleanor corresponded with him occasionally about specific matters, and several times she had invited him to social events at the White House. Like her husband, Eleanor Roosevelt knew who her friends were. And she looked after them.

John visited the White House for tea on March 25, 1945, and again two days later, while he was in Washington researching *Inside U.S.A.* The president was fading quickly at the time—he died just three weeks later—and John did not see him on either occasion. He did, however, have a unique opportunity to learn more about Roosevelt. On March 27, Eleanor asked John if he would like to see her husband's private study. John spent an hour there poking around, and trying to get a feel for the man "whose *santum sanctorum* this was," as he later put it. "I reflected [that] it seemed to be the room of a man who was packing up, who knew that he was about to go away."[20]

John's portrait of the late president entitled, *Roosevelt in Retrospect: A Profile in History*, was published in May 1950. John told Frances in one of his letters that he was pleased with the final product. "[It] in a way is the best book I ever wrote, from the point of view of craftsmanship and the like, and is certainly the best job of its kind that has been done on FDR."[21]

Unfortunately, book sales slumped badly in the early 1950s, for a variety of reasons, not the least of which was the emergence of television as a form of mass entertainment. That situation was reflected in disappointing sales for *Roosevelt in Retrospect*. Harper & Brothers sold only about 45,000 copies in the U.S.—which still made it the company's top seller for the year!—and another 17,000 copies in Great Britian.

Reviews were tepid. Some critics chided John for not making more of an effort to analyze the Roosevelt presidency; others decried his "uncritical admiration, reflecting on occasion the author's actual bedazzlement with his subject's more glittering aspects."[22] Raymond Swing was one of the few reviewers who seemed to grasp the essence of what John had tried to do. "He writes about FDR as a continent," Swing observed in *The Nation* on June 3, 1950. "But since FDR was not a continent, it is clear that Mr. Gunther does not write about him because he understands him and feels compelled to share his understanding. He is searching, and we share his search."

The Roosevelt book was serialized in the *New York Post*, and despite slow sales it attracted considerable attention. John received a flood of letters, some praising *Roosevelt in Retrospect*, others damning it and its author. One letter writer accused John of having been paid to make the Roosevelts look good. Another—this one from John's hometown of Chicago—dismissed FDR as "the greatest fraud who ever lived." From Washington came a five-page, single-spaced letter from Grace Tully, Roosevelt's private secretary, taking exception with some of the things that John had written.[23] Most important of all, however, from John's perspective was the reaction of Eleanor Roosevelt.

On June 2, 1950, she wrote him a cryptic note praising *Roosevelt in Retrospect*. Mrs. Roosevelt said that she thought it "extraordinary" that he had achieved such understanding of FDR with so little personal knowledge of him. "I know you wrote with admiration and a desire to be completely fair. There are certain things you did not understand and of course certain things that neither you nor anyone else knows anything about outside the few people concerned."[24]

As it eventually became clear, what the former first lady was alluding to was a romance between FDR and Lucy Mercer, Eleanor's one-time social secretary. The affair had blossomed in 1917 while FDR was serving as assistant secretary of the Navy. When Eleanor came across some of the love letters, she confronted her husband. There followed the inevitable ugly scene, which ended with FDR promising to end the relationship. He did not entirely.

Although Mercer married in 1920, she and FDR maintained a loose contact for many years afterwards, and on numerous occasions he discreetly invited her to political functions. She was present for his acceptance speech at the Democratic National Convention in 1936. Mercer and Roosevelt began to meet regularly again in 1941. Secret service agents would drive the president to a spot in the countryside outside Washington, where Mercer waited in her car. She and FDR would then drive around talking for an hour or two before he returned home. In 1943 and 1944, Mercer occasionally even visited the White House for tea or dinner when Eleanor was away. Always on these occasions she was accompanied by her daughter, or one or two of her step children.

Eleanor Roosevelt in 1949 had written a memoir called, *This I Remember* (Harper & Brothers). The decision about whether or not to publicly disclose FDR's relationship with Mercer was one that she had agonized over for a long time. In the end, she did not. The full story did not come out until many years later, after Eleanor, too, had died.

CHAPTER THIRTY-FIVE

John and Jane Gunther set off for Japan and the Far East the last week of May 1950. John had accepted an assignment from Gardner Cowles, the editor-publisher of *Look* magaine. Cowles had helped to fund the Gunther's trip to Eastern Europe, and now he was eager to have John write about developments on the other side of the world, where tensions between the U.S. and Communist China were rising. There was growing concern that a military confrontation between the two countries was imminent.

Cowles, like most observers, felt that if war occurred the man in the thick of it would be General Douglas MacArthur, the Supreme Commander for the Allied Powers (SCAP) in the Pacific. MacArthur was headquartered in Japan, where as commander the American occupation army, he also served as military governor. He was a *de facto* dictator whose self-appointed mission was to democratize Japan in the image of America. MacArthur boasted that it would be the greatest reformation of a people ever attempted.

The Gunthers arrived at Tokyo airport on June 3, 1950. They were met by a military limousine sent by MacArthur, and put up in a comfortable suite at the Hotel Imperial, a grand building designed by the prominent American architect Frank Lloyd Wright. Rumor had it that the hotel had been built on a bed of vaseline so that if an earthquake struck, the structure would oscillate without falling down. Military authorities had declared the Imperial strictly "off-limits" to all Japanese, unless they were invited in by hotel guests. And with the Imperial's rooms normally reserved for senior military officials and civilian VIPs, few Japanese were ever seen there.

But John's fame had preceded him to Tokyo.

He was interviewed at the hotel by local reporters, and received scores of letters from ordinary Japanese. Some were heart-wrenching pleas for help with personal problems. Some were fan letters. Others offered bits of information or suggestions for things to write about.

What struck John about this admittedly small sampling of Japanese public opinion was the underlying despair that pervaded the letters. Japan, a proud country with an ancient culture, had been devastated by the war. Now it was suffering the indignity of being forcibly "modernized" in a western sense by the conquering allies. John mused about how little most Americans in Japan really knew—or cared to know—about the country that they had occupied. What's more, John had doubts about the validity of some of the policies being pursued by the military administration headed by General Douglas MacArthur.

The general did not share any such uncertainties. Nor did he even care to consider them.

MacArthur never socialized with the Japanese. And his contact with Japanese officials was limited to meetings with the emperor himself, the prime minister, and a few other high ranking individuals. Aside from the members of his personal staff, MacArthur was almost as inaccessible to Americans. He rarely ventured out of the American Embassy, other than to make the short drive to his office. MacArthur lived in splendid isolation in one of Asia's most populous countries.

In the five years between September 1945 and the outbreak of the Korean War in June 1950, he left Tokyo just twice; what is more, he had not been in the continental U.S. since 1937. He seldom received visitors, or granted interviews with journalists. That he made an exception in John's case was probably only due to the intercession of Secretary of Defense Louis A. Johnson, who had written to MacArthur on John's behalf.

John and Jane were invited to lunch on June 9 with MacArthur and his wife, Jean. The Gunthers, uncertain about the reception they would receive, were pleasantly surprised. MacArthur and his wife were gracious hosts, and the general, himself, made a strong positive impression. As John later wrote, "[MacArthur] is extraordinarily handsome . . . not merely from the point of view of conventional good looks, but with a magnetism, a vitality that comes from within."[1]

With the general's comments being "off the record," he felt free to speak his mind, and did so almost non-stop. Happily, the conversation was lighthearted and wide-ranging. Jane came away dazzled by MacArthur's "grand air," as did her husband. Wrote John, "I have seldom met anybody who gives such a sense of the richness and flexibility of the English language; he draws out of it—like Winston Churchill—as out of some inexhaustible reservoir."[2] That was for public consumption.

However, recounting the meeting in a letter to Frances written on December 19, 1950 John was somewhat more skeptical. "MacArthur is remarkable—archaic in a lot of ways, modern in some others," he wrote. "What he believes in most, I think, is the defense of the U.S. and he is quite genuinely a reformer and an idealist, but he certainly goes about 'defending' us in an idiotic way."[3]

What MacArthur thought of John is not clear. But he seems to have formed a favorable opinion for a few days later he arranged an audience with the Emperor Hirohito for John and Jane. That the general could do so was an indication of how much things had changed in Japan. Such a meeting would have been inconceivable prior to the war. On John's previous visit to Tokyo in 1938, he had not even dared to request an interview with the emperor.

Hirohito, forty-nine years old at the time, was the 124th Emperor in an unbroken dynasty that stretched back 2,611 years; even in the wake of the war, "the son of the sun" was treated as a deity by the Japanese people. Hirohito still did not meet with most foreigners. Audiences were rare, and the only American who saw him regularly was MacArthur.

There may have been an element of simple human curiosity involved in Hirohito's willingness to grant John an audience. Although he did not speak English, indications are that he may have been familiar with at least one of the *Inside* books; John was taken aback by two references to *Inside Asia* that came from members of the royal household. "I was astonished that any Japanese close to the throne had even heard of [the book], much less had ever read it, because the first chapter contains sharp criticism of the Emperor," John later wrote.[4]

The audience with Hirohito took place at the Imperial Palace in a room that was decorated with western furnishings, apart from a large Japanese screen. The hour-long meeting was tightly structured (as tightly as John's first meeting with the Duke and Duchess of Windsor one day in 1935 at Lady Oxford's London home.) At first, John was seated next to the empress, while Jane sat next to the emperor. They conversed via interpreters. After twenty minutes, a signal was given by one of the retinue standing discreetly in the background. When John and Jane changed places, he then had about a half-hour to chat with Hirohito.

John discovered the emperor was a soft-spoken, impeccably polite man. He seemed almost as interested in his hobby of marine biology as in affairs of state. John noted that Hirohito seldom made eye contact as he spoke; most of the time, his eyes were averted or wandered to the window.

Yet Hirohito expressed himself with great self-confidence. He took exception to allegations by some westerners that he had been responsible for Japanese war crimes. The conflict between Japan and the United States, he stressed, had been "a tragedy" that he had tried to prevent. Given that he had failed, he accepted defeat, and conceded that his kingdom was forever changed. He said that in his opinion the reform process begun by General MacArthur would endure long after the American occupation had ended.

Direct quotation of Hirohito's comments was forbidden, and so John spent the time listening intently and studying his host. Hirohito was compactly built and youthful looking, with thick oval glasses. He wore western clothes for this audience, an old suit of gray tweed. John's eyes were drawn to one of the garters holding Hirohito's socks, which kept slipping down his leg. It seems even emperors sometimes have problems keeping their socks up![5]

The meetings with MacArthur and Hirohito were the high points of the Gunthers' one-month stay in Japan. But John and Jane met many other people, Japanese as well as American. They also they took several trips out from Tokyo, making use of MacArthur's private rail car, which he had never used. It was on June 25, while they were on one such trip to Nikko, a picturesque mountain village ninety miles north of the city, that they learned that North Korea, backed by Chinese troops, had invaded South Korea. By the time they returned to Tokyo later that day, the city was buzzing with speculation about the U.S. response.

John was bemused that evening as he dined with Japanese who were seized with passionate alarm. His hosts compared the North Korean action to Hitler's 1938 invasion of Austria. They expressed the hope that Washington would retaliate swiftly and effectively or else risk losing all of Asia to communism. "Such talk of the Rhineland, *Anschluss*, and Munich came strangely from the men who made Pearl Harbor," John observed.[6]

As history records, on the following day, June 26, President Truman authorized American forces to assist South Korean troops operating south of the 38th parallel. On June 27, the United Nations Security Council, acting in the absence of the Soviet representative (who boycotted the session), followed suit in adopting a resolution on armed intervention in Korea. Many people feared that the world was on the brink of yet another war.

John and Jane were apprehensive about continuing their tour, even if transportation could still be arranged. When they found it could, they decided to go ahead with quick visits to Hong Kong and India. They had five days in the latter, and one evening there they dined with Prime Minister Nehru. It was not entirely a pleasant occasion.

John was struck by a couple of things: how quickly anti-Americanism had replaced anti-British sentiment in India, and how naive Nehru seemed. India's leader expressed minimal interest in the ominous events taking place in Korea, and he professed to know nothing of recent developments in Japan. Nehru was far more concerned about Soviet intentions. Publicly, John was still of the opinion that "Nehru is by all odds the most important Asiatic in Asia."[7] Privately, he had grown scornful of the Indian leader's manner.

John's impressions of Nehru, MacArthur, and others he had met on the trip were written in haste because of the pace of events in Korea. *The Riddle of MacArthur*, was published in mid-December, 1950. Despite some factual slips made in the scramble to publish the book before it was rendered out of date by the pace of world events, John's reviews were seldom better.

"John Gunther's new book is as timely as tomorrow morning's newspaper, and in places seems to have been written as hurriedly as tomorrow's headlines," foreign correspondent Hallett Abend commented in a review in the *Saturday Review of Literature* (February 13, 1951).

Of more concern than reviews just now, however, was the realization that interest in MacArthur was strangely lacking. Why that was the case proved to be the *real* riddle of MacArthur. Only about 35,000 copies of *The Riddle of MacArthur* were sold in the U.S., leading John to muse that if it had not been for Truman's controversial April 1951 decision to relieve the General of his command, the book would have been a total flop.

In the face of this and other recent setbacks, a note of self-doubt crept into John's life for the first time in many years. Most people believed the rumors about how wealthy and successful he had become, and his lifestyle and high public profile did nothing to dissuade them. Like Ernest Hemingway, the man whom Louis Sobol had compared him to, John had become an easy target. Some critics and a few old colleagues, who still eyed John's success with envy, were only too eager to see him fall from grace.

Typical of this small group was veteran *New Yorker* writer Richard Rovere, who had written a meanspirited profile of John in the early summer of 1947. Rovere later admitted he had initially intended the article as a full-scale literary assassination. "I found [Gunther's] work superficial and sometimes irresponsible, and I felt that someone ought to show him up for what he was," Rovere wrote in his 1957 memoirs, *Arrivals and Departures*.[8]

With that goal in mind, he had spent several weeks observing John, and had even accompanied him on his daily visits to the hospital to see Johnny. It was a time in John's life when his guard was down. He was preoccupied with work on *Inside U.S.A.*, and worried sick about his dying son. John had simply accepted Rovere as a colleague doing a job; he had taken him into his confidence in good faith, and been friendly towards him in what were trying circumstances. John welcomed the diversion Rovere presented, and he seized the opportunity to talk about better times. It was Johnny, heavily sedated and in great pain, who sensed that Rovere was not the friend he pretended to be. Writing in *Death Be Not Proud*, John quotes Johnny as saying that he felt Rovere might be a "hatchet man."[9]

In the end, when Rovere had John in his sights he could not pull the trigger. Corny as it sounds, the journalistic hit man found that he had actually come to *like* and admire John as a person, and to empathize with his troubles.

"Gunther is one of the gentlest and most amiable of men," Rovere conceded. And he continued, "Gunther's worldwide popularity is greater than that of any other living writer. A few other authors may outsell Gunther in one or two countries, but nobody comes up to him as an all-round international favorite."[10]

Rovere's article, in the August 23, 1947 edition of the *New Yorker* was "not fiercely critical but critical nonetheless," as Rovere put it. Rereading it ten years later, he confided that this was "the only example of such a compromise in my work" since he had softened the article to make his points "in language that would not cut as deeply as the language I might otherwise have used."[11]

John was aware that there were people like Rovere who envied his success and were keen to see him fail. Envy may well be a kind of praise, as the poets say; even so, John was uneasy. He knew full well that declining book sales and his own financial needs necessitated that he would have to change his metier to continue earning a living. Hence his interest in writing a film script for Garbo, and his willingness to tackle another of his trademark series of *Inside* books. Because of persistent problems with timing, John had was still reluctant to do *Inside Washington*. Instead, he agreed to do a revised edition of *Inside U.S.A.* The original book was still selling, and Cass Canfield was convinced the time was ripe for an updated version that could sell in a mass market paperback edition.

Before undertaking that project, John and Jane made a quick trip to Paris in the spring of 1951 on another *Look* assignment. Gardner Cowles was keen to have John profile Dwight Eisenhower, the man that most pundits were convinced would be an easy winner in the 1952 presidential election, if he decided to seek office.

The only real questions were whether or not Ike would do so, and if he did, whether it would be as a Republican or a Democrat. Polls indicated that he could win as the candidate for either party.

Bored with his job as president of Columbia University, Ike had been quick to accept when, in October 1950, President Truman asked him to assume command of the Supreme Headquarters, Allied Powers in Europe (SHAPE), the military arm of the newly created North Atlantic Treaty Organization (NATO).

John found Eisenhower and his wife Mamie residing in a comfortable house just outside Paris, which was provided by the French government. Ike greeted John warmly.

"What are you after, John?" he said.

"You," John replied.

"What? Inside Ike?" Eisenhower asked incredulously.[12]

John nodded. That was exactly what he hoped to write—an intimate portrait. "I have always liked Eisenhower," John told Frances in one of his letters, "though he has severe limitations, one of them being a lack of sense of humor."[13]

John did two lengthy articles about Eisenhower for *Look*. Both were severely cut for publication. Aware that he had a mass of good material left over after writing the magazine articles, and that there seemed to be considerable interest in Ike, John proposed a short book. When Canfield said he would publish it, John spent five weeks writing a 45,000-word biographical sketch, which he finished a week before Christmas. *Eisenhower: The Man and the Symbol* appeared in early 1952.

If readers were expecting a bland, deferential account of the life and times of Dwight D. Eisenhower, most were taken aback. John's analysis had a critical bite to it that surprised everyone, including Ike. There was no disguising the facts that John was an Eisenhower admirer, or that he felt that the general would make a fine president; John painted him as a simple, honest, and decent man, determined to "take the leadership of the middle," as he put it.[14]

Where John raised hackles was in suggesting that Ike was an intellectual lightweight with no coherent philosophy. John later admitted his enjoyment at reporting a coarse joke that made the rounds when Eisenhower became president of Columbia. It had poked fun that Ike was "the first president of that estimable institution who had never read a book."[15]

In fact, Ike read a lot as a youth, and in later years he loved to relax with pulp westerns. He was understandably slighted, and for some time thereafter was cool towards John.

As it turned out, although *Eisenhower: The Man and the Symbol* was well received by critics, the book had little impact upon public opinion. The Eisenhower-for-President bandwagon was rolling, and America's mind was made up. By the time the book was published in early 1952, it was already out of date as far as most readers were concerned. This proved to be another disappointment to John, who confided to Frances and others that he was feeling worn out.

There was, he intimated, a strong possibility that he would tackle *Inside Africa* next. He was convinced the book would be the best seller that he badly needed to pay the bills. Both John and Cass Canfield felt that the disintegration of the old colonial in Africa was destined to reshape the continent, and affect the course of world events.

CHAPTER THIRTY-SIX

John plunged into the daunting task of researching the history of Africa in early 1952. David Bruce, the undersecretary of state at the time, put him in touch with the handful of American officials in Africa. (Having historically had little stake in Africa, the State Department did not even have an African division until 1943. Even then, U.S. policy makers were slow to take note of the nationalist movements that were springing up all across the continent.)

With Jane's help, John wrote scores of letters to the British, French, and Portuguese foreign offices, as well as to various African political, tribal, and cultural leaders. He also contacted the heads of all of the independent governments on that vast continent. At the time there were just five.

John and Jane retreated for the summer to the Perry family cottage in Vermont. Here they hoped to finalize plans for Africa, and to recover from what had been a devastating spring. John had been hit with a variety of nagging ailments several times before finally visiting his doctor for a complete check-up. Although he was pronounced fit, the doctor ordered him to curb his eating, drinking, and smoking.

More disturbing to John than his own health problems was the news that two of his closest friends had died. James (Herc) Mulroy, one of his pals from his youth in Chicago had died suddenly on April 29,[1] and his friend Albert Lasker, the advertising industry pioneer and humanitarian, had succumbed to cancer on May 30.[2] John felt both losses deeply.

Compounding his unhappiness were his on-going financial woes. Not only did he face the enormous cost of paying for the trip to Africa, there were the everyday expenses involved in maintaining the house in New York while he and Jane were traveling, with no money coming in. John had already borrowed from a number of people, including Cass Canfield and Albert Lasker. His plans for repaying the loans were dealt a blow when the Eisenhower book flopped; John realized only about $11,000 in royalties. To make up the shortfall, he wrote a series of political articles, and used the money he made to repay Lasker's estate. He then dashed off a children's book about Alexander the Great for Bennett Cerf at Random House. And "a spiggot got turned on in me," as he told Frances; he wrote six short stories, all of which his agent dutifully informed him were not "commercial."[3]

John sensed that he was running to stand still. Far more troubling, however, was that as yet he had no idea of how he would finance the African expedition. He and Jane scraped together the money to start the Africa trip only by emptying their savings accounts, pre-selling a series of three articles to *Reader's Digest*, borrowing yet again from Cass Canfield and Hamish Hamilton against future royalties, and even by accepting a loan from Frances. She and John also reached an agreement by which John would temporarily reduce her monthly alimony payment, and later make it up in a lump sum.

With this money in the bank, John finalized his African travel arrangements and confirmed interview appointments in countries along the planned route. This was no easy task, given the difficulties of getting around Africa at the time, and given the harshness of the climate, the difficulties in communicating with people in a continent where more than 700 languages were spoken, and the primitive conditions in many places—such basics as food and sanitation were major concerns.

In 1952, most of Africa was ruled still by colonial governors, and so John turned for help and advice to British and French government press offices in New York. Officials from both countries helped to arrange travel and accommodations in the areas of Africa that were under their control.

As always, the British proved to be especially helpful. C.B. Ormerod, the director of British Information Services, provided John with a letter of introduction, and the colonial office, the foreign office, and the Commonwealth office all volunteered to provide the Gunthers with three weeks of briefings in London prior to their departure for Africa.

Time spent in the British capital proved invaluable in another way, too. In the early 1950s London had become the "unofficial" headquarters of many of the nationalist movements that were set to reshape the face of modern Africa. London was teeming with African nationalists of every political stripe, and so John was able to make valuable contacts there.

Knowing that he intended to meet with as wide a range of groups as possible in Africa, the British attempted to influence him in a subtle and unexpected way. "[They] are extremely adept at public relations, which of course depend on private relations," John later wrote in his book *A Fragment of Autobiography*. "No one in London ever told us that it would happen and to this day I do not know who was responsible, but, with one exception, we were put up at Government House in every British territory we visited."[4]

While this was convenient and saved John money, it also created some minor embarrassments. It was awkward to meet nationalist leaders—some of whom were revolutionaries—while staying as a guest of the British government. Fortunately, most of the British colonial governors astutely sensed this, and did not question John about his itinerary, or whom he was meeting. That was just as well, because the list was as varied as it was exhaustive.

John and Jane departed from New York in September 1952, for an eleven-month African odyssey. During that time they traveled 40,000 miles, interviewed 1,500 people in 31 countries, and visited more than 100 cities and towns. The continent of Africa is four times larger than the U.S., and it was a grueling schedule relieved by only a couple of days off during that entire time (they rendezvoused with Frances in Cairo, where the three of them spent some time together.) Neither John nor Jane complained about the workload; it was an astounding trip, the likes of which no American had ever undertaken.

In South Africa, Sir Ernest Oppenheimer, the head of DeBeers Consolidated Mines (which at that time controlled about 95 per cent of the world's diamond production), showed them his mining operations. And they toured the notorious black townships, which John regarded as being among the most wretched slums he had ever seen.

In Egypt, John interviewed General Gamal Abdel Nasser, who not long afterward seized power in his country.

In Ethiopia, John and Jane were received by another staunch nationalist, the Emperor Haile Selassie, and they interviewed a Mau Mau terrorist.

In the French West (now Gabon) Equatorial Africa, they spent a week with famed medical missionary Dr. Albert Schweitzer, who gave them a tour of his bush hospital for lepers. John found the good doctor to be of the more cantankerous people he met on the trip.

"I emerged with something of a minority report," he told Frances in a letter dated October 10, 1953. "He is very old, a fearful autocrat, politically somewhat to the right of Louis XIII, and without a very high opinion of most Africans."[5]

John recounted in *Inside Africa* how Schweitzer had explained that he paid each of his African helpers seven bananas per day. When John asked him if these people would work better if they got eight bananas, Schweitzer replied, "No. That would disturb discipline and morale."[6]

Having formed such a mixed opinion of Schweitzer, John found it difficult to write about him. In relating the story of Schweitzer's good deeds, he could not avoid mentioning that the doctor seemed to have little rapport with the people among whom he worked.

Of course, Schweitzer had been awarded the Nobel Peace Prize in 1952 for his work, and John's announcement was at odds with his popular image as a benign humanitarian. But at least one person who knew Schweitzer wrote John to reassure him that his analysis was correct. "The truth never tarnishes a man as great as

Schweitzer and it is good to tell the truth," the man wrote.[7]

Meeting so many important Africans proved to be fascinating, but it was also exhausting. During the long hours spent aboard trains or airplanes and late into the night wherever they were staying, John organized his notes and read the file folders full of press clippings that he always used to background himself before interviews. Jane looked after travel arrangements every mile of the way, and sometimes prodded her husband to visit some remote areas of the continent that he might otherwise have bypassed owing to laziness or lack of interest. One such place was the Sahara Desert, which John described in a chapter he aptly titled, "Inside Nowhere."[8]

Complicating the travel plans were a couple of problems. One being commitments which John had made to write articles for *Reader's Digest* and other magazines. No sooner had he and Jane arrived in Morocco from Spain than John was obliged to sit down at his typewriter. He spent other valuable days holed up writing in various places. All totaled, John wrote nine lengthy articles as he and Jane traveled. The other problem was even more frustrating.

Just two weeks into the journey John realized that he was slowly going blind as a result of cataracts. For most of the next forty-four weeks he was able to continue his exploration of the darkening continent only because Jane helped him to keep notes, digest reams of background material, and take the photos he used to help him in his writing. It was not until after returning to New York that Jane convinced him to take three months off to have the first of two operations to remove the cataracts. He could delay no longer. Even thick glasses did not allow him to see well enough to work.[9]

That eye surgery was not the routine procedure that it is nowadays. The time needed for John's recovery was just one of the obstacles that made writing of *Inside Africa* almost as big a challenge as the travel had been. Work continued off-and-on until early 1955, with interruptions that became too numerous to recount. John stopped several times to produce the magazine articles that he was obligated to write. Then, too, he had to drop everything to fulfill a commitment made years before to do a six-week lecture tour.

It was a familiar story for John. The Book of the Month Club had chosen *Inside Africa* as its featured selection for September 1955; Cass Canfield was impatient to have the completed book in his hands so he could arrange the details of printing and get the book into stores while it was still fresh and topical. And as always, financial pressures weighed heavy on John's shoulders. He and Jane had almost no money coming in. Jane made some money writing some magazine articles, but it was not enough to pay the bills.

Even as John wrote, the pace of events in Africa had quickened alarmingly. Now, in scenes that were reminiscent of the writing of *Inside Europe*, that first *Inside* book almost two decades before, events in Africa dictated that he rewrite portions of the manuscript. In Egypt, for example, General Mohammed Naguib, the man who had in July 1952 deposed King Farouk, was himself ousted by Nasser in February 1954. All of this took time, precious time that John could ill afford.

Finally, on June 17, 1955 an impatient Cass Canfield sent John a stern memo setting out deadlines for the last four chapters, which dealt with South Africa. (As was his habit, John was writing chapters out of the sequence in which they were eventually published.) Noon of July 8 was set as the appointed hour for delivery of the last chapter. Canfield also demanded to know the length of that last chapter to within 100 words so that it could be slotted into the material that was already typeset and ready for the presses.

With the help of Jane (to whom he dedicated the book), John worked feverishly to meet each successive deadline. Miraculously, on the morning of July 8 he was wrapping up the last chapter with a couple of hours to spare. But a final reading revealed slightly more than the 3,700 words that John had promised. In cutting the chapter to size, a few too many words were edited out. Thus, when *Inside Africa* was published in September 1955, page 556 was blank. Since it was the back of a chart outlining the organization of De Beers mining interests in South Africa, the flaw was not readily apparent to most readers.[10] One other interesting typo, which was caught in the proof-reading stage was a reference to "Christ's *manager*"; John had written "manger."[11]

The release of *Inside Africa*—the fifth of the *Inside* books—created a sensation. The book tackled head on some highly provocative questions, including the future of European involvement in Africa, the race issue, and the East-West rivalry that was emerging as a mid-twentieth century version of the scramble that had taken place a century earlier to carve up the continent. This time, however, foreign powers were grasping for hearts and minds more than territory. The question was whether communism or western-style democracy would rule the day.

John cautioned that with its grinding poverty, masses of poorly educated people, and anti-colonial, anti-western biases Africa was a fertile breeding ground for Soviet and communist Chinese proselytizing. "We should give Africa our most seasoned, scrupulous, and long-minded attention," he wrote.[12] "The two things Africa needs most are development and education."[13]

Not surprisingly, reaction to *Inside Africa* was as intense as it was wide-ranging. In the U.S. and England, the reviews were generally favorable; John was especially pleased by the one written for the *New York Herald-Tribune* by the celebrated South African author Alan Paton, which termed *Inside Africa* "a monumental book," and lauded the chapters on South Africa.[14] Paton's praise served as a counterweight to the less than cordial reception the book received in some of the African countries about which John had written critically.

In Liberia, where he pointed out that annual government spending on public health was less than for brass bands, he was attacked by the editor of the *Liberian Age* newspaper for "[making] Goebbels look childish, and the Russian propaganda machine like child's play."

In Mozambique, *Inside Africa* was banned outright, and for several years copies were seized from travelers entering the country.

The Belgian, French, and Portuguese colonial authorities were displeased with the way John had described their colonial administrations, and when translations of *Inside Africa* appeared, a French version was delayed three years. John understood why when *L'Autre Afrique* finally appeared in 1959. Every line having to do with French territories in Africa had been deleted.[15]

None of the themes raised in *Inside Africa* was easy, and at almost 1,000 pages and 400,000 words, the book stood as the most comprehensive look at Africa ever written by a western reporter. And with total hard cover sales of half a million copies in North America and Great Britain alone, it was by far and away the most widely read. That it was read elsewhere was made clear not long afterwards when Andrei Gromyko, the Soviet foreign minister, upon meeting John casually mentioned that he felt that there should be a Russian edition of *Inside Africa*. Nothing ever came of it, but

John was flattered nonetheless to find out how influential his books were.

Some people, whom John conceded knew more about Africa than he did, chided him for stressing nationalism too strongly. In retrospect, he realized that he had actually erred on the side of caution; he had not stressed nationalism enough![16]

John felt that he had erred, too, in stating the prevailing western view of the day, namely that colonialism had on balance been good for Africa—particularly British rule. Most historians today would disagree; the entire imperial experience in Africa has come to be regarded as one of the darker chapters in modern western history.

Despite the flaws time has exposed, *Inside Africa* was an important book at the time. Even today it is a standard reference for most authors writing about African affairs. When *Los Angeles Times* foreign correspondent David Lamb wrote *The Africans*,[17] his critically acclaimed 1982 study of Africa, he used *Inside Africa* as a source. And what's more, the dust jacket touted Lamb as writing "in the tradition of the late John Gunther."

Inside Africa was a richly detailed historical snapshot of a continent poised on the brink of changes so wide ranging, changes so profound, as to alter the course of history, and reshape the lives of millions of ordinary Africans. It is a process—sometimes evolutionary, but more often than not bloody and revolutionary—that is still underway today.

Writing in his 1962 book *A Fragment of Autobiography*, John mused that "the chief virtue of *Inside Africa* is . . . the way it explored an important region which at the time was much neglected."[18]

In the long term, that analysis has proved valid.

CHAPTER THIRTY-SEVEN

In late May of 1956, John Gunther underwent the second of two successful operations to remove the cataracts which had been clouding his vision, and making it difficult for him to work. "My eyes are all right," he reported to Frances, "but it is a bore to have to wear heavy glasses all the time."[1]

Happily, the success of *Inside Africa*, published the previous fall, had eased John's financial woes. He announced that he planned to "sit in the sun somewhere," as he put it, and do nothing for a time. The urge was understandable, given his prolific output in recent years, and given that he and Jane had in late 1955 adopted a baby boy named Nicholas, whom John adored. However, even the addition to the family of the baby, and having the second eye operation could not stifle John's urge to write; work had become "a drug," as he told Frances.

While recovering from his surgery, he "relaxed" by collaborating with Bernard Quint, *Life* magazine's art director, to do a picture book entitled, *Days to Remember: America 1945-1955.*[2] John dashed off 45,000 words of text, while Quint edited a selection of 400 black-and-white photographs.

Before the book was even published in the autumn of 1956, John was already working on his next project—a book about the Soviet Union, a country which had always fascinated him.

He had been mulling over the possibility of a long trip to Australia, New Zealand, and possibly Antarctica, since they represented the only continents he had not visited, and writing about them would complete a grand scheme that had emerged in his mind. He hoped to complete a literary snapshot of the entire world. Those plans were shelved for now when Robert Graff of NBC asked John to become involved in a television project about the Soviet Union. What Graff had in mind was the video equivalent of an *Inside* book. He proposed five months of travel aboard a private aircraft to film the U.S.S.R. from one end to the other. John would act as show's narrator or host.

It was an intriguing proposal. But John doubted that the Soviet government would issue the necessary visas. As it turned out, he was right.

When word of this reached New York, *Collier's* called to ask John if instead he would go to Russia on the magazine's behalf, if it could be arranged. John agreed, and to his surprise, visas for he and Jane promptly came through. So he signed a contract with *Collier's* for five articles.

Preparations for Russia were almost as exhaustive as for Africa. William Benton, the publisher of the *Encyclopaedia Britannica*, had recently returned from the Soviet Union, and he gave John a large package of valuable memoranda. John also called on a number of Russia experts, visited the State Department in Washington for some briefings, gathered press clipings and a library of several hundred books.[3]

He also wrote personal letters in both English and a Russian translation to more than forty Soviet prominent writers, political leaders, and scientists requesting interviews; he was disappointed to receive only three written replies. Several of those to whom he wrote told him when he chanced to encounter them in Russia that while they had received his letters, they had been "too busy" to respond.

On October 1, 1956, John and Jane flew from New York to London, where friendly officials in the British foreign office provided them with two weeks of background briefings.

The original visas that had been issued to the Gunthers were only for a month. However, they succeeded in arranging a couple of one-week extensions, thus giving them six weeks in the country. The time was spent flying to various parts of the country, including the southern republics of Tashkent and Samarkand, as well as the Ukraine, and visiting the cities of Leningrad and Moscow. Encountering the dour Andrei Gromyko (who had not yet been appointed foreign minister) on these travels, John was greeted with another in what had become an endless string of *Inside* jokes. "Ha! So now you are inside us," he said with a laugh.

"No. I'm outside you, really!" John replied quickly.

He and Jane were in the Soviet capital during the last week of October, when international tensions soared. In the Middle East a brief Arab-Israeli war flared, and in eastern Europe the Kremlin sent troops into Hungary to crush an anti-communist uprising. Oddly enough, the Hungarian invasion helped John in a rather unexpected way. When Dimitri Shepilov, the Soviet foreign minister, appeared before the United Nations General Assembly to defend the Soviet invasion, he compared it to "Operation Anvil," the code-name for the British response to the Mau Mau uprising in Kenya four years earlier. In doing so, Shepilov quoted from John Gunther's book, *Inside Africa*. When *Pravda*, the official Soviet Communist party newspaper reprinted the speech in its entirety, including the *Inside Africa* reference, John found that doors suddenly began opening for him. Except for one.

His request for a formal interview with Nikita Khrushchev was turned down. Nonetheless, he did encounter the first secretary of the Soviet Communist party at several diplomatic receptions. At one such function, John looked on in amazement as Khrushchev downed eleven glasses of champagne before switching to tomato juice; he was still functioning quite well.

On another occasion, at the Turkish embassy, American ambassador Charles E. Bohlen introduced John to Khrushchev, explaining that he was a well-known writer and journalist. Khrushchev, never one known for his social tact, looked disdainful. He snorted something to the effect that journalists were low lifes. At that instant, John brazenly motioned towards Soviet foreign minister Shepilov, a former editor of *Pravda*. "If you've got such a low opinion of journalists, why did you make one your foreign minister?" he asked.

Khrushchev responded, "He's the only good journalist in Russia, and so we had to give him a job."[4]

The more John saw of Khrushchev, and the more he learned about him, the more convinced he was that what one saw was not necessarily what one got. Khrushchev was a man who enjoyed the limelight. Having risen from a humble peasant background, he had never lost his rough edge, he distressed even some of his Kremlin comrades with his untimely indiscretions. At one diplomatic party, when a member of a visiting delegation commented on the fact that so many Soviet women work, Khrushchev shot back, "Yes, our women work, and they are honest women—not like women in France, who are all whores!"[5]

That Khrushchev delighted in shocking people was further evidenced by his policy speeches, which were boastful and truculent. On one occasion he boasted to the west, "We will bury you!" On another, while addressing the United Nations, he took off his shoe and hammered the lectern with it for emphasis. Khrushchev was fond of telling the leaders of smaller nations how many atomic bombs he thought it would take to destroy them.

Rumors swirled in the diplomatic community the Russian leader drank too much, that he was an unpredictable character. It was an image he did nothing to downplay. But John Gunther saw another side of Khrushchev. As he later told a *Newsweek* interviewer, "Those who think of him as just a rowdy drunk couldn't be more wrong. Like all of us, he may occasionally take a few too many drinks. But he is one of the toughest, smartest, quickest, most brilliant men I've met in 35 years of journalism."[6]

The Soviet leader retained his hold on power until 1964, when his luck ran out. He was deposed in a swift coup led by an equally shrewd, tough comrade named Leonid Brezhnev.

Brezhnev has just been appointed to the Politburo, the powerful fifteen-member Communist "cabinet" that ruled the Soviet Union in February 1956, just prior to John's visit. Khrushchev had brought comrade Brezhnev into the inner circle in an effort to broaden his own base of regional support, little suspecting that

Brezhnev would one day be the Brutus who emerged from the shadows to betray him.

Although John did not come to know Leonid Brezhnev, he was certainly aware of him, noting that the former party boss of Kazakhstan was at age fifty-one one of the most powerful men in the Soviet Union. What little was known about Brezhnev in the West was, as John reported, that he was "reputed to be tough and able."[7]

Apart from the disappointment of not obtaining a personal interview with Khrushchev, John's Russian visit proceeded smoothly until October 24, the day before he and Jane were to return home from Moscow. John received distressing news from New York. *Collier's* had gone out of business, another victim of the changing times and America's changing tastes.

By the mid-1950s television had become the nation's most popular form of mass entertainment. The first generation ever—the children of the so-called post-war Baby Boom that followed the return home of millions of GIs—was being weaned on television. And their parents were every bit as much addicted to the flickering black-and-white video images. All of this meant declining sales for books, newspapers, and magazines, as well as slumping audiences at neighborhood movie theatres.

John had noticed the initial effects of this trend when his MacArthur and Eisenhower books flopped. Now, the fate of *Collier's* was another harsh reminder of how rapidly the world was changing. The writing was already on the wall for most of the mass circulation, photo-oriented magazines, for television provided the same news and pictures for free, as the events happened.

Fortunately, John's efforts were not wasted. He found a cable from Harold Ober, his agent, awaiting him on a stopover at the Copenhagen airport; Gardner Cowles at *Look* had agreed to take over the *Collier's* contract and publish the articles he had planned to write.

John had vowed to write nothing during the Russia trip, and so he produced his profiles of Khrushchev, Brezhnev, and other Soviet leaders following his return to New York. The *Sunday Times* in London carried some of what John wrote, and *Look* (April 2, 1957) published a 14,000-word article, the longest that the magazine had ever featured.

The *Look* article appeared just as Khrushchev was moving to consolidate his hold on power. This created intense interest in the west in any news from Soviet Union, and so Cass Canfield and Hamish Hamilton were eager to have John's Russia book as soon as possible.

The start of work on the book was delayed as John and Jane took a brief holiday in Jamaica, and John dashed off the text for an annual report of the Pfizer pharmaceutical company.[8] It was the sort of job that he had often vowed he would never do. But it was an offer he could not refuse. Writing *Inside Pfizer* earned him a quick $12,500, which he used to pay some of the bills from the Russia trip. The report appeared as a unbylined supplement to the *New York Times* and several other major newspapers on March 31, 1957.

The writing of *Inside Russia Today*, the sixth volume in the *Inside* series, took from March 1957 to late January 1958. It was one of the most difficult books John Gunther ever wrote. "I had to haul it out of myself, or rather the material I'd painfully collected inch by inch. I've never had so much trouble with a book," wrote John to Frances. "Subject matter is, I do not need to state, very complex and contradictory, and it is hard to be fair-minded and truly objective without becoming wishy washy. No one gives much of a damn what happens in Uganda. But everything about Russia is important."[9]

Like most old newspaper reporters, John was a two-finger typist. But what took the most time was the incredibly complex job of organizing, culling, and digesting the thousands of pieces of information he had accumulated. John kept his notes on filecard size bits of paper. Hundreds of these notes categorized by subject, plus newspaper clippings, books, and photos would be scattered around his study as he wrote.

John frequently cut up his typewritten pages to paste them back together in revised order. (Such was the writer's craft practised in the era before the invention of the word processor.) Sometimes he did so for creative reasons, other times because the course of events dictated as much. The scene as he wrote was chaos personified, yet somehow out of the confusion would emerge a book. It was a torturous, slow process that never got easier, no matter how many times John went through it.

Progress on the Russia book was slowed by the need to revise the manuscript to reflect developments in the Soviet Union, where Khrushchev had chased his rivals out of the Kremlin, and on October 4, 1957, the Soviets had shocked the world by launching the first Sputnik. It was also a laborious process checking facts and spellings of Russian names. Cass Canfield hired Russia expert Theodore Shabad, who later served as the *New York Times* correspondent in Moscow, to go over the manuscript.

Despite Canfield's objections, John announced that he planned to call the book *Inside Russia Today*—the suffix "today" being added, as he explained in *A Fragment of Autobiography*, to "vary the pattern . . . and indicate that the book dealt with a Russia vastly changed from that which I had seen and written about before the war."[10]

Inside Russia Today appeared in book shops in April 1958, six months late. That did not affect sales. With interest in the Soviet Union at a fever pitch across North America and western Europe, *Inside Russia Today* was featured as the Book of the Month Club selection for May, and chapters were widely syndicated in newspapers and magazines. "Some idiots have even worked out plans for a musical to be based on it," John marveled.[11] The book became a best seller. This development surprised John, who did not feel it was as good as a book as *Inside Africa*. The public and critics did not agree.

Translations of *Inside Russia Today* appeared in Italian, Chinese (the copyright pirates were at work again), Hebrew, and Japanese; John was chagrined by the latter, a two-volume set that had Khrushchev's picture on one, and John's on the other!

What gave the book its wide appeal, and what differentiated it from anything else that had been written was John Gunther's ability to avoid Cold War invective while examining the nature and realities of Soviet life in a cool, no-nonsense way. *Inside Russia Today* was a remarkable book for its day. It was one of the few books written during the Cold War—arguably the first—by an American journalist, that examined the human side of the Soviet menace, and brought the debate down to a level that people could understand and deal with. "With the future of the world, no less, at stake, we at least owe it to ourselves to be informed, and without facile optimism either," John wrote in his foreword.[12]

As he had done in writing *Inside Europe* in 1936, John sounded a warning; echoing sentiments he had expressed in *Behind the Curtain*, he argued that peaceful co-existence, not military confrontation, was the best way to face down the Soviet challenge. The same nation that had launched Sputnik and made such remarkable strides in other areas of science and education, still could not manufacture flashlights that worked, or even grow enough food to feed its people. John made a strong case for the notion that the Soviet system, with its emphasis on oppression, state-terror, and rule by a communist party oligarrchy, would eventually crumble, as would Soviet domination of eastern Europe. "No dictatorship is eternal," he observed.[13]

(Although *Inside Russia Today* offered no predictions on when or how the Cold War might end, one suspects that John Gunther would not have been surprised by the remarkable events of 1990 and 1991, when the Iron Curtain, rusted and worn, collapsed under its own weight.)

Advocating such a tolerant, common sense approach to the Soviet Union was in 1958 risky business. Publication of *Inside Russia Today* exposed John to attacks from moss-backed conservatives and other red-baiters in the United States. The anti-Soviet hysteria of the Cold War had not yet run its course, not by a long shot. Sensing this, some of John's friends and colleagues went out of their way to speak out on his behalf. Veteran *New York Times* foreign correspondent Harrison Salisbury, reviewing the book in that newspaper on April 13, felt obliged to note, "[Gunther] is as American as apple pie and as democratic as a New England town meeting, and precisely because of this is determined to see Soviet Russia clear and whole."[14]

Salisbury added that while *Inside Russia Today* was not without flaws, it was excellent for what it purported to be—"a well-written primer to Soviet Russia, the first step toward measuring the dimensions of the vast challenge that confronts America."

Other informed readers shared Salisbury's opinion. When then-Vice President Richard Nixon journeyed to Moscow in 1959, he reportedly took along with him seven copies of *Inside Russia Today* as background reading for himself and his staff. At FBI headquarters in Washington, ever-vigilant agents pored over the text. They looked for references to the agency or its director, and checked for subversive statements. A four-page analysis prepared for J. Edgar Hoover outlined some disagreements the report's authors had with aspects of what John had written (that Karl Marx was "a devoted, affectionate husband and father . . . ." wrankled them), however, the comments were for the most part favorable. *Inside Russia Today* was summarized as "an extremely valuable reference book."[15]

Meanwhile, in the Soviet Union itself, although the book was not on sale in shops, and there was no Russian translation, it was reviewed in *Pravda* and other publications, negatively for the most part, albeit respectfully.

What amused John were reports that copies of *Inside Russia Today* were selling in the Moscow black market for $10 U.S.—about the same cost as a Frank Sinatra record album.

CHAPTER THIRTY-EIGHT

When *Time* magazine on April 14, 1958, featured a cover story on "Reporter John Gunther," the article pointed out that no other American journalist had ever "plowed or plucked on [his] gargantuan scale." At six-foot-one and 238 pounds, John was described as a "hulking legman" who had traveled more miles, made more money, and written more successful books than any other newsman. The article estimated his *Inside* books had sold more than two million copies, and been translated into eighty-seven languages.[1]

The *Time* reporter's estimate was far too conservative. Figures compiled in 1952 by Harold Ober, John's agent, indicated that the first four *Inside* books *alone* had sold at least 2.7 million copies worldwide.[2] (It was difficult to determined the exact total because of the existence of many "pirated" editions.) If a final count could somehow be done today, and if it included the other five *Insides*, as well as the thirty-eight other books that John Gunther wrote, it would show total sales in excess of 4.5 million hard cover copies. A few—some of his early novels—sold no more than a few thousand copies, while several of the *Inside* books topped the best seller lists. The paperback version of *Death Be Not Proud* continues to sell even today.

Author-writer Clifton Fadiman once described John Gunther as "the best-known, widest ranging and probably best-informed journalist of his generation;"[3] in the late 1950s few people would have argued with that summation. Indeed, mere mention of the adjective *Inside* brought instant recognition of John's name. One reviewer had even coined the word "guntherize" to describe the kind of encyclopedic, yet eminently readable books John wrote.[4] He had clearly ceased to ge an "ordinary" legman.

Such journalists did not sit down with General Douglas MacArthur, Marshal Tito, Emperor Hirohito of Japan, or Dwight D. Eisenhower.

Ordinary legmen were not invited to audiences with the pope. Nor did they sip tea with Prime Minister Nehru of India, dine with the Duke and Duchess of Windsor, or stroll with Garbo through the streets of New York.

For more than thirty years John had been at or near the epicenter of many of the world's major political developments—from the U.S. to Europe, the Soviet Union, and even the far East. A macabre joke among the journalistic fraternity was that whenever John Gunther appeared in some distant foreign capital it was a sign to take cover—the shooting was about to start.

The appearance of each new *Inside* book had become an eagerly awaited publishing "event." A famous cartoon by Helen Hokinson in the *New Yorker* years before had made that point nicely. It depicted a woman in a bookshop asking the clerk, "Isn't it about time that another one of John Gunther's 'Insides' came out?"[5]

Reflecting upon what it was that made Gunther unique, and gave him his worldwide appeal, John's colleague and friend Theodore (Teddy) White noted two qualities: "One is his outgoing warmth and attention to all people, as individuals, be they prince or premier, reporter or apprentice. The other is a unique discipline of craft, as distinctively his as is [Ernest] Hemingway's mastery of the novel."[6]

This mastery was at once John's greatest strength and his greatest weakness. He wrote with a precision and fluidity that was deceptive. He made it all seem deceptively easy.

But it was not.

The medical analogy in the *New Yorker* cartoon about John's "insides coming out" was more accurate than most people realized. The *Inside* books were demanding work, and with each passing year, he found the effort involved in writing a new one left him exhausted—physically and emotionally. Even he sometimes wondered how many more books he had left in him. He had come to grips with the reality that times and reading tastes had changed since he began the *Inside* series a quarter-century before.

Thus, when the *Time* magazine interviewer asked John what he believed in, it was a question he had pondered much over the years. Although life with his second wife and adopted son had finally given him peace of mind, he had often mused about his own beliefs. The deaths of an infant daughter and a teenaged son, as well as the anguish of an star-crossed first marriage had given him ample reason to do so. "I believe that we are all part of a universe that has certain forms, patterns, interrelations, and compensations, even for the worst of personal tragedies. But I do not know enough to know why I think this," John had once written.[7]

The answer that he provided to the *Time* interviewer's question echoed that same inner turmoil, while the candor of his response surprised many people, among them perhaps John Gunther.

"I believe in myself, with fingers crossed," he said. Then drawing on his ever-present Marlboro cigarette, he added, "I'm terribly limited. I completely lack intensity of soul. I'm not original. I'm really only a competent observer who works terribly hard at doing a job well."[8]

It was an analysis with which few friends, colleagues, and fans agreed. But it was typical. John never took his phenomenal success for granted. That was one of his qualities that people found so disarming.

As the peaceful, prosperous 1950s dissolved into the fast, frenetic 1960s, John continued "doing his job well." At an age when most of his colleagues had begun to slow down, he remained as active and as prolific as ever. John told the *Time* interviewer that after finishing the Russian book he had plunged into a short biography of Albert Lasker, another of the "small books . . . that I play with my left hand,"[9] as he liked to joke. Included among them was a successful series of children's books consisting of excerpts from recent *Insides*, which had been specially re-edited for young readeers.

John also mentioned plans for the long-awaited companion volume to *Inside U.S.A.*, plus an *Inside Australia*, and maybe a biography of novelist Sinclair Lewis, who had died in 1951.

The Lasker book was one that for several years friends had urged John to write. The story of Albert Lasker, one of the great innovators of the American advertising industry, had all the ingredients of a good biography. It was one of those Horatio Alger success stories that is at the core of the American dream—boy from humble background rises through pluck, luck, and sheer determination to the pinnacle of his profession; in the end, sadder but wiser, he chucks it all to devote himself to humanitarian causes.

John had met Albert Lasker in India in 1938. When the two began bumping into each another at the homes of mutual friends, they became close; John described Lasker in one of his letters to Frances as "practically our best friend, and really a wonderful old man."[10] Nevertheless, after cancer claimed Lasker in 1952, John resisted the pleas of those who wanted him to write a biography. His reticence was not unusual. Over the years, John received a steady stream of suggestions for books and articles from friends and fans; for a variety of reasons, he ignored most of them.

Hamish Hamilton had prodded him to do an *Inside England*, which had enormous sales potential in Great Britian, where John's books had always been popular. He dismissed the idea, feeling that to do it right would take many years of painfully hard work. Similarly, he evaded an idea that Frances had pitched to him repeatedly, even after their divorce. What she had in mind was a popular book about the world's great religions, to be called, *Inside God*. Each time Frances raised the idea in one of her letters, John simply ignored it in his reply. After all their years together, Frances still did not understand the reason. Finally, in frustration, she demanded to know whether or John he was interested in the project; only then did he admit that he was not.

John initially displayed the same reluctance to tackle a Lasker book. He had felt the pain of Lasker's death too deeply, and feared that knowing the subject as well as he had, he could not write a balanced biography. He changed his mind in late 1957 after commiting himself to do a half-hour, weekly television show for

ABC beginning in the fall of 1959. He felt that his involvement in the show would preclude him from starting another *Inside* book for a while.

John visited Mary Lasker her at her home in La Quinta, California, in early 1958, before spending the spring and summer interviewing dozens of his friends who had known Lasker. He then packed up his notes, his battered Smith-Corona typewriter, and his family, and departed for Europe.

They stayed in England for several weeks, renting a Tudor house in Kent from novelist Arthur Koestler. It was too damp and cold for John's liking, but he delighted in the massive sixteenth century fireplace. It was big enough, he quipped, "to roast Orson Welles and Quentin Reynolds together, without dismembering either."[11]

The Gunthers made their way to a St. Maxine, a tiny village on the French coast, not far from Nice. Jane swam in the Mediterranean, Nicholas played on the beach, and John spent six weeks working on the Lasker book. It was a relaxing time, and so the family did not return to New York until a week before Christmas.

The product of John's efforts, in Cass Canfield's hands by March 1959, was called *Taken at the Flood: The Story of Albert D. Lasker.* The book was published late that year to generally favorable reviews. "There is an immense amount of stuff about Jews in it, a lot of which will, I imagine, amuse you quite a lot," John told Frances in a letter dated January 7, 1960. "As you probably know, Lasker went to Israel a short time before his death, when he was 70, and it was one of the most moving experiences of his life."[12]

Not long after completing the Lasker book, John was in Chicago to receive a University of Chicago alumni association award from the hand of his long-time friend and colleague Fanny Butcher, the *Chicago Tribune* literary editor. "[John's] reputation and the sales of his books [had] become astronomical," Butcher wrote in her memoir, *Many Lives—One Love* (1972). "But he was always to me the same eager young reporter I had happily watched succeed."[13]

In an interview with a *Daily News* reporter following the award dinner, John outlined plans for three new books: *Inside Red China*, *Inside Australia*, and possibly a book on Chicago. The companion volume to *Inside U.S.A.* was now a dead issue. John had concluded that he simply did not have enough time to do the book for the beginning of a new president's term either in 1960 or 1964. Besides, his friend Teddy White had carved out a niche for himself in this area with his splendid "Making of the President" series. And at this point in John's life, other projects simply interested him more.

He was especially hopeful, but not optimistic, about the possibility of visiting China again. Discreet inquiries had been made on his behalf to obtain the necessary visas. Cass Canfield had written to the State Department, and a formal request went from there to the Chinese government. However, Sino-American relations being cool, the request was denied.

John began work in the summer of 1959 on his new ABC television show. He was apprehensive. After all, he had not done a lot of broadcasting in recent years, apart from some brief appearances on radio and TV to promote his books, and an interview he and Jane had given Edward R. Murrow for his *Person to Person* TV show on CBS on October 21, 1955. What induced John to try his hand at a weekly show was one thing: the promise of easy money. Nothing more. Like most old newspapermen, he was skeptical about television journalism.

John Gunther's High Road to Adventure debuted on ABC on September 7, 1959. The show featured travel films narrated by John. Some of them were done expressly for the purpose, others were bought from free-lance film makers. The show was forgettable for the most part, aside from a brief furor over a film that included some scenes of bare-breasted African women.

John was neither disappointed nor surprised when the show was cancelled after just a year. He had found that this foray into television was a lot more work than he had envisioned, largely because the scripts supplied to him by the show's producer had been so poor that he had to rewrite most of them. Still, he had fun dabbling in what was a new medium for him. John confided to Frances, "Oddly enough, I rather enjoy filming although I am, frankly, nervous and upset before a camera."[14]

His next project, another impromptu effort with the promise of more easy money, began one day in early 1960 after a conversation with *Reader's Digest* editor Hobart Lewis. He called to remind John that the twenty-fifth anniversary of *Inside Europe* was fast approaching. What Lewis proposed was for John to visit Europe, and to write an article comparing the situation there in 1936 to the situation in 1961. Such an invitation was irresistible.

John abandoned research for an Australia book, and he and

Jane left in the spring of 1960 on a whirlwind European tour. It was reminiscent of a similar tour of the continent that he had undertaken in the summer of 1935. This time, however, he and Jane flew rather than traveled by train. They made stops in London, Paris, Berlin, and Rome. Along the way, John interviewed many people, including British Prime Minister Harold Macmillan, Chancellor Konrad Adenauer of Germany, West Berlin mayor Willy Brandt, and, of course, General Charles de Gaulle, the president of France.

John had first met de Gaulle in London in 1941, while he was in exile with the French resistance. At that time, the general had impressed John as a man certain to make his mark in history. Now, two decades later, that destiny had been fulfilled. At seventy-one, de Gaulle, as egotistical, passionate, and Olympian as ever, had become a living legend. John recalled having interviewed him in the mid-1950s; at that time, de Gaulle asked him what other French political figures he had seen. Hearing the names, the general smiled, and announced, "Ah! But you have met nobody but the pro-Americans!"

"Who else is there?" John asked.

"*Moi*! de Gaulle answered, only half in jest.

When John later told that story to an aristocratic English lady friend, she sniffed, "It's a wonder he didn't, like a king, say, 'Nous!'"[15]

John recounted his latest interview with de Gaulle, as well as his overall impressions of the *new* Europe in a lengthy article that ran to 42,000 words—far longer than anything Hobart Lewis had contemplated. While Lewis obligingly trimmed the article for the *Digest*, it still ran in three installments. John had another use in mind for the full-length version.

Cass Canfield and Hamish Hamilton had for years been urging him to revise *Inside Europe*, and for just as long he had resisted doing so. Now, he suggested they might reprint the entire Europe article as he had written it. When Canfield insisted on something longer, John set to work. The result was "a full-dress book," which concluded that despite the bloodiest war in history, not all that much had really changed in the quarter-century since the appearance of the original *Inside Europe*. In John's mind, Germany remained the key to the future of the continent.

Inside Europe Today[16] was published in August 1961 to enthusiastic reviews, even from reviewers too young to have recalled the original *Inside Europe* a quarter-century before. Foreign correspondent Cyrus Sulzberger of the *New York Times* praised the book as "another first-class job."[17] Reviewer Charles Rolo of the *Atlantic* touched upon what was becoming a key question from John's perspective: had the *Inside* formula withstood the test of time? Rolo felt it had.

"There has been a great deal of [critical] scoffing at Gunther's *Inside* books, at the absurdity of writing up continents on the run, so to speak," he wrote. "But I submit that in this age of narrow specialization and of group journalism, there is something admirable about Gunther's willingness to make the whole world his beat, and to do all his own legwork."[18]

Fans of the *Inside* books agreed. *Inside Europe Today*, was chosen as the Book of the Month Club's feature selection for August 1961, and it sold so briskly that Canfield asked John to do a revised edition. That book appeared in April 1962, in both hard cover and mass market paperback—for the first time ever for a new Gunther book. It was a sign of the changing times. So, too, was the sad news from Lisbon, Portugal, of the death by heart attack on January 30, 1961, of John's dear friend Dorothy Thompson. She had been only sixty-eight years old.

Almost as unsettling was the news that another close friend, Raymond Swing, had suffered a serious heart attack the month before. And from Jerusalem came word that Frances was in failing health. One by one, the ranks of those who had been close to him were beginning to thin.

Then, in late June the world was shocked by the suicide death of Ernest Hemingway, certainly the preeminent writer of his day, and Chicago's most famous native son. John had never known Hemingway well; he was merely an acquaintance. But Hemingway had cast a giant shadow across the generation of American writers who came of age during the 1920s and 1930s. John, more than most, felt his loss.

John, himself, for several years had been dropping hints—conscious and otherwise—in letters and conversations that indicated he had started to seriously contemplate death. Not that he was preoccupied with such thoughts, or that he was in poor health, simply that he was beginning to feel and act his age.

All things considered, he felt reasonably well. His doctors assured him that despite some minor aches and pains, he was in excellent condition, albeit overweight. And there was no denying that he smoked too much, or that the thick glasses he was now obliged to wear after his eye surgery were a nuisance. As John's sixtieth birthday came in August 1961, he was bothered by a lower back ailment, which necessitated a brief stay in hospital.

In the fall of that year, he and Jane sold the big house on Sixty-second Street, and moved to an apartment on the upper West Side of Manhattan. John in 1959 had already begun to donate his notes, original manuscripts, and many other personal papers to the University of Chicago library. In anticipation of the impending move, and with the deaths and illnesses of people who had been close to him whispering intimations of mortality in his own ear, he accelerated the process of cleaning out his jammed filing cabinets and closets.

Doing so prompted him to write a lengthy memorandum detailing the orgin of the materials that he gave the U of C. The editors of *Harper's* magazine had asked him several years earlier to write an account of how he had created the *Inside* books. In late 1960 he had written two articles. These formed the basis of a series of memorandums that he now sent to Chicago along with his papers. They also formed the core of a short book that was published in the fall of 1962 under the title *A Fragment of Autobiography: The Fun of Writing the Inside Books.*

That 116-page book provided readers with an intimate glimpse into John's life and working habits. It amounted to an introspective "nuts-and-bolts" discussion of how the *Inside* books were created; indeed, the last chapter, "Inside the Insides," amounted to a master's primer in the art of journalism. Like Somerset Maugham's *A Writer's Notebook* (1949), it provided rare insight into the craft of writing. John outlined his technique for such basics as how to take notes, do interviews—he included a list of thirty-sixth basic questions he liked to ask subjects—and even how to type a manuscript.

The book was intended it as a warm-up to *Inside Gunther,* an autobiography that John planned to write soon. The necessity for getting started was underlined by another stay in hospital, this one for a June 1963 attack of phlebitis.

CHAPTER THIRTY-NINE

The saying is that time heals all wounds. But the emotional scars that Frances Gunther had suffered as a result of her 1944 divorce, and the death of her son three years later were too deep to ever disappear. Thereafter Frances wore her grief like a cloak that she took off only briefly.

She had drifted without purpose or direction in the wake of her divorce. In a note to Jawaharlal Nehru written just after the break was finalized, Frances was calm and rational. "I tried with all my might to maintain all the disciplines, but there came the time when the clean cut had to be made," she said. "It wasn't done frivolously or irresponsibly."[1]

In the long, lonely months and years that followed, this fine veneer of self-control gradually eroded. While she lacked for nothing material, hers was a life that was emotionally threadbare.

Frances and Johnny lived comfortably enough in the big house at Madison, Connecticut, on a $600-per-month alimony payment from John, plus some income investment, and some money that she received from her brother Bernie Fineman. He had made a fortune in the 1920s producing Hollywood movies, and later married the adopted daughter of legendary director-producer Cecil B. DeMille.

Relations between Frances and her brother were for many years strained by their differences over Zionism. Frances was outspoken in her opposition to a Jewish homeland in Palestine; she pursued the quixotic dream of a Palestine where Jews and Arabs would live together in peace. As in so many other aspects of her personality, Frances was a study in contradictions. The irony was that a woman who lived her personal life with such intensity should be so cerebral and universalist where the fate of Palestine was concerned. Then, as now, it was an emotionally charged issue.

Frances' brother Bernie did not share her sentiments. He was adament in his Zionism. His daughter, Judith deMille Donelan, recalls that her father had been an officer in the national guard during the war, and afterwards he maintained close ties to the guard in California.

"In 1948-49, he used his contacts there to acquire armaments, which he shipped to Israel. Bernie was eventually indicted by a Grand Jury, and at that point left the country and spent a couple of unhappy years in Israel," she says.

"I believe the State Department sort of winked at all this because they knew that if Israel wasn't getting arms from us, they'd have gotten them from the communist countries. Evidently this was embarrassing for Washington, and so Bernie was allowed to skip out."[2]

Frances joined her brother in Israel in 1949.

Her attitude to Zionism had warmed somewhat in the early 1940s, as the terrible reality of the Holocaust became known. Frances involved herself in Hadassah, the women's Zionist organization, and she supported various lobby efforts pressuring the Roosevelt administration to play a more vigorous role in aiding the millions of Jewish refugees who had fled Europe.

While Johnny was alive, Frances devoted herself to his care and upbringing; all other concerns in her life remained secondary. His death left an enormous gap in her life—both emotionally, and in terms of how she spent her time. Frances needed structure in her life. As a result, she groped for a renewed sense of purpose.

Judith deMille Donelan remembers visiting her aunt Frances at Madison in the summer of 1947, not long after Johnny's death. Says Donelan, "I have the strongest recollection of her saying, 'Let's have lunch.' I went to open the refrigerator, and there was a wilted lettuce and a container of yogurt growing mold. That was lunch. Frances had absolutely no interest in food. After Johnny's death, she ate less and less.

"Frances would sit there talking great metaphysical things, and I honestly couldn't comprehend. Being a smartsy New York teenager at the time, I wasn't even interested. I mean, she probably was saying wonderful things, if I'd listened to her. But I missed most of it.

"My basic impression of Frances was that for someone who'd lived, and traveled, and experienced as much as she had, she was *utterly* out of touch with reality . . . I do think that her grasp on reality was extremely tenuous. Some of her ideas, particularly in the geopolitical sphere were just, you know, cuckoo. But, again, who was I to judge them?"[3]

In 1948, Frances considered going to India, where she dreamed of taking her place at Nehru's side. In her heart, she had long wanted to go; in her mind, even she had begun to sense that doing so was an impossible dream for a variety of reasons. Some people who knew knew Frances—mostly John's friends—wondered aloud how much of the relationship between her and Nehru was reality, and how much was the product of a fanciful imagination. After all, Frances and Nehru had seen one another one another only a handful of times during the 1940s (and 1950s).

The depth of Nehru's feeling for Frances Gunther is not easy to gauge. It is clear that he was a man to whom women were attracted; that he responded to their attentions is equally clear. It is his motivation that remains obscure.

It may have simply been male ego that led to his involvements with Frances, Edwina Mountbatten, Madame Chiang Kai-shek, and other married women.

It may have been a genuine desire for love; after all, Nehru was widowed in 1936, at the age of forty-seven.

It may have been nothing more than a desire to use these women to get close to their husbands and other influential people; Nehru certainly knew of John Gunther's reputation, and he was eager to encourage his support for the cause of Indian indepenence.

Or it may have been a combination of all three reasons.

In the beginning, at least, Nehru's relationship with Frances began like most of the others—with a brief intimacy. Whether this was physical or platonic is uncertain, although the former seems likely. What is important is that in Frances' mind Nehru became a symbol. Like her, he was alone and vulnerable. Like her, he was struggling to define his beliefs. Their relationship took on an added dimension, and endured more than two decades via the mail. Early on, at least, the intensity of Frances' devotion to Nehru and to Indian nationalism befuddled him. Sometimes his letters hinted at his sense of confusion; at other times there was real affection in them.

According to Dr. Alexander Rafaeli, the Jerusalem doctor who became Frances' executor and one of her closest friends after her move to Israel, the bond between Frances and Nehru "was very emotional on both sides. They were not only lovers, but sincere friends and sharp critics."[4]

In addition to the correspondence that passed back and forth, there were romantic poems, and sometimes small gifts. Frances mostly sent Nehru books, while he would remember her birthday or Christmas with personal items, such as silk scarves. Says Rafaeli, "When Frances died, I burned some of her letters because I felt they were too personal for others to read. Some of Nehru's letters that were of interest to the public and historians, I turned over to the Nehru Institute in Bombay.

"This I can tell you, the letters between Frances and Nehru were warm and loving, especially in the days before Indian independence. You must remember that it was difficult for Nehru to write to Frances because he was in jail much of the time, and because his family, as Brahmans, disapproved strongly of any such relationship. Nehru's sister was in love with a Muslim man, and the Nehru family would not permit her to marry him. The two were forced to live parallel lives."[5]

Having concluded that her future lay not in the U.S., Frances sold the house in Madison following Johnny's death, and in 1949 emigrated to Israel. Early the following year she visited India, as the guest of Indira Nehru Gandhi, Nehru's daughter. Frances met with Nehru himself, saw some old friends, and toured a United

Nations observation post on the India-Pakistan border.[6]

She recounted her impressions of the trip in a letter to John, which has unfortunately been lost. However, in a reply dated May 30, 1950, John noted that her brief letter from India "had a tantalizing quality" and that she "must have had a revealing time." He asked for more details.[7]

The Indian visit was indeed "revealing," in more ways than one. It provided Frances with a sharp reminder of just how much had changed in her life, and in the life of Nehru. As the prime minister of India, he had lost the cachet of the struggling revolutionary. Nehru had ceased to be the object of Frances' romantic fantasies; he was now just a friend, albeit a very special one.

Apart from several trips to the U.S. for medical treatment, Frances made her home in Israel for the rest of her life. Being friends with President Chaim Weizmann, U.N. ambassador Abba Eban, and various other Israeli leaders, she had many contacts in the upper echelons of the government. Frances sought to take advantage of the situation, applying for work as the Jerusalem correspondent for the *New Yorker*, and other American and British publications. She had no luck. Likewise, her efforts to find a journalism job in Israel proved fruitless.

In the quarter century since Frances' youthful dreams of a career as a foreign correspondent had been dashed, not all that much had changed. Few females were in the field; only a small handful of talented women had succeded, and managed to maintain their personal dignity. Dorothy Thompson, Ann O'Hare McCormick of the *New York Times*, and Sigrid Schultz, the Berlin correspondent for the *Chicago Tribune* ("the dragon lady from Chicago," as Hermann Goering dubbed her), had been the few real exceptions. All were able to do so only through sheer force of personality.

Compounding Frances' difficulties were gnawing feelings of inadequacy; she was bereft of self-confidence. After all, she had not worked as a journalist since the Vienna years, when she had been the local correspondent for the *London News Chronicle*. "You know how insecure I feel about myself at all times, and especially now, as an unattached female, divorced, and jobless," Frances confided to John in one of her letters.[8]

Her insecurities were not lessened by the reception accorded the job applications she sent out. Frances lamented to John that one of the few serious job offers she received had come from a magazine editor who was interested in more than her writing skills. When Frances resisted his sexual advances, she did not get hired.

Such experiences were frustrating and demeaning, yet Frances perservered.

She appealed for work to General William E. Riley, the chief of the United Nations Armistice Commission in the Middle East, whom she had met at a party at the home of the Weizmanns. Frances had ambitious plans. She told John in a letter dated July 22, 1951, "Special job I want to create is: assistant for psychological peacefare, long range (APPL). This type of job should be set up all over the place, Korea, etc." Unfortunately, the U.N. proposal came to naught; Riley asked Frances to work as a spy, a request she flatly rejected. "I am not intelligence stuff, but . . . simply intelligent and serious," she quipped to John.[9]

When Frances managed to find some work writing press releases for the Israeli information office, she did not enjoy the experience. "It just ties my guts up in knots, and I can't [do it]," she told John.[10]

Instead, Frances turned to freelance writing. For a time in the early 1950s her byline appeared on a semi-regular basis in the *Jerusalem Post*, the local English language daily. Mostly she wrote book reviews and articles. She also lectured and wrote on Indian affairs, and she did a short two-part series on the Ulpan method of Hebrew education, which was designed to immerse immigrants in all aspects of life in Israel. Education was of special interest to Frances, and she donated prize money for essay competitions on various topics.

She began work, too, on another book project with the lofty title, *Theo-politics & Transmission*. After more than twenty years of futility, Frances had abandoned her treatise on the nature of empires, and was intent on investigating the impact of theology on all aspects of life—everything from education to politics. She was convinced that "theo-politics" was destined to be one of the cornerstones of what she termed "the coordinated political sciences of the future." It was an ambitious, complex topic.

Although she was almost sixty, Frances' idealism burned as intensely as ever. She was convinced that if she had a nice apartment, she could invite groups of Arabs and Jews there to socialize, and in this way she would break down some of the hostilities that had grown up between the two peoples. In theory, her humanism made sense; in practice, it proved to be yet another exercise in frustration.

Frances found a two-bedroom apartment, which she furnished with items that she had shipped to her from New York. "It's quite little, compared to some of the enormous old places, but it's turned out quite comfortable: tiny kitchen and very small bedroom, little study, and long graceful living room, made by knocking down partition between two small rooms. And the terrace looking over the hills," she told John.[11]

Alexander Rafaeli remembers Frances inviting groups of friends to her apartment—"Jews and Arabs, some Muslim, some Christian, mostly junior university teachers." He says there were the "standard discussions" about the Middle East. Sometimes Frances gave a cocktail party for a visiting American or British friend. Journalist Edgar Snow came calling, so did Dorothy Thompson, publisher Hamish Hamilton, literary critic Edmund Wilson, and many others.[12]

Like everything Frances did, in the end her good intentions mostly came to naught. One of the few projects that she undertook successfully was a Hebrew translation of *Death Be Not Proud*.

As always, her own writing got nowhere; she resurrected the idea of a book called *Inside God*, and when John repeated his disinterest in the project, she begged him to help her find someone else to collaborate with her on it, Jimmy Sheean perhaps. John ignored these requests. It had become painfully evident to him and to Frances that no matter how hard she tried she could never write "an orderly organized rational book of the kind I so deeply admire when written by other people," as she put it.[13]

Frances' efforts to reconcile Jews and Arabs began to seem equally futile, equally pointless.

"When I first came I had all those God-illusions about helping to make peace between Israel and the Arabs, but I have had no power to. I took this lovely flat for people to meet and be friends, and a few did—but now . . . even the bit of power is drained out of me, and I feel oddly isolated in total powerlessness," she wrote in one of her letters.[14]

As Frances' idealism unraveled, the emptiness of her life started to wear her down. She grew moody and resentful.

A letter to John written in early February 1955, provided a

glimpse into the miasma of her situation. "I see few people," she said. "But I did see Edmund Wilson twice when he was here last year. Last time I saw him . . . when we said good night, he gave me a little peck of a kiss on the forehead, in a kindly way, feeling sorry for me. I'm so goddam sick of people feeling sorry for me."[15]

According to her friend Dr. Alexander Rafaeli, Frances tried to fill the void in her life by finding romance. She had several brief relationships during her years in Jerusalem. For a while she dated a Russian diplomat, for a while an Arab teacher. Says Rafaeli, "Frances was a very lonely woman. She was divorced, and had lost her children. She suffered a great deal during those years. All of her friends here tried to help her, although probably not enough. She had always been a very active woman, who loved people and company."[16]

By the spring of 1957, Frances mused about chucking it all, to retreat to a convent somewhere or maybe go off to sail the Mediterranean. But she admitted that these were nothing more than fantasies. "I'm so busy punishing myself for all my failures that there's no time left for anything amusing," she wrote.[17]

Frances' overall condition was worsened by a growing list of physical ailments. She complained of having suffered several bad falls while walking at night in the Jerusalem streets, many of which were unpaved. Then in the spring of 1957 she was hospitalized for what she termed "routine removal of cyst or tumor on right ovary."[18] She returned to hospital for a second operation in early August 1957.

John, who was concerned both about her health and her financal situation, sent some money to help pay expenses. Frances destroyed the cheque, and announced that she had more than enough money. Then she returned to John some of the alimony money that had accumulated in the bank, and instructed him to reduce her alimony from $600 per month to $400.[19]

As her bouts with depression deepened and became more frequent, she began sending John and Jane jewelry and other small personal items. She put money in a bank account to help pay for Nicholas' education. Frances' will to live was waning; her letters from this period reflect a growing fatalism.

On November 1, 1958, she told John, "For me, personally, nothing seems possible that I want—my wants as you know are not many but intense—or were so. And were realizable, achievable, and were achieved, made real, lived. But now there's nothing I want that's possible. I've just faced up to that, and it has both terrified and stumped me." [20]

In a letter to Jane Gunther that same day, Frances made a bizarre, heart-wrenching admission, one that reflected the fragility of her troubled mind. "In a strange way John has become Johnny, and you are not only John's bride, but Johnny's bride, and also Johnny's sister Judith—and as you [are] just as you are, are just what I would have dreamed and wanted my daughter and my daughter-in-law to be, and what I wanted John's wife to be, you are all those in one to me."[21]

This was not the first time Frances had articulated those kind of ideas. In her own mind, Johnny was still very much alive; his memory was her constant companion. Mary Sanders, one of Johnny's childhood schoolmates, recalls how Frances suddenly "adopted" her in late 1946. Although she had not seen Johnny for almost five years, she got a phone call "out of the blue" one day inviting her to a small birthday party for Johnny, who was suffering at the time with the cancer that ultimately killed him. Mary saw Johnny several times during his last months of life, and to Frances she had become the girlfriend that Johnny never had or never would have.

Frances kept in touch after her move to Israel. Says Mary, "I think maybe she latched onto us (Mary had by that time married Leo von Euler, a young Yale medical student) as a link to her son's generation. Perhaps, too, she had some illusions that if Johnny had lived I might have been the girl he'd have married."[22]

Reacting to such notions was not easy.

Nor was it easy for John to deal with the growing moodiness that Frances began to display in her correspondences. In a rambling, angry letter written in late 1958, for example, she lashed out at John for having created her predicament. In her mind, he was responsible for the sorry mess that her life had become. Citing reference after reference that she had culled from twenty years of John's articles and books, she alleged that by not fully acknowledging that *she* had been the inspiration behind the success of the first two *Insides*, John had made it impossible for her to find a job. Not being able to support herself was the ultimate indignity. "Without this help from me, you would never in all the world have become the author of any *Inside* of anything . . . " she charged.[23]

While Frances' letter was not totally without merit—she certainly had helped with the research and had urged John to write both *Inside Europe* and *Inside Asia*—to suggest that she alone was responsible for those books is nonsense. John had always turned to the people closest to him for encouragement; the essence of good writing is communication, and no writer works in a vacuum. John Gunther certainly did not.

In his youth, he had looked first to his mother and his aunts and uncles for support. In school, his talents had been nurtured by his teachers, particularly James Weber Linn at the U of C. During his days as a young reporter at the *Chicago Daily News*, editors such Henry Justin Smith and Harry Hansen had worked with him to polish his prose. Later, when Helen Hahn entered his life, it was she who began critiquing his writing. As the relationship between John and Frances developed, Frances naturally succeeded Helen as John's chief critic and muse. And following the divorce and John's subsequent remarriage, his wife Jane had happily and very capably assumed those roles in his life, to the discomfort of Frances.

In her letters in the late 1950s, she repeatedly asked John if she could read and critique chapters of his books in progress; he wisely did not respond. That chapter of his life was closed.

John Gunther never made any secret of the help that he received. In fact, throughout his lifetime he was generous in praising the work of others, particularly promising new talents or people who had helped or inspired him with his own writing. In 1926, he dedicated *The Red Pavilion*, his very first book, "To my mother, with no explanations"; *Inside Europe* had been dedicated, "To my wife in love and friendship"; *Inside Asia* to "Johnny who suggested it"; *Inside Africa* to Jane Gunther because, "The 'I' in this book is mostly 'we.'"

One of the qualities that William Shirer remembers best about John Gunther was his quiet determination to succeed; his easy-going manner could be deceptive. "He had great ambition and drive," says Shirer. During those pivotal years in Vienna, he remembers that Frances helped John with his job, encouraged him, prodded him to excel. "She was a very determined woman. I think at the time we [other foreign correspondents] thought she was very good for John. She would restrain his enthusiasms, and I think she was very concerned with furthering his career."[24]

Shirer makes the point that John Gunther, like every other good foreign correspondent, was a master "brain picker"; it was an integral part of doing the job well. Particularly after the success of *Inside Europe* some people envied John's success—H.R. Knickerbocker, who had turned down the chance to write the book, was one. "Some people resented it, but I never did because, I suppose, we were such close friends," says Shirer.[25]

Says Evan Thomas, one of the editors at Harper & Brothers who worked with John for many years, "Gunther was a charmer. He always gave others a lot of the credit for his success." Thomas recalls how John inscribed a copy of *Days to Remember*, the picture book they had worked on in 1956 along with photo editor Bernard Quint: "To my co-author and co-stimulator."[26]

Jane Gunther was not surprised by Frances' angry outburst. She recalls that as a writer Frances was impractical and indecisive, two shortcomings that were largely responsible for her inability to complete her own projects. Frances worked on her book about empires for two decades; she spent the last fifteen years of her life wrestling with another book about "theo-politics."

Apart from her short book about Indian nationalism and assorted newspaper and magazine articles, Frances never completed any of the many projects that she started. There is no denying that she was an immensely talented, intelligent woman, however, hers were talents that were ultimately wasted. She simply did not have the temperament to see her through the writing of a book. Had she never met John Gunther that summer in Paris in 1925 it seems improbable that she ever would have found fame or success on her own; Frances was simply too deeply troubled, her personality too fatally flawed. And such was the temper of the times; Frances had been born a generation too soon.

In the summer of 1961, she was back in the U.S. to visit the von Eulers and to undergo another operation for the cancer that was again growing within her. In a letter written to John in August, Frances inquired about the ashes of Judith and Johnny. She had come up with a plan to move Johnny's ashes to a burial site on the property of Deerfield Academy; it was a bizarre idea, and John gently dissuaded her from attempting to do so.[27]

Thoughts of death were with her more and more now. Indeed, following her return to Jerusalem she knew that she was terminally ill and did not have much longer to live. A photo taken of her by Mary von Euler on a visit to New Haven, Connecticut, depicts a tired, graying woman whose baleful eyes speak of the profound sadness that had seized her soul.

Frances' last few years were marked with more bitterness, confusion, and extreme shifts of mood. "She was often extremely depressed. But then an old friend would drop by for a visit, and she suddenly would become the same strong, logical person she had once been. It was amazing," says Alexander Rafaeli.[28]

Contact between John and Frances during these last years was sporadic. John had wearied of her outbursts, which were painful for everyone concerned. There occurred another in late 1962, when John sent Frances an inscribed copy of *A Fragment of Autobiography*.

Frances studied it carefully, making note of how many places she was mentioned. There were, she pointed out, just three. Despite John's acknowledgement that "she was very much part of this whole process" of writing the first two *Inside* books, Frances was incensed. She sent him another rambling, indignant letter that accused him of "cowardice, and a moral degeneration." She went on to reiterate her now familiar argument that, "Next to your mother and father, I created, molded, much of what you are today." The five-page harangue ended with the plea that John think long and hard before responding. There was no deadline, Frances observed, "Only a death line which I for one for myself await with open arms."[29]

If John reacted to this last outburst, Frances did not keep a copy of his letter. There were no further letters from him to her among her papers when she died. The next time that Frances was in touch with him was via Jane, who in June 1963 wrote to say that John had been in hospital with an attack of phlebitis.

Frances's own health deteriorated steadily in late 1963 and early 1964. By February, she was bedridden. In early April it was clear that she had only days to live.

The end came for Frances on April 6, 1964, at the Notre Dame Hospital for the terminally ill in Jerusalem. She was only sixty-seven. "I saw her, and she was in great pain. Her last words to me were, 'I am so tired. Let me sleep,'" says Alexander Rafaeli.[30]

Frances' brother Bernie arrived the following day and took charge of her remains. Frances had left her body to the Medical School of the Hebrew University of Jerusalem, and donated her brain to Columbia Presbyterian Hospital in New York, in the hope that by analyzing the organ the researchers there might find some genetic clue linking her to the brain cancer that had killed Johnny.

"A year later, as Jewish law prescribes, Frances' body was returned for burial," says Alexander Rafaeli. "We buried her in the Givat Shaul Cemetary at the western entrance to Jerusalem. She rests there on a high rock between the Judean Desert and the Mediterranean Sea. From there, you can see the sea on a clear day.

"Engraved on her headstone are the words of God to Abraham: 'Go from your native land to the land of your fathers, which I promised you and your people.'"[31]

Frances was wrapped in a warm, eternal embrace by the sandy soil of Israel, a land she had once scorned. At long last, she had found the peace that she had always denied herself.

CHAPTER FORTY

He knew that she was a sick woman, dying of cancer, yet the telegram that John received bearing the news of Frances' death came as a shock. Despite their differences, his ex-wife had been a part of his life for almost forty years. He knew that she had gone to her grave loving him, in her own peculiar way. Death had put an end to a bittersweet relationship that had begun one fine Paris spring day in 1925, and suddenly seemed so long ago.

Happily remarried, John had made a new life for himself with Jane and his adopted son Nicholas. He no longer felt any bitterness towards Frances—if ever he had. He felt only a profound sadness that she had not found the kind of happiness he had.

John spent a long time reflecting on the nature of his relationship to Frances, and about his early journalism career. Both elements were at the heart of his novel *The Lost City*, which was published in the spring of 1964. A rambling, wistful tale of love lost and then rediscovered, it revolves around the adventures of a young American foreign correspondent named Mason Jarrett, and his wife Paula; the pair bear more than a passing resemblance to John and Frances. This was essentially the book that John had struggled to publish in 1937 as *Ring Around Vienna*. At that time, lawyers warned it was libelous. Although such fears had by now ceased to be a serious concern, the book carried a disclaimer stating that the characters and situations were fictional.

The Lost City was a selection of the Literary Guild book club, and inital sales were strong. Critics praised aspects of the novel, especially what a reviewer for the *New Yorker* termed the "sunlit" evocation of Vienna of the early 1930s.[1] But sales quickly fell off. In most peoples' minds, the name John Gunther had become synonymous with one thing only—the *Inside* books.

That was the standard by which the critics judged his fiction. It was also an impossible standard to meet.

Says critic and friend Clifton Fadiman, "John Gunther was essentially a social person. He led an interesting enough life to produce good fiction, only he didn't have the novelist's touch. His life was based on contact, whereas the novelist's life—no matter how busy he or she is—is basically a matter of digging into the mind. That wasn't John's beat."[2]

From childhood on, books had been at the core of John Gunther's life. They were his private world, his refuge. Writing fiction was for him an emotional outlet, a means of expressing all of the things that he could not articulate. At heart, John was an incurable romantic, and such a gentle soul that he could not bear to hurt anyone, nor to leave any wrong unrighted. Writing was his way of healing hurts.

"I believe it was William James who said that the chief value and virtue of life was to give you a chance to do something that will outlast it," John once wrote.[3] To the generation of writers who came of age during the 1920s and 1930s, that meant just one thing: novels. Journalism was merely a means to an end. The day's headlines would be forgotten tomorrow. Great fiction endured.

A lifetime of observing people had given John a keen sense of humanity's foibles and frailities, particularly his own. It had shown him how people said and did hurtful things. He had come to the realization that in the end, none of that mattered. As Leonora Hornblow notes, "John Gunther was such a warm, kind man, that he bore no grudges."[4]

It is no coincidence that the *Lost City* (like *The Red Pavilion*, 1926) ends with the reconciliation of Mason and Paula, the estranged couple. In his own mind, in reexamining his own life, it was as if John had finally arrived at a kind of peace with Frances, and himself.

Whether by design or happenstance, the late 1960s were among the busiest and most productive years of his life. He began work on another novel. He wrote short stories that appeared in such magazines as *Playboy* and *Esquire*, and he produced a flurry of nonfiction books and articles. Completion of the *The Lost City* had been delayed briefly when John accepted an invitation to write an informal history of the University of Chicago.

The U of C, like many other American universities, was under siege in the early 1960s, both from within and without. Student radicals questioned the nature and quality of the education that the school was providing, and senior officials in the administration were eager to show the other side of the story, namely that the university had always been and remained one of the world's great academic institutions. Their problem, of course, was to find a credible, unbiased voice who could say as much. John Gunther seemed the ideal candidate for several reasons: he was one of the world's best-known and most respected liberal journalists. He was also a 1922 graduate. And having had little to do with the university in the years since had allowed him to maintain an outsider's perspective. The only real question was whether or not he could be persuaded to take on the assignment, even for a handsome fee.

University of Chicago President George Beadle and Board of Trustees Chairman Fairfax Cone were delighted when John agreed to do so, despite a daunting backlog of work. At the time, Cass Canfield was impatient for *The Lost City* manuscript; plans were in the works for another *Inside* book, and the editors of *Look* magazine were breathing down his neck for a survey article he had promised on the course of the twentieth century. "I am bursting to tell you that while I can't possibly undertake the assignment I am going to do it anyway!" John told Cone.[5]

He visited the U of C campus, where he spent several days rediscovering all of his youthful haunts, and reliving his memories.

It was a grand homecoming. John dined with university officials, and chatted with students eager to share with him their criticisms of the school, which revolved around what they regarded as a "moldy" approach to education, and a tardiness in hiring black faculty and encouraging black students. John looked into many of these complaints, concluding that while the U of C undeniably had problems, they merely reflected broader concerns that were troubling society in general.

That the task of writing about his alma mater was a labor of love was clear. John refused any payment for writing *Chicago Revisted*, which was published in 1965 by the university. The slender book, ninety-eight pages of text, was a loving tribute to the university, and to the memory of many old friends. John compared the campus to a principality in the midst of the surrounding city. The U of C, he said, was "still the most exciting university in the world."[6]

Hot on the heels of that book, in June 1965, Harper & Row published *Procession*. This was a collection of profiles of world leaders and prominent people culled from the seven *Inside* books, as well as from articles written during the course of a long career. *Procession* delighted long-time fans and showed new ones why John Gunther had remained popular and influential for so many years. Critics, many of whom were too young to have read the first *Insides*, liked the book. To them John's early writings seemed fresh and alive. So, too, did his intimate style, and his gift for capturing a person or situation in a few lines of prose. "The essence of an age is here," exclaimed J.M. Allison of the *Saturday Review*.[7]

The reception accorded *Procession* delighted John, who was already working in earnest on what would be the next book in the *Inside* series. That it would take barely two years to complete is astonishing, considering that John was no longer a young man and suffered from a variety of aches and pains.

The next *Inside* was originally to have been about Australia. Those plans were put on hold once more when Hobart Lewis, the president and executive editor of *Reader's Digest*, asked John to instead update the South American chapters of his 1941 book, *Inside Latin America*. Events in that area of the world had exploded into the headlines, and the interest of the American public rose, especially after President Lyndon Johnson sent the Marines into the Dominican Republic, which was in the throes of civil strife. Johnson had moved on April 28, 1965, to protect American citizens on that Caribbean island, and to prevent the establishment of a Communist government.

As the White House responded to that threat, and to the escalating level of Soviet-and Cuban-backed guerrilla activities, media reports painted a grim picture. It seemed as though there was scarcely a country in South America that was not on the brink of revolution. As a result, a growing number of people feared that the entire continent was a powder keg ready to explode at America's back door. President John F. Kennedy had articulated that view, warning that Latin America had become more crucial to the United States than any other region of the world, even Southeast Asia. John Gunther was coming to share that opinion.

Armed with knowledge acquired in a series of briefings given to him by friends and Latin American experts in New York and Washington, John and Jane set out in late 1965 on a ten-country tour, mostly by airplane. They traveled from Venezuala in the north to Cape Horn in the south. As had become the custom, Jane made all of the travel arrangements, leaving John free to conduct interviews, and write the articles which helped to pay the costs of the trip. As always, the workload was dizzying. In an effort to ease it, Jane tried without success to add a new wrinkle to John's approach: she introduced him to the convenience of using a portable tape recorder to record interviews. He would have none of it, since he was convinced that it was a distraction that would certainly malfunction during interviews.

With trusted pencil and notebook in hand, John visited Jorge Luis Borges, the aging Argentinian short-story writer, essayist, poet, and man of letters.[8] Borges was one of the first Latin American writers to achieve fame on the national and international stage. His remarkable talents had come to the world's attention in 1962, when he shared the Formentor International Publishers' Prize with British playwright Samuel Beckett.

Borges' writing was unmistakably local in its settings, but universal in its themes; his work inspired a generation of young writers. Sadly, a congenital disease had robbed him of his sight. Like the poet Milton, he continued to write only by dictating to a secretary. Having suffered from cataracts, John empathized with Borges' condition. He urged the writer to travel to the U.S. to see opthalmological specialists there. Borges only sighed. His condition was "incurable" he said; it was a burden that he was resigned to bear stoically.

Late in the day, just as they were concluding the interview, Borges intimated to John how and why he had begun writing the stories which had made him world famous. He explained that he had suffered a bad fall, and during the long months it took him to recover, he feared that he had lost his gift for verse. So he started to write fiction because it was a new departure for him; readers would not be able to compare his old work with the new.

That Borges interview was one of the most memorable of John's experiences in South America. In total, he interviewed more than 770 people in the ten countries that he visited; among them were thirteen presidents. This peculiarity came about because in the brief time that he was in Ecuador, that nation went through four leaders! More than anything else, this example of "musical governments" underlined the continent's political volatility.

But what truly shocked John was the realization that in the quarter century since he had last visited, South America had been "frozen into a kind of derelict immobility," as he put it.[9] He argued that what was underway in South America was a race between reform and chaos. He did not share the prevailing wisdom that the continent was in danger over being overrun by communists. In John's mind, the real dangers in South America were posed by military dictatorships, and the problems of uncontrolled urbanization. Already a booming population was spawning squalid shanty towns which ringed the urban core areas of most South America cities. Millions of desperately poor, hungry people with no present and even less prospect for the future, threatened the continent's long-term stability and development, and hence, America's peace of mind; the illegal drug traffic had not yet become a concern.

Inside South America concluded that what the 160 million inhabitants of that continent wanted most was a better standard of living, and to be treated with dignity. "South America needs us, but the whole great quivering bunch of grapes of a continent is determined to establish its own destiny. South Americans are, in fact, just like us—they want to be for themselves," John wrote.[10]

John articulated those views in a series of articles for *Reader's Digest* and other magazines. Then, as had become his custom, he revised and expanded upon what he had written. The result was the book, *Inside South America*, which was published in February 1967. Like all of the previous *Insides*, it was a "selection" of the

Book of the Month Club. This ensured strong sales and wide reviews.

John Gunther's liberal opinions found a receptive audience, at least in some corners of a nation that was tearing itself apart over the Vietnam War. Unfortunately, with America preoccupied with events in southeast Asia, the important message in *Inside South America* was drowned out by the cacophony of competing voices. The book's impact was much less than it otherwise would have been. An observation made by James Reston of the *New York Times* echoed in John's mind: "Somehow the people of the United States will do anything for Latin America except read about it."[11]

None of this dampened John's spirits. Thus when Hobart Lewis next proposed that John write a series of profiles of the world's great cities, he accepted the assignment eagerly. Lewis paid most of the bills part of the way as John and Jane took a series of four trips, touching down in cities that had once been stops on John's world-wide journalistic beat. They traveled to London, Western Europe, the Far East, and Eastern Europe, the Soviet Union and the Middle East. In contrast to the harried routine of researching an *Inside* book, this was a paid holiday. John wrote some travel sketches for the *Digest*, and for *Harper's* magazine, and later recycled much of the material for a book entitled *Twelve Cities*,[12] which he dedicated to DeWitt and Lila Wallace, the founders of *Reader's Digest*. The book, published in 1969 by *Harper & Row*, appeared briefly on the best seller list, and spurred John to plunge into work on a book that Cass Canfield and other friends had for years been urging him to do. An *Inside Australia* would complete a grand scheme to chart the political history of all the continents.

John and Jane spent five months touring Australia, New Zealand, and New Guinea before returning home in early February 1970. Both were bone weary after the long, arduous trip, but John immediately began writing. It was agonizing work; he was listless and so very tired.

In early May, John took a day away from his desk to attend a memorial service for Joe Barnes, an old newspaper pal who had died of cancer. William Shirer delivered the eulogy. He recalls, "I was supposed to return that evening to Lenox [Massachussets], where I was now living, but John said, 'Let's have a drink,' so we went to a pub and had a long chat for two or three hours."[13]

Shirer was struck by how pale and gaunt his old friend looked.

John was short of breath as he talked, and stopped frequently to cough. Although he still was trying to quit smoking, he attributed his lung problems to the asthma that had dogged him since childhood. Shirer had his doubts, but he said nothing as the two old men fell to talking mutual friends, about their lives, and about their writing.

Shirer's career had been resurrected by the phenomenal success of *The Rise and Fall of the Third Reich* in 1960. He had followed up with two more best selling books in the next two years. In May 1970, he was being praised for a new book about the collapse of the third French republic. John told Shirer that he, too, had been busy. He was finishing off yet another novel, and working hard on *Inside Australia*. That book would be the last of the series because when it was done, John said that he intended to take "a helluva long rest."

John and William Shirer shook hands as they parted. "That was the last time I ever saw him," Shirer says, his voice growing soft. "He was dead a few weeks later."[14]

Looking back, Jane Gunther, too, now recognizes that by the spring of 1970 her husband was a very sick man. What neither John nor his family as yet knew was that cancer was slowly draining the life from him. It is now evident that John had suffered from cancer for about a year, but all of his other nagging health complaints masked the symptoms.

Complaining of exhaustion, John entered the Harkness Pavilion of the Columbia-Presbyterian Medical Center, the last week of May. It was the same hospital in which Johnny had died. John hoped that his stay would be brief. The Australia book was only partially done, and he had a lot more writing to do. He would never have the opportunity.

Doctors discovered that John had been suffering from cancer of the esophagus, and it had spread to his liver. There was no hope. He was failing fast.

John's last days were a blur of confusion and disbelief for himself, his family and friends. No one was ready for this; no one suspected that he was as ill as he really was.

On May 29, 1970, his suffering came to a merciful end. John Gunther died of liver cancer.[15] He had told a reporter for *Time* back in a 1958 interview, "What disturbs and upsets me is that there is not time or freedom or energy enough to do all the things I would like to do."[16] That thought echoed through the minds of those who loved him. He had been too young too die; he had too much still to do.

John's family and friends were devastated by his sudden passing. His family was filled with guilt that they had not somehow been able to stop him from smoking. They had tried everything, including urging John to see a hypnotist. It was maddening, but nothing worked for more than a few weeks; John had smoked too long, for too many years. The terrible irony was that although John had been a victim of cancer, it was a cancer that probably was not related at all to his smoking.

John Gunther's funeral was held at St. James Episcopal Church in Manhattan on June 3, 1970. The church was filled with family, friends, colleagues, and admirers. Messages of sympathy poured in from around the world. News of the death of "Mr. Inside," as *Newsweek* dubbed him, touched people far and wide. It was page one news in the *New York Times*, and in many other major newspapers around the world. CBS newsman Eric Sevareid paid tribute in his evening radio broadcast, and so did many other commentators. Said Sevareid, "He was one of the inventors of a kind of literary form, the book length reporting, which brought distant, misty realities to life and colored them bright, enthralling millions of readers and inspiring hundreds of young men and women to go forth and do likewise . . . More than diplomats or politicians, it was they who told America what was happening and what was going to happen to the civilization of the west."[17]

New York Post people columnist Leonard Lyons, another dear friend, reported an anecdote that to him summarized John's personality. It seems that British novelist Michael Arlen, who had been one of John's inspirations in his university days, had once given John a letter of introduction to the editor of the *London Daily Express*. Many years later, Arlen was in New York, where he and John chanced to meet.

"Say, whatever happened at the *Daily Express*?" Arlen asked.

"I didn't get the job," John said, seemingly oblivious to the fact that by this time he had become one of the world's best known journalists. It simply never occurred to him that his fame had far outstripped that of Arlen and most of the other literary gods he had once worshipped.[18]

New York Post columnist Pete Hamill expressed much the same sentiments. Although he was a generation younger, Hamill recognized his genius. "[Gunther] was one of the great reporters, a worshiper of facts, with not a pretense of his own importance," Hamill wrote.[19]

John's old friend Whit Burnett penned a "Letter to the Editor" a few days later thanking Hamill for his kind words. He went on to offer his own observations on what it was about John Gunther that had made him so special to so many people: his kindness, his generosity, and his concern for others. Wrote Burnett, "Probably only John himself knew how many good things he did, and he was not one to talk about them. But many others knew how generous he was, not only to his friends he kept a lifetime, but to many, many others in his profession."[20]

At the time of his death, John left two books unpublished. One was a short novel called *The Indian Sign*, the other was the Australia book.

The novel was complete, and ready for publication. It was a story about a love affair between a famous one-footed news broadcaster and the wife of a brilliant alcoholic newspaper reporter. Friends of John who read the book instantly recognized him as the one-footed narrator, a thinly disguised H.R. Knickerbocker as the husband, and Agnes Knickerbocker as the woman caught in the middle.

"I told him that he should never publish that book. It was terrible," says William Shirer. "I thought it was in bad taste. 'Why air this thing?' I asked him. He had been in love; it was a difficult situation, and I told him that I thought he should leave it at that."[21]

Leonora Hornblow and others, including Jane Gunther, were also opposed to the book being published. But for reasons of his own, John insisted. And so it was published, with predictably painful results. The book was a flop, and the few reviews it received were poor. "Needless to say, the book is not so much a novel as something resembling a series of extracts from a journal. If the protagonists aren't fictionalized real people, they sure as hell sound like it," observed one critic.[22]

Inside Australia was another matter. At the time of his death, John had completed only a couple of chapters. He left behind forty thick notebooks filled with interview notes, hundreds of scraps of paper with random scribbled thoughts, more than 150 reference books he had collected, and a desk piled high with newspaper and magazine clippings.

Several weeks after the funeral, Cass Canfield and Jane Gunther decided that they owed it to John to finish the book. But the obvious question was who should do so? Jane, who had written only magazine articles, did not want to attempt the project herself. Canfield made some inquiries, and the name William Forbis was suggested to him by Richard Clurman, a vice president of Time, Inc. Forbis was living what he describes as a life of "sportive idleness" after twenty years as a writer, senior editor, and correspondent for *Time* magazine.[23]

Cass Canfield rang Forbis early one morning in July 1970, at his home in Missoula, Montana, with a proposition: was he interested in finishing John Gunther's Australia book? Forbis had retired the previous year with a vague idea of writing books, and the Gunther proposal struck him as an ideal way to get started.

When Jane Gunther met him, she agreed that Forbis was the right man for the job, a deal was struck. Forbis, who was paid a flat fee for the job, went to Australia and New Zealand for a couple of weeks to get a feel for the country. He then began the nine-month task of sorting through John's research notes, and writing the rest of the book, which was published in 1972 as *John Gunther's Inside Australia*. It was not an easy task, even with Jane Gunther's help.

Says Forbis, "John Gunther was a man with great zest. As I read through his notes, I got the sense that he must have been aware that his time was running down. I got intimations of that. There were some days when he couldn't get to work, and that was painful. He had always loved life, always loved journalism.

"His books suited the times. But by the 1950s many people were getting their information from TV. Gunther was sensationally good in those first *Inside* books. Nobody before had ever done what he did. He had such a eye for detail, for snappy quotes, and good sum-ups. I think now that by the time *Inside Australia* was finished the 'inside' idea had run its course. It was a throwback to another time, a time when the world was a very different—and in some ways simpler—kind of place."[25]

AFTERWORD

If there are such people—and I firmly believe there are, John Gunther was a born reporter; one cannot think of him as anything else. I and my family should know. He became an intimate of our household because, as a boy scarcely out of high school, he feel in love with my sister, Helen, and was thereafter a fixture in the house—at least until he left Chicago in late 1924 to seek fame and fortune as a foreign correspondent. I believe he was unhappy at home, though he never said so. He had a passionate interest in current events, large and small, and a vivid way of talking of them, but more often he just soaked things up. My brother-in-law was interested in him, and once, after an evening during which I talked at length about some class uproar, Mitchell said, "Did you see how John listened to all that? Not a word was lost."

"But it hadn't anything to do with him!" I said.

Mitchell laughed and shook his head. "Everything has something to do with him," he replied. "He may never use this material, but it hasn't been wasted."

Not long afterward, John got what he had long wanted, a newspaper job abroad, and as the cliche has it, "he never looked back." He was a remarkable figure for his time, a sort of boy wonder. If Ken Cuthbertson is correct in saying that few people today recognize John's name—though considering the popularity of his books this is hard to believe—I suppose it is because a reporter is born to reflect the happenings of his age, his age and no other. Among his thirty-five books are seven novels, five biographies, and seven juvenile books, yet only once did John successfully depart from the subjects of politics and national movements, when tragedy struck him in a very personal way. His son died, and John wrote a book in his memory—*Death Be Not Proud.*

One other personal matter occurs to me: later, he and his second wife, Jane, adopted a child, who one day strolled into his nanny's bedroom and for the first time noticed a crucifix hanging on the wall.

"Get that man down off that stick!" he demanded.

"Son," said John, "people have been trying to do that for the past two thousand years."

John Gunther reported faithfully, intelligently, and with never-flagging enthusiasm. What more can one say in praise of a reporter?

Emily Hahn

Emily Hahn, a native of St. Louis, grew up in Chicago, Illinois. She is the sister of Helen Hahn, John Gunther's first love. Ms. Hahn is the author of more than fifty books, and has been a contributor to the New Yorker *magazine for forty years. She divides her time between homes in New York and England.*

NOTES

LEGEND

AR	Dr. Alexander Rafaeli, Jerusalem, Israel (papers since transferred to the Hebrew University of Jerusalem
D of J	Department of Justice, Washington, D.C.
HE	Dr. Henry Eisner, Philadelphia, Pa.
MvE	Mary von Euler (papers since transferred to Schlesinger Library, Radcliffe College, New York)
NL	Newberry Library, Chicago, Ill.
SD	Department of State, Washington, D.C.
U of C	Special Collections, The Regenstein Library, University of Chicago, Chicago, Ill.

NOTES

The initials "J.G." refer to John Gunther. Footnotes designating the U of C as a source, which are followed by an asterik (*), are from the unpublished papers of John Gunther, housed in the Department of Special Collections at the University of Chicago library and are cited by special permission. Other citations of material in the Gunther collection are from *John Gunther: Inside Journalism* by Jay Pridmore, a catalogue prepared for a 1990 exhibition of Gunther's papers at the University of Chicago. Author interviews designated with the word "from. . . ." were conducted by telephone. All others were conducted in person.

INTRODUCTION

1 Eric Sevareid, CBS Radio transcript, June 2, 1970 (cited hereafter as Sevareid transcript).

2 *New York Post*, June 3, 1970.

3 Jay Pridmore, *John Gunther: Inside Journalism* (U of Chicago, 1990), 33 (cited hereafter as *Inside Journalism*).

4 *New Yorker*, Aug. 23, 1947, 30.

5 *Time*, Apr. 14, 1958, 42.

6 Ibid.

7 *The New Yorker*, Aug. 23, 1947, 30.

8 *Time*, Apr. 14, 1958, 42.

9 *New Yorker*, Aug. 23, 1947, 30.

10 *New York Times*, May 30, 1970, p. 1.

11 Sevareid transcript, op. cit.

12 John Gunther, *A Fragment of Autobiography* (New York: Harper & Row, 1964), 5 (cited hereafter as *F of A*).

13 *Time*, Apr. 14, 1958, 42.

14 Julia Edwards, *The Women of the World: The Great Foreign Correspondents* (Houghton-Mifflin, 1988), 4 (cited hereafter as Edwards).

15 Vincent Sheean, *Personal History* (Modern Library, 1935), 4 (cited hereafter as Sheean).

16 *F of A*, op. cit., 19.

17 *New York Post*, May 26, 1939.

18 *Time*, Apr. 14, 1947, 47.

19 Ibid.

20 John Gunther, "Man Made God," in *This I Believe*, ed. Edward R. Murrow (New York: Simon & Schuster, 1954), 61 (cited hereafter as *This I Believe*).

21 *Time*, Apr. 14, 1947, 50.

22 John Gunther, *Procession* (New York Harper & Row, 1965), xii (cited hereafter as *Procession*).

23 *Inside Journalism*, op. cit., vii.

24 *Inside Journalism*, op. cit., 51.

CHAPTER 1

1 John Gunther, *Inside U.S.A.* (New York: Harper & Brothers, 1947), xvi (cited hereafter as *Inside U.S.A.*).

2 *New Yorker*, Aug. 23, 1947, 33.

3 Standard Certificate of Death, Cook County, Ill., Aug. 23, 1927.

4 The course of Eugene Gunther's career has been pieced together using information obtained from Chicago City Directories, as well as interviews with family members.

5 Author interview with Gretchen Corazzo, J.G.'s cousin, June 19, 1986, Chesterton, Ind.; also interview with Joseph Schoeninger, J.G.'s cousin, Sept. 22, 1986, from Dealfield, Wisc.

6 Author interview with Marco Zur, J.G.'s cousin, June 17, 1986, from Stratford, Conn.

7 Ibid.

8 John Gunther, "Autobiography in Brief," *Story*, May 1938, 89 (cited hereafter as Story).

9 Interview with Gretchen Corazzo, June 19, 1986; also interview with Jean Gunther, J.G.'s sister, Aug. 23, 1986, Holyoke, Mass.

10 Report of Birth, Cook County, Ill., Aug. 30, 1901.

CHAPTER 2

1 *Story*, op. cit., 89.

2 Cited in *Inside Journalism*, op. cit., 2.

3 Interview with Gretchen Corazzo, June 19, 1986; also Marco Zur interview, June 17, 1986.

4 Interview with Jean Gunther, Aug. 23, 1986.

5 Ibid.

6 *Story*, op. cit., 89.

7 Ibid, 90.

8 Cook County Board of Education School Records, 1911-1914.

9 *Story*, op. cit., 90.

10 Interview with Jean Gunther, Aug. 23, 1986.

11 Ibid. According to *Inside Journalism*, op. cit., John Gunther recalled that his family also spent some summer vacations at Ephraim in Door County, Wisc.

12 *Story*, op. cit., 91.

13 *Inside Journalism*, op. cit., 3.

CHAPTER 3

1 *Story*, op. cit., 91.

2 Robert H. Ferrell, *Woodrow Wilson & World War I: 1917-21* (New York: Harper & Row, 1985), 189. Finley Peter Dunne (1867-1936), a self-educated second-generation Irish-American, became city editor of the *Chicago Times* in 1888 at the age of twenty-one. Five years later, he began writing a satirical column narrated by a character named "Mr. Dooley." Once a week, Mr. Dooley polished his bar and commented to one of his regular customers, "I see be th' paapers Hinnissy . . ." Dunne's column, which skewered Washington politicians and deflated assorted egos, became a popular fixture for the next twenty-five years in the *Chicago Evening Post*, and a syndicate of newspapers.

3 Sheean, op. cit., 12.

4 Ibid, 3.

5 *Saturday Review*, Oct. 16, 1965, 87.

6 T. Aylesworth and V. Aylesworth, *Chicago: The Glamour Years (1919-41)* (New York: Gallery Books, 1986), 103.

7 Mark Schorer, *Sinclair Lewis: An American Life* (New York: McGraw-Hill, 1961).

8 Marion K. Sanders, *Dorothy Thompson: A Legend in Her Time* (Houghton-Mifflin, 1973), 112 (cited hereafter as *Dorothy Thompson: A Legend*).

9 *Story*, op. cit., 91. The essay was entitled, "James Branch Cabell: An Introduction," *Bookman*, November 1920, 200-06.

10 Author interview with Arvid C. Lunde, J.G.'s classmate, Mar. 18, 1936, from Chicago.

11 Author interview with Jean Brand (married name Bennedsen), J.G.'s classmate, Oct. 2, 1986, from Orinda, Calif.

12 *Story*, op. cit., 92.

13 "Review of Reviews," *Daily Maroon*, Oct. 7, 1921, 2.

14 "Literary Leaders," *Daily Maroon*, Oct. 7, 1921, 2.

15 *Smart Set*, April 1922, 62-77.

16 *Inside Journalism*, op. cit., 7.

17 Ibid, 7. Mencken and J.G. continued to correspond, however, comments which Mencken wrote in his diary suggest that he was privately scornful towards John. For example, on May 14, 1945, he wrote, "Gunther, in general is a third rater, but in [Inside Asia], at least, he did a really good job." Quoted in *The Diary of H.L. Mencken*, ed. Charles Fecher (New York: Knopf, 1989), 366.

18 *Cap & Gown*, University of Chicago yearbook, 1922, 500.

19 *Inside Journalism*, op. cit., 10.

CHAPTER 4

1 Paul Scott Mowrer, *The House of Europe* (Houghton-Mifflin, 1945), 72 (cited hereafter as *The House of Europe*).

2 *Story*, op. cit., 92.

3 Author interview with "Buddy" Lewis, former CDN crime reporter, Oct. 5, 1986, from Chicago. The scene in the CDN newsroom is also described in Ben Hecht's novel, *Erik Dorn* (Putnam, 1921), ch. 3.

4 Ben Hecht, *A Child of the Century* (New York: Simon & Schuster, 1954), 250 (cited hereafter as *A Child of the Century*).

5 Smith outlined his theories of journalism in a book entitled, *It's the Way It's Written* (Mariano, 1940). This was a collection of three lectures which Smith had delivered years earlier to Medill School of Journalism at Northwestern University in Chicago. The details of Smith's life and newspaper career are set out in his memoir, *Deadlines* (Covici-McGee, 1923).

6 Harry Hansen, *Midwest Portraits* (Orlando, Fla.: Harcourt, Brace & Co., 1923), 10.

7 Hecht described his early newspaper career in Chicago in two books, *A Child of the Century*, op. cit., and *Gaily, Gaily* (Doubleday, 1965).

8 *Inside Journalism*, op. cit., 21.

CHAPTER 5

1 Author interview with Helen Hahn (married name Smith), J.G.'s college sweetheart, Dec. 15, 1986, from New York.

2 Ibid.

3 F. Scott Fitzgerald, "Echoes of the Jazz Age," *Scribner's Magazine*, November 1931.

4 *New Yorker*, Aug. 23, 1947, 35.

5 This anecdote is related in *Story*, op. cit., 92.

6 John Gunther, "The Return of Joe Vesley," *Chicago Daily News*, Dec. 27, 1923.

7 *Story*, op. cit., 93.

8 Interview with Gretchen Corazzo, June 19, 1986.

9 *New York Times Book Review*, Oct. 26, 1941, 28.

10 Author interview with Leonora Hornblow, J.G.'s friend, May 29, 1987, in New York.

11 Interview with Helen Hahn, Dec. 26, 1986, in New York.

12 *New York Times*, May 30, 1970.

13 Author interview with Emily Hahn (Boxer), Gunther friend, Mar. 14, 1987, from New York.

14 "The Reporters Who Travel with Presidents and Princes," *Reader's Digest*, June 1927.

15 Author interview with William L. Shirer, Gunther friend, Nov. 10, 1986, at Lenox, Mass.

16 This comment, one that was said about John by newspaper friends in good-natured jest, appeared in *The Lost City*, op. cit., 5. John used it in describing the Mason Jarrett character. The self-effacing quip was typical of J.G.'s sense of humor.

17 Interview with Helen Hahn, Dec. 26, 1986.

18 Ibid.

19 Emily Hahn, *Times & Places* (New York: Crowell Co., 1970), 37.

20 John Gunther, *The Red Pavilion* (New York: Harper & Bros., 1926) (cited hereafter as *The Red Pavilion*).

21 This exchange was recorded in John's novel *The Red Pavilion*. According to Helen Hahn the dialogue was a verbatim account of the conversation that day. Interview with Helen Hahn, Dec. 26, 1986, in New York.

22 *Story*, op. cit., 93.

23 Malcolm Cowley, *Exile's Return* (New York: Norton, 1934).

24 *Chicago Daily News*, May 8-9, 1971, 6.

CHAPTER 6

1 J.G. to Helen Hahn, Oct. 24, 1924, U of C.*

2 Ibid.

3 *Chicago Daily News*, Oct. 26, 1924, 2.

4 J.G. to Helen Hahn, Oct. 24, 1924, U of C.*

5 Ibid.

6 George V to Prince of Wales, quoted in *The Windsor Story* by J. Bryan III and Charles Murphy (New York: Morrow & Co., 1979), 61.

7 Ibid, 179.

8 J.G. to Helen Hahn, Oct. 26, 1924, U of C.*

9 *Chicago Daily News*, Nov. 1, 1924, 2.

10 J.G. to Helen Hahn, Oct. 26, 1924, U of C.*

11 *New York Times Book Review*, op. cit., 2.

12 J.G. to Helen Hahn, Nov. 1, 1924, U of C.*

13 *Newsweek*, June 2, 1952, 104.

14 Paul Scott Mowrer, *The House of Europe* (Boston: Houghton Mifflin, 1945), 440.

15 J.G. to Helen Hahn, Nov. 2, 1924, U of C.*

CHAPTER 7

1 J.G. to Helen Hahn, Nov. 6, 1924, U of C.*

2 Raymond Gram Swing, *Good Evening* (Orlando, Fla.: Harcourt, Brace & World, 1964), 154.

3 "The Blue Eyed Tornado" was the title of a tribute to Dorothy Thompson that John wrote for the *New York Herald-Tribune*, Jan. 13, 1935.

4 *Dorothy Thompson: A Legend*, op. cit., 65.

5 Victoria Glendinning, *Rebecca West: A Life* (Weidenfeld & Nicolson, 1987), 96 (cited hereafter as *Rebecca West: A Life*)

6 J.G. to Helen Hahn, Dec. 21, 1924, U of C.*

7 *Rebecca West: A Life*, op. cit., 102.

8 J.G. to Helen Hahn, Nov. 16, 1924, U of C.*

9 J.G. to Helen Hahn, Nov. 28, 1924, U of C.*

10 J.G. to Helen Hahn, Jan. 30, 1925, U of C.*

11 J.G. to Helen Hahn, Jan. 23, 1925, U of C.*

12 J.G. to Helen Hahn, Nov. 17, 1924, U of C.*

13 *The House of Europe*, op. cit., 533.

14 J.G. to Helen Hahn, Nov. 28, 1924, U of C.*

15 J.G. to Helen Hahn, Jan. 10, 1925, U of C.*

16 J.G. to Helen Hahn, Mar. 3, 1925, U of C.*

17 J.G. to Helen Hahn, Mar. 18, 1925, U of C.*

18 J.G. to Helen Hahn, Mar. 24, 1925, U of C.*

19 J.G. to Helen Hahn, Mar. 24, 1925, U of C.*

20 J.G. to Helen Hahn, Mar. 27, 1925, U of C.*

CHAPTER 8

1 J.G. to Helen Hahn, Mar. 29, 1925, U of C.*

2 J.G. to Helen Hahn, Mar. 30, 1925, U of C.*

3 J.G. to Helen Hahn, Apr. 16, 1925, U of C.*

4 As reported in an undated clipping from *Chicago Tribune*, MvE. Included among the papers of Frances Gunther were stacks of newspaper clippings which she had saved over the years. Both John and Frances were habitual newspaper "clippers"—most correspondents of the day shared this habit. John maintained extensive clippings files, which he used as background in his own journalism. Frances, who for many years helped maintain John's files, was never as diligent about recording sources and dates of

items in her own library. This helps to explain the difficulties she experienced in attempting to write.

5 "Menelaus and Helen" in *Collected Poems of Rupert Brooke* (Sidgwick & Jackson, 1918), 92.

6 J.G. to Helen Hahn, June 13, 1925, U of C.*

7 J.G. to Helen Hahn, May 23, 1925, U of C.*

8 J.G. to Helen Hahn, May 29, 1925, U of C.*

9 J.G. to Helen Hahn, June 7, 1925, U of C.*

10 Undated clipping from the *New York Post*, circa 1945, MvE.

11 Ian Norrie, *Publishing & Bookselling*, vol. 2 (Cape, 1974).

12 *Saturday Review*, 1924, 577.

13 *New York Times*, Jan. 3, 1977, 24.

14 Interview with Helen Hahn, Dec. 26, 1986.

CHAPTER 9

1 *F of A*, op. cit., 5.

2 J.G. to Charles Dennis, June 11, 1926, NL.

3 Undated press clipping in Frances Gunther's files, circa 1940.

4 *Chicago Daily News*, June 14, 1926.

5 J.G. to Charles Dennis, June 11, 1926, NL.

6 *Editor & Publisher*, Feb. 5, 1927.

7 *Saturday Review*, July 17, 1926, 74.

8 James Weber Linn review in *Chicago Daily News*, July 1926.

9 *Spectator*, June 10, 1926.

10 *New York Times*, Jan. 30, 1927, 8.

11 *The Bohemian*, May 1927.

12 Author interview with Emily and Helen Hahn, Dec. 15, 1986, from New York.

13 Charles Dennis to J.G., July 22, 1926, NL.

14 Interview with Helen Hahn, Dec. 26, 1986.

CHAPTER 10

1 *New York Times*, Apr. 7, 1964; Academic records of Barnard College.

2 Author interview with Judith de Mille Donelan, Frances Gunther's niece, March 23, 1987, from Easton, Md.

3 *The Review*, Ball High School yearbook, June 1915; Ball High School Academic records.

4 Barnard College records.

5 *New York Times*, Feb. 11, 1925, VII-2; *New York Times*, Sept. 27, 1925, VII-2.

6 Interview with Helen Hahn, Dec. 26, 1986.

7 Ibid.

8 Interview with Leonora Hornblow, May 26, 1986.

9 Interview with Helen Hahn, Dec. 26, 1986.

10 Atti di Matrimomonio #08824 (Marriage Certificate), Rome, Italy, Mar. 16, 1927.

11 *Chicago Daily News*, March 17, 1927.

12 Interview with Helen Hahn, Dec. 26, 1986.

CHAPTER 11

1 J.G. to Dorothy Thompson, quoted in *A Legend*, op. cit., 146.

2 Author interview with William Shirer, Nov. 10, 1986.

3 *New York Times*, Mar. 17, 1975, 32.

4 Ibid.

5 "London on Edge," *Atlantic*, April 1937, 395-96.

6 Interview with William Shirer, Nov. 10, 1986.

7 John Gunther, "A Macedonian Robin Hood," *North American Review*, October 1929, 417-21.

8 *Chicago Daily News*, Jan. 28, 1928.

9 Cable from George Grier, U.S. Embassy in Constantinople, to secretary of state, Jan. 24, 1928.

10 Author interview with George Seldes, retired foreign correspondent, Jan. 20, 1989, from Hartland-4-Corners, Vt.

11 *F of A*, op. cit., 5.

12 *Chicago Daily News*, Aug. 20, 1928, 2.

13 *Chicago Daily News*, Aug. 23, 1928, 2.

14 Ibid.

15 Ibid.

16 Undated *Chicago Daily News* clipping.

17 Junius Wood, "Russia of the Hour," *National Geographic*, November 1926, 537.

18 Rebecca West to J.G., 1928, quoted in *Rebecca West: A Life*, op. cit., 120.

19 Report of Birth, American Consulate, Paris, France, Sept. 25, 1928.

CHAPTER 12

1 *Chicago Daily News*, Dec. 13, 1928.

2 Interview with Marco Zur, June 17, 1986.

3 *Chicago Daily News*, Jan. 18, 1929.

4 *Chicago Daily News*, Jan. 28, 1929.

5 Dr. L.E. Holt, Johns Hopkins Hospital, to Frances Gunther, June 7, 1929, MvE.

6 *The Lost City*, op. cit., 24.

7 Dr. Julius A. Miller to Frances Gunther, Feb. 28, 1929, MvE.

8 Interview with Gretchen Corazzo, June 19, 1986.

9 Author interview with John Gershgorn, friend of Bernie Fineman, June 3, 1987, from Los Angeles.

10 *Chicago Daily News*, Jan. 4, 1930.

11 *Chicago Daily News*, July 20, 1929.

12 John Gunther, "The High Cost of Hoodlums," *Harper's*, October 1929, 529.

13 *Death Be Not Proud*, op. cit., 3.

CHAPTER 13

1 *Inside Journalism*, op. cit., 12. According to Pridmore, pay for *CDN* foreign correspondents in the 1930s was about $6,500, plus a $3,000 annual expense account. While this seems like a generous amount during the Great Depression, it did not go far. The cost of living in many European capitals was high, and out of the $3,000 expense money, a correspondent was expected to meet all of the costs involved in travel, accommodation, eating, and maintaining a network of paid informants in the countries which were part of his/her beat.

2 *The Lost City*, op. cit., 68.

3 Interview with William L. Shirer, Nov. 10, 1986.

4 *The Lost City*, op. cit., 394.

5 *Story*, op. cit., 94.

6 Interview with William L. Shirer, Nov. 10, 1986.

7 *The Spectator*, Feb. 6, 1932, 230.

8 *Times of London*, Mar. 31, 1932, 230.

9 Interview with William Shirer, Nov. 10, 1986.

10 Marcel Fodor, *South of Hitler* (Allen & Unwin Ltd., 1937), 3.

11 John Gunther, "Trotsky at Elba," *Harper's*, April 1933, 589.

12 *The Lost City*, op. cit., 13.

13 J.G.'s *Daily News* colleague A.R. Decker, quoted in *Dorothy Thompson: A Legend*, op. cit., 94.

14 *F of A*, op. cit., 6.

15 *Inside Journalism*, op. cit., 21.

16 *F of A*, op. cit., 5.

17 Ibid.

18 John Gunther, "Funneling the European News," *Harper's*, April 1930, 636.

19 Ibid.

20 Author interview with George Seldes, Jan. 20, 1989.

21 *Esquire*, January-June 1935.

22 Interview with William Shirer, Nov. 10, 1986.

23 Vincent Sheean, *Dorothy & Red* (Boston: Houghton-Mifflin, 1963), 212.

24 Author interview with William Shirer, Nov. 10, 1986.

CHAPTER 14

1 Interview with William Shirer, Nov. 10, 1986.

2 *New York Post*, Apr. 14, 1947.

3 *The Lost City*, op. cit., 56.

4 John Gunther, "Dateline Vienna," *Harper's*, July 1935, 201.

5 George Gedye. Born in Cleavedon, Somerset, U.K., on May 27, 1890, George Gedye was a graduate of the U of London. He began a distinguished journalism career in 1922, and during the course of his forty-eight years as a newsman made a name for himself with his hobby: "irritating the conventional." Gedye was one of the more col-

orful members of Vienna's foreign press corps. Marcel Fodor's son Denis recalls Gedye, who in the early 1930s was the Vienna correspondent for the *Times of London*, as having a schnauzer that launched into ferocious fits of barking and growling at the command of "Hitler!"

6 Author interview with Denis Fodor, Marcel Fodor's son, Dec. 1, 1986, from Munich, Germany.

7 Author interview with Sen. William Fullbright, June 6, 1987, from Washington, D.C.

8 Ibid.

9 Author interview with Denis Fodor, Dec. 1, 1986.

10 "Hitler," *Harper's*, January 1936, 59.

11 Author interview with Denis Fodor, Dec. 1, 1986.

12 Whit Burnett, *The Literary Life & the Hell with It* (New York: Harper & Brothers, 1939), 269 (cited hereafter as *The Literary Life & the Hell with It*).

CHAPTER 15

1 Author interview with Leonora Hornblow, July 12, 1991.

2 Author interview with William Shirer, Nov. 10, 1986.

3 Author interview with Leonora Hornblow, May 29, 1987.

4 Author interview with William Shirer, Nov. 10, 1986.

5 Author interview with Denis Fodor, Dec. 1, 1986.

6 Author interview with William Shirer, Nov. 10, 1986.

7 Author interview with Luise Rainer, Feb. 2, 1987, from Vico Morcote, Switzerland.

8 Ibid.

9 Author interview with William Shirer, Nov. 10, 1986.

10 John Gunther, "Has Hitler a Mother Complex?" *Vanity Fair*, October 1934. In this article John Gunther outlined Stekel's theory about the nature of dictatorship.

CHAPTER 16

1 Arthur M. Schlesinger, Jr., *The Crisis of the Old Order: 1919-33* (Boston: Houghton-Mifflin, 1957), ch. 24.

2 Sinclair Lewis, *It Can't Happen Here* (P.F. Collier, 1935).

3 Raymond Gram Swing, *Forerunners of American Fascism*, (J. Messner, 1935).

4 Ezra Pound, *Jefferson and/or Mussolini* (Liveright, 1935), 12.

5 *Inside U.S.A.*, op. cit., xv.

6 Charles Dennis to J.G., Aug. 3, 1926, NL.

7 Charles Dennis to J.G., Aug. 16, 1926, NL.

8 Charles Dennis to J.G., Nov. 29, 1926, NL.

9 John Gunther, "Policy by Murder: The Story of the Killing of Dollfuss," *Harper's*, November 1934.

CHAPTER 17

1 *Saturday Review of Literature*, Sept. 5, 1931, 100. When the identities of the authors of *Washington Merry-Go-Round* became known, both Drew Pearson and Robert S. Allen lost their jobs. As a result, in 1932, they launched a syndicated newspaper column entitled, "Washington Merry-Go-Round." The column proved to be popular, and over the ten years that Allen and Pearson did the column together it incurred the wrath of many politicians, and earned a well-deserved reputation for muckraking.

2 *New Republic*, Aug. 12, 1931, 346.

3 *F of A*, op. cit., 6.

4 Transcript of Cass Canfield interview with Columbia University Oral History Project, 1966, 206 (cited hereafter as Canfield transcript).

5 Ibid.

6 *Story*, op. cit., 95.

7 H.R. Knickerbocker won a Pulitzer Prize in 1931 for his coverage of the Moscow show trials. Knickerbocker covered many important news stories, and authored several books. His illustrious career was cut short on July 12, 1949, when the Dutch airliner on which he and forty-five other persons were traveling crashed in Indonesia. He was just fifty-five at the time of his death.

8 Cass Canfield, *Up & Down & Around* (Harper's Magazine Press, 1971), 123 (cited hereafter as *Up & Down & Around*).

9 *F of A*, op. cit., 7.

10 Canfield transcript, op. cit., 208.

11 Author interview with Cass Canfield, Jr., Mar. 27, 1987, in New York City.

12 "Cass Canfield, a Titan of Publishing is Dead at 88," *New York Times*, Aug. 28, 1986.

13 *Up & Down & Around*, op. cit., 123.

14 *F of A*, op. cit., 8.

15 Ibid, 8.

16 *The Lost City*, op. cit., 580.

CHAPTER 18

1 *F of A*, op. cit., 8.

2 John Gunther, "Inside England," *Atlantic*, April 1937, 272 (cited hereafter as "Inside England"). This was the second installment of John's London diaries, which were published in *Atlantic* magazine after he abandoned plans to turn them into a book. A portion of the diary manuscript remains unpublished (cited hereafter as J.G.'s London Diary). All of this material now is part of the Gunther Collection at the University of Chicago library.

3 *F of A*, op. cit., 9.

4 "Inside England," op. cit., 272.

5 *F of A*, op. cit., 10.

6 Author interview with Denis Fodor, Dec. 1, 1986.

7 Author interview with George Seldes, Nov. 1, 1987, at Hartland-4-Corners, Vt.

8 Author interview with Kenneth Knickerbocker, Mar. 22, 1987, from Knoxville, Tenn.

9 J.G. to Cass Canfield, March 2, 1936, U of C.*

10 John Gunther, *Inside Europe* (New York: Harper & Brothers, 1936), ix (cited hereafter as *Inside Europe*). This was the first of seven editions of *Inside Europe*. All totaled, the book went through ninety-five printings in the U.S. and foreign editions.

11 *F of A*, op. cit., 12-13.

12 "Inside England," op. cit., 266.

13 *F of A*, op. cit., 12.

14 Ibid.

CHAPTER 19

1 John Gunther, "London on Edge," *Atlantic*, April 1937, 389. This was the first installment of John's London diaries. See note 2, ch. 18 (cited hereafter as "London on Edge").

2 Ibid, 393.

3 J.G.'s London Diary (unpublished portion), 102, U of C.*

4 *London Evening Standard*, Apr. 8, 1936.

5 *The Times of London*, July 30, 1945, 6.

6 *New York Times*, July 29, 1945, 39.

7 "Inside England," op. cit., 267.

8 J.G. to Eugene Saxton, Dec. 7, 1936, U of C.*

9 "Inside England," op. cit., 276.

10 Ibid.

11 Ibid.

12 *F of A*, op. cit., 16.

13 *Chicago Daily News*, Apr. 17, 1936.

14 "London on Edge," op. cit., 385.

15 J.G. to Bernice Baumgarten, May 29, 1936, U of C.*

16 J.G.'s London Diary, July 20, 1936, U of C.*

17 Ibid, July 24, 1936, U of C.*

18 Ibid, Aug. 18, 1936, U of C.*

19 J.G. to Frances Gunther, Sept. 1, 1936, MvE.

20 J.G.'s London Diary, Aug. 24, 1936, U of C.*

21 Ibid, Sept. 4, 1936, U of C.*

22 Ibid.

CHAPTER 20

1 *New York World-Telegram*, Oct. 3, 1936.

2 As quoted in the *New Yorker*, Aug. 23, 1947, 36.

3 *The Nation*, Mar. 4, 1936, 285.

4 *New York Herald-Tribune*, Feb. 8, 1936, 9.

5 *The Literary Life & the Hell with It*, op. cit., 144.

6 *F of A*, op. cit., 22.

7 J.G. to Cass Canfield, Sept. 27, 1937, U of C.*

8 J.G. to Hamish Hamilton, Sept. 27, 1937, U of C.*

9 *F of A*, op. cit., 26.

10 *The Sphinx*, Sept. 13, 1937; *Egyptian Mail*, Sept. 13, 1937.

11 Frances Gunther to Johnny Gunther, Nov. 18, 1937, MvE.

12 Frances Gunther to Johnny Gunther, Nov. 18, 1937, MvE

13 John Gunther, *Inside Asia* (New York: Harper & Brothers, 1939), 500 (cited hereafter as *Inside Asia*).

14 Ibid.

15 Ibid, 499.

16 John Gunther, "The Realities of Zionism," *Harper's*, June 1930, 202.

17 Author interview with Dr. Alexander Rafaeli, Frances Gunther's executor, Oct. 25, 1991, from Jerusalem, Israel.

18 "Message to Islam." Some of Frances Gunther's papers were left with Mary von Euler (nee Sanders) of Washington, D.C., a friend of Johnny's with whom Frances developed a warm friendship. These papers have subsequently been donated to the Schlesigner Library, Radcliffe College. The balance of Frances' personal papers were left with Dr. Alexander Rafaeli, a former member of the Jewish underground movement, the Irgun. Rafaeli became a close personal friend of Frances' during the last fifteen years of her life, which were spent in Israel. He donated the papers in his possession to the Hebrew University of Jerusalem.

CHAPTER 21

1 J.G. to Cass Canfield, Dec. 14, 1937, U of C.*

2 *Inside Asia*, op. cit., 463.

3 Ibid, 465.

4 Frances Gunther to Johnny Gunther, Dec. 18, 1937, MvE.

5 Frances Gunther to Johnny Gunther, Dec. 25, 1937, MvE.

6 *New York Post*, June 2, 1939.

7 Frances Gunther to Johnny Gunther, Jan. 5, 1938, MvE.

8 Cass Canfield to J.G., Jan. 10, 1938, U of C.*

9 Cass Canfield to J.G., Jan. 13, 1938, U of C.*

10 Hamish Hamilton to J.G., Jan. 18, 1938, U of C.*

11 J.G. to Cass Canfield, Jan. 27, 1938, U of C.*

12 Author interview with Leonora Hornblow, May 29, 1987.

13 *Inside Asia*, op. cit., 409.

14 B.N. Pandy, *Nehru* (New York: Macmillan, 1976), 224.

15 *Inside Asia*, op. cit., 344.

16 *New York Post*, Jan. 31, 1948.

17 *Inside Asia*, op. cit., 345.

18 J.G. to Cass Canfield, Jan. 27, 1938, U of C.*

19 Frances Gunther to Johnny Gunther, Feb. 6, 1938, MvE.

20 Hamish Hamilton to J.G., Feb. 15, 1938, U of C.*

21 J.G. to Hamish Hamilton, Feb. 21, 1938, U of C.*

22 Ibid.

23 *Manila Tribune*, Mar. 9, 1938.

24 *Inside Asia*, op. cit., 287.

25 *F of A*, op. cit., 34.

26 Author interview with Emily Hahn, Dec. 15, 1986, from New York.

27 *New York Times*, Apr. 7, 1938.

28 Frances Gunther to Nehru, Apr. 14, 1938, MvE.

29 Ibid.

30 Frances Gunther to Johnny Gunther, Apr. 29, 1938, MvE.

31 *Inside Asia*, op. cit., 29.

32 Ibid, 572.

CHAPTER 22

1 Nathan Miller, *FDR: An Intimate History* (New York: Doubleday, 1983), 418.

2 J. Blum, et al., *The National Experience (Part II)* (Orlando, Fla.: Harcourt, Brace & Janovich, 1973), 664.

3 *Time*, June 21, 1938.

4 *The Literary Life & the Hell with It*, op. cit., 177.

5 *Inside Journalism*, op. cit., 27.

6 J.G. to Cass Canfield, Jan. 11, 1939, U of C.*

7 An excellent source of information on DeWitt and Lila Wallace and the growth of *Reader's Digest* is Charles Ferguson, "Unforgettable DeWitt Wallace," *Reader's Digest*, February 1988, 77-147.

8 J.G. to Hamish Hamilton, Mar. 7, 1939, U of C.*

9 *New York Post*, Apr. 14, 1939.

10 *New York Post*, May 26, 1939.

11 *Miami Herald*, May 21, 1939.

12 *New Yorker*, June 10, 1939.

13 *New York Times Book Review*, June 11, 1939, 1.

14 *Time*, June 12, 1939.

15 John Gunther, *The High Cost of Hitler* (Hamish Hamilton, 1939), 9 (cited hereafter as *High Cost of Hitler*).

16 *New York Herald Tribune*, (Paris) July 2, 1939.

17 J.G. to Frances Gunther, July 9, 1939, MvE.

18 *New York Post*, Oct. 10, 1939.

19 *High Cost of Hitler*, op. cit., "Broadcast from Geneva, July 23, 1939," 29.

20 Ibid, "Broadcast from Warsaw, Aug. 13, 1939," 43.

21 J.G. to Frances Gunther, Aug. 8, 1939, MvE.

22 *High Cost of Hitler*, op. cit., "Broadcast from London, Sept. 3, 1939," 121.

23 Ibid, "Broadcast from London, Aug. 28, 1939," 63.

24 Ibid, "Broadcast from London, Sept. 1, 1939," 99.

25 Ibid, "Broadcast from London, Sept. 3, 1939," 121.

26 *Procession*, op. cit., 138.

27 *New York Post*, Sept. 19, 1939.

CHAPTER 23

1 Nehru to Frances Gunther, Nov. 16, 1939, AR.

2 The manuscript entitled *Empire* was found among Frances Gunther's papers when she died. It consists of several hundred typewritten pages, plus accompanying file folders filled with newspaper clippings and some handwritten notes.

3 Nehru to Frances Gunther, Aug. 3, 1939, AR.

4 Frances Gunther to Nehru, Aug. 28, 1939, AR.

5 Author interview with Leonora Hornblow, May 29, 1987.

6 Author interview with Kenneth Knickerbocker, Mar. 22, 1987.

7 Ibid.

8 Author interview with Leonora Hornblow, May 29, 1987.

9 John Gunther, *The Indian Sign* (New York: Harper & Row, 1970), 86 (cited hereafter as *The Indian Sign*).

10 Interview with William Shirer, Nov. 10, 1986.

11 Author interview with Leonora Hornblow, May 29, 1987.

12 J.G. to Hamish Hamilton, July 25, 1939, U of C.*

13 J.G. to Cass Canfield, Sept. 9, 1939, U of C.*

14 *New York Times*, Nov. 14, 1939, 21.

CHAPTER 24

1 Author interview with Nancy Barnett, Gunther's secretary, May 24, 1986, at Great Barrington, Mass.

2 *F of A*, op. cit., 36.

3 Ibid.

4 J.G. to Frances Gunther, Sept. 28, 1940, MvE.

5 *New York Times*, Oct. 6, 1940, 33.

6 *F of A*, op. cit., 38.

7 *The Bronx Home News*, Apr. 10, 1947.

8 John Gunther, *Inside Latin America* (New York: Harper & Brothers, 1941), 6 (cited hereafter as *Inside Latin America*).

9 *Time*, Apr. 14, 1958, 42.

10 *Inside Latin America*, op. cit., 30.

11 *Procession*, op. cit., 263.

12 John Gunther, *Roosevelt in Retrospect: A Profile in History* (New York: Harper & Brothers, 1950), 24.

13 Ibid.

CHAPTER 25

1 J.G. to Frances Gunther, Apr. 12, 1941, MvE.

2 Ibid.

3 J.G. to Frances Gunther, May 1941, MvE.

4 *F of A*, op. cit., 37.

5 W.G. Bannister, special agent to J.E. Hoover, FBI director, Apr. 23, 1942, D of J.

6 *Catholic World*, December 1941, 368.

7 J.G. to Eleanor Roosevelt, Jan. 14, 1942, U of C.*

8 *F of A*, op. cit., 39.

9 Author interview with Leonora Hornblow, May 29, 1987.

10 Frances Gunther to Nehru, Spring 1940, AR.

11 Nehru to Frances Gunther, Aug. 27, 1941, AR.

12 Frances Gunther to J.G., October 1941, AR.

13 Ibid.

CHAPTER 26

1 Winston Churchill, *Their Finest Hour* (Boston: Houghton-Mifflin, 1949), 307.

2 *New York Times Book Review*, Oct. 26, 1941, 2.

3 *Inside Journalism*, op. cit., 31. This figure is presumably for the 1940 taxation year.

4 Author interview with Helen Hahn, Dec. 26, 1986.

5 Author interview with Nancy Barnett, May 24, 1986.

6 Frances Gunther to Nehru, Nov. 14, 1942, AR.

7 *Inside Journalism*, op. cit., 33.

8 *New York Times*, Dec. 24, 1941.

CHAPTER 27

1 Jan Morris, *Manhattan '45* (Oxford Univ. Press, 1987), 138.

2 A full account of the Baker incident is given in *The Jazz Cleopatra: Josephine Baker in Her Time* by Phyllis Rose (New York: Doubleday, 1989), 216-31.

3 *New York Post*, Oct. 12, 1939.

4 *New York Post*, Oct. 14, 1944.

5 *Inside Journalism*, op. cit., 33.

6 Ibid.

7 Bennett Cerf, *At Random: The Reminiscences of Bennett*

Cerf (New York: Random House, 1977), 42.

8 *Inside Journalism*, op. cit., 32.

9 Clifton Fadiman, ed., *The Little, Brown Books of Anecdotes* (Boston: Little, Brown & Co., 1985), 259.

10 *Inside Journalism*, op. cit., 34.

11 Ibid.

12 Ibid, 32.

13 Ibid.

CHAPTER 28

1 John Gunther, *D-Day* (New York: Harper & Brothers, 1941) 2 (cited hereafter as *D-Day*).

2 Ibid, 5.

3 Ibid, 10.

4 Ibid, 12.

5 Ibid.

6 Ibid, 18.

7 Ibid, 23.

8 Ibid, 42.

9 Ibid, 47.

10 Ibid, 52.

11 Ibid, 48.

12 Ibid, 50.

13 Ibid, 53.

14 Ibid, 55.

15 Ibid, 56.

16 Ibid, 57.

17 Ibid, 61.

18 Ibid, 71.

19 John Gunther, *Eisenhower* (New York: Harper & Brothers, 1952), 157 (cited hereafter as *Eisenhower*).

20 *D-Day*, op. cit., 87.

21 Ibid, 90.

22 Ibid, 92.

23 Ibid.

24 Ibid, 108.

25 Ibid, 124.

26 Ibid, 168.

27 Ibid, 276.

CHAPTER 29

1 Author interview with Leonora Hornblow, May 29, 1987.

2 Author interview with Nancy Barnett, May 24, 1986.

3 *New York Times*, Nov. 23, 1943, 31.

4 Frances Gunther to Nehru, Sept. 19, 1943, AR.

5 Author interview with Nancy Barnett, May 24, 1986.

6 Frances Gunther, *Revolution in India* (Washington, D.C.: Island Press, 1944), Frances dedicated her only book to John Gunther. It was a softcover book that was printed on the sort of pulpy stock used for many books when wartime rationing was in effect. Although the book went into a second printing, it is no longer generally available. Given the poor quality of the paper and binding, it seems unlikely that many copies have survived.

7 Nehru to Frances Gunther, May 4, 1946, AR.

8 *Chicago Daily News*, Dec. 12, 1940.

9 Undated newspaper clipping regarding Virginia Safford, a Minneapolis newspaper columnist who Frances had ap-

parently told she was writing a book to be called "Inside Gunther," MvE.

10 "Earth" by Frances Gunther (unpublished poem found among Frances Gunther's papers when she died), MvE.

11 Dorothy Thompson to Frances Gunther, undated note in Frances Gunther's papers, circa 1952, MvE.

12 *F of A*, op. cit., 43.

13 As quoted in *Inside Journalism*, op. cit., 31, U of C.*

14 Author interview with Leonora Hornblow, July 25, 1988, from New York.

15 Author interview with William Shirer, Nov. 10, 1986.

16 *The Indian Sign*, op. cit., 121.

17 Author interview with Leonora Hornblow, July 12, 1991, from New York.

18 *The Indian Sign*, op. cit., 152.

19 Ibid, 143.

20 Interview with Leonora Hornblow, July 25, 1988.

21 Interview with Kenneth Knickerbocker, Mar. 22, 1987.

22 Author interview with Leonora Hornblow, June 19, 1991, from New York.

23 Author interview with Leonora Hornblow, July 12, 1991.

24 *The Indian Sign*, op. cit., 144.

25 Author interview with Dorothy Olding, H. Ober & Associates.

26 Cass Canfield to J.G., Feb. 21, 1944, U of C.*

27 *Chicago Daily News*, Mar. 14, 1944.

28 J.G. to Hamish Hamilton, July 25, 1944, U of C.*

29 Thomas Mann to J.G., Nov. 28, 1944, U of C.*

30 Somerset Maugham to J.G., Dec. 10, 1944, U of C.*

31 *New York Times*, Feb. 4, 1945, 7.

32 *New York Herald Tribune*, Dec. 17, 1945.

33 John Gunther, *Inside U.S.A.* (New York: Harper & Brothers, 1947), ix (cited hereafter as *Inside U.S.A.*).

34 J.G. to Cass Canfield, Oct. 16, 1941, U of C.*

35 Eugene Saxton to J.G., Aug. 7, 1942, U of C.*

36 *Procession*, op. cit., 264.

37 J.G. to Hamish Hamilton, July 25, 1944, U of C.*

38 Ibid.

39 *Inside Journalism*, op. cit., 37.

40 Ibid.

41 Ibid.

42 J.G. to Hamish Hamilton, July 25, 1944, U of C.*

43 Author interview with Leonora Hornblow, July 12, 1991, from New York.

44 *New York Daily News*, Dec. 7, 1944.

45 Author interview with Leonora Hornblow, July 25, 1988.

CHAPTER 30

1 *F of A*, op. cit., 43.

2 J.G. to Hamish Hamilton, July 25, 1944, U of C.*

3 *Inside U.S.A.*, op. cit., xiii.

4 Ibid, ix.

5 *F of A*, 48.

6 *This I Believe*, op. cit., 61.

7 J.G. to Carl Brandt, Aug. 14, 1945, U of C.*

8 *F of A*, op. cit., 49.

9 Ibid, 50.

10 Ibid, 51.

11 Ibid, 52.

12 Ibid, 53.

13 J.G. to Cass Canfield, July 14, 1945, U of C.*

14 J.G. to Frances Gunther, Apr. 30, 1945, MvE.

15 Ibid.

16 J.G. to Carl Brandt, Aug. 14, 1945, U of C.*

17 Cass Canfield to J.G., Nov. 14, 1945, U of C.*

18 Cass Canfield to J.G., Nov. 27, 1945, U of C.*

19 *F of A*, op. cit., 49.

20 Ibid, 54.

21 Ibid, 55.

CHAPTER 31

1 F. Boyden, Deerfield Academy, to Frances Gunther, July 14, 1945, U of C.*

2 Ibid, Jan. 15, 1946, U of C.*

3 John Gunther, *Death Be Not Proud* (New York: Harper & Brothers, 1949), 11 (cited hereafter as *Death Be Not Proud*). This is the only book that John Gunther wrote that is still in print today.

4 Author interview with Dr. Henry Eisner, Johnny Gunther's friend, Sept. 17, 1991, from Philadelphia, Pa.

5 Author interview with Bertha Brenner, friend of Frances Gunther, Sept. 21, 1991, from Layhill, Md.

6 Dick Cutler, Treetops counsellor, to Frances Gunther, Sept. 14, 1938, U of C.*

7 Mrs. D. Haskelle, Treetops counsellor, to Frances Gunther, Oct. 5, 1940, U of C.*

8 *Death Be Not Proud*, op. cit., 17.

9 Ibid, 810.

10 Ibid, 35.

11 Ibid, 42.

12 Johnny Gunther's diary, May 31, 1946, MvE.

13 *Death Be Not Proud*, op. cit., 107.

14 Author interview with Bertha Brenner, Sept. 21, 1991.

15 Author interview with Henry Eisner, Sept. 17, 1991.

16 *Death Be Not Proud*, op. cit., 236.

17 Author interview with Henry Eisner, Sept. 17, 1991.

18 *Death Be Not Proud*, op. cit., 61.

19 Ibid, 74.

20 Ibid, 76.

21 Johnny Gunther to Henry Eisner, Nov. 3, 1946, HE.

22 J.G. to H. Scherman, Oct. 28, 1946, U of C.*

23 *F of A*, op. cit., 58.

24 Author interview with Nancy Barnett, May 24, 1986.

25 Cass Canfield to Hamish Hamilton, Jan. 24, 1947, U of C.*

26 *F of A*, op. cit., 55.

27 Gunther detailed reader and media reaction to *Inside U.S.A.* in *A Fragment of Autobiography*, op. cit., 62-65.

28 *Time*, June 2, 1947, 104.

29 *New York Times Book Review*, June 1, 1947, 1.

30 *F of A*, op. cit., 61.

31 Author interview with Henry Eisner, Sept. 17, 1991.

32 *Death Be Not Proud*, op. cit., 168.

33 Ibid, 171.

34 Ibid, 183.

35 Ibid, 189.

36 Borough of Manhattan Death Certificate, July 3, 1947.

CHAPTER 32

1 *Death Be Not Proud*, op. cit., 261.

2 Author interview with Henry Eisner, Sept. 17, 1991.

3 Undated newspaper clipping in Frances Gunther files, MvE.

4 *Death Be Not Proud*, op. cit., 250.

5 Author interview with Bertha Brenner, Sept. 21, 1991.

6 Ibid.

7 Author interview with Helen Hahn, Dec. 15, 1986.

8 John Gunther for many years negotiated his own book contracts with Cass Canfield, since the two men were close friends. In addition, he had a good working relationship with DeWitt Wallace at *Reader's Digest*. Thus, when John ran into financial troubles in the mid-1940s, he grew dissatisfied with Brandt & Brandt, his agent. He complained that the firm was not doing enough to market his freelance articles, and sought the standard 10 per cent fee for book contracts for which he felt that he did much of the negotiating. According to Carl Brandt, Jr., when Gunther approached Carl Brandt, Sr., about reducing the agency's cut on his books, Brandt refused "as a matter of principle." As a result, Gunther left Brandt & Brandt for the Harold Ober agency.

9 *Philadelphia Inquirer*, June 8, 1947.

10 *New York Times*, Apr. 30, 1948.

11 Undated clipping from the *New York Post*, MvE.

12 *New York Times*, May 1, 1948.

13 *New York Daily Mirror*, May 1, 1948.

14 *New York Post*, Mar. 21, 1948.

15 Eric Sevareid transcript, op. cit.

16 *New Republic*, Feb. 12, 1936, 22.

17 FBI Memo to HUAC, May 5, 1958, regarding *Daily Worker*, Sept. 13, 1937, D of J.

18 W.G. Bannister, FBI special agent to J. Edgar Hoover, Apr. 23, 1942, D of J.

19 Transcript of radio show, FBI Memo to J. Edgar Hoover, Sept. 29, 1943, D of J.

20 *Dangerous Dossiers: Exposing the Secret War Against America's Greatest Authors* (New York: Fine, 1988).

21 The author obtained copies of many of the documents in the Department of Justice's Gunther files using the Freedom of Information Act, however, some documents in those files remain classified. While it is evident that FBI agents kept an eye on John Gunther, there is no evidence that he was ever subject to ongoing active surveillance.

22 J.G. to J. Edgar Hoover, Western Union cable, Nov. 25, 1947. Handwritten comment by Hoover on bottom of page with query to C. Tolson, D of J.

23 *PM Magazine*, Mar. 25, 1947.

24 Not surprisingly, Edward R. Murrow saw the incident differently than did Shirer. There is an excellent account in *Murrow: His Life and Times* by A.M. Sperber (Freundlich Books, 1986), 279-90. Sperber suggests that there may have been something of a personal rivalry between the two men, as well as professional disagreements.

25 Author interview with Leonora Hornblow, May 29, 1987.

26 Ibid.

27 J.G. to Cass Canfield, Aug. 1, 1947, U of C.*

28 *Death Be Not Proud*, op. cit., 3.

CHAPTER 33

1 Author interview with Leonora Hornblow, July 12, 1991.

2 For details of the life of John Vandercook, see his obituary in *Time*, Jan. 18, 1963, 74.

3 Author interview with Leonora Hornblow, May 29, 1987.

4 A wedding story appeared in the *New York Times*, Mar. 8, 1948, 15.

5 J.G. to Cass Canfield, Mar. 17, 1948, U of C.*

6 Interview with Nancy Barnett, May 24, 1986.

7 *Time*, Apr. 26, 1948, 25.

8 *The Traitor*, op. cit.

9 J.G. to Frances Gunther, June 24, 1948, AR.

10 *Death Be Not Proud*, op. cit., 251.

11 J.G. to Cass Canfield, June 23, 1948, U of C.*

12 J.G. to Frances Gunther, July 1948, MvE.

13 *Procession*, op. cit., 356.

14 The interview with Tito is described in detail in *Behind the Curtain* by John Gunther (New York: Harper & Brothers, 1949) 79.

15 Department of State telegram (#1409), from U.S. Embassy in Budapest to Secretary of State, Washington, D.C., Sept. 3, 1948.

16 Author interview with Leonora Hornblow, May 29, 1987.

CHAPTER 34

1 Cass Canfield to J.G., Mar. 1, 1949, U of C.*

2 Author interview with Henry Eisner, Sept. 17, 1991.

3 *New York Times*, Feb. 4, 1975, 67.

4 Whitelaw Reid to Cass Canfield, Feb. 23, 1949, U of C.*

5 *Behind the Curtain*, op. cit., 351.

6 *New Statesman*, Oct. 1, 1949.

7 *New York Sun*, Dec. 11, 1948.

8 *Time*, Apr. 14, 1958, 50. Vincent Auriol was president of France from 1947 to 1954.

9 Author interview with Leonora Hornblow, May 29, 1987.

10 J.G. to Frances Gunther, Dec. 18, 1951, AR.

11 J.G. to Frances Gunther, Jan. 20, 1950, AR.

12 J.G. to Frances Gunther, June 28, 1951, AR.

13 Author interview with William L. Shirer, Nov. 10, 1986.

14 J.G. to Frances Gunther, June 28, 1951, AR.

15 Author interview with William L. Shirer, Nov. 10, 1986.

16 Author interview with William Shirer, Nov. 10, 1986.

17 J.G. to Frances Gunther, Feb. 10, 1952, AR.

18 *New York Journal-American*, Feb. 23, 1951.

19 J.G. to Frances Gunther, Jan. 20, 1950, AR.

20 *Roosevelt in Retrospect*, op. cit., 362.

21 J.G. to Frances Gunther, June 28, 1951, AR.

22 *San Francisco Chronicle*, June 5, 1950.

23 Grace Tully to J.G., June 26, 1950, U of C.*

24 Eleanor Roosevelt to J.G., June 2, 1950. As quoted in *Eleanor: The Years Alone* by Joseph Lash (New York: Norton, 1972), 189.

CHAPTER 35

1 John Gunther, *The Riddle of MacArthur* (New York: Harper & Brothers, 1951), 49 (cited hereafter as *The Riddle of MacArthur*).

2 Ibid, 27.

3 J.G. to Frances Gunther, Dec. 19, 1950, MvE.

4 *The Riddle of MacArthur*, op. cit., 112.

5 The substance of this interview with Hirohito is described in detail in *The Riddle of MacArthur*, op. cit., 111-15.

6 Ibid, 168.

7 Ibid, 215.

8 Richard Rovere, *Arrivals and Departures* (New York: Macmillan, 1957), 181 (cited hereafter as *Arrivals and Departures*).

9 *Death Be Not Proud*, op. cit., 94.

10 *New Yorker*, Aug. 23, 1947.

11 *Arrivals and Departures*, op. cit., 181.

12 John Gunther, *Eisenhower: The Man and the Symbol* (New York: Harper & Brothers, 1951), 4 (cited hereafter as *Eisenhower: The Man*).

13 J.G. to Frances Gunther, Dec. 18, 1951, AR.

14 *Eisenhower*, op. cit., Feb. 10, 1952.

15 Ibid, 24.

CHAPTER 36

1 *New York Times*, Apr. 30, 1952.

2 John Gunther, *Taken at the Flood: The Story of Albert Lasker* (New York: Harper & Brothers, 1960), 345.

3 J.G. to Frances Gunther, Aug. 18, 1952, MvE.

4 *F of A*, op. cit., 73.

5 J.G. to Frances Gunther, Oct. 18, 1953, AR.

6 John Gunther, *Inside Africa* (New York: Harper & Brothers, 1955), 724 (cited hereafter as *Inside Africa*).

7 Rev. Homer A. Jack to J.G., Dec. 1, 1955, U of C.* As quoted in *Inside Journalism*, op. cit., 43.

8 Ibid, ch. 9.

9 J.G.'s cataract problems were mentioned in *Time*, Apr. 14, 1958, 48.

10 *F of A*, op. cit., 78.

11 Ibid, 80.

12 *Inside Africa*, op. cit., 439.

13 Ibid, 883.

14 *New York Herald-Tribune Book Review*, Oct. 2, 1955.

15 L'Autre Afrique is mentioned in *F of A*, op. cit., 79.

16 Ibid, 81.

17 David Lamb, *The Africans* (New York: Random House, 1982).

18 *F of A*, op. cit., 82.

CHAPTER 37

1 J.G. to Frances Gunther, May 5, 1957, MvE.

2 John Gunther and Bernard Quint, *Days to Remember: America 1945-55* (New York: Harper & Brothers, 1956).

3 *F of A*, op. cit., 84.

4 *Procession*, op. cit., 492.

5 John Gunther, *Inside Russia Today* (New York: Harper & Brothers, 1958), 104 (cited hereafter as *Inside Russia Today*).

6 *Newsweek*, Apr. 14, 1958, 118.

7 *Inside Russia Today*, op. cit., 508.

8 *Time*, Apr. 14, 1958, 44.

9 J.G. to F.G., Feb. 10, 1958.

10 *F of A*, op. cit., 92.

11 J.G. to Frances Gunther, Nov. 25, 1958, MvE.

12 *Inside Russia Today*, op. cit., xx.

13 Ibid, 501.

14 *New York Times Book Review*, Apr. 13, 1958, 1.

15 Justice Department Memo, Apr. 28, 1958, Dept. of Justice.

CHAPTER 38

1 *Time*, Apr. 14, 1958, 42.

2 Author interview with Dorothy Olding, Harold Ober Agency, Feb. 12, 1987, in New York City.

3 *Book of the Month Club News*, September 1955.

4 *F of A*, op. cit., 95.

5 *New Yorker*, Oct. 7, 1944.

6 *Book of the Month Club News*, Midsummer, 1961, 6.

7 *This I Believe*, op. cit., 61.

8 *Time*, Apr. 14, 1958, 50.

9 Ibid, 50.

10 J.G. to Frances Gunther, June 28, 1951, MvE.

11 J.G. to Frances Gunther, Nov. 25, 1958, MvE.

12 J.G. to Frances Gunther, Jan. 7, 1960, MvE.

13 Fanny Butcher, *Many Lives—One Love* (New York: Harper & Row, 1972), 311.

14 J.G. to Frances Gunther, Nov. 25, 1958, MvE.

15 *Procession*, op. cit., 483.

16 John Gunther, *Inside Europe Today* (New York: Harper & Brothers, 1961).

17 *New York Times Book Review*, July 23, 1961, 1.

18 *Atlantic*, September 1961, 99.

CHAPTER 39

1 Frances Gunther to Nehru, 1947, AR.

2 Author interview with Judith de Mille Donelan, Mar. 23, 1987, from Easton, Md.

3 Ibid.

4 Author interview with Dr. Alexander Rafaeli, Oct. 24, 1991, from Jerusalem, Israel.

5 Ibid.

6 Frances gave details of her visit to India in a Letter to the Editor, *Jerusalem Post*, May 24, 1950. The letter was apparently written in an effort to squelch rumors about her relationship with Nehru, or as Frances put it, "to keep the record straight and the protocol correct."

7 J.G. to Frances Gunther, May 30, 1950, AR.

8 Frances Gunther to J.G., July 22, 1951, AR.

9 Ibid.

10 Ibid.

11 Frances Gunther to J.G., July 4, 1953, AR.

12 Author interview with Dr. Alexander Rafaeli.

13 Frances Gunther to J.G., May 20, 1957, AR.

14 Ibid.

15 Frances Gunther to J.G., Feb. 3, 1955.

16 Author interview with Dr. Alexander Rafaeli.

17 Frances Gunther to J.G., May 20, 1957, AR.

18 Ibid.

19 Frances Gunther to J.G., Dec. 7, 1957, AR.

20 Frances Gunther to J.G., Nov. 1, 1958, AR.

21 Frances Gunther to Jane Gunther, Nov. 1, 1958, AR.

22 Author interview with Mary von Euler, Frances' friend, Apr. 19, 1986, at Bethesda, Md.

23 F.G. to John Gunther, 1958, AR.

24 Author interview with William L. Shirer, Nov. 10, 1986.

25 Ibid.

26 Author interview with Evan Thomas, former Harper & Brothers editor, Mar. 27, 1987, at New York City.

27 J.G. to Frances Gunther, Sept. 1, 1961, AR. (The author was unable to locate a copy of Frances' original letter, if one still exists.)

28 Author interview with Dr. Alexander Rafaeli.

29 Frances Gunther to J.G., Dec. 1962, AR.

30 Author interview with Dr. Alexander Rafaeli.

31 Ibid.

CHAPTER 40

1 *New Yorker*, Sept. 26, 1964, 205.

2 Author interview with Clifton Fadiman, June 12, 1988, from Santa Barbara, Calif.

3 *This I Believe*, op. cit., 61.

4 Author interview with Leonora Hornblow, July 12, 1991.

5 John Gunther, *Chicago Revisited* (U of Chicago, 1965).

6 *Chicago Sun-Times Midwest Magazine*, Dec. 12, 1965, 14.

7 *Saturday Review*, July 10, 1965, 38.

8 John Gunther, *Inside South America* (New York: Harper & Row, 1967), 218 (cited hereafter as *Inside South America*).

9 Ibid, xi.

10 Ibid, 527.

11 Ibid, xiii.

12 John Gunther, *Twelve Cities* (New York: Harper & Row, 1969).

13 Author interview with William Shirer, Nov. 10, 1986.

14 Ibid.

15 *New York Times*, May 30, 1970, 1.

16 *Time*, Apr. 14, 1958, 50.

17 Sevareid transcript, op. cit.

18 *New York Post*, June 1, 1970.

19 *New York Post*, June 3, 1970.

20 "Letter to the Editor," *New York Post*, June 11, 1970.

21 Author interview with William Shirer, Nov. 10, 1986.

22 *Book World*, June 21, 1970.

23 Author interview with William Forbis, author, Mar. 18, 1987, from Big Arm, Mont.

24 John Gunther and William Forbis, *John Gunther's Inside Australia* (New York: Harper & Row, 1972).

25 Author interview with William Forbis, Mar. 18, 1987.

INDEX

Aga Khan, 162
Air Transport Command (ATC), 228-29
Albert, Eddie, 307
Alexander, General Sir Harold, 234
Algren, Nelson, 5
Allen, Jay, 130, 147, 225
Arias, Dr. Arnulfo, 203
Arlen, Michael (Dikran Kuyumjian), 34, 50, 371
Asquith, Herbert H., 140
Asquith, Margot (Lady Oxford), 103, 140 (early life), 216
Auriol, Paul, 306
Avila Camacho, General Manuel, 199

Baker, Josephine, 221
Baldwin, Stanley, 153
Bankhead, Tallulah, 181
Barnett, Nancy (J.G.'s secretary), 214, 227, 244, 264, 276, 297 (leaves J.G.'s employ)
Baruch, Bernard, 311
Baumgarten, Bernice (J.G.'s agent), 125, 146, 179, 206
Beadle, George, 365
Behind the Curtain (1949), 303, 305
Ben-Gurion, David, 160
Bennett, Enoch Arnold, 52
Benny, Jack, 239
Benton, William, 333
Best, Robert, 103, 148, 164, 240, 251, 297-98 (treason trial)
Billingsley, Sherman, 220, 221
Bookman, 19
Borges, Jorge Luis, 367-68
Bourke-White, Margaret, 227
Brand, Jean (nee Bennedsen), 20
Brandt, Carl (J.G.'s agent), 43, 227, 262, 264, 265, 285, 286f
Brenner, Bertha, 269, 284, 285, 299
Brenner, Edgar, 269, 284
Brereton, Major General Lewis H., 239
Brezhnev, Leonid I., 335
Bright Nemesis, The (1932), 94
Browder, Earl, 177
Brown, Constantine, 56
Budberg, Baroness Moura, 103, 139
Burnett, Whit, 94, 108, 152, 372
Butcher, Fanny, 345
Butcher, Harry C., 231, 239

Cabell, James Branch, 19
"cablese," 98
Canfield, Cass (J.G.'s publisher), 48 (meets J.G., 1924),

125-26, 143, 147, 150, 152, 154, 155, 168, 169, 178, 182, 195, 198, 206, 238, 250, 254, 264, 265, 275, 292, 296, 297, 299, 304, 321, 323, 325, 328, 329, 337, 338, 365
Canfield, Cass, Jr., 126
Capote, Truman, 307
Capra, Frank, 223
Cardenas, General Lazaro, 199
Carlyle, Thomas (historian), 133
Castagneta, Grace, 256
Central Intelligence Agency (CIA), 79
Cerf, Bennett, 59, 224, 244, 307, 325
Chamberlain, Neville, 185
Chase, Stuart, 181
Chesterton, Gilbert Keith (G.K.), 50 (meets)
Chiang Kai-shek, General, 170-71, 172
Chiang Kai-shek, Madam, (*see Soong Mei-ling*)
Chicago, 4-5
Chicago Daily News, 20, 39, 98 (overseas service)
Chicago Revisited (1965), 366
Chou En-lai, 173
Churchill, Sir Winston, 136, 185-87, 212-13
Clayton, John, 72
Cockburn, Claud, 139
Communism, 118 (in America, 1930s), 287-89 (fear of, 1940s)
Cone, Fairfax, 365
Cooke, Alistair, 243
Corazzo, Gretchen (J.G.'s cousin), 32
Covici-McGee Booksellers, 28
Cowles, Gardner, 296, 315, 321, 336
Cowley, Malcolm, 39, 288
Crump, E.H. (Ed), 263

Daily Maroon, The, 19-20
Daladier, Edouard, 178
Dane, Patricia, 223
Daniels, Joseph, 199
Davis, Bette, 224
Days to Remember: America 1945-1955 (1956), 333
Death Be Not Proud (1949), 292-93, 303, 304, 305
Death Be Not Proud (TV movie), 304ff
D-Day (1944), 229, 250
de Mille, Agnes, 139
Dennis, Charles, 25, 31, 33, 60, 66, 67, 120, 126
de Tocqueville, Count Alexis (French historian), 1, 253, 259
Dietrich, Marlene, 224, 307
Dietz, Howard, 286 (*Inside U.S.A.* musical)
Dollfuss, Dr. Engelbert, 102, 120-21
Donald, W.H., 172
Donelan, Judith de Mille (Frances' niece), 351, 352
Doyle, Sir Arthur Conan, 50 (meets)
Dreiser, Theodore, 17, 76
Dugdale, Major Nigel, 238
Dunne, Peter Finley, 15
Duranty, Walter, 82, 154, 177, 303

Earle, George, 240
Eban, Abba, 354
Eden, Anthony, 136
Eden for One (1927), 74-75 (see *Peter Lancelot*)
Edward VIII (Duke of Windsor), 35 (meets), 42, 44, 141 (lunch with), 153, 286, 306
Einstein, Albert, 271

Eisenhower, General Dwight D., 169 (meets), 227, 231, 233, 234, 236, 239, 305, 321-23
Eisenhower: The Man and the Symbol (1952), 322
Eisner, Dr. Henry, 269, 272-73, 275, 282, 304

Fadiman, Clifton, 154, 182, 199, 201, 206, 225, 255, 342, 364
Farson, Negley, 128
Fineman, Bernard (Frances' brother), 69, 88, 205, 351, 361
Fineman, Dennis (Frances' father), 68
Fineman, Sonia (nee Paul, Frances' mother), 68
Fitzgerald, F. Scott, 177
Fitzgerald, Geraldine, 224
Fodor, Denis, 106, 114
Fodor, Marcel (J.G.'s friend and colleague), 76, 94, 95, 103, 105-06 (early life), 107, 133, 164, 170, 184, 205
Forbis, William, 373-74
Ford, Ford Madox, 58 (meets)
Forte, Ralph, 130
Foster, Preston, 223
Fragment of Autobiography: the Fun of Writing the Inside Books, A, (1962), 349
Frick, Wilhelm, 265
Fullbright, Senator J. William, 105-06
Fuqua, William N., 16

Gallico, Paul, 200
Gandhi, Indira Nehru, 353
Gandhi, Mahatma, 166, 167
Garbo, Greta, 224, 308-09
Gedye, George, 105, 240
George, Major-General Harold L., 228
Gervasi, Frank, 239
Gilbert, Morris, 130
Gilbert, W.S., 140
Gillard, Frank, 233
Gilling, Ted, 231, 233, 237, 238
Gladstone, William, 140
Golden Fleece, The (1929), 85, 88
Goldman, Emma, 50, 139
Gort, Field Marshal Lord, 233
Graff, Robert, 333
Gromyko, Andrei A., 330, 334
Gunther, Eugene McClellan (J.G.'s father), 5-6, 10, 12, 34 (like J.G.), 62, 262
Gunther, Frances Powell (nee Fineman, J.G.'s first wife), 57 (meets), 68-71 (early life), 80, 83 (first child born), 111 (writing), 130 (role in *Inside Europe*), 148, 157, 167 (affair with Nehru), 172, 183, 184, 187 (illness), 188-90, 193, 205, 206, 214, 224, 242, 245, 247-48 (divorce), 255, 269, 279, 283-84 (and anti-Semitism), 292, 310 (emigrates to Israel), 320, 348, 350-61 (life in Israel), 361-62 (death)
Gunther, Jane (nee Perry, J.G.'s second wife), 294 (early life), 295 (marries J.G.), 299, 300-01, 303, 317-18, 332, 367
Gunther, Jean (J.G.'s sister), 10 (birth), 11, 32, 146, 148, 155, 217, 310
Gunther, John (J.G.'s paternal grandfather), 5
Gunther, John, 8 (birth), 11-12

(early education), 13, 14 (enrolls at U of Chicago), 17, 19 (wins literary prize), 20, 41, 48, 56, 61 (becomes "swing man"), 66 (alleged plagiarism), 72 (first marriage), 80, 83, 86 (first radio broadcast), 90 (in Vienna), 107 (on Gestapo death list), 134 ("Inside" title), 143 (*Inside Europe* published), 146 (quits *Chicago Daily News*), 149 (returns to U.S.), 155, 157, 182, 191, 202 (meets F.D. Roosevelt), 214, 220 (nightlife), 233, 234 (and Eisenhower), 245, 247-48 (divorce), 248-49, 255, 277 (*Inside U.S.A.*), 289-90 (FBI surveillance), 294 (courts Jane Perry), 296 (remarries), 306, 308-09 (Garbo friendship), 318, 328, 332, 337-38 (work habits), 346 (TV show), 370
(death)
Gunther, Johnny (J.G.'s son), 89 (birth), 149, 155, 156, 157, 205, 209, 227, 243, 255, 268-70 (early life), 271-75 (illness), 279, 280 (death), 282-83 (funeral), 292 (*Death Be Not Proud*), 321, 360
Gunther, Judith (J.G.'s daughter), 83 (birth), 87 (death)
Gunther, Louise (nee Kraeger, J.G.'s paternal grandmother), 5
Gunther, Lizette (nee Schoeninger, J.G.'s mother), 7, 11, 86-87 (death)
Gunther, Nicholas (J.G.'s son), 332 (adopts), 357

Hahn, Dauphine, 35-36, 37
Hahn, Emily, 30, 37, 114, 171 (in China)
Hahn, Helen, 30 (meets), 35 (on J.G.'s looks), 38ff, 57, 66, 114 (on J.G.'s fiction), 191, 214, 246, 247, 285, 359
Haile Selassie, Emperor (of Ethiopia), 327
Haley, Jack, 286
Hamill, Pete, 372
Hamilton, Hamish (J.G.'s British publisher), 127, 139, 147, 148, 155, 164, 168, 178, 180, 195, 216, 251, 254, 256, 258, 293, 325, 337, 344
Hansen, Harry, 28, 42, 59, 76, 359
Hart, Moss, 191, 286
Hecht, Ben, 21, 22, 25, 26-27, 28
Heifetz, Jascha, 139
Hemingway, Ernest M., 58 (meets), 177, 348 (death of)
High Cost of Hitler, The (1939), 195
Hirohito, Emperor (of Japan), 174, 317-18
Hitler, Adolf, 107, 133, 136, 178, 202
Hoffman, Paul, 264
Hokinson, Helen, 342
Hoover, J. Edgar, 289, 340
Hopkins, Miriam, 224, 227, 256
Hopper, Hedda, 252
Hornblow, Arthur, 302, 307
Hornblow, Leonora (nee Schinasi, J.G.'s friend), 35, 72, 112, 165, 191, 243, 249, 256, 294, 296, 302, 365, 372
Howitt, Arnold, 286
Humphrey, Hubert, 263

Huston, John, 224
Hutton, Barbara, 162
Huxley, Aldous L., 139

Indian Sign, The, 372
Inside Africa (1955), 323, 329, 330
Inside Asia (1939), 180-81
Inside books (The), 341 (sales of)
Inside Europe (1936), 128, 132-37, 143-44
Inside Latin America (1941), 366, 368
Inside Russia Today (1958), 337-38
Inside South America (1967), 368
Inside U.S.A. (1947), 275-79, 286 (Broadway musical)
Irgun Zvai Leumi (Israeli underground, 1940s), 243
Ivens, Joris, 177

John Gunther's High Road to Adventure (TV show), 346
John Gunther's Inside Australia (1972), 344, 369, 373
Johnson, President Lyndon, 366
Jumblatt, Lady Nazira-el-, 64

Keynes, John Maynard, 139
Khrushchev, Nikita S., 334-35, 338
King Farouk (of Egypt), 239-40, 329
Knickerbocker, Agnes, 190, 196, 208-09, 213, 215, 224, 242, 246, 247, 248-49, 372
Knickerbocker, Hubert Renfro, 100, 106, 125 (and *Inside Europe*), 131, 146, 183, 190, 215, 249, 360, 372
Knickerbocker, Kenneth (H.R. Knickerbocker's brother), 132, 191, 192
Knickerbocker, Ronald (H.R. Knickerbocker's brother), 191, 249
Koestler, Arthur, 345
Kung, Dr. H.H., 171

LaGuardia, Mayor Fiorello Henrico (of New York), 243
Lamb, David, 331
Landon, Governor Alfred (of Kansas), 263
Lascelles, Captain Alan, 44
Lasker, Albert, 325, 344
Lasker, Mary, 345
Laski, Harold, 139
LeHand, Marguerite (Missy), 203
Lewis, Hobart, 346, 366, 369
Lewis, Sinclair, 18 (*Main Street*), 47, 65, 100, 119, 151, 170, 222, 264, 278-79, 280, 344
Lilienthal, David E., 264
Lillie, Beatrice, 286, 287
Lindbergh, Charles, 119
Linlithgow, Viceroy of, 168
Linn, James Weber, 19, 21, 75, 359
Litvak, Anatole, 223
Loos, Anita, 18
Losch, Tilly, 256
Lost City, The (1964), 363-64
Lunde, Arvid, 20
Lyons, Leonard, 183, 219, 222, 256, 287, 371

MacArthur, General Douglas, 169 (meets), 315-17, 318
MacDonald, J. Ramsay, 134
MacLeish, Archibald, 177, 181, 196, 255
Mallory, Walter, 181
Mankiewicz, Herman J., 139
Mankiewicz, Joseph, 307
Mann, Thomas, 252
Maschwitz, Eric, 52, 55-56

Masters, Edgar Lee, 22, 39
Maugham, Somerset, 252
Maxwell, Elsa, 227, 256
Mayer, Louis B., 115
McCarthy, Senator Joseph (of Wisconsin), 287
McCormick, Anne O'Hare, 225, 354
McKellar, Senator Kenneth (of Tennessee), 263
Mencken, Henry Lewis (H.L.), 18, 21, 22ff, 264
Mercer, Lucy, 313
Mihailov, Ivan, 78
Millay, Edna St. Vincent, 21
Mitchell, Margaret, 185
Moderwell, Hiram (Hi), 64, 67
Montague, Evelyn, 233
Montgomery, Field Marshal Bernard, 233, 237 (meets)
Morley, John, 140
Morris, Jan, 219
Mosley, Sir Oswald, 137
Mountbatten, Lord Louis, 233
Mowrer, Edgar, 100, 107, 147
Mowrer, Paul Scott, 46, 52, 56, 78, 95, 145, 146
Mowrer, Richard, 230
Mulroy, James, (Herc), 16-17 (Pulitzer Prize), 19, 325
Murrow, Edward R., 226, 255, 261, 291, 307
Mussolini, Benito Juarez, 142, 178

Nasser, General Gamal Abdel, 327, 329
Nehru, Jawaharlal, 139 (meets), 165, 167, 172, 188, 189, 209, 215-16, 243, 244, 246, 306, 319, 350, 352
Nehru, Kamala (wife of Jawaharlal Nehru), 164
Nehru, Motilal (father of Jawaharlal Nehru), 165
Nicholson, Harold, 144
Nicholson, Meredith, 200
Nixon, Vice-President Richard M., 339

Ober, Harold (J.G.'s agent), 285, 336, 341
O'Brien, Howard Vincent, 250
O'Brien, Marianne, 256
Odets, Clifford, 115
O'Flaherty, Harold (Hal), 46, 54, 67, 76, 86, 120, 126, 145
Operation HUSKY (Invasion of Sicily), 231, 234-35
Oppenheimer, Sir Ernest, 327
Ormerod, C.B., 326
Orwell, George, 306

Paley, William, 291
Parker, Dorothy, 227, 256, 291
Parmelee, Anna, 283
Parsons, Louella, 223
Paton, Alan, 330
Patton, General George S., 235
Penfield, Dr. Wilder, 274
Peter Lancelot (1927), (see *Eden for One*)
Phillips, Lieutenant-Colonel Joseph P., 231
Pilsudski, Josef, 131
Pius XII, Pope, 299-300
Pound, Ezra, 119
Prescott, Orville, 278
Pridmore, Jay, 92ff
Priestley, John Boynton (J.B.), 53 (meets)
Prince Bernard (of the Netherlands), 222
Prince Fumimaro Konoye (of Japan), 174
Procession (1965), 366

Pulitzer, Joseph, 264
Putnam, Dr. Tracy, 3, 270

Quezon, Manuel, 169, 180

Radio broadcasting, 86, 226
Rafaeli, Dr. Alexander, 159, 160ff, 353, 356
Rahn, Muriel, 221
Rainer, Luise, 114-16
Rankin, Representative Jeanette, 217
Red Pavilion, The, 65-66
Reid, Whitelaw, 304
Revolution in India (1944), 244
Reynolds, Quentin, 254, 345
Riddle of MacArthur, The (1951), 320
Riley, General William E., 355
Ring Around Vienna, (see *Troubled Midnight*), 161
Rintelen, Dr. Anton, 120
Robinson, Edward G., 139, 291
Rogers, Ginger, 252
Rommel, General Erwin, 231, 239
Roosevelt, President Franklin Delano, 176, 202-04, 217, 222, 254, 293 (death), 297, 311
Roosevelt, Eleanor, 207, 222, 311
Roosevelt in Retrospect (1950), 312
Rovere, Richard, 2, 320
Rubel, Herbert, 20
Russell, Ned, 233

Safford, Virginia, 245
Salisbury, Harrison, 339
Sandburg, Carl, 4, 18, 22, 25-27
Sanina, Valentina Nicolaevna (Valentina), 308
Saunders, Margaret (Rakham Holt), 13
Saxton, Eugene, 142, 253
Schary, Dore, 309
Schermann, Harry, 179, 206, 275
Schlee, George, 308
Schlesinger, Arthur M., Jr., 118
Schoeninger, Joseph (J.G.'s maternal grandfather), 7-8
Schoeninger, Julius (J.G.'s maternal uncle), 13, 75
Schoeninger, Lisetta (nee Kraeger, J.G.'s maternal grandmother), 7-8
Schoeninger, Lizette (*see Gunther, Lizette*)
Schultz, Sigrid, 354
Schwartz, Arthur, 286 (*Inside U.S.A.* musical), 287
Schweitzer, Dr. Albert, 327
Seabrook, William B., 66
Secker, Martin, 58
Seldes, George, 79, 252, 289
Seldes, Gilbert, 252
Sevareid, Eric, 287, 371
Shabad, Theodore, 338
Shah of Iran, 157-58
Shaw, George Bernard, 51 (meets), 103, 141
Shaw, Irwin, 230, 307
Sheean, Vincent (Jimmy), 16, 76, 100, 144, 147, 166, 170, 173, 219, 227, 307, 356
Shepilov, Dimitri, 334
Shertok, Moshe, 160
Sherwood, Robert, 311
Shirer, William Lawrence, 17, 76, 77, 99-100, 105, 112-13, 117, 154, 166, 184, 205, 215, 219, 287-88, 290, 292, 298, 307, 308, 310, 370, 372
Shirer, Theresa (nee Stiberitz), 112-13
Simon, Simone, 256
Simpson, Wallis (Duchess of Windsor), 141-42, 153

Sinmay, Zau, 171
Smith, Henry Justin, 26, 39, 61, 76, 145 (death), 359
Snow, Edgar, 205, 284, 356
Somoza, Anastasio, 200
Soong, Ai-ling (wife of Dr. H.H. Kung), 171
Soong, Ching-ling (wife of Sun Yat-sen), 171
Soong, Mei-ling (wife of Chiang Kai-shek), 171, 172
Stekel, Dr. Wilhelm, 116-17 (treats the Gunthers)
Stevenson, Governor Adlai (of Illinois), 17
Stewart, Donald Ogden, 177
Stimson, Henry, 79, 204
Stoneman, William B., 147
Sullivan, Ed, 219, 221
Sulzberger, Cyrus, 240
Sun Yat-sen, 171
Swing, Raymond Gram, 48, 58, 76, 83, 106, 119, 152, 154, 225, 274, 291, 312, 348
Swope, Herbert Bayard, 135

Taken at the Flood: The Story of Albert D. Lasker (1960), 345
Tehran, Iran, 157
Tennyson, Alfred, 140, 247
Thalberg, Irving, 88
Thomas, Evan, 360
Thompson, Dorothy, 48, 76, 100, 106, 151, 154, 170, 205, 246, 261, 292, 307, 309, 348, 356
Thompson, Francis, 58, 105
Thorsen, Joan, 256
Tierney, Gene, 223
Todd, Michael, 222
Tong, Hollington K., 172
Tito, Marshal (Josip Broz), 300-01 (meets)
Traeger, Dr. Cornelius, 280
Trotsky, Leon, 96 (meets), 104
Troubled Midnight, The (1945), 251-53
Truman, President Harry S., 278, 290ff, 319
Tully, Grace, 313
Twelve Cities (1969), 369

Uris, Mickey, 223
University of Chicago, 15-16, 365-66

Vallee, Rudy (J.G. on radio show), 152
Vandercook, John, 226, 291, 294-95
van Doren, Mark, 254, 255
Vienna, Austria, 90-92, 104 (coffee houses), 301
Villard, Oswald Garrison, 102, 244
von Euler, Mary (nee Sanders), 358, 360
von Schuschnigg, Dr. Kurt, 122

Wallace, DeWitt (Wally), 179-80 (starts *Reader's Digest*), 201, 369
Wallace, Lila (wife of DeWitt Wallace), 179-80, 369
Walpole, Sir Hugh, 47
Warner, Jack, 88, 223
Washington Merry Go Round (1931), 123ff
Watson, General Edwin (Pa), 203
Wauchope, Sir Arthur, 158
Weil, Leonard, 16, 19, 54
Weizmann, Chaim, 139, 158, 160, 354
Welles, Orson, 254, 345

Welles, Sumner, 198, 202, 207, 311
Wells, Herbert George (H.G.), 103 (meets), 139
West, Dame Rebecca (Cicily Fairfield), 49, 53, 58, 103, 139, 143, 148, 216
White, Theodore (Teddy), 342, 346
Willkie, Wendell, 237, 240
Wilson, Edmund, 356, 357
Wilson, President Woodrow, 4, 15
Wilson, R.C., 169
Winchell, Walter, 219, 220-21 (at the Stork Club), 225, 256
Winsloe, Christa, 100
Winsor, Kathleen, 220, 256
Wood, Junius B., 80
Woolf, Virgina, 140

Zanuck, Darryl, 223